FUELING ONE BILLION

AN INSIDER'S STORY OF CHINESE ENERGY POLICY DEVELOPMENT

Yingzhong Lu

Published in the United States by
Washington Institute Press
1015 18th Street, N. W., Suite 300
Washington, DC 20036

First printing: October 1993
Printed in the United States of America
Design and typesetting by Kelley Graphics

Library of Congress Cataloging-in-Publication Data
Lu, Yingzhong, 1926-
Fueling one billion: an insider's story of Chinese energy policy development / Yingzhong Lu
      p.   cm.
Includes bibiographical references (p.   ) and index.
ISBN 0-88702-064-X: $29.95. — ISBN 0-88702-065-8 (pbk): $19.95
      1. Energy policy — China. 2. Energy industries — China.
I. Title.
HD9502.C62L8 1993
333.79'0951 — dc20
                        93-36004
                        CIP

PREFACE

I

Energy provides the basis for modern civilization. No other single category of material supply has proved so critical. Two recent oil crises triggered worldwide economic recessions. The third crisis led to an all-out war. Although the 1991 conflict with Iraq was not officially a "war for oil," it is clear to everyone that the Middle East's rich oil resources are always a factor in the endless conflicts in that restless region. Blood is now being mixed with oil. Western energy policy based on oil imported from the Middle East has proved to be full of potential hazards.

Another Damocles' sword balanced over our heads is the suspicion that a disastrous global warming could possibly be caused by the emission of CO_2 from the burning of fossil fuels. Such an impending evil casts more uncertainty into a world already entangled in so many predictable troubles. Many governments, as well as the people of most countries, are alarmed. As a result, the International Panel of Climate Change (IPCC) has been established to deal with the question of global warming. Better energy policy should be drawn up worldwide to avoid impending catastrophe.

For developing countries with frail economies, energy shortage has become a nightmare. A number of them have run into debt beyond redemption because of skyrocketing oil prices. Others are obliged to hold back economic growth and leave their people in poverty. For those fortunate, rapidly growing developing economies, ever rising energy demands present a formidable challenge — not only to these countries themselves but to the whole world. In the coming decades, the energy demand from developing countries will exceed that of the developed countries. Then the world will be facing a far more serious energy crisis and a much greater threat of climate change. It is therefore the major concern of energy-environmentalists to look for a policy providing an alternative energy supply for the developing economies.

Energy policy therefore appears on the stage at a critical moment of human history.

II

China is the most populous rapidly developing country and consumes the largest share of energy in the third world. Its economy grew tenfold from 1953 (the beginning of its First Five-Year Plan) to 1989, and its energy consumption has increased eighteenfold, already crossing the threshold of its first billion tons of standard coal.

Although China suffered from severe energy shortages before 1980 because of the lack of a sound, consistent energy policy, substantial progress in formulation and implementation of a scientific energy policy has been made during the past decade of economic reform, and hence the energy situation has been greatly improved. Generally speaking, China has successfully found the fuel for its fast-growing economy. In 1980 a policy was launched to quadruple China's production by 2000, using only its own resources, and this course is to be followed until the turn of the century. Much has been learned from the profound changes in the past decade.

However, ensuring China's future energy supply remains a daunting task. According to forecasts from various sources, Chinese energy demand will reach the next threshold, consumption of five billion tons of standard coal, around the middle of the twenty-first century. By 2025, CO_2 emission from China will be 2.8 times that from India and 13 times that from Brazil, as estimated in an IPCC report. China is now becoming a focus of global energy-environmental concern. An adequate policy for the reduction of energy intensity, the improvement of energy structure, and the mitigation of CO_2 emissions will be of great importance not only for China itself but also for the world as a whole.

In view of all the above, it is not surprising that in every international conference on energy-environmental issues I have been asked the same set of questions: What is the energy situation and energy policy in China? How long can China afford to meet the energy needs of its one billion people and its fast-growing economy on a self-reliant basis? How much energy will China need in the next decades?

Will China continue to export oil or become another greedy buyer in the world oil market? Is it possible for China to reduce its CO_2 emissions, and to what extent can its coal-predominant energy structure be improved?

III

This book is an attempt to answer these questions. In addition, it is a summary of China's experiences in developing and pursuing a consistent, scientific energy policy during the past decade of economic reform. The author happened to be one of the earliest pioneers and the most enthusiastic promoter of a scientific approach to Chinese energy policy; much of the information in this book is based on personal experience and first-hand information. Since Chinese political and economic institutions have been undergoing profound changes during the past ten years, the formulation and implementation of energy policy had to overcome numerous obstacles. As a consequence, although most of the positions taken in this volume have been adopted by Chinese policymakers and are included in the government's formal policy, some of them are still under discussion. However, based on the experience of the last decade, science and rationality can be expected to eventually triumph over prejudice and arbitrariness in policymaking.

FUELING ONE BILLION consists of three parts. Part I, "The Evolution of a Scientific Energy Policy," is a comprehensive description of all major aspects of the Chinese energy situation and relevant energy policies. In chapter 1 the historical background of the initiation and development of the current, scientific energy policy is introduced. The implications of creating such a policy extend beyond the energy community: that event was in fact the very beginning of reform in all aspects of Chinese economic policymaking. Chapter 2 presents an overview of the characteristics of the Chinese energy-economic situation, providing an understanding and correct diagnosis of conditions in many fields, not just in the energy sector. On the foundation of this information, the reader may easily understand the next four chapters dealing with different aspects of Chinese energy policy. Chapter 3 deals with energy consumption and conservation in China, chapter 4 with energy production and its relevant policies. In chapter 5 the very complicated issue of the fuel needs of the 800 million rural people and Chinese experi-

ence in dealing with the fuel problem are described. Chapter 6 gives a forecast of future Chinese energy demands and policy concerning their serious energy-environmental impacts.

In Part II six case studies on critical energy issues are included, taken from the original work carried out by the Institute of Nuclear Energy Technology and the Institute for Techno-Economics and Energy System Analysis since 1980. The outcomes of these studies have provided methodology, data base, and other valuable information needed for government policymaking. In chapter 7 the outline of the Medium- and Long-Term Energy-Economic Model System is described. This model has been adopted by the State Planning Commission as a standard tool for energy forecasting. The outcome of this study was commended by the government in 1987 for its important contribution to Chinese energy policymaking.

Chapter 8 gives detailed information on the very successful rural energy program causing 90 million improved wood stoves to be distributed during the past decade. Such an achievement is a decisive step toward mitigating rural energy shortages and provides some ecological protection. Audits of representative plants in five energy-intensive industrial branches are given in chapter 9, together with findings and recommendations for energy conservation. In chapter 10 details are given of the process and methodology of energy-environmental assessment and planning in a typical northern city. In chapter 11 the issues and prospects of the most critical energy sector, the power sector, are analyzed, and in the last chapter, a report is made on a very comprehensive joint research project comparing the energy situations and policies of China and India, including many observations and recommendations.

The third part of this book is the Appendix. Along with the full text of the official Energy Technology Policy, six sets of energy data and one energy flow diagram are included. It is the author's opinion and experience that all correct decisions on econo-technical policy must be made on the basis of sufficiently detailed quantitative analysis in addition to purely qualitative judgment. In fact, in the first stage of development of the scientific policy in China, much emphasis was put on the creation of the data base. Only recently has the government published energy statistical data in its yearbooks. Since some of the data quoted in the text are based on research done during the creation stage of the national data base, a collection of consistent sets of such data from the most recently published official sources is considered helpful to foreign researchers in the energy field and is therefore included.

The major weakness of Chinese energy policy lies in the lack of powerful vehicles to activate the economy. This seems to be the common failing of centralized, socialist economies. Though it is in the process of being reformed, there is still a long way to go before an effective, rational economic system can be established in China. The author has to leave this vital issue to the future.

Yingzhong Lu
January 18, 1991, at Oak Ridge

Acknowledgments

The writing and the publishing of this book has been sponsored by the Washington Institute for Values in Public Policy during a very special period in the history of the People's Republic of China. I am most grateful to Dr. Alvin M. Weinberg, who has been supporting this work from its embryo stage and who introduced me to my sponsor. I am also indebted to Neil Albert Salonen for all his help in creating a favorable environment for carrying out this work.

Special thanks are given to all my colleagues in China who have worked and are still working for the development, implementation, and research of Chinese energy policy. The contents of this book are in fact a brief summary of the collective effort carried out by all of them during the past decade.

I am also grateful to all the American professors and my colleagues at Stanford University and at the University of California at Berkeley and Davis who hosted me during the past two years and provided so much support to facilitate my work. Thanks to Rebecca Salonen and her colleagues in editing my manuscript and improving the readability of the text.

Finally, I should express my deep gratitude to my dear wife, Huaiqing Chen, for her work in typing and editing of the text, tables, and figures. Without her help, this book could not have been completed in such a short period.

FOREWORD

The future of the world's energy system cannot be discussed intelligently without taking into account the role of China. With a population of over a billion people, it is all but inevitable that China's energy future will profoundly influence all aspects of the world energy system during the next century: economics, resources, and perhaps most important, environmental and ecological impact. Yet because China has been a closed society, energy analysts in the outside world have been unable to take into account China's energy situation in a fully realistic way.

In his book, FUELING ONE BILLION, Yingzhong Lu has provided the first authoritative account of energy in China by an insider. As director of the Institute for Techno-Economics and Energy System Analysis at Tsinghua University in Beijing, Professor Lu had access to the most comprehensive analysis of China's energy situation. Much of the work he summarizes in FUELING ONE BILLION was conducted under his supervision, or with his active participation, and represents the combined efforts of many Chinese energy experts. The overall result is a brilliant, and entirely authoritative, estimate of the history and the likely future of energy in China. The world community of energy analysts owes Professor Lu an immense debt for providing this extraordinary yet realistic account of the energy situation in China, the world's largest nation.

A. M. Weinberg

CONTENTS

LIST OF TABLES

LIST OF FIGURES

LIST OF ACRONYMS AND ABBREVATIONS

Bbl .... barrel
CEC .... Commission of the European Community
CERS .... China Energy Research Society
ECOMOD ... Ecological Model
EDM .... Energy Demand Model
EEE .... Energy-Economic-Ecology Model
EEEOM .... Energy-Economic-Ecology Optimization Model
EIM .... Energy Impact Model
EI/OM .... Energy Import/Export Model
ESDPM .... Energy Supply, Distribution and Planning Model
ESROM .... Energy Supply Base Development Model
ESSM .... Energy Supply Strategic Model
FORMOD ... Forecasting Model
Gcal .... gigacalorie (10^9 calorie)
GDP .... Gross Domestic Product
GJ .... gigajoule (10^9 joule)
Gm^3 .... giga-cubic meter
GNP .... Gross National Product
Gt, Gton .... gigaton (10^9 ton)
GWe .... gigawatt (10^9 watt) electricity
GWh .... gigawatt-hour (10^9 watt-hour)
GWt .... gigawatt thermal (10^9 watt heat energy)
ha .... hectare
HEGO .... Huaneng Electricity Generation Corporation
HIEDC .... Huaneng International Electricity Development Corporation
HTGR .... High-Temperature Graphite Reactor
IDRC .... Internatiuonal Development Research Center (Canada)
INET .... Institute of Nuclear Engineering (China)
ISE .... Institute for Syustem Engineering (China)

ITEESA .... Institute for Techno-Economics and Energy System Analysis
J .... joule
kcal .... kilocalorie
kgce .... kilogram coal equivalent
kgoe .... kilogram oil equivalent
KV .... kilovolt
KVA .... kilovolt-amp
kWe .... kilowatt
kWh .... kilowatt-hour
Mcal .... megacalorie (10^6 calorie)
MMEM .... Macro-Economic Model
MPa .... megapascal (10^{-13} atmospheres)
Mt, Mton ..... megaton (10^6 ton)
MWe .... megawatt (10^6 watt) electricity
MWh .... megawatt-hour (10^6 watt-hour)
MWt .... megawatt-thermal (10^6 watt heat energy
Mu .... Chinese acreage unit, equal to about 1/6 acre
NI .... National Income
NOEMOD .. Non-Biomass Energy Model
REP .... Rural Energy Planning
REDM .... Regional Energy Demand Model
RMB .... *Renminbi*, Chinese currency unit
SEC .... State Energy Commission of the PRC
SPC .... State Planning Commission of the PRC
SSTC........... State Science and Technology Commission of the PRC
t .... ton
tce .... ton coal equivalent
toe .... ton oil equivalent
TWh .... tetrawatt-hour (10^{12} watt-hour)
UNDP .... United Nations Development Program

PART I

THE EVOLUTION OF A SCIENTIFIC ENERGY POLICY

CHAPTER ONE

BREAKING INTO A FORBIDDEN CITY

How a Scientific Approach to Energy Policymaking Was Born

THE ELASTICITY CURVE AND ITS STORY

Anyone who looks at the energy consumption elasticity curve for the People's Republic of China from 1953 to 1987 (figure 1) may be surprised by two

Fig. 1.1 Energy Consumption Elasticity

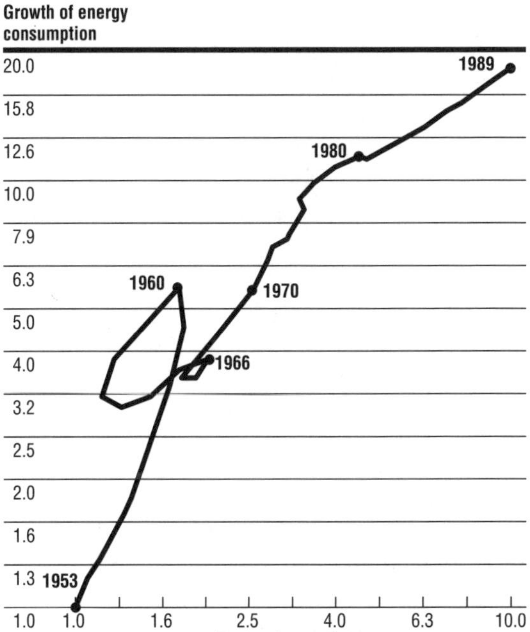

SOURCES: Data from *China Statistical Yearbooks, 1980–1989* (Beijing: International Center for the Advancement of Science & Technology, Ltd., 1989), and State Science and Technology Commission, *Guide to China's Science and Technology Policy (1986) —White Paper on Scinece and Technology* (Beijing: China Academic Publishers, 1987).

strikingly peculiar features: one is the pair of loops between 1959 and 1969, and the other is the leveling off after 1980. The former abnormality is the reflection of the disastrous economic setbacks caused by the failure of the Three Red Banners campaign in 1959 and the political turmoil during the Cultural Revolution. Further analysis of this period is not the subject of the present book.

The second interesting phenomenon reflects the implementation of energy conservation policies beginning in 1980. In fact, the elasticity of energy consumption in this period decreased from the former average value of 1.66 (1953-1979) to 0.51 (1980-1987), as shown in table 1. It is expected that such a low elasticity will be maintained throughout the next few decades. It is in fact a miracle in the history of the Chinese economy. How and why did this happen? What lessons can be learned from such an achievement? These are the questions to be answered in this book.

1.1. THE MELTING OF THE ICE

In December 1979, at the beginning of Chinese economic reforms, about a dozen senior experts in the Chinese energy community were called together in a small meeting room of the State Science and Technology Commission by Fang Yi, then the chairman of the commission, to speak out from their

Table 1.1 Energy Consumption Elasticities (1981 to 1987)

	1981	1982	1983	1984	1985	1986	1987	Average
GDP growth rate, %	4.87	8.27	9.83	13.48	13.14	7.97	10.50	9.68
Energy growth rate, %	−1.37	5.38	5.42	7.37	8.63	5.01	4.47	4.95
Elasticity	−0.28	0.65	0.55	0.55	0.66	0.63	0.43	0.51

SOURCE: Derived from data taken from *China Statistical Yearbooks, 1980-1989.*

"private" viewpoints about the real Chinese energy situation. Most of the participants were not only famous pioneers in various energy sectors, including coal, petroleum, electricity, hydropower, and rural and nuclear energy, but were also well-known "technical dissidents" in their fields, used to holding opinions that differed from the inadequate and unscientific technical and even political policies of the past regime. As a result, all of them had been bitterly persecuted in the Anti-Rightists Campaign and/or in the Cultural Revolution. However, patriotism and conscience continued to compel them to contribute their wisdom for the welfare of the people.

Fang Yi, an intellectual and an accomplished Chinese painter and calligrapher, was not only fully sympathetic but also respectful in listening to these elderly authorities in the energy field. He sincerely asked the participants to "tell the truth" about the actual energy situation in China and to give their recommendations.

The unprecedented economic reform of the period was giving great impetus to the emergence of all kinds of unusual events in China. Reform-minded government officials were eagerly looking for new concepts and novel approaches to formulate policies for reviving the shattered economy, brought to the brink of bankruptcy by the notorious Cultural Revolution. The patriotic Chinese elite were also ready to respond; they had always been enthusiastic about making contributions. Very soon, therefore, this handful of intellectuals turned the small commission meeting room into a tiny volcano exploding with shocking facts and sharp critiques. A picture of the Chinese energy crisis was painted before Fang's artist's eyes: the blackout of an entire urban district, the unheated homes with crying babies, the exhausted peasants complaining over cold food they had been unable to cook, the idle industrial equipment sidelined by power shortages, and the suffering miners in the bankrupt coal industry. It was then clear that Chinese economic reform could not be successful without adequate supplies of energy.

Fang immediately decided to repeat this kind of meeting on an enlarged scale to look for a solution. He convened the "First All-China Energy Symposium" in late December 1979, attended by more than a hundred senior energy experts and some senior energy technocrats responsible for energy administration, to discuss the energy crisis and energy policies of the People's Republic of China. This unusual symposium was a turning point not only in Chinese energy policymaking but also in Chinese policymaking in general: it implied that the Chi-

nese elite had begun to stand up and participate in the national policymaking process.

The symposium was held in the newly opened Wang Villa Hotel on the beach of the charming West Lake in Hangzhou. It had been one of Mao's beautiful villas and happened also to be the very place where the 1965 Central Committee Workshop of the Chinese Communist party was held when it initiated the disastrous Cultural Revolution. At that time the Chinese Communist leaders had criticized the elite and launched mass persecution. After just fourteen years, the wind had turned 180 degrees: the persecuted elite now stood up to criticize the party's policy.

The keynote of this gathering was patriotism —"Tian Xia Xin Wang, Pi Fu You Zhe" (Everyone has a share of responsibility for the fate of his country). Participants revealed numerous astonishing facts about the catastrophic consequences of the past mistaken energy policies and sharply criticized the irrational decisions made by the late Chairman Mao and his successor, Hua Guofeng, of the Communist party.

Such a discussion had not occurred in a public meeting since the Anti-Rightists Campaign in 1957. Mistakes of each ministry responsible for energy issues were also explained, and many constructive proposals were put forth. Most of the speakers in that symposium were so emotional that someone later recalled the atmosphere as being "full of a smell of gunpowder."

Those party leaders who were reform minded greatly appreciated the courage and the contributions of the participants. A vice-chairman of the State Science and Technology Commission, Tong Dalin, attended the meeting and declared that he would henceforth believe that "Criticizing is meritorious" rather than the old Chinese saying, "Criticizing is not guilty."* He explained, "Why should there be guilt attached to any criticism that seeks the people's welfare?"

Three follow-ups were decided upon in that symposium: (1) to submit immediately a report on the findings of this meeting to the top leaders in both the central government and the Central Committee of the Communist party, using language "as sharp as possible" to attract their attention; (2) to carry out a one-year research program on the energy situation and policy issues of the PRC, the findings to be published and distributed to all relevant gov-

---

*In ancient times in China, criticism of officials might result in imprisonment, or even a death sentence. "Criticizing is not guilty" expressed the hope of not being found guilty.

ernment agencies and institutions; and (3) to establish a policy-oriented academic society serving as a standing organization to pursue policy study and provide consultants to the government. These resolutions were all first-of-a-kind initiatives at that time in the PRC.

The elite thus began to break into the "forbidden city" of state-level policymaking. The winter was over; the ice was melting.

1.2 DISASTROUS POLICYMAKING: "PATTING THE HEAD"

The focus of the critiques in the Hangzhou Symposium was on the disastrous consequences of the senseless energy policies made in the past according to the "patting the head" process — a characteristic policymaking practice in all highly centralized politico-economic systems. Within such a system, all the decisions on major political and economic policies are made by the supreme leader of the party based on only his intuition. As a result, political interests inevitably override all economic considerations. Furthermore, fear of political persecution inevitably distorts economic information.

Since Chairman Mao's words were at that time honored as the "Supreme Instructions" and were not to be questioned by anybody, his decisions on economic policies, however inconsistent with reality, had also to be implemented unconditionally. Officials submitted information catering to the sensitivities of the Supreme Leader, even if it conflicted with the truth. As a result, most of the major economic policies, including energy policies, were based on information sharply differing from reality and thus led to disaster.

Serious mistakes resulting from past policies were found in every energy sector. These policies had eventually produced dangerous energy shortages in China. Before 1980, however, those who dared to point out such mistakes were usually accused of being "rightists" or of harboring "disloyalty to the party line" and were persecuted. As a result, even those policies which were obviously harmful to the economy were enforced under political pressure.

1.2.1. THE COAL SECTOR: "REVERSE THE TREND OF COAL TRANSPORTATION FROM THE NORTH TO THE SOUTH"

The geographical distribution of China's coal resources is quite uneven and does not coincide with

Fig. 1.2 Distribution of National Income and Coal Reserves

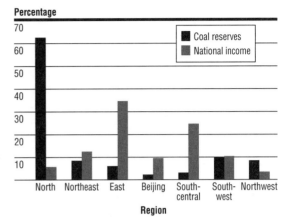

Percentage

SOURCE: Data from *China Statistical Yearbooks, 1980–1989* and Wu, Zongxin, "The Effects of Energy Policies on Demand Management," paper presented at the Seminar on Structural Change and Energy Policy, ESCAP, Bangkok, 1987.

industrial and population patterns. Of the total measured coal reserves (mostly of high quality), 62.4 percent are located in northern China, where income amounts to only 5.78 percent of the national total. But in south-central and eastern China, where 59.12 percent of the national income is created, only 9.1 percent of the national coal reserves are found, as shown in figure 1.2.

However, instead of looking for an optimal solution based on scientific evaluation of overall costs and benefits, Chairman Mao decided on a policy solely by his "lofty inspiration" to "reverse the trend of coal transportation from the north to the south" and, at the same time, also to "reverse the trend of grain transportation from the south to the north." According to his policy, the economically favorable coal reserves in northern China were abandoned, and the poor reserves in eastern and southern China were exploited, with unjustifiable effort. Most of the coal mine design institutes and coal mine exploration and construction companies in northern China were ordered to move to eastern and southern China during the Cultural Revolution. As a result, the productivity and economic efficiency of the coal industry dropped substantially, and the growth rate of coal production decreased. Enormous waste of both financial and human resources resulted. Fewer and fewer new state-owned coal mines were opened up since few large new coal reserves could be found in eastern and southern China.

Coal is China's major energy source. The declining growth rates of coal production resulted in ever more acute energy shortages. After Mao's death and the termination of the Cultural Revolu-

Table 1.2 Oil Burned Directly in China (Mton)

Year	Oil Produced	Oil burned				Percentage of oil burned
		Crude	Fuel	Diesel	Total	
1966	14.54	0.01	2.32	0	2.34	16.10
1967	13.76	0.03	2.75	0	2.79	20.30
1968	15.99	0.67	4.32	0.15	5.15	32.21
1969	21.74	2.19	4.71	0.70	7.61	35.02
1970	30.64	1.36	8.63	0.75	10.75	35.09
1971	39.41	1.53	11.87	1.58	15.00	38.07
1972	45.67	4.95	11.99	1.37	18.32	40.12
1973	53.61	7.71	13.24	0.65	21.61	40.31
1974	64.85	8.97	15.61	0.82	25.42	39.20
1975	77.05	12.41	17.20	0.58	30.20	39.20
1976	87.15	14.54	19.84	0.33	34.72	39.84
1977	93.63	14.85	21.57	0.20	36.63	39.12
1978	104.04	13.49	24.25	0.09	37.84	36.37
1979	106.14	11.31	24.70	0.24	36.26	34.16
1980	105.94	7.15	27.90	0.45	35.51	33.53

SOURCE: Song, Jian, et al., *Population Cybernetics* (Beijing: Scientific Press, 1990).

tion in 1976, the Ministry of Coal began to call some design institutes and construction companies back to northern China to enhance coal production. However, enormous difficulties were then encountered in relocating hundreds of thousands of workers and staff members and their families. Many of the experienced workers and engineers had grown old, had died, or were lost over the intervening decade. The backbone of the central-government controlled coal industry was thus substantially weakened.

1.2.2. THE OIL SECTOR: "BURN OIL"

Intoxicated by the successful exploitation of the Daqing oil field in the sixties and seventies, Chinese leaders overestimated potential Chinese oil resources and decided to demonstrate their motto, "Superiority of Socialism over Capitalism," in the midst of the world oil crisis of the time. -They issued the instruction, "Burn Oil," which meant oil was to be burned directly as fuel in many sectors, despite the waste of valuable oil resources. -A number of oil-fired power plants were built during the seventies, and a large quantity of crude oil was burned as fuel without being refined.

In Chinese refineries, the fraction of light products was far lower than in most other countries, and a large proportion of lighter hydrocarbons was left behind in heavy fuel oil burned (see table 1.2). The fraction of oil burned in the seventies is estimated to have been as high as 39 to 40 percent of the total oil produced. In table 1.3 the increasing

share of fuel oil produced in refineries from 1960 to 1981 is shown.

The policy of using oil as fuel should not be taken to imply that China really had an extensive oil supply. On the contrary, road transportation and agricultural mechanization in China were quite underdeveloped, and strict quotas on gasoline and diesel oil use have continued throughout the past decades. At least a billion barrels of oil were simply wasted by burning as a heat source. Later, in the eighties, oil shortages forced these oil-burning power plants to be retrofitted to burn coal. Several hundred million yuan of investment were thus wasted.

The overoptimistic attitude toward potential Chinese oil resources continued after the end of the Cultural Revolution. Mao's successor, Hua, boasted

Table 1.3 Proportion of Light and Heavy Oil Products

Year	Light products, %	Fuel oil, %
1960	56.78	6.51
1965	56.97	18.26
1970	49.21	31.66
1975	48.81	34.82
1976	47.48	34.92
1977	46.87	35.46
1978	47.44	34.94
1979	49.59	34.94
1980	46.46	38.12
1981	47.48	36.03

SOURCE: Song, Jian, et al., *Population Cybernetics.*

in 1979 that China would open ten more giant oil fields the size of Daqing by 2000, and the annual oil output would then reach 500 million tons (about 10 million barrels per day). This ambitious expectation was obviously based on false information about Chinese oil reserves provided by ingratiating officials. Such an unrealistic plan made the critical energy shortage even worse. At the time of the Hangzhou Symposium in 1980, top political leaders still dreamed of China as a "second Middle East." The very sharp critiques of the prevailing oil policy offered in that symposium incurred furious responses from some high officials.

1.2.3. THE NATURAL GAS SECTOR:
THE SECHUAN-SHANGHAI "STRATEGIC"
GAS PIPE LINE

The Chinese discovered and utilized natural gas in Sechuan as early as the second century B.C., more than two thousand years ago. However, the present known gas reserves are exceptionally limited compared to coal and oil. During the Cultural Revolution, party leaders received exaggerated information that enormous natural gas reserves had been discovered in Sechuan Province. They thought the utilizing of this fuel presented the ideal solution to the energy shortages in eastern China, where most Chinese industries were concentrated. Since this false report particularly suited Mao's ambitious Third Front (Strategic Rear Base) program, it immediately attracted the attention of the Supreme Leader. In the mid-seventies, Mao hastily launched a mammoth project to build a huge gas pipeline over 1,500 miles, from Sechuan to Shanghai, together with a parallel "strategic superhighway," as a part of his favored Third Front Construction Program. Construction of the gas pipeline started at once. Since the reported reserves were so huge, non-energy use of this resource was also planned. Construction also began on several large synthetic fertilizer plants along the pipeline intended to use natural gas as feedstock. Equipment for these factories was procured from abroad.

After Mao's death, the purported huge gas reserve was exposed as a fraud; there was not enough gas for even local consumption. This elaborate "patting the head" project was scrapped, but hundreds of millions of yuan worth of investment had been wasted. The fertilizer plants under construction had to change their feedstock from gas to naphtha, and the cost of fertilizer was increased substantially. No organization had ever accepted any responsibility for this horrible loss by the time the Hangzhou Symposium was held.

1.2.4. THE HYDROPOWER SECTOR:
THE THREE GORGES DAM

Hydropower resources are abundant in China. The exploitable resource is estimated to be 380 gigawatts (GWe), of which less than 5 percent had been developed by 1980. Many economically favorable dam sites are found along the major rivers, most in the multi-gigawatt range. In normal practice, to make better use of water power and to facilitate construction, stepwise development is favored in building dams. Dams on side streams and upper streams of a large river are usually built first, and downstream dams on the main stream are considered later. However, since Mao was intensely interested in mammoth projects and had written a well-known poem on the "Three Gorges Dam," this hydropower project became a political mission. Thus the rational sequence of the systematic exploitation of hydropower was exactly inverted, and the most difficult and highly uncertain project, the largest dam downstream, was planned to be built first.

In fact, the Three Gorges Dam project is unique in the world. The total installed capacity would have been over 25 GWe as it was first proposed. The height of the dam was originally to be as high as 200 meters, and at least 1.4 million people were to be relocated. The project's enormous engineering, economic, social, and environmental problems would have been impossible to solve in a short period. Sufficient analysis and experimentation should have been done in advance. However, under heavy political pressure, this project was begun prematurely. Hundreds of thousands of workers were moved to the site, and construction of a tail dam (Gezhouba) below the main one was begun during the Cultural Revolution. Because of the lack of preparation for the project, very soon after construction began an unexpected geological fault was discovered under the dam's foundation and reinforcement had to be added, wasting a great deal of investment and causing delay. Unfortunately, the responsible officials apparently did not learn their lessons, and enormous human and financial resources continued to be injected into this project. As a result, construction of hydro stations in many other more favorable sites was postponed indefinitely because of lack of resources.

1.2.5. RURAL ENERGY: NOBODY'S CONCERN

Rural energy issues were entirely ignored before 1980. This was a logical consequence of the lopsided industrialization policy, not limited to the energy sector alone. As implied by the popular slogan, "Steel Is the Key Link in the Economy," a priority in Chinese economic policy was put on the most energy-intensive sector, heavy industry. Much less attention was paid to light industry, and the service sector was almost ignored. Although the rural sector was a source of primary input to the whole economy, it received very little material feedback from other sectors. Overemphasis was put on human motivation and physical power and effort in agricultural production, as Mao prescribed in his preface to the "Collected Works on the High Tide of Socialistic Agricultural Collectivization." Only an insignificant amount of commercial energy was supplied for agricultural production, while the energy consumed in rural life depended entirely upon biomass and other local energy sources (figure 1.3.).

It was estimated that the average energy supply (about 3,500 kilocalories per family per day) was 20 percent below the baseline of energy demand for

rural livelihood (4,500 kilocalories per family per day). Peasants in some areas did not have even one cooked meal every day. As most of the agricultural wastes were burned as fuel, very little organic material could be returned to the fields or composted. Excessive deforestation had already caused serious soil erosion. Firewood was almost unavailable in most rural areas. Thus, the fertility of arable land continuously deteriorated, and agricultural productivity declined. The result has been the vicious cycle shown in figure 1.4.

Ironically, despite such a critical situation, no ministry in the government was assigned responsibility for rural energy issues. No specific rural energy policy was ever formulated before 1980. The daily life of 800 million rural people seemed to be entirely forgotten by their leaders!

1.2.6. CONSEQUENCES OF THE CHINESE ENERGY CRISIS

The serious mistakes in energy policies before 1980 led not only to direct financial losses of hundreds of millions of yuan, but also to a profound energy crisis in China. The disastrous consequences of the crisis may be summarized as follows:

1. Loss of about 30 percent of industrial production due to chronic energy shortages, in particular serious power shortages
2. Prolonged rationing of most energy commodities, in both productive and residential sectors, thus lowering productivity and quality of life
3. Energy availability for rural households of 20 percent less than the baseline of minimum daily requirements
4. Emergence of the vicious cycle in rural ecology, thus reducing agricultural production

Fig. 1.3 Energy Structure in Chinese Rural Regions

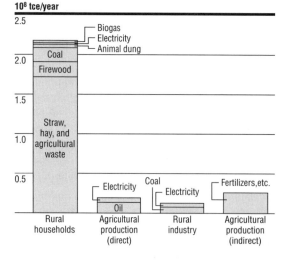

Fig. 1.4 Vicious Cycle of Energy Shortages in Rural China

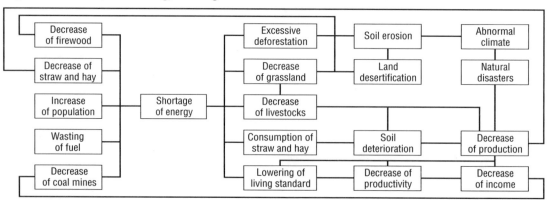

SOURCE: See Lu, Yingzhong, "An Analysis of the Substitution of Coal with Nuclear Energy," *Research in Econometrics and Techno-economics* 10 (1983).

5. Enormous difficulties in the energy industry threatening to further decrease the energy supply
6. Serious waste of energy and high energy-intensities in many sectors
7. Resultant critical energy shortages as the most serious constraint on the development of the national economy

In 1980, the Chinese government announced its ambitious goal of the Four Modernizations, that is, "to quadruple the national product by the year 2000," which required an annual economic growth rate of 7 percent to be maintained for the twenty years after 1980. It was quite clear that, without a rational energy policy for fueling the rapidly growing economy, the "quadrupling" target would be only a "paper tiger," even laughable.

1.3. BIRTH OF A SCIENTIFIC APPROACH TO ENERGY POLICY

1.3.1. FIRST REPORT ON THE CHINESE ENERGY CRISIS

According to the resolutions made at the Hangzhou meeting, a report entitled "The Critical Energy Situation of the PRC" was very soon drafted and sent to most of the top leaders through various channels. It resulted in fierce responses. It was the first report addressing the Chinese energy crisis, describing the real energy situation, and documenting the disastrous consequences of the wrong energy policies. At that time, this was a bold violation of a taboo — the word "crisis" could never be used in referring to a socialist economy.

The fact that these dissident intellectuals dared to criticize the party policy even after the Anti-Rightists Campaign of 1957 was itself a shock to the ruling regime. Some reform-minded leaders applauded the courage and patriotism of the elite, but others stamped their feet in fury. The executive chairman of the symposium, Lin Hanxiong, then the leader of the Energy Bureau of the SSTC, was bitterly scolded and threatened by one "overlord" in the Chinese energy administration. It was said that Lin even lost his opportunity for promotion for several years afterward as a penalty for his disloyalty. However, the audacious report had in fact challenged the party's monopoly on policymaking. Later on, more and more meetings similar to the Hangzhou symposium were sponsored by reform-minded leaders, and such activities eventually led to general reform of policymaking and the adoption of a more scientific approach in the decisionmaking process within the bureaucratic superstructure of the PRC.

1.3.2. FORMATION OF A CENTER FOR ENERGY POLICY RESEARCH

The second resolution of the First All-China Energy Symposium was implemented one year later. At the end of December 1980, the Second All-China Energy Symposium was held in Beijing. Stemming from that meeting, the first Chinese non-governmental academic policy research organization, the Chinese Energy Research Society (CERS), was founded in January 1981. The second energy report, entitled "Thirteen Proposals: Toward Alleviating the Energy Crisis in the PRC," was drafted by the same meeting and submitted immediately to the government.

Soon after the CERS came into being, it became the focus of Chinese energy policy research. Over five hundred senior energy experts from 170 institutions all over China joined the CERS and began conducting comprehensive research on all aspects of the Chinese energy situation and relevant policies. One year later, in January 1982, the Third All-China Energy Symposium was held in Zhengzhou (Henan Province), where the research findings were discussed. In October 1982, the first comprehensive academic report, entitled "Research Report on Chinese Energy Policy," the outcome of the collective work of some 270 co-authors, was published and circulated internally. It later served as the basis of the official Chinese energy policy.

The broad Chinese economic reform promoted an evolution of energy policymaking. Reform leaders advocated that all government officials should study modern sciences and technologies to increase their ability to manage a modern economy. At the initiation of the late party secretary-general, Hu Yaobang, a group of senior scientists were invited to Zhong-nan-hai, the headquarters of the Chinese Communist party and the central government, to give a series of lectures for the top leaders beginning in July 1980. One topic of these lectures was "Ways to Eliminate the Energy Crisis from the Viewpoint of Energy Technology Development." The term "energy crisis" attracted the attention of the top reform leaders. Immediately the State Science and Technology Commission and the General Office of the Central Government were authorized to ask CERS to organize a series of lectures on energy and energy policy for over a thousand senior officials (ministers and bureau leaders and the equivalent). It was the first large-scale training program of its kind for government officials on the sciences and the scientific approach to policymaking. Chinese intellectuals had been considered an alien stratum deserving only "re-education" during the Cultural Revolution. But the re-educatee reassumed the mantle of educator.

Seven popular lectures on basic knowledge, "Energy and Energy Forecasting," "Energy Conservation," "Coal," "Oil and Natural Gas," "Electricity," "Nuclear Energy," and "Rural Energy," were given, and they received the serious attention of most attendees. Energy suddenly became a focus in national economic planning. One year later, energy was officially recognized in formal government documents to be the most critical issue in the development of the Chinese economy.

1.3.3. OBSTACLES TO SCIENTIFIC POLICYMAKING

The way to a scientific methodology for energy policymaking was not straightforward. Ideology was the first barrier to overcome. Before the recent economic reform, particularly during the Cultural Revolution, what was considered common sense in Western economies was heresy or even criminal in China, since it was contradictory to the then-prevailing crude doctrines of Maoism. Policies giving priority to profit or development of technology were bitterly denounced as revisionism. Instead, "Politics in Command" and "Class Struggle as the Key Link" were then the unquestionable "Supreme Instructions."

Ideological bias always overrode economic considerations in policymaking. As a result, many basic concepts and common practices in Western economies were absolutely banned in China. For instance, even the concept of elasticity was not understood and was therefore unacceptable to most Chinese economic officials and planners at that time. The basic idea of the "cost" of money was once considered a terrible heresy to the Marxist Labor Theory of Value.

In such a repressive environment, how could a scientific methodology of integrated energy-economic modeling be applied to Chinese energy policymaking? In fact, some liberal economists openly expressed their fear of being persecuted as counterrevolutionaries when they introduced Western econometric methodology into energy-economic forecasting. In such an approach, two productive factors, capital and labor, were assumed to be mutually substitutive, which directly contradicted Marx's Labor Theory. Bitter personal experiences in the Anti-Rightists Campaign and the Cultural Revolution had made many intellectuals "trembling in talking about a tiger" on politics, so they preferred to keep their distance from politically sensitive issues such as energy-economic policymaking.

The second barrier was that, for the sake of political security, responsible officials often preferred to go along with the opinions of their direct superiors rather than to credit the findings of scientific research. In fact, the report on the first forecast of Chinese energy demand was locked in the desk drawer of the vice-chairman of the State Planning Commission (SPC), simply because the result was considered to deviate too far from the thinking of his direct superiors.

The third obstacle was unreasonable security regulations. National economic statistics were then considered top secret, and no academic researcher was allowed to access information needed in policy analysis and forecasting. Under such circumstances, the statistical data gathered by the central government were far from adequate, and they were insufficient for policymaking. For instance, no official input-output table had been developed before 1980, even though the State Planning Commission had to balance the input-output of every economic sector when formulating and implementing the five-year plan. The planners followed the most primitive trial-and-error, hand-calculation methods, and they always left some gaps between supply and demand. As a result, energy research in China had to start from scratch; that is, basic data collection had to be conducted before methodology development could proceed.

Even the state financing system imposed some additional obstacles. The funds for scientific research in China were allocated among the natural, technological, and social sciences. Finances in the former two categories were allocated to the SSTC and the Academy of Natural Sciences, and those for the social sciences went to the Academy of Social Sciences. Research on energy policy was not considered to fit into any of these three categories, so CERS energy policy research could not get even a little seed money from the state financing system. Donations had to be sought among the member institutes, and the CERS office had to be operated solely by "loan" staffs from the Institute of Nuclear Energy Technology (INET) for several years. The INET in turn got its funds through international cooperative energy research projects sponsored by the United Nations Development Program (UNDP), the Commission of the European Community (CEC), and the International Development Research Center (IDRC) in these years, rather than through the official channels from SSTC and the Ministry of Education, to which it belongs. Not until 1984 was policy research, a so-called "soft science," formally recognized by the Ministry of Finance and given its piece of the pie in the state budget of China.

1.3.4. INTRODUCTION OF SCIENTIFIC METHODOLOGY IN ENERGY SYSTEMS ANALYSIS

With the strong support of reform-minded leaders, the above obstacles were overcome one after another, and a very progressive research program on Chinese energy policy was at last carried out. Under the sponsorship of the SSTC and SPC, the INET of Tsinghua University and the Institute of Systems Engineering (ISE) of Tianjing University cooperated in developing the first Chinese Medium- and Long-Term Energy-Economic Model System. This comprehensive model was completed in 1982 and includes the economic development model, the multisector input-output model, the linear programming optimization model, the regional energy demand and supply model, and the national accounting model. (See chapter 7.) At the same time, a very detailed official input-output table consisting of some 124 sectors was edited by SPC with the advice and participation of INET. With all these basic tools prepared, Chinese energy policymaking eventually bade farewell to the "patting the head" tradition and entered a new era of scientific analysis.

1.3.5. OFFICIAL EFFORTS ON ENERGY POLICY REFORM

The Chinese economic reform of the early eighties gave great impetus to techno-economic policy study. After January 1983, the three highest administrative organizations in the Chinese government — that is, the State Science and Technology Commission, the State Planning Commission, and the State Economic Commission — under the guidance of the State Council organized over 2,000 senior experts and responsible senior officials to discuss and draft technical policies in thirteen sectors and areas — energy, transportation, communications, computers, integrated circuits, consumer goods, materials industries, building materials, urban and rural construction, urban and rural housing, and environmental protection.

The energy sector was a focus and hence was most thoroughly investigated. The research outcomes of CERS were extensively referred to, and in fact all the leaders and most of the participants of the energy policy drafting group were members of CERS. As a result, the viewpoints in CERS' past research were basically included in the final draft of the official "Energy Policy Outline" which was published as Blue Paper No. 4 of the SSTC, 1984. Later on, all the technical policies of the thirteen sectors and areas were published in a total of eleven volumes of blue papers.

The technical policies of the energy sector included

1. promoting the production and improvement of the structure of primary energy;
2. energy-economic zoning of the whole nation, establishing the integral energy-economic complex in each zone, and gradually adjusting the geographical distribution of industries;
3. enhancing coal production;
4. emphasizing general exploration for petroleum resources and increasing the economic efficiency of oil fields;
5. giving priority to the exploitation of hydropower, a renewable energy source;
6. building nuclear power stations in those regions economically advanced but short of energy;
7. putting equal emphasis on the exploitation of natural gas and the exploitation of oil;
8. accelerating the construction of power plants
9. actively developing and utilizing new energy sources;
10. improving energy utilization efficiency and strictly enforcing energy conservation measures;
11. rationalizing the utilization of oil and natural gas resources, improving processing of crude oil and the allocating of oil products;
12. modernizing the technologies of coal processing, burning, and conversion, improving of coal allocation, and enhancing the comprehensive utilization of coal;
13. establishing a rational rural energy structure and terminating the severe energy shortages in rural regions as soon as possible;
14. improving the urban residential energy structure and meeting the reasonable energy demands of urban residents;
15. elevating the quality and technical levels of energy equipment; and
16. giving more attention to environmental protection in energy production and use.

In May 1986, the State Council of the PRC approved the publication of these sectoral technical policies in the form of a white paper, volume 1, of SSTC. The full text of the "Main Points of the Technical Policies of Energy Sources" in this white paper is included in Appendix A.

By the beginning of the Seventh Five-Year Plan (1986-1990) of the PRC, the energy sector (as well as the other twelve sectors, in various degrees) thus had a consistent set of comprehensive technical policies based on extensive scientific research carried out by hundreds of experts. The "patting the head" approach of the former party leaders was no longer in control.

The implications of such an achievement extended far beyond the energy sector. It was essentially a first step toward political reform. In July 1986, an "All-China Symposium on Soft Sciences" was held in Shanghai. The theme of this symposium was "The Democratization of Decisionmaking." Vice-Premier Wan Li made the keynote speech at that gathering. An editorial entitled "Carry Out Soft Science Research, Promote the Democratization and Scientification of Decisionmaking" was published in the official newspaper, the *People's Daily*. It was reported that some 420 institutes with 15,000 researchers were involved in "soft science" research (including policy study) by 1986, and 1,735 projects had been carried out. Later, in 1986 and 1988, the research outcomes under the "National Energy Model System" and the "Chinese Energy Policies" blue papers, respectively, were commended by the Chinese government.

The efforts made by Chinese energy experts eventually bore fruit. A scientific methodology of energy policymaking had been at last established and adopted.

CHAPTER 2

THE INESCAPABLE DENOMINATOR — ONE BILLION

Rediscovery of Chinese Energy Reality

2.1 REALITY AND SPECIAL FEATURES OF THE CHINESE ENERGY-ECONOMY

Ignorance of the real situation and the special features of the Chinese energy economy was one of the major causes of the disastrous mistakes in Chinese policymaking described in the previous chapter. Thus, reform of Chinese energy policy could only begin with the rediscovery of the relevant facts.

China is a huge developing country of over one billion people and 9.6 million square kilometers of territory. In the past forty years, both its economy and its energy production have grown rapidly, as shown in tables 2.1 and 2.2 and figures 2.1 and 2.2, respectively. From 1953 to 1989, the national income increased 895.7 percent, while energy production increased 1,858.5 percent during the same period. Total energy production attained almost 1,017 million tons coal equivalent (tce) in 1989, the third-greatest national production in the world. However, since China's population also increased substantially in those years, the per capita value of energy consumption still remains very low in China as compared with many other countries.

China has adopted a policy of self-reliance in developing its economy. The energy industry in China has developed very rapidly. Presently most equipment for coal mines, oil fields, refineries, and fossil-fuel and hydropower plants is manufactured inside China, and more advanced technologies such as nuclear plants and fluidized bed boilers are under development. Chinese industry is now able to supply all the major equipment for the large oil fields (annual production up to 350 million barrels per field), underground coal mines (annual production up to 3 to 5 million tons per mine), hydropower plants (up to 2.71 GWe per station), thermal power

Fig. 2.1 Gross Value of Agricultural and Industrial Production and National Income

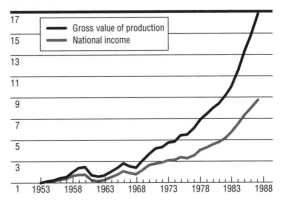

Fig. 2.2 Energy Production in China

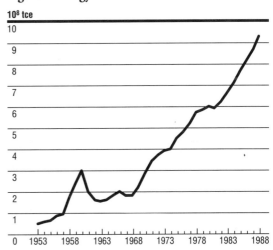

plants (up to 1.62 GWe per station), and nuclear power plants, including nuclear fuel (300 MWe per unit). In figure 2.3 major energy production bases and potential sites are shown schematically, indi-

Table 2.1 Growth of Gross Value of Industrial and Agricultural Products and National Income of the PRC

Year	Amount (100 million yuan) Gross value	Net income	Growth indices (1953=100) Gross value	Net income
1953	960	709	100.0	100.0
1954	1,050	748	109.4	105.8
1955	1,109	788	121.1	112.5
1956	1,252	882	135.9	128.4
1957	1,241	908	146.7	134.2
1958	1,649	1,118	194.0	163.8
1959	1,980	1,222	231.6	177.2
1960	2,094	1,220	244.1	174.6
1961	1,621	996	168.3	122.8
1962	1,504	924	151.2	114.8
1963	1,635	1,000	165.7	127.1
1964	1,884	1,166	194.8	148.1
1965	2,235	1,387	234.5	173.2
1966	2,534	1,586	275.1	202.6
1967	2,306	1,487	248.7	188.0
1968	2,213	1,415	238.3	175.7
1969	2,613	1,617	294.9	209.6
1970	3,138	1,926	371.0	258.4
1971	3,482	2,077	416.0	276.6
1972	3,640	2,136	434.8	284.5
1973	3,967	2,381	474.7	308.1
1974	4,007	1,348	481.3	311.6
1975	4,467	2,503	538.6	337.5
1976	4,536	2,427	547.7	328.5
1977	4,978	2,644	606.4	354.1
1978	5,634	3,010	680.9	397.7
1979	6,379	3,350	738.8	425.5
1980	7,078	3,688	794.2	452.9
1981	7,581	3,941	830.8	474.8
1982	8,294	4,258	903.8	513.7
1983	9,211	4,736	996.1	565.0
1984	10,831	5,652	1,147.5	641.8
1985	13,337	7,020	1,340.2	728.5
1986	15,207	7,859	1,467.6	784.5
1987	18,489	9,294	1,687.7	864.4
1988	24,089	11,716	1,979.7	960.3
1989	28,552	13,000	2,128.2	995.7

SOURCE: *China Statistical Yearbooks, 1980-1989.*

Table 2.2 Growth of Energy Production in the PRC

Year	Total	Coal	Oil	Natural gas	Hydro-power
1949	2,374	2,285	17	1	71
1950	3,174	3,070	29	1	74
1951	3,903	3,784	44	—	75
1952	4,871	4,712	63	1	95
1953	5,192	4,998	89	1	104
1954	6,262	5,998	113	2	149
1955	7,295	6,997	139	2	157
1956	8,242	7,854	166	3	219
1957	9,816	9,353	209	9	290
1958	19,845	19,278	323	15	229
1959	27,161	26,347	533	36	242
1960	29,637	28,346	744	138	409
1961	21,224	19,849	759	196	420
1962	17,185	15,708	822	161	494
1963	17,009	15,494	927	136	452
1964	17,232	15,351	1,213	141	527
1965	18,824	16,565	1,617	146	496
1966	20,833	17,993	2,081	178	581
1967	17,494	14,708	1,985	194	607
1968	18,715	15,708	2,287	186	534
1969	23,104	18,992	3,109	261	742
1970	30,990	25,276	4,383	382	949
1971	35,289	27,989	5,636	497	1,167
1972	37,785	29,274	6,531	644	1,336
1973	40,013	29,774	7,666	795	1,778
1974	41,626	29,488	9,274	1,001	1,863
1975	48,754	34,415	11,020	1,177	2,142
1976	50,340	34,486	12,464	1,343	2,047
1977	56,396	39,270	13,391	1,612	2,123
1978	62,770	44,125	14,879	1,826	1,840
1979	64,562	45,339	15,179	1,930	2,114
1980	63,735	44,297	15,136	1,898	2,404
1981	63,227	44,404	14,461	1,694	2,668
1982	66,778	47,596	14,589	1,587	3,006
1983	71,270	51,039	15,135	1,624	3,454
1984	77,855	56,375	16,374	1,652	3,454
1985	85,546	62,307	17,843	1,720	3,676
1986	88,124	63,861	18,670	1,830	3,762
1987	91,266	66,285	19,163	1,847	3,970
1988	95,801	69,993	19,578	1,897	4,333
1989	101,687	75,248	19,626	2,034	4,779

SOURCE: *China Statistical Yearbooks, 1980-1989.*

cating the tremendous scale of development and the extreme effort made by the Chinese people in their own energy industry.

However, the Chinese energy-economy has some peculiar features which are radically different in most other countries. Failure to recognize these features in policymaking will cause mistakes and even lead to disasters.

Besides some characteristics common to developing countries, such as the large proportion of rural

14

Fig. 2.3 Energy Production Bases in the PRC

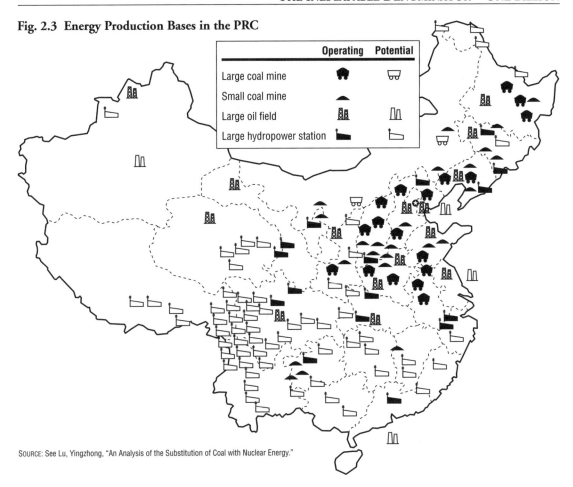

SOURCE: See Lu, Yingzhong, "An Analysis of the Substitution of Coal with Nuclear Energy."

population and agricultural production, the extensive use of noncommercial traditional fuels, and the low per capita income, the Chinese energy-economy has certain paradoxes more critical to energy policymaking. These might be summarized as four "coexistences," that is, (1) the coexistence of abundance and shortage, (2) the coexistence of vastness and diversity, (3) the coexistence of modernization and backwardness, and (4) the coexistence of central planning and market economy.

2.2 THE COEXISTENCE OF ABUNDANCE AND SCARCITY

2.2.1. EFFECT OF THE ONE-BILLION DENOMINATOR

In the early stages of energy policy study in 1980, much effort was made to convince overoptimistic senior government policymakers to recognize the "dual nature" of Chinese energy reality. On the one hand, China has enormous energy resources and ranks third in the world in energy production. Based on these facts, China would seem to be an "energy power" with great potential for energy exports, and hence a country where an energy crisis could never appear. On the other hand, when the impressive figures on energy resources and production are divided by the huge number of people in the country, namely, by a factor of one billion, then both the per capita resources and the per capita product rank very low among the countries of the world.

Hence, chronic energy shortages have struck every sector of the Chinese economy and threatened the fulfillment of the Four Modernizations. This paradox arises from the enormous population of China, the huge denominator of one billion, and determines the energy policy in the country. The key point in the report of the First All-China Energy Symposium was the analysis of the two-sided nature of the Chinese energy situation, and it urged recognition of the Chinese energy crisis.

This argument is self-evident today, but at that time it was not easily comprehended by those who were biased, for various reasons. It took a long time

15

to convince senior Chinese leaders to accept such an irony in their policymaking.

Since energy will be eventually consumed by all the people, either directly or indirectly, energy resources and supply should be calculated on a per capita basis. The population of China is the greatest of any nation; it reached a billion by 1981. Any amount of resource or production divided by this astronomical denominator will be reduced by nine orders of magnitude. Then the picture will be changed entirely. In figures 2.4 and 2.5, the total and per capita energy consumption of the twelve largest energy consumers in the world are shown; China's rank descends from third in terms of total quantity to eleventh in terms of per capita value, just above that of India. The per capita energy consumption of the Chinese people is less than a tenth of that in the United States and Canada, less than a fifth of that in most developed countries. How could China be an energy power with such a low level of per capita energy consumption?

Two more examples of the energy paradox, with important policy implications, should be mentioned here. The first concerns evaluation of China's oil export potential. The prevailing opinion in the late seventies in China was that it would become a great oil exporter, even a "second Middle East." A second example has to do with determining the respective roles of energy conservation and exploitation, and the opinion among policymakers that energy conservation alone would solve the acute energy shortage in the Chinese economy. In fact, even some knowledgeable foreign energy experts have made the same mistakes in these two cases by neglecting the two-sided nature of China's energy situation.

2.2.2. IS CHINA POTENTIALLY A GREAT OIL EXPORTER?

China has sizable oil resources, 20.5 billion barrels as reported in 1980 (see table 2.3). However, when counted on a per capita oil reserve basis, the situation turns out to be quite different, as shown in table 2.4. The per capita oil reserve in China was just twenty-one barrels in 1980, barely enough for one year's per capita oil consumption in 1986 in the United States. In figures 2.6 and 2.7, the total and per capita oil reserves of the thirty largest oil-producing countries are depicted side by side. It is quite clear that, while the total reserve of China ranks tenth among these countries, China's per capita reserve rank drops to twenty-eighth. Anyone who looked seriously at figure 2.7 would never dream that China could become the "second Middle East"!

In fact, the supply of oil products in China is far from sufficient to run a modern society. The quota of gasoline in Beijing for each institute-owned

Fig. 2.4 Comparative Total National Energy Consumption in 1986

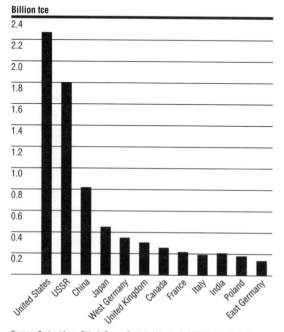

SOURCE: Derived from *China's Energy Statistics Yearbook, 1989* (Beijing: China's Statistics Press, 1990).

Fig. 2.5 Comparative National Per Capita Energy Consumption in 1986

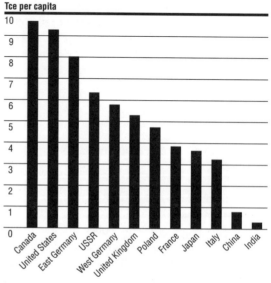

SOURCE: Derived from *China's Energy Statistics Yearbook, 1989.*

Table 2.3 Proven Oil Reserves in 30 Countries, 1980 (Billions of barrels)

Country	Reserves	Country	Reserves
1. Saudi Arabia	165.0	16. Canada	6.4
2. Kuwait	64.9	17. Norway	5.5
3. Soviet Union	63.0	18. Qatar	3.6
4. Iraq	57.5	19. Malaysia	3.0
5. Mexico	44.0	20. Egypt	2.9
6. United Arab Emirates	36.5	21. India	2.6
7. Iran	30.0	22. Argentina	2.5
8. United States	26.4	23. Australia	2.4
9. Libya	23.0	24. Oman	2.3
10. China	20.5	25. Syria	1.9
11. Venezuela	18.0	26. Brunei	1.7
12. Nigeria	16.7	27. Tunisia	1.6
13. United Kingdom	14.8	28. Brazil	1.3
14. Indonesia	9.5	29. Angola	1.2
15. Algeria	8.2	30. Ecuador	1.1

Table 2.4 Per Capita Oil Reserves in 30 Countries (Barrels)

Country	Reserves	Country	Reserves
1. Kuwait	44,721	16. Tunisia	260
2. United Arab Emirates	36,460	17. Soviet Union	237
3. Saudi Arabia	19,713	18. Malaysia	223
4. Qatar	16,296	19. Nigeria	217
5. Brunei	9,000	20. Syria	216
6. Libya	7,718	21. Angola	170
7. Oman	2,626	22. Australia	161
8. Iraq	2,294	23. Ecuador	132
9. Iran	1,535	24. United States	116
10. Norway	1,345	25. Argentina	91
11. Venezuela	1,290	26. Egypt	69
12. Mexico	612	27. Indonesia	63
13. Algeria	441	28. China	21
14. Canada	267	29. Brazil	11
15. United Kingdom	265	30. India	4

Source: *Energy Statistics* (Chicago: Gas Research Institute, 1980).

car is as low as 20 to 25 gallons per car per month, while the number of privately owned cars is still negligible. Current Chinese gasoline production would not be sufficient to maintain an increase in private cars in China. The export of Chinese crude oil is merely a measure to earn hard currency; oil revenues amounted to 25 percent of total revenue from exports before the collapse of oil prices in 1986. Some Chinese experts charged that such a policy was "selling one's blood for bread."

The policy implication of the above analysis is that the momentum of Chinese crude exports should

Fig. 2.6 Proven Oil Reserves

Billions of barrels

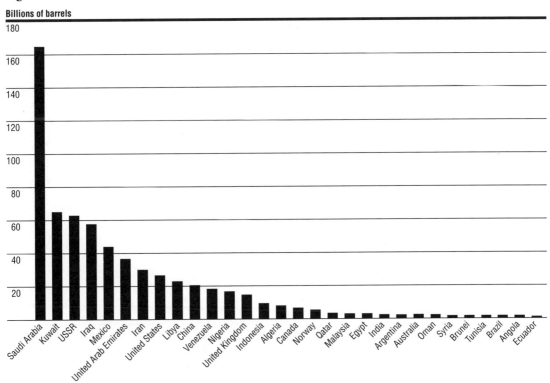

Fig. 2.7 Per Capita Oil Reserves

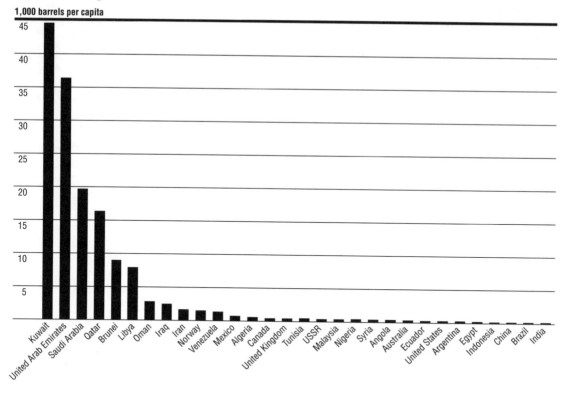

1,000 barrels per capita

be slowed. It is estimated that one ton of oil could create at least ten times more value if it were used to produce other commodities for export. Ironically, due to serious energy shortages, the government has even allowed some local trading companies in eastern and southern China to "import" Chinese crude from northern China and pay for it with hard currency they had earned from exporting other commodities! It is therefore expected that the oil exports of China will steadily decrease.

2.2.3. ENERGY EXPLOITATION AND CONSERVATION

A more important implication of the "one-billion denominator" problem is the recognition of the equal importance that should be given to energy exploitation and conservation in Chinese energy policy. Another example can be given of misunderstanding on the part of some knowledgeable energy experts as well as some policymakers.

A hot debate had been waged in the embryonic stage of policy research on the respective roles of energy conservation and energy exploitation. Because the energy intensity per unit value created in the economy was several times higher in China than in developed countries, some experts maintained that the energy shortage in China could be terminated

by merely promoting energy conservation. Others argued that since the per capita energy consumption in China was so low, even if energy conservation was successfully implemented, a rapid increase of energy demand would be inevitable if modern-

Fig. 2.8 Distribution of Coal Resources in China

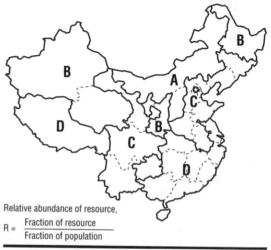

Relative abundance of resource,

$$R = \frac{\text{Fraction of resource}}{\text{Fraction of population}}$$

A	10 < R	Extremely abundant	**C**	0.1 < R < 1	Relatively poor
B	1 < R < 10	Relatively abundant	**D**	R < 0.1	Extremely poor

SOURCE: See Lu, Yingzhong, "The Prospect of Energy in the PRC," paper presented at the Training Program on Energy Planning and Management at State University of New York, Stony Brook, October 1980.

ization targets were to be pursued. (Such a situation has already been shown in figure 2.5.) How could one imagine that China could match the standard of living in advanced countries with a per capita energy consumption of less than a tenth or a fifth of the consumption in those countries?

The paradox of very high energy intensities per unit value and very low energy consumption per capita was partly attributed to the differences in respective energy pricing systems. The actual conservation potential was not so great when technological potential alone was considered. Hence, at the same time that efforts were being made to decrease energy intensity, substantial increases in energy supplies would also be indispensable in promoting modernization programs. Even doubling the energy supply, the per capita energy consumption in China by 2000 (about 1.3 tce) will still be far behind many advanced countries. Thus the low per capita energy consumption level must always be kept in mind in policymaking.

2.3. COEXISTENCE OF VASTNESS AND DIVERSITY

The vastness of Chinese territory leads naturally to diversity. However, in energy policymaking, the two interrelated factors have special implications.

2.3.1. PROBLEMS ASSOCIATED WITH GEOGRAPHICAL DISTRIBUTION

In chapter 1 the mistake caused by ignoring the effect of the uneven distribution of Chinese coal resources was addressed. However, restoring priority to the exploitation of the more favorable resources in northern China does not imply a solution of the

problems accompanying the uneven distribution of coal reserves. On the contrary, as coal production increases, the transportation difficulties become more and more acute, and this may eventually turn out to be a major restraint on Chinese energy supply and coal exploitation.

As already seen in chapter 1, most of the coal resources are concentrated in northern China, and most centers of consumption are located in eastern and southern China. The implementation of the government's recent "open policy" will further accelerate the economic development of coastal regions and thus will further increase this discrepancy. Early in 1980, a coal resource distribution zone map based on the per capita reserve of each region was drawn (see figure 2.8). A forecast based on such zoning was then made, which predicted the pending energy shortage in northeast China, in contrast with the prevailing opinion at that time that this region was an important energy production base. Later on, in the mid-eighties, energy shortages struck northeast China exactly as forecasted. About 24 million tons of coal had to be imported from Shanxi to this region in 1985, and the amount is steadily increasing.

The share of coal production in northern China between 1980 and 2000 is expected to increase from 33 percent to 46 percent of the national total (see table 2.5). About 400 million tons of coal will have to be shipped from the north to eastern and southern China. Thus transportation can be predicted to become the bottleneck of the future Chinese energy supply system. The construction of more railroads will be obstructed by the massive mountain ranges between the coal bases and the coastal region, and the limited capacity of available harbors along the coasts will further restrict the amount of coal trans-

Table 2.5 Coal Reserves and Production by Region

Region	Measured reserves 10^9 ton	%	1985 (actual), 10^9 ton Production	Consumption	Transportation	2000 (forecast), 10^9 ton Production	Consumption	Transportation
Shanxi, Shaanxi, Inner Mongolia	480.0	62.4	0.257	0.130	0.127	0.60	0.150	0.450
Northeast	64.1	8.3	0.147	0.171	−0.024	0.24	0.315	−0.075
East	46.9	6.1	0.127	0.181	−0.054	0.20	0.390	0.190
Beijing, Tianjing, Hebei	17.8	2.3	0.071	0.101	−0.030	0.09	0.155	−0.065
South-central	23.4	3.0	0.131	0.153	−0.022	0.16	0.235	−0.074
Southwest	74.3	9.7	0.095	0.088	0.007	0.14	0.148	−0.007
Northwest	63.0	8.2	0.043	0.041	0.002	0.07	0.060	0.008
Total	**769.2**	**100.0**	**0.871**	**0.865**	**—**	**1.50**	**1.453**	**—**

SOURCE: Wu, Zongxin, et al., *China's Energy Demand by 2050* (Beijing: INET, 1988).

ported to the east and south. Water shortages will force the multi-gigawatt mine-mouth power plants to adopt dry cooling — an expensive option even if it is technically feasible.

This situation is critical for the Chinese energy system. Such a bottleneck may eventually become a serious constraint on further development of a coal-dominant energy structure. Thus the uneven geographic distribution requires not only substantial expansion of the transportation system in China but also radical readjustment of industrial distribution and the energy mix. The policy addressing the establishment of the integral "energy-economic zones" reflects such a consideration.

2.3.2. DIVERSE ENERGY SITUATIONS AND DIVERSE SOLUTIONS

Casual analysts and policymakers often neglect the crucial fact that the situations are entirely different in Chinese urban and rural regions. In fact, the commercial energy data usually cited is relevant only for urban regions. The rural regions have to maintain themselves on very small amounts of energy, mainly noncommercial agricultural wastes. If the situation in Chinese urban areas is considered an energy crisis, it would not be an exaggeration to say that the energy situation in Chinese rural regions is an energy famine.

Since over 81 percent of China's total population lives in the countryside, the development of the rural economy is particularly significant to the national economy. In fact, the situation of Chinese rural regions became nearly explosive as a result of the catastrophic policy of the People's Communes. The stagnation of per capita average rural income implies that a sizable fraction of rural people were actually impoverished during the three decades after 1949. The rural economy was then on the verge of bankruptcy. The rural energy policy thus acquired strategic significance beyond the energy sector.

However, the Chinese rural economy is characterized by its highly decentralized and technically backward nature. The low income level and the vast rural territory make the distribution of large amounts of commercial energy extremely difficult. As a result, the solution of Chinese rural energy issues must be based on principles entirely different from those applied to the urban situation. The policy as stated in the white paper was: "Conforming with local conditions, mutual supplementing of various energies, comprehensive utilization, and attachment of importance to economic returns as far as energy construction in rural areas is concerned."

In short, this policy was based on diversification. (Chapter 5 is devoted to the discussion of Chinese rural energy policy.)

2.4. COEXISTENCE OF MODERNIZATION AND BACKWARDNESS

The modernization of the life of one-fifth of the world's population requires centuries, not decades. As a result, the coexistence of modernization and backwardness will be a reality in Chinese society for many decades to come. In particular, one cannot ignore the historical background of the present Chinese energy-economic situation.

China successfully advanced its industrialization program during the turbulent years from 1958 to 1979 totally isolated from the rest of the world. This fact accounts for many peculiar features in the Chinese energy-economic system. The Russians terminated their commitments and deserted their intimate ally after 1958, and the import of Russian technologies almost stopped after 1960. The only trade remaining with the Soviet Union was the Chinese repayment of the debts of the fifties with the agricultural and raw materials so badly needed by China's own people. On the other hand, Western countries had conducted an economic blockade against the People's Republic since the Korean War in 1950, and the economic relationship was not normalized until 1979, when the reform regime declared its "open door policy." However, during this long isolation period, China almost tripled its national income and established a complete domestic industrial system based on the Russian technologies imported during the fifties. The Chinese also succeeded in developing some high technologies for national defense such as nuclear weapons, nuclear submarines, and missiles, but the country lagged far behind in most civilian areas, such as materials, manufacturing, petrochemicals, electronics, computers, and most consumer goods.

The Chinese energy system reflects all these techno-economic features. On the one hand, the self-reliance line guaranteed very rapid growth of energy production, almost 8.9 percent per year, or a 650 percent growth in the twenty-three years after 1957. On the other hand, the irrational economic structure and the backwardness of most technologies increased the energy intensity of the economy from 1.06 kilograms coal equivalent (kgce) per yuan in 1957 to 2.04 kgce/yuan in 1980, almost doubling during that period. Should this trend continue, the ambitious plan of quadrupling the national product by 2000 would require multiplying the energy supply by a factor of eight — something totally incredible and beyond the reach of any economy. Energy shortages thus threatened every economic sector, and further economic development was seriously restrained by energy supply. This was one of the most critical issues that the Chinese reformers faced at the beginning of the recent economic reform in 1979.

The official slogan in 1980 was "Double the Energy Supply to Guarantee the Quadrupling of Production." At that time the energy planners had in fact a very hot potato on their hands as they began to look for a novel approach to the Chinese energy economy: to double the energy supply within two decades while reducing the energy intensity by a factor of two.

The policy implications of such a complicated situation are twofold. On the one hand, obsolete technologies waste energy and keep intensity high. On the other hand, however, since development is rapid, the newly built production capabilities will dominate the economy within two or three decades. Thus, new technology will lead if correct policies are implemented to favor energy-saving targets. Events have already proved this argument. Energy consumption elasticity has dropped from an average value of 1.27 between 1953 and 1979 to 0.5 in the eighties, after the scientific energy policies were formulated and implemented.

2.5. COEXISTENCE OF CENTRAL PLANNING AND THE MARKET ECONOMY

The present Chinese energy policy was born at the beginning of an unprecedented economic reform. One of the most radical aspects of this reform was the recognition and incorporation of market mechanisms in the context of a centrally planned economy, which had been claimed to be the essence of socialism.

The analysis of the adequacy, the limits, and the theoretical implications of such an interesting experiment is beyond the scope of the present book. However, since this novel duality has profound effects on Chinese energy policy, it is interesting to analyze the effects of the hybrid economic system.

The rapid growth of the Chinese economy and its energy industry had been achieved in a centrally planned context. The merit of such a system was generally recognized to be its potential to concentrate necessary resources for the implementation of a particular long-term or very large project. This is not a method unique to the Chinese economy. Many Western market economies have adopted and still pursue central planning for special tasks under certain conditions in order to guarantee their success, such as the Manhattan Project and the NASA programs in the United States. Besides, the energy industries in many developing (and even some developed) countries are under the direct control of their governments, which implement various types of central planning. Under such circumstances, economic benefits are often not the main concern, and government subsidies will be offered for the sake of long-range national goals.

However, the total abandonment of the market mechanism in all economic sectors, as implemented in the PRC and many socialist countries regardless of the political implications attributed to such a system, has inevitably led to inferior economic efficiency, which has eventually resulted in the stagnation of their economies. In fact, the respective sectoral productivity in both Chinese urban and rural sectors had not increased before the start of the current reform (1979), as shown in figure 2.9, and the apparent increase of the aggregated productivity was

Fig. 2.9 Stagnation of Urban and Rural Productivity

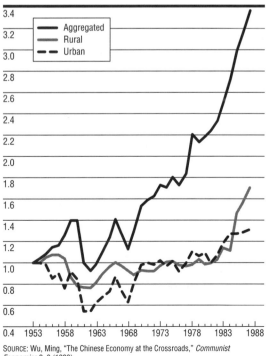

SOURCE: Wu, Ming, "The Chinese Economy at the Crossroads," *Communist Economies* 2, 3 (1990)

entirely a result of shifts in the rural-urban population mix. This was the major reason for the current radical economic reform. In the energy sector, both the specific investment and the lead time of construction of energy projects increased steadily. The irrationally low prices had brought the coal industry to bankruptcy and reliance on government subsidies. The energy industry was unable to finance its own further development.

In the course of reforms, several economic policies have been adopted to revitalize the energy industry. A dual pricing system has been implemented giving all energy producers the right to sell their surplus products on a "free market" basis with "negotiable prices." Larger shares of profits were allowed to be retained by the enterprises for self-development, and capital investment could be raised from outside the state budget — for example, from the local governments, the collective organizations, and private and foreign investors. As a result, the Chinese energy sector began to "walk on two legs" and grow faster than ever before.

CHAPTER 3

THE "FIFTH ENERGY SOURCE"

Energy Consumption and Conservation

3.1 ENERGY CONSUMPTION IN THE PRC

China is known for its high specific energy consumption. In order to formulate effective energy conservation policy, an in-depth study on the causes of China's abnormally high consumption was carried out.

Energy consumption and its structure in the PRC are shown in table 3.1 and figure 3.1. Energy consumption in different sectors is shown in table 3.2 and figure 3.2. Energy intensity per unit of national income (converted to a comparable basis) is shown in table 3.3 and figure 3.3. From all these basic data, the following particular features of Chinese energy consumption can be identified:

1. A high growth rate of energy consumption, increasing 94 percent from 1953 to 1988
2. High energy intensity per value added, even though the intensity decreased after 1980
3. A high percentage of coal in the consumption structure, decreasing in the seventies but increasing again in recent years
4. A high percentage of total energy consumed by the industrial sector and low proportion used by transportation and other sectors

The most striking fact and the issue causing most concern for policymakers is the high energy intensity and the accompanying high growth rate of energy demand. As a result, from the beginning of the research on Chinese energy policy, great emphasis has been put on the potential and measures of energy conservation.

3.2. REASONS FOR HIGH ENERGY INTENSITY

The Chinese economy is energy intensive as compared with either developed countries or other developing countries (see table 3.4). The per GDP energy consumption of the PRC in 1980 was about twice that of Canada or India, about three times those of the United States and South Korea, or about four times those of Japan, most European countries, and Argentina. In order to reduce the energy use intensity in China and achieve the target of quadrupling industrial and agricultural production while only doubling energy consumption, great effort was necessary in energy conservation.* As a first step, the real reasons for China's high energy intensity had to be analyzed.

Based on in-depth analysis of the statistical data and extensive on-the-spot surveys, five responsible factors were identified — structural, technological, managerial, economic, and statistical.

3.2.1 THE STRUCTURAL FACTOR

Both the sectoral structure and the branches or product-mixes inside each sector of an economy affect its energy intensity. In 1980, the Chinese industrial sector accounted for more than 60 percent of the total GDP, while the service and commerce sectors accounted for only 5 percent. However, industry consumed more than five times as much energy per dollar value created than the commerce and

---

*In the Chinese energy community, energy conservation is sometimes called the "fifth energy source," emphasizing that it is equally as important as any of the other four primary energy sources — coal, oil, natural gas, and hydropower.

Table 3.1 Chinese Energy Consumption and Its Structure

Year	Total Consumption (10⁴ tce)	Coal	Oil	Natural gas	Hydro-power
1953	5,411	94.33	3.81	0.02	1.84
1954	6,234	93.45	4.33	0.02	2.20
1955	6,968	92.94	4.91	0.03	2.12
1956	8,800	92.73	4.83	0.03	2.41
1957	9,644	92.32	4.59	0.08	3.01
1958	17,599	94.62	3.92	0.06	1.40
1959	23,926	94.68	4.05	0.14	1.13
1960	30,188	93.90	4.11	0.45	1.54
1961	20,390	91.31	5.47	0.94	2.28
1962	16,540	89.23	6.61	0.93	3.23
1963	15,567	88.93	7.20	0.81	3.06
1964	16,637	97.97	8.04	0.73	3.26
1965	18,901	86.45	10.27	0.63	2.65
1966	20,269	86.24	10.17	0.67	2.92
1967	18,328	84.77	10.89	0.84	3.50
1968	18,405	83.79	12.09	0.76	3.36
1969	22,730	81.93	13.76	0.82	3.49
1970	29,291	80.89	14.67	0.92	3.52
1971	34,496	79.19	16.00	1.44	3.37
1972	37,273	77.51	17.17	1.73	3.59
1973	39,109	74.84	18.58	2.03	4.55
1974	40,144	72.14	20.72	2.49	4.65
1975	45,425	71.85	21.07	2.51	4.57
1976	47,831	69.91	32 .00	2.81	4.28
1977	52,354	70.25	22.61	3.08	4.06
1978	57,144	70.67	22.73	3.20	3.40
1979	58,588	71.31	21.79	3.30	3.60
1980	60,275	72.15	20.76	3.10	3.99
1981	59,447	72.74	19.96	2.79	4.51
1982	62,067	73.67	18.91	2.56	4.86
1983	66,040	74.16	18.14	2.44	5.26
1984	70,904	75.27	17.45	2.37	4.91
1985	76,682	75.81	17.10	2.24	4.85
1986	80,850	75.83	17.20	2.26	4.71
1987	86,632	76.21	17.02	2.13	4.64
1988	92,997	76.17	17.05	2.06	4.72
1989	96,000	75.80	17.20	2.10	4.90

SOURCE: *China's Energy Statistics Yearbook, 1989.*

Fig. 3.1 Structure of Chinese Energy Consumption

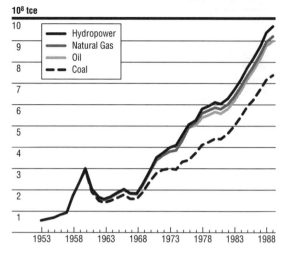

10⁸ tce

Fig. 3.2 Sectoral Energy Consumption

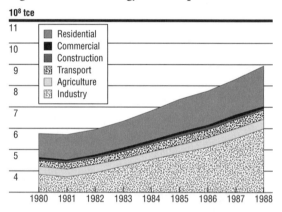

10⁸ tce

centage-point drop in the heavy industry share would reduce the national total energy consumption by 0.46 percent.

The product-mix within each sector played an even more important role in per GDP energy intensity. In the Chinese centrally planned system the gross physical volume of products in each sector, instead of the varieties of commodities for meeting consumers' needs, was adopted as the production index. For instance, the total tonnage of steel production per year was considered the most important criterion to judge economic growth. As a result, the dollar value per physical unit produced might be rather low, since, for instance, steel ingots and thin tubes were all counted by weight, though the dollar value of the former was only a fraction of the latter. Thus the energy intensity per dollar of value produced tended to be high due to the large share of the low value-adding raw products counted in each sector.

service sectors did. Inside the industrial sector, China put more emphasis on heavy industry, with the share of the latter reaching 56.9 percent in 1979. The energy intensity per dollar value for heavy industry was about 350 percent that of light industry. As a result, since the industrial sector consumed some 65 percent of the total primary energy, each per-

Table 3.2 Final Energy Consumption by Sectors (10^8 tce)

Year	Total	Production Sector	Agriculture	Industry	Construction	Trans-portation	Commerce	Non-production	Residential
1980	5.751	4.610	0.347	3.829	0.096	0.286	0.052	0.183	0.958
1981	5.688	4.502	0.346	3.727	0.079	0.291	0.059	0.179	1.006
1982	5.942	4.724	0.350	3.917	0.086	0.308	0.063	0.186	1.031
1983	6.329	5.036	0.361	4.187	0.096	0.322	0.070	0.202	1.091
1984	6.798	5.405	0.384	4.498	0.102	0.341	0.080	0.216	1.176
1985	7.359	5.780	0.404	4.802	0.130	0.367	0.077	0.246	1.332
1986	7.744	6.132	0.424	5.109	0.122	0.395	0.083	0.254	1.358
1987	8.300	6.593	0.447	5.521	0.126	0.408	0.091	0.275	1.432
1988	8.923	7.056	0.471	5.933	0.116	0.428	0.108	0.314	1.553

SOURCE: *China's Energy Statistics Yearbook, 1989.*

Table 3.3 Energy Intensity in the Chinese Economy (kgce/yuan)

Year	Intensity	Year	Intensity
1953	0.665	1972	1.607
1954	0.724	1973	1.557
1955	0.760	1974	1.580
1956	0.841	1975	1.652
1957	0.882	1976	1.787
1958	1.320	1977	1.815
1959	1.659	1978	1.764
1960	2.122	1979	1.690
1961	2.039	1980	1.634
1962	1.769	1981	1.550
1963	1.504	1982	1.494
1964	1.380	1983	1.448
1965	1.340	1984	1.370
1966	1.228	1985	1.310
1967	1.197	1986	1.279
1968	1.285	1987	1.240
1969	1.330	1988	1.199
1970	1.390	1989	1.194
971	1.530		

SOURCE: *China's Energy Statistics Yearbook, 1989.*

Fig. 3.3 Energy Intensity in China

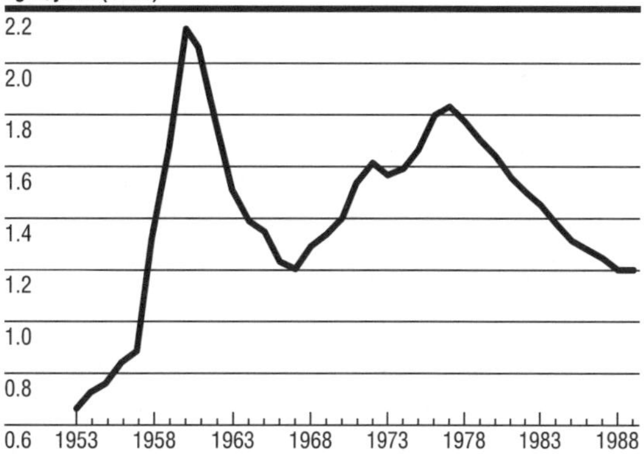

kgce/yuan (1980)

3.2.2 THE TECHNOLOGY FACTOR

Inferior technology is an obvious cause of wasted energy. However, in-depth analysis found the actual situation in China was very complicated. Inferior technology was the result of many other factors, such as historical background, scale effects, the energy structure, and the unavailability of state-of-the-art technologies.

Before 1978, most of the technologies used in the Chinese economy were those which had been imported from the USSR in the fifties. After the break in its relationship with the USSR, China endured a series of internal political disruptions and external blockades for more than two decades. As a result, until 1980 most technology used in the PRC remained at the level of the early fifties. "One design stands for thirty years," the Chinese joked in considering their domestically produced trucks. That was an exact description of most Chinese industrial products. Consequently, the energy efficiencies of equipment and processes were inevitably low.

The second technical factor was the smaller size of plants and equipment. This was not only because any developing economy had to start with smaller plants because of limited available resources and experience, but also because a particular political line, that is, the "Mass Movement," had been advocated by the Chinese Communist party before 1980. This policy encouraged small, backyard enterprises — small blast furnaces, small fertilizer plants, small cement kilns, small coke retorts, and small refineries — all extremely wasteful of energy. In table 3.5, a comparison of the energy intensities of synthetic ammonia (fertilizer) plants of different sizes shows that the small plants consume about twice as much energy as the large ones.

Table 3.4 Comparison of National Energy Intensities, 1980 (kgce/U.S.$)

	Primary commercial energy consumption per unit GDP	Total primary energy consumption per unit GDP*	Residential/ commerical energy consumption per unit GDP*
Developing Countries			
China	2.13	2.90	1.14
Argentina	0.44	0.49	0.10
Brazil	0.61	0.88	0.19
Mexico	0.80	0.84	0.11
India	1.05	1.77	0.83
South Korea	1.06	1.12	0.48
Developed Countries			
Canada	1.39	1.39	0.45
France	0.45	0.45	0.14
Italy	0.53	0.53	0.16
Japan	0.51	0.51	0.13
United Kingdom	0.57	0.57	0.22
United States	1.05	1.05	0.35
West Germany	0.49	0.49	0.18

* Including noncommercial energy such as biomass.

SOURCE: World Bank, *China: The Energy Sector* (Washington: World Bank, 1985).

The third technological factor was the difference in energy efficiency using various kinds of energy. For instance, steam locomotives are still widely used in China for railway transportation. The average efficiency of those engines is only 6 percent, or about one-fourth that of diesel locomotives. The efficiency of coal as a cooking fuel is only half to a third that of natural gas. Even synthetic ammonia plants using coal as feedstock consume 25 percent more energy than those using natural gas. Since coal constitutes over 70 percent of the Chinese primary energy supply, the efficiency of the Chinese energy system is inevitably lower than that of systems using petroleum products.

The fourth factor was the lack of state-of-the-art energy-saving technologies. Since most of the advanced energy-saving technologies are invented in developed countries, they are not always readily available to developing countries. Great amounts of foreign exchange have to be paid for the import of new technologies.

3.2.3 THE MANAGEMENT FACTOR

Before 1980, very little attention was paid to Chinese energy management. No specific element of the government was administratively responsible for energy management issues, and no energy audit or management system had ever been established in most factories.

At the beginning of energy policy research in 1980, no energy consumption data was available from the State Statistics Bureau. Energy experts had to collect the energy sale records from commercial departments to estimate the possible use of these commodities. In fact, sometimes the management had been so chaotic that part of the industrial energy supplies had been diverted to non-productive uses. Since most large enterprises have their own residential communities, the energy consumed by the workers at home was also counted in the specific energy consumption for production in that sector. Thus, before 1980, energy management actually did not exist in most enterprises.

3.2.4 THE ECONOMIC FACTOR

A fatal defect in the centrally planned economy is the lack of the capacity for self-adjustment by enterprises. Since all the production targets of these enterprises are set by government planning offices and all the products are turned over to governmental commercial departments, the cost and the quality of these products are irrelevant to the managers. No economic incentive exists for improving the efficiency of any factor input. The relatively low prices of energy in China made the situation even worse. The overall energy cost constituted only about 3 percent of the total production cost. Thus the managers had virtually no enthusiasm for reducing energy

Table 3.5 Scale Effect on Energy Intensity

	Specific energy consumption (Gcal/t)					
	1980	1981	1982	1983	1984	1985
Sector average	17.92	17.13	16.43	15.62	15.11	14.73
Large plants	10.18	10.09	9.94	9.79	9.76	9.64
Medium plants	17.07	16.67	16.63	16.32	15.84	15.64
Small plants	21.15	20.40	18.74	17.45	16.68	16.57

SOURCE: Qiu, Daxiong, et al., "Industry Energy Conservation in China: Preliminary Report on Energy Auditing in Five Demonstration Plants," report to Asian Development Bank, July 1989.

Table 3.6 Energy Consumption and Intensity in China and India, 1985

	Unit	China	India
Industrial energy consumption	Mtoe	28.8	60.6
Industrial energy consumption intensity	toe/1,000 US$	1.83	1.28
Crude steel	toe/ton	1.00	1.32
— Coke consumption	kg coke/ton	558	723-1,056
Cement	kcal/ton clinker	400	1,330
— Wet process	Kcal/ton clinker	1,480	1,500
— Dry process	Kcal/ton clinker	1,340	1,100
Paper and paperboard	kgoe/ton	0.88	0.95
Ammonia: Feed stock			
— Natural gas	Gcal/ton	9.5	12.3
— Naphtha	Gcal/ton	10.2	13.4
— Fuel oil	Gcal/ton	11.7	17.2
Electricity generation	kcal/kWh	2,786	3,201

SOURCE: See Lu, Yingzhong, *Comparison of the Energy Supply, Consumption, and Policy of the PRC and Some Developing Countries* (Washington: The Washington Institute, 1989).

consumption. On the contrary, they preferred to fulfill the planned targets by consuming more energy.

3.2.5 THE STATISTICAL FACTOR

China's irrational energy pricing system not only caused the wasting of energy but also led to a paradox in the comparison of energy intensities of different countries.

Since the price for a commodity may vary substantially in different countries, the comparison of energy intensities per unit value created often loses its meaning. For instance, in 1985 the per GDP energy intensity in China was about 230 percent that of India. However, when comparing the energy intensities of various products based on physical output, it has been found that the energy intensities of Chinese products are in general lower than those of India. The low prices of many Chinese commodities tend to exaggerate the difference in energy intensities, or even to appear to reverse the facts. This situation is illustrated in table 3.6. Although the energy intensity per dollar value of Chinese industry is about 50 percent higher, the specific energy consumption per physical unit output in China is in general lower than that for products in India, except for cement production.

A more rational comparison of energy intensities among different countries would be based on the adjusted dollar value of national production, according to internationally recognized pricing systems. However, this is too complex and is also unre-

liable. As a compromise, it is preferable to compare energy intensities based on energy consumption values per physical unit output.

Special attention should be paid to the exchange rates used in those comparisons, since many countries adjust their exchange rates periodically to control trade deficits. China adjusted its RMB exchange rates to U.S. dollars from 1.5:1 in 1980 to 4.71:1 in 1990. If the current exchange rate is used, the energy intensity of the Chinese economy in 1987 and 1980 would appear to be 3.36 and 2.45 kgce/dollar, respectively — a 37 percent increase! This is entirely contrary to the fact. Energy elasticity decreased substantially, to 0.51, from 1980 to 1987, as shown above (table 1.1). Comparison of production variables between countries is therefore better carried out in physical rather than monetary units of production. Thus the apparent high per capita energy intensity in China is partially due to the statistical paradox caused by the irrationally low energy prices and varying exchange rates.

3.3. CHINESE ENERGY CONSERVATION POLICY

3.3.1. GENERAL AND SPECIFIC POLICIES

In the light of the five factors identified above, the General Policy of Energy Conservation in China was formulated as follows: "Put equal emphasis on energy conservation and energy provision." Following this general policy, four specific policies on energy conservation were implemented:

1. Adjustment of economic structure toward a less energy-intensive economy, including the adjustment of the relative shares of various sectors and changing of the product-mix within each sector. The service sector should be developed faster than industrial sectors, and light industries faster than heavy industries. Within each sector, deep processing or refining of products should be encouraged in order to create more value from the same amount of energy or raw material consumed.

2. Innovation in technologies, including adopting energy-saving technologies, processes, and equipment and phasing out obsolete energy-wasting technologies, processes, and equipment.

3. Improvement in management, including the establishment of a hierarchy of energy management, assigning responsibilities and authority,

Table 3.7 China's Energy Savings from Imports

	Rolled Steel (Mt)	Energy Equivalent (Mtce)	Fertilizer (Mt)	Energy Equivalent (Mtce)	Annual Savings (Mtce)
1980	5.51	8.3	10.02	5.0	13.3
1981	3.55	5.3	5.55	2.8	8.1
1982	3.77	5.7	6.06	3.0	8.7
1983	9.63	14.4	7.99	4.0	18.4
1984	12.30	18.5	9.23	4.6	23.1
1985	20.03	30.0	7.61	3.8	33.8
1986	18.37	27.6	5.10	2.6	30.2
1987	12.40	18.6	10.90	5.5	24.1
Total	**85.56**	**128.4**	**62.46**	**31.3**	**159.7**

SOURCE: *China Statistical Yearbooks, 1980-1989.*

Table 3.8 Changes in Sector Shares in China (%)

Year	Agriculture	Industry	Construction	Transportation	Commerce
1980	35.95	48.92	5.02	3.42	6.69
1981	38.30	46.70	4.91	3.31	6.78
1982	40.44	45.71	4.90	3.52	5.43
1983	40.61	45.15	5.48	3.39	5.37
1984	39.84	44.52	5.37	3.60	6.66
1985	35.56	45.00	5.65	3.57	10.24
1986	40.26	39.55	6.51	3.90	9.78
1987	32.54	46.94	6.76	3.60	10.16

SOURCE: Zhou, Dadi, et al., "The Experience and Prospects of Energy Conservation in China," paper presented at Lawrence Livermore Laboratory, Berkeley, California, December, 1989.

Table 3.9 Change in Shares, Heavy and Light Industries (%)

Year	Heavy industry	Light industry
1980	53.06	46.94
1981	48.57	51.43
1982	49.53	50.47
1983	50.36	49.64
1984	50.43	49.57
1985	50.40	49.60
1986	53.49	46.51
1987	53.21	46.79

SOURCE: Zhou, Dadi, et al., " Experience and Prospects of Energy Conservation in China."

Table 3.10 Changes in Shares by Industrial Branches (%)

Branch	1980	1985	1987
A. Heavy industry	**53.06**	**50.41**	**53.21**
1. Metals	8.62	8.01	9.71
2. Power	3.77	3.29	3.19
3. Coal	2.48	2.51	2.45
4. Petroleum	5.05	4.49	5.45
5. Chemicals	12.46	6.65	7.34
6. Machine building	25.51	19.88	19.38
7. Building materials	3.64	4.23	5.18
8. Forest products	1.74	0.98	1.36
B. Light industry	**46.94**	**49.58**	**46.79**
9. Food processing	11.38	11.47	13.22
10. Textiles	14.73	15.35	11.93
11. Tailoring	2.70	2.40	1.99
12. Leather products	1.02	0.92	1.04
13. Paper	1.28	1.30	1.98
14. Arts and crafts	2.24	2.57	2.49
15. Household chemicals	—	4.52	6.07
16. Light machine building	—	7.07	6.16
17. Furniture manufacturing	—	0.63	0.82

SOURCE: *China Statistical Yearbooks, 1980-1989.*

setting up energy audits and accounting systems, promulgating energy conservation norms and regulations, implementing energy conservation programs, and using rewards and penalties to achieve goals.

4. Use of incentives with economic measures, including the partial deregulation of energy prices and the provision of energy conservation investments, loans, and subsidies.

3.3.2. ADJUSTMENT OF THE ECONOMIC STRUCTURE

Four levels of economic structural changes affect energy intensities, as follows:

1. National Level:

Change in foreign trade policies to increase imports of energy-intensive products and prohibit the export of such products. The most notable change was the increase in imports of rolled steel and synthetic fertilizer — corresponding to some 1.5 tce and 0.5 tce per ton of product, respectively. In table 3.7, it is shown that the saving of energy due to these imports attained 159.7 Mtce, or 15 percent of the total saving

from all the domestic measures. This factor is sometimes overlooked by outside investigators.

2. Sectoral Level:

Decreasing the relative shares of energy-intensive sectors to reduce the energy intensity of the whole economy. In table 3.8 the changes in various sector shares are shown. However, these changes are not simply increasing or decreasing but fluctuating, since they are very sensitive to factors other than energy conservation. Although it is generally expected that, in the long run, the decrease of industrial share and the increase of commercial and service shares will

Table 3.11 Generalized Structural Energy Savings (Mtce)

Year	Direct savings (Technological innovation)	Indirect savings (General structural savings)
1981	29	71
1982	54	46
1983	34	66
Average	39	61

SOURCE: Zhou, Dadi, et al., " Experience and Prospects of Energy Conservation in China."

Table 3.12 General Structural Savings by Branches (Mtce)

Product	Direct savings (Technological innovation)	Indirect savings (General structural savings)
Steel	21.8	78.2
Fertilizer	15.4	84.5
Electricity	50.0	50.0
Petroleum	50.0	50.0

SOURCE: Zhou, Dadi, et al., " Experience and Prospects of Energy Conservation in China."

substantially reduce the overall energy intensity, the contribution of this change in the near term is less than from other levels of structural change. As a result, this factor should not be overemphasized in energy conservation analysis.

3. Branch Level:

The changes in the respective shares of economic branches within sectors, such as in the heavy and light industries and among the various modes of transportation, will change the overall energy intensity of those sectors. However, contrary to the general belief that the most important effect results from the changes in relative shares of heavy and light industry, it can be seen from table 3.9 that such an outcome is not assured. A detailed analysis of more branches for a given year is shown in table 3.10. It is noted that this effect is quite uncertain in most cases.

4. Product-Mix Level:

Changes in product-mix within each branch are not reported explicitly in official statistics, and thus they are often overlooked. In fact, the energy savings in each branch includes two parts: one is the result of actual technological innovation, and the other comes from product-mix changes. In the literature (see reference 5), this difference has been identified; an estimate is given in tables 3.11 and 3.12. The so-called "generalized structural energy savings" is about twice the "direct savings" produced by technological innovations (table 3.11). Of course, the effect

shown in this table includes the changes made at all three levels — sectoral, branch, and product-mix. Since the changes at sectoral and branch levels are not obvious, the major contribution is believed to come from the changes in product mixes, even though this could not be explicitly determined in statistical data.

3.3.3. MANAGEMENT IMPROVEMENTS

Management is the key to energy conservation. A strong administration or hierarchy is indispensable for the formulation and enforcement of effective energy conservation policy.

In 1980, the State Energy Commission (SEC) was established, under which a Bureau of Energy Conservation was set up. Since the final decisions on allocating resources was made by the State Planning Commission, an Energy Conservation Section was established under the Bureau of Comprehensive Planning of SPC. Later, in 1982, when SEC was merged into SPC, this section was expanded into a Bureau of Energy Conservation in the new SPC. In 1984, a Standing Convention under the State Council was established to coordinate the energy conservation efforts of the state commissions, the ministries, and the provinces. Corresponding organizations were also set up at local and enterprise levels. As a result, a hierarchy or network of administrative organizations for energy conservation was created (figure 3.4). With the establishment of the management network, several important measures were adopted to enhance energy management.

1. Energy Conservation Planning

A planning group for drawing up the Energy Conservation Plan for the Sixth Five-Year Plan was formed under the direct leadership of the vice-chairman of the SPC and supported technically by the official Institute of Energy Research. Based on extensive surveys by special groups of experts covering critical issues and situations all over China (such as the heat supply system, industrial furnaces, and home cooking stoves, among others) the potential benefits of energy conservation were carefully estimated and appropriate measures and policies recommended. The Energy Conservation Bureaus, sections, and offices at various levels then drew up their own energy conservation plans in line with the National Energy Conservation Plan. As a result, a multi-level Energy Conservation Plan was formulated conforming to reality in every sector and enterprise and then implemented.

Fig. 3.4 Energy Intensities in 13 Countries, 1980

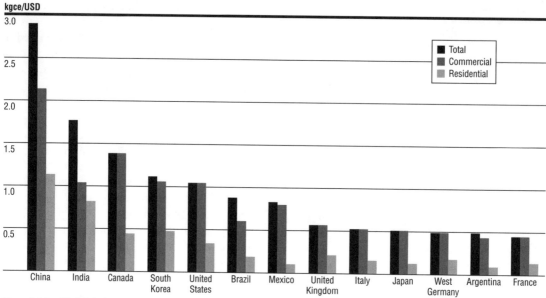

SOURCE: Data from World Bank, *China: The Energy Sector.*

2. Regulations and Standards for Energy Conservation

A series of regulations, norms, and standards for energy conservation were formulated and enforced. From 1981 to 1984, five specific "Instructions on Energy Conservation" were issued by the government, including "Reducing the Consumption of Oil in Boilers and Furnaces," "Conservation of Petroleum Products," "Conservation of Coal in Industrial Boilers," and "Enhancement of Coal Washing." Another general instruction, "Some Measures of Energy Conservation in Industrial Enterprises and Urban Areas," was also issued and enforced.

In order to conduct energy audits and maintain controls, more than 500 regulations, norms, and standards have been drawn up and implemented. In fourteen major energy-intensive sectors or branches, a total of twenty-six "Design Norms for Energy Conservation" were issued. Documentation systems for energy conservation and energy management were established. More important, the achievement of energy conservation goals for all state-owned enterprises was officially designated one of the major criteria for evaluating their performance.

3. Rewards and Penalties

Both material and psychological rewards were granted by the government administrations at all levels to enterprises in which energy conservation programs were successfully carried out and/or where the energy intensities of their products were the lowest among similar enterprises. At the same time, extremely high fines were imposed on those who consumed energy exceeding the applicable norms. For instance, each enterprise or household consuming electricity above its quota had to pay a tariff 500 to 1,000 percent higher. As a result, managers and residents were very concerned about their electricity consumption, and many conservation measures were adopted.

4. Demonstration of Energy Conservation Technologies

A number of demonstration projects for advanced energy-saving technologies were set up to create and disseminate successful experiences under the Sixth Five-Year Plan. For instance, the technologies of retrofitting a small fertilizer plant, of cogeneration and district heating, of continuous casting and rolling in steel mills, and of fuel-saving stoves in rural regions were all successfully demonstrated and diffused.

5. Technical Support and Training

A total of eighty-seven service centers for energy conservation were established throughout the country, covering all the provinces and municipalities, to provide technical support on energy audits, measurement, management, technology transfer, feasibility studies, and training.

3.3.4. TECHNOLOGICAL INNOVATIONS

Energy conservation programs were established in all sectors. Tens of thousands of such programs have now been successfully implemented. It is estimated that technological innovations in the six major areas have created an annual conservation capability of

Fig. 3.5 Hierarchy of the Energy Conservation Administration

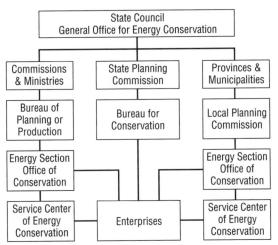

SOURCE: Zhou, Dadi, et al., "Experience and Prospects of Energy Conservation in China."

45 million tce, of which 25 million tce are commercial energy. This corresponds to the direct savings part of the total energy conservation in the Sixth Five-Year Plan period.

1. Replacement and renovation of obsolete processes accounts for about 10 Mtce of annual conservation capability. The most important achievements include the retrofitting of 147 small fertilizer plants, which resulted in a reduction of 23 percent energy intensity; the increasing share of continuous casting and rolling in steel mills; and the recovery of off-gases in petroleum industries.

2. Utilization of waste heat accounts for about 7 Mtce of annual conservation capacity, an increase of 500 MWe cogeneration units.

3. Comprehensive utilization of fuel, including the use of gangue and stone coal, contributes about 2 Mtce annual conservation capacity.

4. Adoption of new, energy-saving motors and other equipment makes up about 4 Mtce of annual conservation capacity. A total of 1,413 new kinds of energy-saving electrical and mechanical equipment have been designed, manufactured, and used.

5. Diffusion of coal briquette and gaseous fuel for cooking accounts for about 2 Mtce of annual conservation capacity. About 10 million tons annual production capacity of coal briquettes was added in the Sixth Five-Year Plan; this increased the percentage of coal briquettes in total coal used for cooking from 21.6 percent in 1981 to 32.6 percent in 1985. At the same time, the percentage of gaseous fuel for cooking was also increased.

6. Energy conservation in rural regions yields about 20 Mtce of annual conservation capability through the diffusion of more efficient devices, such as 40 million fuel-saving stoves and 2.5 million new biogas digesters. However, since only non-commercial energy was used in rural areas for home consumption, such an achievement made no direct contribution to the conservation of commercial energy.

3.3.5. ECONOMIC MEASURES

Two major economic measures have been adopted to promote energy conservation. The first is the partial deregulation of energy prices, the adoption of a dual pricing system. The second step is the financial support of energy conservation programs.

1. The Dual Pricing System. Irrational pricing is the Gordian knot of all centrally planned economies. Theoretically, the problem has no solution in such an economy. However, Chinese reformers tried to improve their situation by adopting a dual pricing system, whereby most energy products were still allocated by the government at fixed prices but the rest could be sold on the free market at much higher floating market prices. The ratio between the allocated and the free market fractions then becomes an additional measure of energy conservation.

However, since energy costs usually amount to a small part of total production costs, and the managers under the Chinese centrally planned system do not care very much about the costs, the effect of such a pricing reform on energy conservation was not as remarkable as it was on energy production. In this case, the existence of a free energy market stimulated the rapid growth of local small industries, which were in general more energy-intensive than their larger counterparts. Besides, dual pricing opened up the opportunity for racketeering. The net effect of the dual pricing system on energy conservation is therefore still a controversial issue.

2. Energy Conservation Investment. The investments in energy conservation programs have brought direct, obvious benefits. It is estimated that during the Sixth Five-Year Plan a total of 10 billion yuan in investment was provided and a total annual conservation capacity of 25 Mtce of commercial energy created. On average, the specific investment was about 300 yuan per ton raw coal annual conservation capacity, while the overall investment of annual production capacity of one ton raw coal (in-

Table 3.13 Effect of Energy Conservation Investments

Project category	Investment (10⁶ yuan)	Annual capacity (10³ tce)	Special investment (yuan/tce)
A. Capital construction:			
1. Cogeneration	1,814	1,380	1,314
2. District heating	312	604	516
3. Retrofitting cement kilns	66	197	330
4. Town gas plants	535	982	545
5. Continuous casting	289	132,106	273
6. Coal washing	143	756	189
7. Scrap recovery	2,190	81,130	168
8. Retrofitting fertilizer plants	542	1,140	475
Total	**3,891**	**6,305**	**617**
B. Technological innovation			
9. Furnace improvements	579	1,640	353
10. Waste heat recovery	781	3,080	254
11. Boiler improvements	750	3,030	248
12. Coal blending	46.7	280	167
13. Gangue utilization	104	740	141
14. Urban coal utilization	91.7	940	98
15. New designs	254.7	750	340
16. Biogas	17.4	8,110	158
17. Coordination	24.2	50	484
18. Others	982.9	NA	NA
Total	**3,680**	**>10,620**	**<347**

SOURCE: Zhou, Dadi, et al., " Experience and Prospects of Energy Conservation in China."

Table 3.14 Chinese Energy Savings, 1981-1987

Year	GDP (10⁹/US$)	Energy consumption (Mtce)	Energy intensity (kgce/US$)	Annual energy saving (Mtce)
1980	245.9	602.8	2.451	...
1981	257.9	594.5	2.305	37.6
1982	286.0	626.5	2.191	74.5
1983	306.7	660.4	2.153	91.3
1984	348.1	709.0	2.037	144.2
1985	393.9	770.2	1.955	195.2
1986	424.7	880.8	1.904	232.1
1987	464.4	845.0	1.820	293.2
Total	**2,481.7**	**5,014.4**	**2.021**	**1,068.1**

SOURCE: China Statistical Yearbooks, 1980-1989.

achievements from these investments are summarized in table 3.13.

3.4. CHINESE ACHIEVEMENTS IN ENERGY CONSERVATION

The advancement of energy conservation in China in the past decade has been remarkable, and a wealth of experience has been amassed. Generally speaking, the average energy consumption elasticity has been reduced from 1.66 (1953 to 1979) to 0.51 (1980 to 1987), as already seen. Thus, in the Sixth Five-Year Plan alone some 550 Mtce of primary energy was saved, as compared with the energy intensity of 1980. However, even more important, the significance of energy conservation has been universally recognized in China and an effective administrative network for energy conservation has been established. The latter achievements will have profound impact on Chinese energy in the future.

3.4.1. ENERGY SAVINGS

The energy savings from 1981 to 1987, based on the energy intensity of 1980, are shown in table 3.14. The savings in these seven years totaled some 1,127 Mtce.

The energy intensity changes in various sectors are shown in table 3.15, and the annual savings in these sectors based on energy intensities of the previous year are shown in tables 3.16 and 3.17. It is interesting to note that the energy savings in heavy industries were predominant in the Sixth Five-Year Plan. Since the savings in these tables were calculated on the basis of annual changes in sectoral energy intensity, the continuous efforts made in each sector could be envisaged. However, due to the

cluding the infrastructure) amounted to 400 yuan in the 1980s. Thus, the return for investment in energy conservation is believed to be higher than that in energy production.

There are two categories of energy conservation investments in the Chinese financial system. Those investments of less than 5 million yuan per project belong to the category of technical innovation, and those equal to or greater than 5 million yuan per project belong to the category of capital construction.

In the first category, a total investment of 5 billion yuan was allocated to 12,500 projects during the Sixth Five-Year Plan. All of these projects were completed within one to three years. Another 5 billion yuan was allocated to capital construction projects including cogeneration, district heating, retrofitting of small fertilizer and cement plants, town gas production and piping systems, coal washing plants, and continuous casting systems. The

Table 3.15 Changes in Energy Intensity (kgce/10^4 yuan)

Year	Total	Agriculture	Industry	Construction	Transportation	Commerce
1980	547.5	224.0	742.0	125.2	1,174.1	118.2
1981	504.7	223.1	675.9	109.9	1,157.5	114.3
1982	482.6	214.7	657.9	100.0	1,087.4	114.7
1983	462.9	205.4	627.6	101.0	1,044.9	115.3
1984	436.0	198.7	585.9	94.7	1,005.8	116.2
1985	410.0	197.6	533.0	102.0	968.7	111.1

SOURCE: Derived from *China Statistical Yearbooks, 1980–1989.*
Note: Based on annual total production value of each sector, thus giving a total intensity different from that shown in table 3.3.

Table 3.16 Annual Energy Savings in Industries (Mtce)

Sector	1981	1982	1983	1984	1985	Total
Industry total	34.23	10.04	18.68	29.31	43.88	136.14
Intensity reduction	9.391	5.92	24.58	31.14	46.61	27.41
Light industry	7.27	0.08	1.01	5.89	6.01	20.18
Heavy industry	8.15	14.48	21.73	23.76	37.71	105.83
Structural change	18.81	−4.06	−4.06	−0.34	0.16	10.05

SOURCE: Derived from *China Statistical Yearbooks, 1980-1989.*
Note: Based on annual total production value of each sector, thus giving a total intensity different from that shown in table 3.3.

limitations of data availability, the effect of changes in the product-mix category could not be singled out. Thus, the contributions entitled "structural changes" in these tables are underestimated since they take into account only the changes in sectoral shares of production.

3.4.2. CHINESE ENERGY CONSERVATION PRACTICE

There are five major elements of Chinese energy conservation practice.

1. The general recognition and acceptance of the significance of energy conservation by government leaders as well as the public through continuous surveys, analyses, argument, demonstrations, propaganda, training, and education are of first importance. Since energy conservation must be the task of nearly all participants inside the economy, no really significant success can be achieved without such a general understanding, acceptance, and determination.

   The Chinese energy community has made great effort in this respect and has successfully convinced the reform leaders in the government, as well as the managers, technical staff, and workers in the enterprises, of the significance of energy conservation. As a consequence, a favorable environment has been created for implementing conservation policies and measures.

2. An effective administrative network has been established to exercise authority over all energy

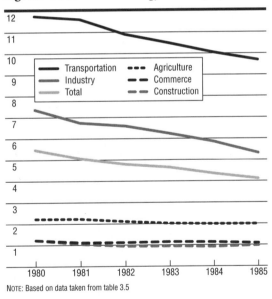

Fig. 3.6 Reduction of Energy Intensity by Sector

Transportation — Agriculture
Industry — Commerce
Total — Construction

NOTE: Based on data taken from table 3.5

conservation efforts, either from the top (governmental planning) or from the bottom (initiatives of the masses).

3. Adequate policies have been formulated based on extensive on-the-spot surveys and scientific analysis.

4. Integrated energy conservation planning has been done covering structural adjustments, managerial improvements, technical innovations, and economic incentives and financial support.

Table 3.17 Annual Energy Savings in Various Industrial Branches (Mtce)

Source of energy savings	1981	1982	1983	1984	1985	Total
Heavy industry, total	8.15	14.48	21.73	23.76	37.71	105.83
Intensity reduction	9.67	13.67	16.82	16.57	25.06	81.78
Metals	2.77	3.02	1.44	2.65	6.12	16.00
Chemicals	3.56	6.19	6.81	4.35	7.65	28.56
Machine building	1.61	2.41	4.97	4.49	8.00	21.48
Building materials	0.45	0.06	1.39	4.71	4.53	11.14
Energy	2.24	1.18	1.60	0.81	−1.89	3.94
Others	−0.96	0.81	0.61	−0.44	0.65	0.67
Structural change	−1.52	0.81	4.91	7.19	12.5	24.04
Light industry, total	7.27	0.08	1.01	5.89	6.01	20.18
Intensity reduction	7.20	0.00	1.04	5.70	5.63	19.57
Food processing	1.13	0.38	−0.66	0.32	−0.07	1.10
Textiles	1.93	−0.64	0.93	2.23	2.35	6.80
Paper products	0.48	0.03	0.27	0.59	0.55	1.92
Chemicals	0.47	0.31	0.19	0.53	1.20	2.70
Machine building	−0.42	0.16	0.33	0.76	1.01	1.84
Others	3.61	-0.24	−0.02	1.27	0.59	5.21
Structural change	0.07	0.08	−0.03	0.19	0.38	0.69

SOURCE: *China Statistical Yearbooks, 1980-1989.*

5. Experiences in energy conservation have been summarized and diffused through demonstration, propaganda, training, and education among all the people concerned.

3.5. POTENTIAL AND LIMITS OF CHINESE ENERGY CONSERVATION

In carrying out medium- and long-term energy planning, the potential for energy conservation was evaluated. Although the energy intensities per unit of physical output in the Chinese economy are lower

Fig. 3.7 Forecast of Long-Term Potential Energy Intensity

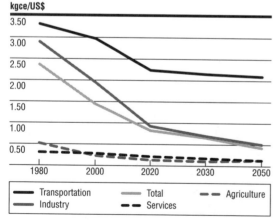

kgce/US$

| Transportation | Total | Agriculture |
| Industry | Services | |

than in some developing countries, they are still high when China is compared with advanced countries. Great possibilities for energy conservation still exist in many sectors of the Chinese economy.

3.5.1. ESTIMATED ENERGY CONSERVATION POTENTIAL BY 2000

According to the technological development target set by the Chinese government, by 2000 the level of energy intensity for major industrial products in China should reach the 1980s level of intensity of the advanced countries. At the same time, waste of energy should have been identified and controlled. Such general targets imply the following specific energy conservation potential:

1. The energy savings for the most energy-intensive products — steel, cement, synthetic ammonia, and thermal electricity — are listed in table 3.18 together with the relevant outputs and energy intensities. The energy conservation potential of these products totals some 90 Mtce.
2. The improved design of seventeen categories of mechanical and electrical equipment will result in a total saving of about 200 Mtce.
3. Raising the efficiency of industrial boilers from 60 percent to 70 percent will contribute some 37 Mtce per year to energy conservation.
4. The recovery of the waste heat in steel mills, chemical plants, petrochemical industries, and light industries will save about 30 Mtce per year.

Table 3.18 Energy Conservation Potential of Selected Products

Product	Output by 2000	Energy intensity	Energy savings
Steel	90 Mt	1,400 kgce/ton	21 Mtce/year
Cement	110 Mt	122 kgce/ton	8 Mtce/year
Synthetic ammonia	132 Mt	1,150 kgce/ton	12 Mtce/year
Thermal electricity	950 TWh	0.38 kgce/kWh	49.4 Mtce/year

SOURCE: Zhou, Dadi, et al., " Experience and Prospects of Energy Conservation in China."

5. Improvements in design and insulation of buildings will save about 8 Mtce annually. However, due to the enormous additional investment needed, further energy conservation potential in buildings cannot be fully realized.

3.5.2. ESTIMATED ENERGY CONSERVATION POTENTIAL BEFORE 2050

For evaluating long-term energy conservation potential, a comparison has been made of Chinese historical records and developing trends with those of other countries. The results are summarized in table 3.19. It is noted that structural change, that is, the growth of the service sector and the decline of the industrial sector, will contribute most to long-term energy conservation.

It should be pointed out that this forecast is based on the assumption of a continuation of the high growth rates of the overheated period of 1987-1988. Later on, the Chinese economy fell back to another "adjustment period." However, although economic growth may slow in the coming decades, the analysis of the variation of sectoral intensities with respect to economic growth levels will remain valid over the long term.

3.5.3 THE LIMITS OF ENERGY CONSERVATION

There are several limitations on energy conservation. First, the diffusion of new technology is not an easy task. According to Chinese experience, shifting to new technologies always requires tremendous effort and needs a very long lead-time. No advanced technology can be disseminated overnight. It took more than a decade to diffuse fuel-saving stoves in half of China's 160 million rural households. The total electrification of these 160 million rural homes, scattered over 9.6 million square kilometers, needs at least half a century. Thus, technically speaking, time and space limitations will make energy conservation a strategic task rather than a tactical one. Thus, while the role of energy conservation in the Chinese economy should not be underestimated, neither should it be overestimated as a quick and easy solution to China's energy problems.

Secondly, the Chinese economy itself will impose a limit on energy conservation. Even though most energy conservation measures are economically justifiable on paper, they may not materialize since the required investment must be provided by hundreds of millions of users whose interests in decisionmaking are as diverse as their faces. No existing mechanism, even in centrally planned economies, could force hundreds of millions of households to invest in energy conservation. Besides, most new technologies are monopolized by developed countries. A developing country like China has to import these technologies from abroad. The level of available technologies in China has always lagged behind that in advanced countries by one or two decades.

The last but most important limitation on energy conservation is the rapid growth of a developing economy. Even though remarkable success has been achieved in energy conservation in the past

Fig. 3.8 Forecast of Long-Term Conservation Potential in China

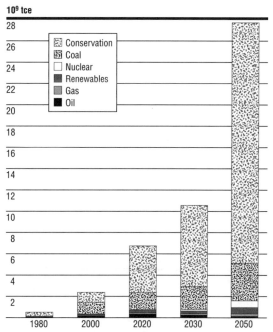

SOURCE: Derived from Wu, Zongxin, et al., *China's Energy Demand by 2050.*

Table 3.19 Long-Term Energy Savings Potential in China

	Unit	1980	2000	2020	2030	2050
Population	10^9	0.987	1.254	1.393	1.441	1.416
GDP	10^9 US$	246	1,003	2,780	4,320	11,300
GDP/capita	US$/person	249	800	2,000	3,000	8,000
1. Industry						
Value added	10^9 US$	123.6	502	1,250	1,730	4,080
Share	%	54	50	45	40	36
Consumption	Mtce	391.43	1017	1,218	1,335	2,129
Intensity	kgce/US$	3.01	2.03	0.974	0.772	0.522
2. Agriculture						
Value added	10^9 US$	88.4	252.6	435	530	787
Share	%	36	25.2	15.6	12.3	6.96
Consumption	Mtce	46.92	59.8	66.8	72.3	97.5
Intensity	kgce/US$	0.53	0.237	0.153	0.140	0.124
3. Transportation						
Value Added	10^9 US$	8.3	38	111	173	452
Share	%	3.4	3.8	4.0	4.0	4.0
Consumption	Mtce	29.02	118.0	259	390	990
Intensity	kgce/US$	3.45	3.11	2.33	2.25	2.19
4. Services						
Value added	10^9US$	16.5	210.4	984	1,807	5980
Share	%	6.6	21	35.4	43.7	52.9
Consumption	Mtce	5.18	60.0	212.7	308.7	725.2
Intensity	kgce/US$	0.315	0.285	0.216	0.171	0.121
5. Total (production)						
Consumption	Mtce	480.55	1,254	1,765	2,108	3,942
Intensity	kgce/US$	1.955	1.660	0.631	0.487	0.348
6. Total (including household)						
Consumption	Mtce	602.75	1,500	2,400	3,000	5,200
Intensity	kgce/US$	2.450	1.495	0.863	0.694	0.460
Elasticity	—	1.622	0.555	0.451	0.443	0.535

SOURCE: Derived from data in *China Statistics Yearbook, 1989.*

decade and great prospects for conservation have been envisioned, the rapid growth of the economy still demands huge amounts of additional energy. This is determined by the process of development of a backward economy. Presently, 70 percent of the Chinese population are still living in rural areas with very low productivity and, hence, very low income. Consequently, people are eager to improve their standard of living. The anticipated industrialization and urbanization of about one billion rural people in the next century will demand an increase in the GDP of an order of magnitude within that time. Any stagnation or slowing down of Chinese economic growth will result in social instability and amount to political catastrophe for the regime in power. As a result, energy consumption can be ex-

pected to at least quintuple, even if energy intensity can be cut to one-fifth its present value in the next few decades.

Table 3.20 shows a forecast of the energy demand increase based on the realization of all the energy-saving potential summarized in table 3.19. It is noted that primary energy equivalent to more than five billion tons of coal will still be required by 2050, and nuclear energy will have to be deployed on a tremendous scale to cope with this formidable challenge. At the same time, annual energy savings of up to 10.57 billion tce can be expected, based on 1980 energy intensity.

In conclusion, we shall return to the general energy policy of China: "Putting equal emphasis on energy production and energy conservation." The

Table 3.20 Forecast of Long-Term Energy Demand in China

	Unit	1980	2000	2020	2030	2050
Total	Mtce	606.8	1,500	2,400	3,000	5,200
Oil	Mtce	125.1	286	358	277	166
	%	20.8	19.1	14.9	9.2	3.2
Natural gas	Mtce	18.7	53	133	167	266
	%	3.1	3.5	5.5	5.6	5.1
Hydropower	Mtce	24.1	100	210	241	320
	%	4	6.7	8.8	8	6.2
New energy sources	Mtce	0	0	10	29	250
	%	0	0	0.4	1	4.8
Coal	Mtce	434.9	1,050	1,626	2,149	3,640
	%	72.1	70.1	67.7	71.6	70
Nuclear power	Mtce	0	10	63	137	558
	%	0	0.7	2.6	4.6	10.7
	TWh	0	30	180	391	1,750

SOURCE: Wu, Zongxin, et al., *China's Energy Demand by 2050*.

significance of this policy can be seen in figure 3.5, in which the cumulative effect of energy conservation is surprisingly high, but on the other hand, the tremendous growth of energy consumption can also be seen. As will be spelled out in the next chapter, China has to walk forward actually on two legs — that is, depending on both conservation and production in order not to be crippled.

CHAPTER 4

WALKING ON TWO LEGS

Issues and Controversies behind the
Rapid Growth of Chinese Energy Production

4.1 ISSUES AND CONTROVERSIES

Chinese energy production has been growing very rapidly during the past forty years. Total energy production increased more than fortyfold from 1949 to 1988, with an average growth rate of 9.68 percent per year. The annual coal production exceeded one billion tons in 1989, having increased by 8.93 percent per year, while oil production attained one billion barrels in the same year, having increased by 19.25 percent per year. The annual production of natural gas and electricity were 14.9 billion cubic meters and 582 tetrawatt-hours (TWh), respectively, in 1989, and their annual growth rates in the past forty years averaged 20.9 percent and 12.9 percent, respectively. The rapid exploitation of all kinds of energy sources is the result of effective policies. In this section the major issues and controversies in formulating and implementing these policies will be addressed first.

4.1.1. THE GENERAL ISSUE: ATTAINING MAXIMUM OUTPUT WITH LIMITED INVESTMENT

This is a common issue for all sectors in a developing economy. However, the issue of financing the development of the energy sector is most critical due to its capital-intensive nature and the longer lead-time needed. The low energy prices and the low economic efficiency in a centrally planned economy make the situation even more difficult. The policy of "Walking on Two Legs" has been adopted in China for dealing with this problem, and the strengths as well as the weaknesses of such a strategy will be discussed below.

4.1.2. LIMITATIONS OF COAL PRODUCTION: THE TRANSPORTATION ISSUE AND THE SOLUTION

The size of China's coal reserves is not a constraint on production for the time being. However, besides the general constraint of the availability of investment, which is particularly serious in the coal sector due to the low price of coal, the necessary transportation of coal presents an increasing challenge because more and more coal production is concentrated in the Shanxi-Shaanxi-Inner Mongolia region. As shown in table 2.5, in 1985 about 127 million tons of coal had to be transported from this region to eastern and southern China, and by 2000 the amount of coal transported is expected to have increased to some 450 million tons. Several options have been studied for the solution of this serious problem: the construction of heavy duty unit-trains for coal transportation, mine-mouth power plants for coal conversion, and a pipeline for pumping coal slurry. Yet none of these options seems to present the final answer to meeting this formidable challenge beyond this century.

4.1.3. CONSTRAINT ON OIL PRODUCTION: LIMITED RESERVES

The picture is quite different for oil production. Finding more oil is always the major concern in the Chinese oil industry. Although theoretically, from the point of view of geology, China's petroleum resources must be enormous, measured reserves have always barely met the increasing demand on oil production. Some Chinese policymakers have been confused by the difference between recoverable oil reserves and potential geological resources. This is one important reason for the overoptimistic attitude of the authorities regarding potential Chinese oil production. Presently China is facing the possibility of decreased oil production after the year 2000. Thus, the policy of conservation of oil resources will be emphasized.

4.1.4. CONTROVERSIES OVER THE THREE GORGES PROJECT

This debate on the Three Gorges Dam has lasted over three decades. It is an example of the effects of Chinese bureaucracy on energy policymaking. About 94 percent of China's annually exploitable hydropower (1,900 TWh) has not yet been developed, so a comprehensive strategy for hydropower

development is needed instead of concentrating on a single mammoth project. The issue of the Three Gorges project became extremely complicated and protracted because of its bearing on the political interests of some responsible officials and institutions. More-scientific policies on hydropower development are therefore needed to accelerate the exploitation of this enormous renewable energy source in China.

4.1.5. THE SLOW PACE OF NUCLEAR POWER DEVELOPMENT

The fate of nuclear power is an area offering another example of Chinese-style bureaucracy. China detonated its first atomic bomb in 1964 and started up its first submarine nuclear reactor in 1971, yet some twenty years later there is still no nuclear power

Table 4.1 Shares of Investment and Revenue of Energy Sector

Year	Revenue	Total energy sector	Oil	Coal Total	Washed coal	Electricity Total	Thermal	Coke
1953	3.87	7.73	0.77	3.96	—	2.90	1.71	0.10
1954	4.13	10.31	1.43	4.61	—	3.96	2.23	0.30
1955	4.70	13.51	1.76	5.93	—	5.33	3.77	0.49
1956	4.62	12.71	2.74	5.18	—	4.66	3.13	0.12
1957	4.90	15.71	2.67	5.25	—	7.43	5.13	0.36
1958	6.79	15.34	1.48	6.04	—	7.62	4.29	0.20
1959	7.30	16.53	1.49	6.22	—	7.88	4.76	0.95
1960	8.04	16.32	2.23	6.31	—	7.63	4.00	0.15
1961	9.66	21.55	3.17	12.25	—	5.99	2.91	0.14
1962	10.47	22.02	4.49	12.42	—	5.00	1.68	0.11
1963	10.10	16.81	4.38	8.37	0.34	3.98	1.81	0.07
1964	9.42	15.04	4.11	6.40	0.31	4.50	2.14	0.03
1965	9.05	14.26	3.46	4.29	0.10	6.50	3.52	0.01
1966-1970	9.56	15.89	3.98	4.78	—	7.03	3.35	0.10
1971-1974	12.02	17.67	4.98	5.32	—	7.29	3.40	0.09
1975	12.50	17.46	5.27	4.56	0.06	7.49	3.68	0.15
1976	13.15	18.56	5.07	4.39	0.04	9.03	4.98	0.07
1977	12.87	20.58	5.43	5.91	0.03	9.08	4.59	0.16
1978	12.32	22.89	6.21	6.35	0.02	10.16	4.66	0.17
1979	12.08	21.20	5.17	6.09	0.13	9.74	3.91	0.20
1980	11.31	20.69	5.97	5.99	0.07	8.61	3.42	0.12
1981	12.25	21.37	6.31	5.23	0.07	9.06	3.29	0.77
1982	11.86	18.40	4.55	5.37	0.25	8.32	3.27	0.15
1983	11.50	21.48	4.89	6.74	0.15	9.67	4.23	0.18
1984	10.87	22.23	4.12	7.42	0.08	10.36	5.15	0.43
1985	10.27	19.11	3.09	5.13	0.10	10.19	4.66	0.70
1986	10.28	22.71	3.28	4.91	0.09	13.74	7.25	0.78
1987	9.64	25.32	4.36	4.44	0.19	15.70	7.94	0.82
1988	8.93	26.88	5.67	4.16	0.10	16.27	9.58	0.78

SOURCE: *China's Statistics Yearbook, 1989.*

plant in operation. The controversies among the three responsible ministries and various institutions have endured throughout the decade, and the lack of objective economic criteria has made the comparison of complicated large-scale projects more or less arbitrary. As a result, the Chinese civil nuclear program had been postponed until the recent economic reform cleared away some of the obstacles.

4.2. WALKING ON TWO LEGS

Chinese energy investment amounts to more than 20 percent of total national investment. However, the revenue earned by the energy sector constitutes only some 8 percent of the gross national product. Both these figures are shown in table 4.1, indicating that the energy sector is unable to finance its own development.

Furthermore, the efficiency of energy investment has fallen lower and lower, as shown in table 4.2. For instance, adding one ton of annual coal

Fig. 4.1 Revenue and Investment in Energy Sector of Chinese Industry

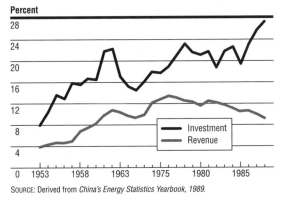

SOURCE: Derived from *China's Energy Statistics Yearbook, 1989.*

production capacity required 45 yuan of investment under the First Five-Year Plan; but now, in the Sixth Five-Year Plan, over 220 yuan is needed. Even taking into account the deflator (in this case, around 1.40 from 1953 to 1985), the specific investment has increased to over 300 percent of its original value. The causes of such an escalation are many-sided, but most are connected with the characteristically low economic efficiency of centrally planned economies. Such a situation cannot be improved from within the energy sector itself.

This problem is becoming more and more serious. The addition of new capacity to energy production has lagged behind the growth of the economy even though the energy intensity is steadily decreasing. A new approach for enhancing energy development must be sought to meet the challenge — and the Chinese policymakers have identified it: Walking on Two Legs.

Multiple implications are taken from the "two-legs" policy. That is, to solve China's energy problems, it will be necessary to (1) construct both large and small facilities, (2) use both modern and traditional technologies, (3) raise both public and private capital, and (4) allow both domestic and foreign investment. In short, departing from the orthodox principle of a centralized, publicly owned economy, the "Walking on Two Legs" policy attempts to mobilize all possible resources to promote energy production.

The effect of this policy has been straightforward. The annual coal production increased to over one billion tons in 1989 and is expected to reach 1.4 billion tons by 2000, a target formerly considered unattainable. Local small mines contributed more than 50 percent of the national total, producing over 500 million tons of coal per year. (The development and the trend of local small mines are

Table 4.2 Specific Investment in the Chinese Energy Sector

		Coal (Yuan/ton/year)		Oil (Yuan/ton/year)		Fossil fuel power (Yuan/kWe)		Hydropower (Yuan/kWe)	
FYP	Year	A	B	A	B	A	B	A	B
1	1953-1957	45.4	—	913.1	—	1,072.6	—	1,598.7	—
2	1958-1962	85.6	65.5	307.7	610.4	666.9	869.8	2,947.2	2,273.0
Interim	1963-1965	112.3	98.9	243.7	275.7	722.5	694.7	1,852.1	2,399.7
3	1966-1970	67.5	89.9	139.9	191.8	554.2	638.4	1,325.9	1,589.0
4	1971-1975	111.7	89.6	216.8	178.4	520.2	537.2	1,200.3	1,263.1
5	1976-1980	207.7	159.7	330.6	273.7	677.6	598.9	2,573.2	1,886.8
6	1981-1985	245.0	226.4	291.4	311.0	941.6	809.6	3,937.0	3,255.1
Average	1953-1988	141.3	141.3	288.6	288.6	714.4	714.4	2,320.4	2,320.4

SOURCE: Derived from data in *China's Statistics Yearbook, 1989.*

NOTE: A = Lead time not considered.   B = 5-year lead time considered.

shown in table 4.3.) The advantages and shortcomings of such a situation will be discussed in the next section. However, this seems to be the only way to meet the tremendous demands for energy in China's rapidly developing economy.

All possible sources of capital investment have been pursued to benefit the energy sector, which was formerly tightly controlled by the government. To supplement domestic sources, foreign investors are sought to open up new energy resources and build energy facilities all over China. The most outstanding example is the joint venture with an American company (Occidental Petroleum) in Antaibao for an open-cast coal mine with a final annual output of 45 million tons of high-quality bituminite. The trend of diversification of energy investments is shown in tables 4.4 though 4.6.

The diversification of capital sources also led to varying kinds of ownership, and the latter has produced better management and hence higher economic efficiency. The Chinese government has unambiguously expressed its desire to introduce Western management practices through joint ven-

tures such as that with Occidental Petroleum in the Antaibao coal mine. However, Chinese officials ignored the fact that Western management is rooted entirely in the capitalist value system, which the

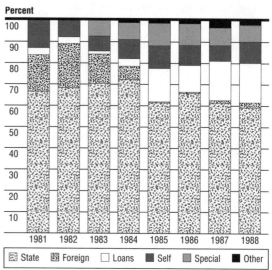

Fig. 4.2 Coal Investment from Various Sources

☒ State ☒ Foreign ☐ Loans ■ Self ▨ Special ■ Other

Table 4.3 Coal Production by Types of Mine Ownership (10⁴ ton)

Type of Mine	1987 Production	1987 % of total	1986 Production	1986 % of total	Rate of Increase (%)	Production Increase
State-owned	42,020	45.3	41,392	46.3	101.52	628
Locally owned	50,789	54.7	48,012	53.7	105.78	2,777
Provincial	6,310	6.8	6,047	6.8	104.35	263
District	4,910	5.3	5,198	5.8	94.46	-288
County	68,934	7.4	6,893	7.7	100.00	0
Collective	29,634	31.9	27,748	31.0	106.80	1,886
Private	2,836	3.1	2,043	2.3	138.82	793
Others	207	0.2	83	0.1	249.39	124
National total	**92,809**	**100.0**	**89,404**	**100.0**	**103.81**	**3,405**

SOURCE: *China's Statistics Yearbook, 1989.*

Table 4.4 Sources of Capital Investment in Chinese Coal Sector (10⁴ yuan)

Year	Total	State	Loans	Foreign	Special*	Self-financed	Others
1981	250,330	166,610	7,530	43,595	—	32,595	—
1982	323,399	195,555	9,310	67,457	—	51,077	—
1983	435,106	306,896	5,656	59,963	31,124	31,280	187
1984	586,481	424,715	21,861	36,250	47,780	52,300	3,875
1985	592,100	364,558	91,950	3,644	62,761	63,119	6,068
1986	619,489	408,987	78,916	3,777	62,598	57,577	7,634
1987	638,267	392,962	116,767	7,747	54,386	46,937	19,468
1988	615,769	366,480	111,124	14,227	48,683	65,042	10,213

SOURCE: *China's Statistics Yearbook, 1989.*

* A special amount of investment has been put aside by the Chinese government to promote the retrofitting of the oil-burning power plants into coal-fired power plants and enhance coal supply to these plants.

current Chinese regime is trying to resist. As a result, a dualism prevails in the Chinese economy and has become a new constraint.

In spite of the increasing economic efficiency brought about through implementing material incentives, the deficits in energy enterprises continue to increase (see table 4.7). The irrational pricing system is the major cause of such deficits. However, the rate of deficit increase has even exceeded the rate of price escalation. It is further noted that this deficit increase happened at the apex of the recent

Fig. 4.3 Oil Investment from Various Sources

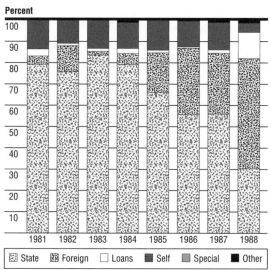

Fig. 4.4 Electricity Investment from Various Sources

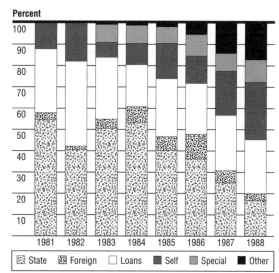

Table 4.5 Sources of Capital Investment in Chinese Oil Sector (10^4 yuan)

Year	Total	State	Loan	Foreign	Special*	Self-financed	Others
1981	290,119	230,884	10,544	10,449	—	38,242	—
1982	295,435	225,209	2,751	35,197	—	32,278	—
1983	297,638	249,801	3,920	5,204	—	38,707	6
1984	283,174	224,923	6,598	14,465	—	35,992	196
1985	344,500	227,282	3,009	65,462	150	48,555	42
1986	418,797	234,111	855	132,470	360	50,668	333
1987	446,191	249,893	5,845	128,660	100	58,591	3,102
1988	610,441	185,166	75,472	317,383	500	25,929	5,991

SOURCE: *China's Statistics Yearbook, 1989.*
*See explanation under table 4.4.

Table 4.6 Sources of Capital Investment in Chinese Power Sector (10^4 yuan)

Year	Total	State	Loan	Foreign	Special*	Self-financed	Others
1981	376,394	205,382	112,286	12,050	—	46,676	—
1982	454,120	183,647	180,263	7,863	—	82,347	—
1983	574,812	289,251	167,800	24,961	49,855	40,624	2,321
1984	761,911	404,764	151,707	56,652	62,526	76,127	10,135
1985	1,072,441	430,748	293,018	68,536	86,828	177,469	15,842
1986	1,490,637	548,439	353,262	172,664	145,660	196,817	73,795
1987	1,813,441	455,126	471,756	101,216	153,166	37,385	256,792
1988	2,083,711	348,358	522,994	72,052	221,109	562,550	356,648

SOURCE: *China's Statistics Yearbook, 1989.*
*See explandation undet table 4.4.

economic reform, when the focus was on improving the economic efficiency of state-owned enterprises. Thus, the present policy of Walking on Two Legs does not seem not powerful enough to deal with the root cause of the low productivity of the energy sector. Could the Chinese reformers take one step further, to consider capitalistic private ownership as one leg to assist the other, socialistic, leg in their long march?

4.3. OPTIMISM AND ANXIETY IN THE COAL INDUSTRY

Coal is the backbone of the Chinese energy sector. Presently coal consumption constitutes over 76 percent of total energy consumption, and its share can be expected to steadily increase. The Chinese government has implemented a series of policies to promote coal production, and the results are en-

couraging. As mentioned above, the annual production of coal has already exceeded one billion tons, and the optimistic target of 1.4 billion tons by the year 2000 is now considered attainable. However, numerous hidden obstacles exist in the coal industry which may threaten its future and hence should be mentioned. In this section the prospects and hidden problems of the Chinese coal industry will be analyzed.

4.3.1. A RESOURCE WITH FORMIDABLE PROBLEMS

Chinese coal resources are considered extremely abundant, based on either the estimated potential geological resource of 3,200 billion tons or the measured reserve of 769 billion tons. However, as mentioned in chapter 2, the geographical distribution of China's coal presents a great difficulty. It is estimated that the coal transported out of the major coal production base, the Shanxi-Shaanxi-Inner Mongolia

Table 4.7 Deficits of the Chinese Energy Industry

Sector	Year	Total Enterprises	Deficit Enterprises	Proportion Deficit Enterprises (%)	Deficit (10^8 yuan) Amount	Net production (%)	Total investment (%)
Energy sector total	1985	21,377	3,387	15.87	17.85	1.76	8.70
	1986	23,808	4,359	18.31	25.73	2.31	9.63
	1987	23,558	4,502	19.11	32.62	2.51	9.59
	1988	23,478	4,736	15.91	51.75	3.40	12.62
Coal sector	1985	8,872	1,943	21.90	15.71	7.10	28.57
	1986	9,976	2,605	26.11	22.18	9.34	38.44
	1987	9,458	2,658	28.10	26.24	10.21	44.03
	1988	9,230	1,954	21.17	30.11	9.51	47.42
Oil sector	1985	23	1	4.35	0.01	—	—
	1986	25	4	16.00	0.18	0.08	0.61
	1987	29	6	20.69	1.99	0.68	4.71
	1988	30	13	43.33	11.42	3.73	18.70
Electricity sector	1985	10,404	1,156	11.01	1.23	0.42	1.12
	1986	11,515	1,451	12.60	2.13	0.68	1.32
	1987	11,407	1,397	12.25	2.70	0.73	1.28
	1988	11,293	1,392	12.33	7.09	1.57	2.86
Refinery industry	1985	388	30	7.73	0.01	—	0.16
	1986	485	31	6.39	0.09	0.03	1.02
	1987	626	46	7.35	0.01	—	0.06
	1988	690	41	5.94	0.02	—	0.08
Coke industry	1985	1,550	257	16.58	0.89	3.00	11.17
	1986	1,807	268	14.83	1.15	3.50	12.53
	1987	2,038	395	19.38	1.68	4.15	15.23
	1988	2,235	336	15.03	3.11	6.23	26.24

SOURCE: *China's Statistics Yearbook, 1989.* Note: NP — Net Production Value in the sector; IV — Total Investment in the sector.

region, will increase to 450 million tons in 2000, a net increment of 320 million tons as compared with 1985. By the middle of the twenty-first century, more than 4 billion tons of coal will have to be moved out of this region annually. Chinese energy policymakers have to face this unprecedented challenge.

The terrain around the coal production areas is unfavorable for transportation. A rugged mountain range runs along the east border of Shanxi Province and separates it from the coastal provinces, with only three zigzag passes allowing the passage of railways. In the south, the river Huang He flows from west to east, cutting off the connection between Shanxi and south-central China. Only two railroad bridges at present cross the river. Recently, one pair of unit-train tracks was completed, from Datong to Qinhuangdao, and about 80 million tons of coal can be transported over this powerful new facility. However, even the maximum capacity of the most powerful unit-trains available for coal transport can move only 100 million tons of coal per year. There is barely enough space to build forty pairs of tracks through the mountains in order to transport the necessary 4 billion tons of coal. Likewise, it will be impossible to find enough harbors in Bohai Bay to further transport the huge amounts of coal required in eastern and southern China. Considering the further challenges to the Chinese energy supply, several other options have been seriously studied.

One alternative mode of coal transport is pumping coal slurry through pipelines. Two key technologies involved in this option have been studied seriously — the stability of the coal-water mixture and the dehydration of the slurry before it is used as fuel at the end of the line. It is believed that both problems are technically solvable. Two other uncertainties still remain, however. One is the economic viability of the coal slurry method: the actual investment needed and the operational cost are totally unknown. Another unknown is the

availability of water at the coal mine for the production of many billions of tons of slurry. More development work is therefore needed before implementation of such a gigantic project.

Another alternative is the conversion of coal into electricity at mine-mouth and transmission of the electricity by high voltage power lines. All the technologies involved are mature, and the overall cost has been estimated to be comparable to the railway option (see table 4.8). Though power lines can be built more easily than railways through mountain ranges, another obstacle emerges. The coal mines are located in an arid region already short of water, and the availability of cooling water for power plants will present a major constraint. Considering that hundreds of millions of tons of coal will need to be converted into electricity, the consumption of cooling water will be enormous, even if advanced cooling towers are used. In order to save water, dry cooling technology has been studied. At the present level of technology, the largest capacity of a single dry-cooled turbo-generator attains only 200 MWe, too small for a modern power station. However, the capacity needed to be installed is still moderate at present, thus the water constraint will not be a serious problem at first. Several mine-mouth stations are already under construction or planned. For instance,

Fig. 4.5 Proportion of Deficit in Coal Sector

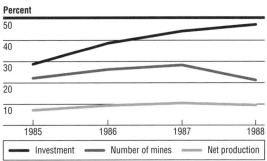

Table 4.8 Comparison of Coal Transportation and Electricity Transmission

	Coal transportation	Electricity transmission
Type	Single Track	Nine 500-KV lines
Distance	1,100 km	1,000 km
Cost Basis	1. Railway at Y 3.6 millon/km	1. Transmission line at Y 300,000/km
	2. 330 locomotives at Y 1.2 million each	2. Substation at Y 120/KVA
	3. 14,300 coal cars at Y 36,000 each	3. Power plant Y 260/kWe
Total capital investment	Y 4.871 billion	Y 5.884 billion
Unit cost of energy transported	30.5 yuan/ton (5,000 kcal/ton)	30.9 yuan/ton (5,000 kcal/ton)

SOURCE: World Bank, *China: The Energy Sector.*

a 2.4 GWe power station has been planned for the vast Junggar coal field. Whether such power stations will be able to digest multi-billion tons of coal in the future remains an issue.

4.3.2. HIDDEN DEFECTS IN BOTH LEGS

China stakes its energy future on the rapid growth of coal production. "Walking on Two Legs" seems to have been very successful in recent years, but energy experts have long been worried about how far the two legs will be able to walk together. Fatal hidden weaknesses exist in both legs. In table 4.9 and figure 4.6 one can see that one leg — the state-owned large coal mines — grew very slowly in recent years. The growth rates dropped from 7 to 10 percent per year in 1982-1985 and fell to 3 to 5 percent per year in 1986-1988, while the specific investment was steadily increasing. The share of production from these large, modern mines dropped to 44 percent of the national total in 1988. The financial situation worsened: the deficit of those mines increased at 24 percent per year in the same period, amounting to about half of the annual capital investment! How can such an unhealthy "leg" be expected to stride into the twenty-first century toward its goal of multi-billion tons of production?

The other "leg" — the local medium-size and small coal mines — grew more rapidly in the same period, as seen in table 4.9. The total output of the local mines has exceeded that of the state-owned mines since 1985, and the rural small mines have increased production most dramatically. The output of local mines doubled from 1980 to 1988, while that of rural mines tripled. The small rural mines use manual labor and backward technology, some of them having not even the most primitive basic equipment — the so-called "four small items," that is, the winch, the pump, the blower, and safe mine lamps. As a result, safety in these rural mines is very poor, and casualties are high. Fatalities per million tons of coal were 5.2 in 1981, about thirty times higher than the same statistic for the United States. Another drawback to expanding small rural mines is the waste of resources: the recovery rate of coal is estimated to be less than 50 percent at small mines, or even lower when the indirect degradation of the whole coal field is considered. Thus, though this strategy retrieves more coal, it is at the expense of wasted resources and lives. Both resources and lives seem abundant in China now, but the situation may be different in the future. The second "leg" thus seems larger but is actually only "swollen." Consequently, very few experts really believe that the local small coal mines will survive as a significant factor into the next century. Highly skilled "surgery" is thus needed to make both legs healthy enough to continue the long march.

4.3.3. THE ENVIRONMENTAL IMPACT OF COAL

Another critical factor affecting the fate of coal consumption has no direct connection with coal production. However, pollution may turn out to be the ultimate constraint on coal output. The environmental impact of coal utilization falls into two categories: the near-term impact, such as air pollution and acid rain, and the long-term impact, such as the CO_2 "greenhouse effect." While detailed analysis will be left to chapter 6, some brief comments should be made here.

Coal is a "dirty" fuel when compared with any other kind of primary energy source, whether oil, natural gas, hydropower, biomass, solar, wind, or even nuclear energy. Since over 75 percent of the primary energy available in China comes from coal, its environmental impact is more serious here than anywhere else in the world. As a result, much emphasis should be put on energy-environmental issues in Chinese energy policy. "Clean" coal technologies must be developed at a faster pace to mitigate the situation, and alternatives should be exploited to replace coal as much as possible over the long term.

Several "clean" coal technologies, coal gasification and direct and indirect coal liquefaction, are being developed in China. The technology of low-pressure synthesis of methanol has also been developed in China, and it has been estimated that the

Fig. 4.6 Growth of Coal Production by Mine Ownership

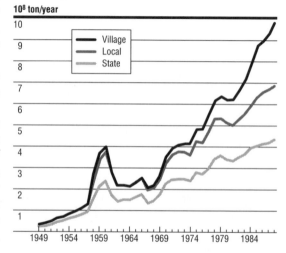

46

Table 4.9 Growth of Production in Various Types of Mines

Year	Total	Production (10^8 ton)			Proportion (%)		
			Locally owned			Locally owned	
		State-owned	Subtotal	Village-owned	State-owned	Subtotal	Village-owned
1949	0.32	0.24	0.08	—	75.00	25.00	—
1950	0.43	0.30	0.13	—	69.77	30.23	—
1951	0.53	0.37	0.16	—	69.81	30.19	—
1952	0.66	0.48	0.18	—	72.73	27.27	—
1953	0.70	0.52	0.18	—	74.29	25.71	—
1954	0.84	0.62	0.22	—	73.81	26.19	—
1955	0.98	0.73	0.25	—	74.49	25.51	—
1956	1.10	0.82	0.28	—	74.55	25.45	—
1957	1.31	0.94	0.37	—	71.76	28.24	—
1958	2.70	1.58	1.12	0.34	58.52	41.48	12.59
1959	3.69	2.16	1.53	0.28	58.54	41.46	7.59
1960	3.97	2.40	1.57	0.22	60.45	39.55	5.54
1961	2.78	1.76	1.02	—	63.31	36.69	—
1962	2.20	1.48	0.72	—	67.27	32.73	—
1963	2.17	1.51	0.66	—	69.59	30.41	—
1964	2.15	1.51	0.64	—	70.23	29.77	—
1965	2.32	1.64	0.68	—	70.69	29.31	—
1966	2.52	1.81	0.71	—	71.83	28.17	—
1967	2.06	1.36	0.70	0.08	66.02	33.98	3.88
1968	2.20	1.47	0.73	0.13	66.82	33.18	5.91
1969	2.66	1.79	0.87	0.18	67.29	32.71	6.77
1970	3.54	2.27	1.27	0.31	64.12	35.88	8.76
1971	3.92	2.47	1.45	0.32	63.01	36.99	8.16
1972	4.10	2.49	1.61	0.36	60.73	39.27	8.78
1973	4.17	2.48	1.69	0.42	59.47	40.53	10.07
1974	4.13	2.43	1.70	0.52	58.84	41.16	12.59
1975	4.82	2.80	2.02	0.57	58.09	41.91	11.83
1976	4.83	2.74	2.09	0.65	56.73	43.27	13.46
1977	5.50	2.95	2.55	0.79	53.64	46.36	14.36
1978	6.18	3.42	2.76	0.87	55.34	44.66	14.08
1979	6.35	3.58	2.77	0.98	56.38	43.62	15.43
1980	6.20	3.44	2.76	1.05	55.48	44.52	16.94
1981	6.22	3.35	2.87	1.17	53.86	46.14	18.81
1982	6.66	3.50	3.16	1.37	52.55	47.45	20.57
1983	7.15	3.63	3.52	1.59	50.77	49.23	22.24
1984	7.89	3.95	3.94	1.95	50.06	49.94	24.71
1985	8.72	4.06	4.66	2.38	46.56	53.44	27.29
1986	8.94	4.14	4.80	2.43	46.31	53.69	27.18
1987	9.28	4.20	5.08	2.61	45.26	54.74	28.12
1988	9.80	4.34	5.46	2.95	44.29	55.71	30.10
1989	10.54	—	—	—	—	—	—

SOURCE: *China's Statistics Yearbook, 1989.*

cost of liquid fuel will be competitive when the factory reaches an annual output of one million tons. Successful experiments combining gasoline with up to 15 percent methanol have been reported. An integral coal-gasification and methanol factory at mine-mouth has been proposed which can process 7.5 million tons of raw coal to produce 2 billion cubic meters of pipeline gas and a million tons of methanol annually. The medium heat-value gas thus produced can be transported though pipelines to be used as a "clean" fuel in cities hundreds of miles away. Thus, coal gasification methanol technology provides another promising mode of "transportation" in connection with "clean" coal utilization.

4.4. THE FUTURE OF OIL AND GAS PRODUCTION

4.4.1 THE RISING STAR: DAQING AND THE OIL INDUSTRY

The Chinese oil industry won a dazzling victory in the early sixties as it leapt forward from almost nothing to fourth place among oil-producing countries. In 1989 China's annual oil production reached 137.5 million tons (about 2.7 million barrels per day), and over 30 million tons of crude oil and oil products were exported. Table 4.10 gives the oil production and the annual growth rates of the past four decades.

The Daqing oil field is located in the Songliao Basin in northeast China. Discovered oil-in-place amounts to 36.37 billion barrels, of which 12.89 billion barrels (35.4 percent) are believed to be recoverable. Chinese oil experts adopted the technology of early water injection (secondary recovery) and have maintained high productivity throughout the past two and a half decades. For the past fifteen years the annual output from this oil field alone exceeded 50 million tons, or more than 50 percent of the national total production. The triumph of the exploitation of Daqing oil field in the sixties terminated the then-prevailing belief that China was a geologically "oil poor" country and made pointless the Soviet oil embargo after 1960. The Daqing field was therefore honored like a national hero and was put forward as the model for all of Chinese industry.

As a result, the prosperous Chinese oil industry has come to be considered the backbone of the Chinese economy. On the one hand, oil is no doubt the blood of modern civilization and national defense in particular. It was unimaginable in the hostile world

Table 4.10 Crude Oil Production and Growth Rate

Year	Production (10^4 ton) Total	Natural	Annual growth rate (%)*
1949	12	7	—
1950	20	10	—
1951	31	14	—
1952	44	20	100.00
1953	62	30	150.00
1954	79	38	126.67
1955	97	43	113.16
1956	116	59	137.21
1957	146	86	145.76
1958	226	146	169.77
1959	373	376	189.04
1960	520	419	151.81
1961	531	482	115.04
1962	575	527	109.34
1963	648	595	112.90
1964	848	794	133.45
1965	1,131	1,076	135.52
1966	1,455	1,393	129.46
1967	1,388	1,357	97.42
1968	1,599	1,581	116.51
1969	2,174	2,135	135.04
1970	3,065	3,014	141.17
1971	3,941	3,,885	128.90
1972	4,567	4,510	116.09
1973	5,361	5,307	117.67
1974	6,485	6,430	121.16
1975	7,706	7,655	119.05
1976	8,716	8,673	113.30
1977	9,364	9,329	107.56
1978	10,405	10,369	111.15
1979	10,615	10,583	102.06
1980	10,595	10,562	99.80
1981	10,122	10,090	95.53
1982	10,212	10,179	100.88
1983	10,607	10,574	103.88
1984	11,461	11,430	108.10
1985	12,490	12,458	108.99
1986	13,069	13,039	104.66
1987	13,414	13,393	102.71
1988	13,705	13,686	102.19
1989	13,745	—	100.30

SOURCE: *China's Statistics Yearbook, 1989.*

*The ratio of the annual production compared with that of the previous year, expressed in percentage, assuming the value previous year = 100.

environment before the 1980 reforms that China could carry out its Four Modernizations without an adequate domestic oil supply. In addition, because of the worldwide oil crisis in the seventies, China got almost a fourth of its hard currency from oil exports until the collapse of world oil prices in 1985. Presently, oil dollars still amount to 10 percent of the annual export revenue.

4.4.2. THE STRUGGLE TO FIND MORE OIL

An examination of the oil production recorded in table 4.10 reveals the problem in the Chinese oil industry. The annual growth rates have dropped from two digits (10 to 50 percent per year) between 1958 and 1978, to 2 percent or less in recent years. The reason is that the addition of new oil reserves has not been enough to meet the expanding oil production demand. The causes are many.

One important reason lies in the misunderstanding existing among Chinese policymakers. Some top Chinese leaders were not fully aware of the differences among various definitions of oil resources and reserves. As a result, they were vulnerable to exaggerated reports and specious figures on Chinese oil resources, and they were always too optimistic about the prospects of domestic oil production. Tables 4.11 and 4.12 list the figures on Chinese oil reserves and resources under various definitions. Proven recoverable oil accounts for less than a third of the oil-in-place actually found by extensive drilling. The remaining two-thirds or more of the oil cannot be extracted with ordinary technology. Some new technologies for enhanced oil recovery, such as steam soaking and injection, CO_2 and chemical injection, can increase the recovery rate to a certain extent, but in the long run more than 50 percent of the original oil-in-place will still remain

underground in the crevices of rocks and on the surfaces of sands.

Furthermore, the estimated undiscovered oil reserves are a matter of complete uncertainty. They should be evaluated at a probability shown in table 4.12. The mean probable value of the undiscovered recoverable crude oil in China is about twice the present recoverable oil reserves. Even if all potential reserves have been discovered, Chinese oil resources will be able to sustain the present production level for less than ninety years. Since the current five-year plan has set the target of producing 200 million tons of crude oil by 2000 (about 4 million barrels per day), production will probably drop after 2029 (see figure 4.11). This fact not only frustrates the hope of China's becoming a "second Middle East," it also emphasizes the serious problem of the long-term supply of liquid fuel in China.

4.4.3. THE OTHER LEG IN THE CHINESE OIL INDUSTRY — NONCONVENTIONAL OIL RESOURCES

The Chinese oil industry will eventually walk on two legs, even though such an issue has not yet been

Table 4.12 China's Crude Oil Resources, January 1986 (billions of barrels)

Resource	Probability distribution of assessment		
	95%	Mean	5%
Ultimate recoverable crude oil	49	87	134
Cumulative production to date plus proved reserves	34	34	34
Undiscovered recoverable crude oil	15	53	100

SOURCE: Gas Research Institute, *Energy Statistics*

Table 4.11 Reserves of Crude Oil in China, January 1986

	Unit	Region				Total
		Eastern	Songliao	Central	Western	
Original oil in place	Mbbl	101,708	36,372	21,425	5,046	128,179
	%	79.35	28.38	16.71	3.94	100
Proved ultimate recovery	Mbbl	28,203	12,887	4,441	1,666	34,310
	%	82.2	37.56	12.94	4.86	100
Cumulative production	Mbbl	9,661	5,550	569	530	10,760
	%	89.79	57.58	5.29	4.29	100
Proved oil reserves	Mbbl	18,542	7,327	3,872	1,136	23,550
	%	78.73	31.11	16.44	4.82	100
Recovery efficiency	%	27.7	35.4	20.7	33	26.8

SOURCE: Gas Research Institute, *Energy Statistics*.

seriously considered by most policymakers. China has a long history of producing shale oil and synthetic oil, due to the lack of oil reserves before Daqing was found. Because of the ultimate limitations of the recoverable oil reserves in China and the insignificant findings in large-scale explorations for offshore oil, nonconventional oil resources and synthetic oils such as heavy oil, oil shale, and coal pyrolysis and liquefaction are more and more important in long-term Chinese energy strategy.

The proven heavy oil reserves account at present for one-sixth of the total oil reserves, and more potential resources have not been extensively explored due to the lack of extraction technology. Kramai oil field in the northwest and Liaohe oil field in the northeast have the largest proven reserves of heavy oil. Steam soaking and injection technology have been actively developed in recent years, and trial production is under way. In order to cope with the future shortage of oil, nuclear heat from high-temperature graphite reactors (HTGR) has been proposed as a heat source for heavy oil recovery. One feasibility study of nuclear steam injection has been carried out in the Shengli oil field.

The proven oil shale reserves in China amount to some 31 billion tons, containing 1.8 billion tons of shale oil. The reserve was estimated one order higher than the proven resources, which is comparable to the total potential oil resources. The output of shale oil reached 790,000 tons in 1959 but had dropped to 30,000 tons by 1980. Since the technology is mature and the cost is not unreasonably high, shale oil is expected to resume its former importance early in the next century.

The final liquid fuel resource in China is the coal itself. Since most varieties of Chinese coal contain a high fraction of volatile matter, flash pyrolysis can produce hundreds of millions of tons of liquid fuel. Several technologies are promising. The "vibrated" bed flash pyrolysis technology under development can co-generate liquid fuel and electricity when integrated with a fluidized-bed boiler, which may provide one attractive technology for liquid fuel supply in the long-term Chinese energy strategy.

When will the Chinese policymakers, particularly those responsible for the oil industry, become really serious about the importance of this second "leg," coal?

4.4.4. AN UNSOLVED PUZZLE — PROSPECTS FOR NATURAL GAS

Though natural gas is a promising alternative to both oil and coal as a clean and convenient energy source, the prospects for natural gas in China are still unclear. The annual output of natural gas is low compared to the production of both coal and oil (see table 4.13). The ratio of natural gas to coal and oil in world energy production was 29 percent by energy content in 1986, but in China it was only 2.2 percent. It is not clear why Chinese natural gas resources are so poor, disproportionately to both oil and coal resources, since the formation processes for gas, oil, and coal are interrelated. More drilling efforts have to be made before this puzzle can be solved.

Fig. 4.7 Prospective Oil Production in China

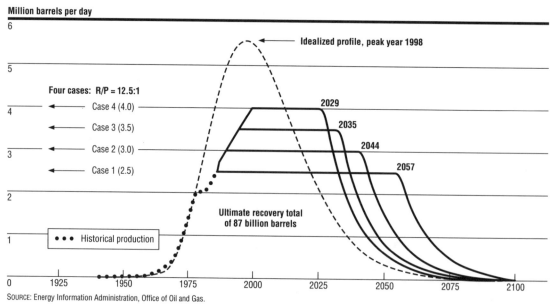

Million barrels per day

SOURCE: Energy Information Administration, Office of Oil and Gas.

Table 4.13 Natural Gas Production and Growth Rate (10^8 cubic meters)

Year	Production Total*	From gas wells	Annual growth rate (%)
1949	0.07	0.06	—
1950	0.07	0.06	Base Year
1951	0.03	0.02	−66.67
1952	0.08	0.06	200.00
1953	0.11	0.08	33.33
1954	0.15	0.11	37.50
1955	0.17	0.12	9.09
1956	0.26	0.21	75.00
1957	0.70	0.63	200.00
1958	1.10	0.85	34.92
1959	2.90	2.52	196.47
1960	10.40	10.15	302.78
1961	14.70	14.38	41.67
1962	12.10	11.52	−19.89
1963	10.20	9.44	-18.06
1964	10.60	9.13	−3.28
1965	11.00	8.98	−1.64
1966	13.40	10.34	15.14
1967	14.60	11.59	12.09
1968	14.00	10.55	−8.97
1969	19.60	13.96	32.32
1970	28.70	20.28	45.27
1971	37.40	25.94	27.91
1972	48.40	29.77	14.76
1973	59.80	34.46	15.75
1974	75.30	39.75	15.35
1975	88.50	47.67	19.92
1976	101.00	55.58	16.59
1977	121.20	67.46	21.37
1978	137.30	77.70	15.18
1979	145.10	79.80	2.70
1980	142.70	70.50	−11.65
1981	127.40	63.70	−8.65
1982	119.30	52.50	−17.58
1983	122.10	53.80	2.48
1984	124.30	54.80	1.86
1985	129.30	56.40	2.92
1986	137.60	58.90	4.43
1987	138.90	59.00	0.17
1988	139.10	59.50	0.85
1989	152.90	—	10.01

SOURCE: *China's Statistics Yearbook, 1989.*

*Includes natural gas produced from both gas wells and oil wells.

There is also an administrative issue which has some bearing on the situation. Natural gas has never been treated as an independent energy sector by the Chinese administrative hierarchy but has been included under the Ministry of Petroleum. As a result, exploration for natural gas was never given adequate emphasis. This can certainly be seen as one reason for the poor understanding of the natural gas situation in China. Due to the limited available investment and the increasing pressure for oil exploration, the position of natural gas in China cannot be expected to improve very much in the foreseeable future.

4.5. THE VANGUARD LAGGING BEHIND: THE CHINESE POWER SECTOR BEGINS TO WALK ON TWO LEGS

4.5.1. QUADRUPLING 1980 POWER GENERATION BY 2000

It has long been a favorite slogan in Chinese policymaking that "Electric power should be the vanguard of the economy," and indeed it was before 1980. Table 4.14 and figure 4.8 illustrate that the growth rates of electricity production were always greater than the growth of national income before 1980, and the elasticity averaged about 1.077. However, due to decreasing economic efficiency in the power sector and the shortage of capital investment, the growth of power production began to lag behind the economy, and elasticity dropped to 0.98. Since the share of electricity in Chinese total energy consumption is still very low (16.9 percent) as compared with the world average (about 35 percent), the modernization process will increase the demand for electricity even if the total energy intensity decreases. Thus an elasticity of electricity consumption of 1.0 is expected in the future Chinese economy, and the target of electricity production by 2000 is set at 1,200 TWh, quadrupling the 300 TWh generated in 1980.

4.5.2. WALKING ON TWO LEGS AND POLICY IN THE POWER SECTOR

How can China reach the ambitious goal of quadrupling its electricity generation in two decades? Accomplishing this difficult task implies that the installed capacity of generating units will have been physically quadrupled, since the utilization factor of Chinese power plants is already very high. The power sector is the most capital-intensive one, and the drop

Table 4.14 Growth of Electricity Generation

Year	Total generation (10^8 kWh)	Thermal (%)	Hydro (%)	Growth rate of generation 1952=100%	Previous year = 100%	Growth of national income Previous year = 100%
1953	92	16.30	83.70	126.03	126.03	114.0
1954	110	20.00	80.00	150.68	119.57	105.8
1955	123	19.51	80.49	168.49	111.82	106.4
1956	166	21.08	78.92	227.40	134.96	114.1
1957	193	24.87	75.13	264.38	116.27	104.5
1958	275	14.91	85.09	376.71	142.49	122.0
1959	423	10.40	89.60	579.45	153.82	108.2
1960	594	12.46	87.54	813.70	140.43	98.6
1961	480	15.42	84.58	657.53	80.81	70.3
1962	458	19.65	80.35	627.40	95.42	93.5
1963	490	17.76	62.24	671.23	106.99	110.7
1964	560	18.93	81.07	767.12	114.29	116.5
1965	676	15.38	84.62	926.03	120.71	117.0
1966	825	15.27	84.73	1,130.14	122.04	117.0
1967	774	16.93	83.07	1,060.27	93.82	92.8
1968	716	17.02	83.94	980.82	92.51	93.5
1969	940	17.69	82.98	1,287.67	131.28	119.3
1970	1,159	18.14	82.31	1,587.67	123.30	123.3
1971	1,384	18.90	81.86	1,895.89	119.41	107.0
1972	1,524	23.32	81.10	2,087.67	110.12	102.9
1973	1,668	24.53	76.68	2,284.93	109.45	108.3
1974	1,688	24.31	75.47	2,312.33	101.20	101.1
1975	1,958	22.45	75.69	2,682.19	116.00	108.3
1976	2,031	21.31	77.55	2,782.19	103.73	97.3
1977	2,234	17.38	78.69	3,060.27	110.00	107.8
1978	2,566	17.77	82.62	3,515.07	114.86	112.3
1979	2,820	19.36	82.23	3,863.01	109.90	107.0
1980	3,006	21.18	80.64	4,117.81	106.60	106.4
1981	3,093	22.70	78.82	4,236.99	102.89	104.9
1982	3,277	24.59	77.30	4,489.04	105.95	108.3
1983	3,514	23.02	75.41	4,813.70	107.23	109.8
1984	3,770	22.50	76.98	5,164.38	107.29	113.5
1985	4,107	21.02	77.50	5,626.03	108.94	113.1
1986	4,495	20.02	78.98	6,157.53	109.45	108.0
1987	4,973	20.11	79.89	6,812.33	110.63	110.5
1988	5,452	20.01	79.99	7,468.49	109.63	111.0
1989	5,847	20.25	79.75	8,009.59	107.25	103.7

SOURCE: *China's Statistics Yearbook, 1989.*

in investment efficiency increases the investment needed. As a result, more than three times the total capital investment before 1980 will be needed from 1980 to 2000. A total of 175 GWe of new power would require more than 580 units generating 300 MWe (presently the largest unit capacity operating in China) or 290 units generating 600 MWe (the largest unit under development in China) to be installed within the next twenty years. This is a challenging task.

The first obstacle is finding a source of capital investment. Formerly all investment in the power industry came from the state budget. It is impossible to triple this budget to meet the requirements

Fig. 4.8 Elasticity of Electricity Generation

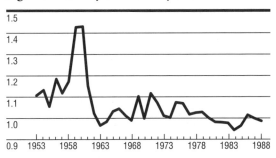

of power plant construction. The only solution is to find another "leg," that is, to raise capital from other possible financial sources. Such a policy was implemented after 1980 and has proved very effective (see table 4.5). In 1981, the share of direct government investment plus loans accounted for 84.4 percent of the total annual investment in power plant construction, where the direct investment share constituted 54.6 percent. In 1988, the government share dropped to 43.5 percent, of which the direct investment share was only 16.77 percent. The major alternative financing source was then "self-financing" (27.0 percent), which, together with investment from "other sources" (17.1 percent), exceeded the share from the state budget. In fact, many industries and local authorities are enthusiastic about investing in the power industry in hopes of getting more electricity for their own needs, and the construction of locally owned small power stations has been booming.

This new financing policy soon justified itself. The target of the Sixth Five-Year Plan was overfulfilled. The target of the Seventh Five-Year Plan is also expected to be overfulfilled, and the deputy minister of power has claimed that the actual electricity generated by 2000 may reach 1,450 TWe, or 120 percent of the original target of quadrupling of power production set in 1980, about which even many optimistic experts had been skeptical. Now there is even discussion about "further doubling the national power production by 2015 with installed capacity reaching 480-540 GWe." The power of the "two legs" policy again asserts itself; it is no less impressive in the case of the Chinese power sector than it was in the case of the coal industry.

4.5.3. THE DEBATE OVER THE THREE GORGES DAM — INSTITUTIONAL REFORM FOR THE FULL DEVELOPMENT OF HYDROPOWER

China's enormous hydropower potential (1,923 TWh per year) and the extremely low level of development (6 percent) present a sharp contradiction.

For many years, numerous Chinese and foreign experts have made strenuous efforts to promote hydropower plant development, and much emphasis has also been made in Chinese official energy policy. However, hydropower development has still lagged far behind, and a number of issues have been discussed over and over again without resolution. The basic reason is not on the technology side but reflects an institutional weakness in the Chinese energy-economic system — or in the economic system in general — which can only be resolved through more radical institutional reform.

We will begin our analysis with the hot debate over the Shanxia Dam project — a multi-decade controversy which is still unresolved. Shanxia (Three Gorges) is the most scenic section of the Chang Jiang (Yangtze River) valley. More than half (53.4 percent) of the national total exploitable hydropower potential is concentrated along this river. A dam 200 meters high would permit a firm 7.3 GWe with an installed capacity of 25 GWe and annual energy production of about 110 TWh. This ambitious project was claimed to be multi-functional, providing power generation, flood control, navigation improvement, water supply to northern China, and irrigation.

Three major specific benefits were often quoted in official documents. First, the electricity generated was to be sent though 500-kilovolt DC lines to Shanghai to mitigate the severe power shortage there. Second, part of the reservoir (about 20 billion cubic meters) was to be assigned to flood control for Hubei Province, downstream of the great dam. Third, the navigation improvement was to guarantee that ships of up to 10,000 tons could reach the city of Chongqing (located behind the reservoir), the largest commercial center in Sechuan Province, which had been the emergency capital of China during the Japanese invasion in 1937-1945. Each of the three benefits were considered indispensable for the development of the economy of the Chang Jiang valley, the heartland of China.

However, both economic and environmental costs and the risks involved in such a mammoth project are extremely high. It was estimated in 1987 that more than $10 billion would be needed (in contrast to the first estimate, of $5 billion, in 1958), excluding the cost of relocating more than 1.4 million people. The nature of the disruption to the ecology, particularly the aquatic environment, due to the inundation of 114,000 acres of farmland remains highly uncertain. Because of these factors, in later plans the height of the dam was reduced to

150 meters, with due reduction of installed generation capacity to 13 GWe. The number of people to be relocated decreased to half a million. However, the changes also dramatically reduced the projected benefits from the dam, and some new issues emerged.

The three major benefits discussed above aroused the skepticism of many experts, in particular those most experienced in the hydropower sector, such as Li Rui, former vice-minister and head of the General Bureau of Hydroelectric Construction. Their major arguments were that the benefits of the Shanxia Dam had been exaggerated and the costs and problems involved had been seriously underestimated. Furthermore, all possible approaches to hydropower development strategy alternative to this single mammoth dam project had never been examined objectively. In particular, neither the impact of the long lead-time on the overall national economic plan nor any possible risks involved in this project had ever been assessed. Thus many experts advocated postponing the construction plans and preferred to continue with more research before beginning the project.

Questions were raised about the three major benefits, the adverse impacts, and the possible alternatives.

First, it remains questionable whether the electricity generated in the Shanxia hydropower station will in fact benefit the Shanghai region. The reduction of dam height in the recent plan already halved the power output (from 25 to 13 GWe). The serious power shortages in regions along the proposed power transmission line would most likely consume all the electricity before it reached Shanghai, just as land in a drought absorbs all the water running through it. Furthermore, the long lead-time would push the date of commissioning of this hydropower plant far into the next century. The pressing power needs in the Shanghai region cannot be relieved by constructing this project any more than the starving peasant can be fed by planting rice. More coal-fired power plants have to be constructed to meet immediate needs, along with the Shanxia project.

Second, the flood control function involves great uncertainty. A review of the history of the disastrous floods of 1870, 1931, 1954, and 1981 reveals that the floods downstream of the proposed Shanxia Dam had no definite correlation with the waterfall upstream. The two most serious downstream floods, in 1931 and 1954, occurred when waterfalls in Sechuan Province were moderate. Thus the storage of upstream floods in the reservoir may not be critical to the control of downstream floods. The rein-forcement of downstream dikes is probably more urgent — indeed, indispensable — and the investment needed to attain the same flood control capability in this way would be much smaller. Furthermore, in recent years the floods in Sechuan Province have worsened due to increasing deforestation. The construction of Shanxia Dam may in fact have an adverse effect on upstream floods, and the touted benefit of flood control seems indeed dubious.

Third, the improvement of navigation has one important precondition: the resolution of the siltation problem. The annual silt accumulation in the Chang Jiang amounted to over 680 million tons in 1987, and the amount is increasing. The planned 150 meters of dam height could lead to the worst siltation occurring in the section of Chang Jiang just below Chongqing and, hence, navigation might become even more difficult. In this case, according to some transportation experts, dredging of the waterways is more important than the building of the dam.

Fourth, adverse environmental impacts have not been sufficiently studied. There is no available data at all on the possible disruption of the environment by the inundation of farmland and the relocation of 100,000 to 500,000 people. The flooding of numerous archaeological sites has also received little attention. More research should therefore be carried out before actual construction is started.

Fifth, a comprehensive comparison among different schemes of hydropower development strategy and an all-around evaluation of these schemes in the context of national economic development have not been adequately conducted. Clearly, this multi-billion-dollar project has not been proved economically sound by any standard.

A more reasonable strategy, argued by many of the dam's opponents, is to first build a series of smaller dams upstream and on the side-streams of Chang Jiang, meanwhile continuing research on the controversial issues involved in the Shanxia Dam. These "small" dams are themselves giants in the multi-GWe range, and their installed capacities will total 5.6 times the capacity of Shanxia Dam (table 4.14). These side dams would also dramatically reduce the silt transported to Shanxia, and the inundation loss would also be much less since most of the dams would be located in sparsely populated regions. On the other hand, because of the limited construction funds available, if the Shanxia project remains on the planning list before 2000, as suggested by the Ministry of Water Resources and Electric Power (see table 4.15), most of these favor-

Table 4.15 Potential Hydropower Sites
(Larger than 2 GWe capacity)

Site	River	Capacity (Gwe)	Planned capacity in use before 2000 (Gwe)
1. Shanxia	Chang Jiang	13.0	13.0
2. Xiluodu	Chang Jiang (Jinsha Jiang)	11.4	0.0
3. Baihetan	Chang Jiang (Jinsha Jiang)	10.1	0.0
4. Longtiaoxia	Chang Jiang (Jinsha Jiang)	6.0	0.0
5. Xiangjiaba	Chang Jiang (Jinsha Jiang)	5.7	0.0
6. Wudongde	Chang Jiang (Jinsha Jiang)	5.6	0.0
7. Pichang	Chang Jiang (Jinsha Jiang)	5.5	0.0
8. Hongmenkou	Chang Jiang (Jinsha Jiang)	4.0	0.0
9. Xiaowan	Lancang Jiang	4.0	4.0
10. Longtan	Hongshui	4.0	4.0
11. Laxiwa	Huang He	3.7	3.7
12. Pubugou	Chang Jiang (Dadu He)	3.3	3.3
13. Banbianjia	Chang Jiang (Jinsha Jiang)	3.0	0.0
14. Jinping I	Chang Jiang (Yalong Jiang)	3.0	0.0
15. Jinping II	Chang Jiang (Yalong Jiang)	3.0	1.5
16. Etan	Chang Jiang (Yalong Jiang)	3.0	3.0
17. Nuozhadu	Lancang Jiang	2.6	0.0
18. Jijiaheba	Chang Jiang (Dadu He)	2.2	0.0
19. Shipeng	Chang Jiang	2.1	0.0
20. Gouptitan	Chang Jiang (Wu Jiang)	2.0	2.0
21. Lianghekou	Chang Jiang (Yalong Jiang)	2.0	0.0
22. Yangfanggou	Chang Jiang (Yalong Jiang)	2.0	0.0
Total		101.2	34.5
Total of Chang Jiang excluding Shanxia		73.9	9.8

SOURCE: *Electric Power Industry in China (In Celebration of National Installed Generating Capacity over 100 GW)* (Beijing: China's Water Research and Electric

able upstream and sidestream dam projects will have to be postponed. From both technical and economic viewpoints, the strategy of building small dams upstream and on side streams is more feasible and more beneficial than the single venture of the Shanxia Dam.

However, in the overcentralized politico-economic institutions of China, techno-economic issues are always overridden by politics. The debate on Shanxia Dam has been interwoven with top-level political struggles inside the Chinese Communist party. The debate began in 1954 between two representative figures, Lin Yishan, the head of the Yangtze Valley Planning Office, and Li Rui, the vice-minister of power. The debate began over the purpose of the Shanxia Dam. Lin approached Chairman Mao and Premier Zhou directly in 1954 suggesting that the

Shanxia Dam should be built mainly for flood control, to avoid another 1954-type flood, in which 30,000 lives were lost, 7.8 million acres of farmland were inundated, and a total of 19 million people were affected. Two years later the Yangtze Valley Planning Office proposed a conceptual design for a 235-meter-high dam and claimed that such a dam could be designed in three years and built in another four years. Li opposed both of Lin's points: he argued for a multifunction project (including power generation, flood control, navigation, and irrigation) and declared it was premature to begin construction.

However, political campaigns put an end to these technical debates. Since Mao wrote the well-known poem in 1958 praising the Shanxia Dam, opposition to this project was considered almost a political betrayal. In the Anti-Rightists Campaign in 1957, experts who opposed the hasty construction of the Shanxia Dam were accused of "challenging the leadership of the Party" and were persecuted as rightists. Li himself was persecuted two years later as a "rightist-opportunist" inside the party. Even after Mao's death, this project continued to play the role of a counter in political conflicts.

A climax was reached in 1986 when the dam's proponents, supported by some of the top leaders, succeeded in getting the project included in the Seventh Five-Year Plan. The Preparatory Working Group of a new administrative area, Shanxia Province, was set up to take responsibility for coordinating all the controversial issues within its jurisdiction. The Shanxia Dam project seemed then to be gaining momentum. The opponents, encouraged by the progress of economic and political reforms, launched a counterattack in the Chinese People's Political Consultative Conference (CPPCC), presenting enormous amounts of information based on comprehensive study of the entire plan and a thirty-eight-day on-site survey along the Chang Jiang valley. Sun Yueqi and Lin Hua, the leaders of the Economic Construction Commission of the CPPCC, expressed clear and eloquent arguments against the hasty construction of the Shanxia Dam. Premier Zhao Ziyang was convinced, and the project once again slowed down.

When Zhao was purged during the Beijing uprising in 1989, the direction of the wind changed again. Chinese economic and political reforms ebbed. As might be expected, in the intense atmosphere of political persecution just after the anniversary of the crackdown in Tiananmen Square, the Shanxia project was again pushed forward despite the difficulty of financing. Political pressure once again paved the way for this premature project. As usual, politics overrode economic and technical considerations in the centralized economy.

The whole story of the ups and downs of the Three Gorges Dam deserves its own book, but one important point should be emphasized here: The most serious troubles in Chinese energy-economics originate from institutional defects rather than from technical difficulties, and the resolution of such issues depends on further reform of the politico-economic system.

One less soul-stirring but not trivial institutional defect hindering the development of hydropower is the economic aspect of the central planning system. No market mechanism is in effect, and no reasonable pricing system exists. As a result, there is no incentive to promote the exploitation of hydropower, which is capital intensive but is fuel cost-free, since the cost of coal is kept so low that it seems to be almost negligible. The solution of such a contradiction again depends on further reform of the whole economic system.

One final comment should be made before concluding this section. The "two legs" policy is also applicable in the hydropower sector, notably in the success of minihydropower construction. Over 63,000 small hydropower stations were put into operation in 1989, and a total of 31 TWh of electricity were generated by them in 1988. The power requirements of a third of China's rural counties and 40 percent of the county-owned industries were supplied by these small hydropower stations. We will evaluate this strategy in the next chapter when discussing rural energy.

4.6. The "Three Kingdoms" in the Nuclear Realm

4.6.1. How a "Nuclear Power" Can Exist without Nuclear Power

Among the world's five "nuclear powers," those countries with nuclear warhead stockpiles, China is the only one which had no nuclear power plant in operation before the end of 1990. China possesses atomic bombs, hydrogen bombs, nuclear submarines, ballistic missiles, and the technologies and resources needed for nuclear power development, including uranium mining and enrichment, reactor design, construction, operation, and reprocessing. However, no experimental, demonstration, or commercial nuclear power plant was constructed

until the late 1980s — about two decades after China detonated its first atomic bomb in 1964, about two and a half decades after the initiation of its first nuclear reactor in 1958, and about three decades after the launching of its nuclear programs in 1955. The reason is neither a technical nor an economic one. Even the extremely low price of coal would not be an argument in a centrally planned system against development of nuclear power capacity. The real cause is again the institutional contradiction, another example of Chinese-style bureaucracy — that is, the friction among the various authorities within a highly centralized economy.

4.6.2. "Three Kingdoms" in the Chinese Nuclear Realm

After China signed the agreement with Russia on nuclear cooperation in April 1955, it launched an ambitious nuclear program including the development of atomic bombs, hydrogen bombs, and ballistic missiles as well as the construction of nuclear submarines. A new ministry, then called the Third Ministry of Machine Building, was founded under the State Council to direct Chinese nuclear programs. Later, in 1958, it was reconstructed as the Second Ministry of Machine Building, responsible for the research, development, design, and operation of uranium mining and enrichment; plutonium production; nuclear bomb development, testing, and production; submarine nuclear power plant development; nuclear fuel fabrication and reprocessing; nuclear instruments and control systems; and isotope production and application. The Atomic Research Institute of the Academy of National Sciences was also under the actual leadership of this ministry. The Chinese nuclear program was assigned a first priority in these years; thus the Second Ministry became the most privileged kingdom in the whole world of Chinese industry.*

However, the scope of this new ministry was so broad that it had to transfer most of the manufacturing of equipment to the First Ministry of Machine Building, originally only responsible for machine building for civil purposes. A special bureau under the First Ministry was therefore formed to administer the military contracts, which were also assigned first priority and were hence fully guaranteed by the government in financing and the supply of other resources. A research institute for nuclear

---

* In ancient times, between 220 and 265 A.D., China was split into three kingdoms, Wei, Shu, and Wu. Endless wars were carried on among them, and a number of interesting stories about their battles were vividly portrayed in the famous novel, *The Romance of the Three Kingdoms*.

equipment development was in preparation in 1960 but was disbanded during the Cultural Revolution. A second kingdom in the Chinese nuclear realm thus matured and grew to control all the major manufacturing capabilities of nuclear power plants with the exception of fuel fabrication.

Third came the Ministry of Power. (In certain periods it combined with the Ministry for Water Resources and formed a larger ministry.) Since the original task of the Second Ministry did not include the civil application of nuclear power, and in all Western countries the development of civil nuclear power was a commercial activity separate from national defense programs, the Chinese Ministry of Power claimed its leading role in nuclear power and began design and research of pressurized water reactors (PWR) as early as 1959, at the very beginning of the Chinese nuclear age. However, since civilian nuclear energy had no policy priority and most nuclear information and materials were classified at that time, the research and development effort in the Ministry of Power was seriously retarded. A division within the Electric Research Institute was established in Beijing for nuclear power research in the 1960s, and later it was transformed into an independent Nuclear Power Research Institute in Suzhou. The Bureau of Nuclear Power in this ministry was established, and a joint venture with the power company in Hong Kong was initiated by the Ministry of Power in the early 1980s in Guangdong to build the first Chinese commercial nuclear station. The Ministry of Power thus struggled vigorously for leadership in nuclear power development over the past three decades.

All the Chinese nuclear programs were then under the direct control of the Central Special Committee (CSC) of the Chinese Communist party, headed by the late Premier Zhou Enlai and consisting of the chairmen of all the state commissions, the relevant ministries, and a number of top experts. After the successful commissioning of the Chinese nuclear submarine prototype in 1971, Premier Zhou considered it was the right time to promote the civil application of nuclear energy, and he convened several sessions of the Central Special Committee to discuss the development of Chinese nuclear power. However, he failed to resolve the disputes among the three ministries on the leadership in nuclear power development, and hence the programs of civilian nuclear power proceeded very slowly.

Only two outsiders were able to carry out their respective research and development proposals on more advanced nuclear power reactors. Proposals for the high-temperature gas-cooled reactor developed by INET, Tsinghua University, and the molten-salt reactor designed by Shanghai Nuclear Research Institute were accepted and development proceeded. The commercial power reactor lagged behind only because of conflict of interests. Later the Shanghai nuclear power program was changed to develop a prototype pressurized water reactor due to technical difficulties in its original liquid-fuel reactor concept. This reactor was code-named "728," the date of first approval, August 1972. The project later evolved into the present 300-MWe Qingshan Nuclear Power Station, scheduled to be in operation by the end of 1990, or eighteen years after the approval date. Still, it will be the first Chinese civil nuclear power reactor ever in operation.

The "728" prototype nuclear power station is by no means a commercial one. The development of a large commercial power plant awaits the solution of the leadership controversy. Premier Zhou failed to cut this Gordian knot, and he died in 1976.

4.6.3. TECHNICAL ISSUES IN THE DEBATE OVER NUCLEAR POWER

It is not the objective of this book to discuss in more detail the quarrels and the solution of the nuclear power leadership in the Chinese bureaucracy. Only techno-economic issues relevant to policymaking will be analyzed further for a better understanding of the current Chinese nuclear energy policy.

There are all together ten major controversial issues on which Chinese policymakers must reach some consensus before achieving consistent policy for the development of nuclear energy. The four most substantial issues are briefly summarized as follows:

1. Reactor Type.

Controversy has persisted for a long time on the choice of reactor for the first-generation Chinese commercial nuclear power stations. Three candidates have been proposed by various ministries and institutes — the Pressurized Water Reactor (PWR), the Heavy Water Reactor (HWR), and the Gas-Cooled Reactor (GCR, CO_2 cooling). The PWR was the most popular and ready-to-import technology on the world market, and domestic experience with the submarine reactor could be applied directly. Enrichment was needed, however, and heavy equipment such as pressure vessels, steam generators, circulating pumps, and high-pressure first-loop piping systems were difficult to manufacture in China.

Both the HWR and the GCR could use natural uranium, and domestic production capacities of both heavy water and nuclear graphite were already established. Most components were considered easier to manufacture in China than those of the PWR. However, these technologies, despite having already been commercialized in certain countries, were not popular. More restrictions existed for importing technologies due to the limited number of suppliers.

Since the proponents of each reactor type had some powerful bureaucratic background, a decision on the reactor type to be developed was deadlocked before 1983. As a result, the commercial nuclear power program was indefinitely postponed.

2. Technical Line.

There existed two opposite lines for developing commercial nuclear power in China. One was the traditional line of self-reliance, backed by successful experience in developing the atomic bomb and the nuclear submarine. No technical obstacle actually existed if China decided to build its own power reactor based on its nuclear submarine technology. However, the lead-time and financial resources needed for independently developing nuclear power technology to the commercialization stage would be formidable. The opposite line — that is, to import the most advanced Western nuclear power technology from abroad — seemed preferable from the economic point of view. Only the "open door policy" adopted after 1980 created the latter opportunity.

Two major drawbacks, however, existed in importing foreign equipment. The first was the need for a large amount of foreign exchange to buy nuclear equipment and technologies. The second was the restriction resulting from China's refusal to sign the Nuclear Nonproliferation Treaty before 1984. The Chinese nuclear power program could not step forward before this controversy was settled.

3. Enrichment Technology.

The additional capacity of uranium enrichment was needed for the civilian nuclear program since the separation production of the first Chinese diffusion plant was very small (estimated around 800 tons SWU), barely enough for the weapons program. Because of the inefficiency of Chinese gas diffusion technology and its energy-intensive nature, the construction of a second diffusion plant was questioned in the 1970s. A more advanced separation technique based on the gas ultra-centrifugal process was favored by many experts. Impressive progress was made in the early 1980s. Although three research institutes (in Beijing, Tianjing, and Shang-

hai) had built centrifuges and carried out experiments successfully, the responsible authorities were hesitant to make the transition from diffusion to ultra-centrifuge technology. Thus the plan of building the second uranium separation plant was indefinitely postponed.

4. Role of Nuclear Heat and R&D for Advanced Reactors.

Since 70 percent of the primary energy in China is consumed in the form of heat, nuclear energy can find applications in the heat market. Although great research and development effort was still needed in the technology of high-temperature nuclear-process heat, Low-Temperature Nuclear Heating Reactors (LTNHR) were much easier to build. However, different institutions held different opinions; hence, the development of nuclear heat was also delayed until 1985, when the first heating reactor program was approved.

4.6.4. THE HUEILONGGUAN MEETING AND CHINESE NUCLEAR ENERGY

In early 1983, when economic reform was proceeding rapidly, the debate over Chinese nuclear energy policy seemed mature enough for a final resolution. A meeting was convened jointly by the State Science and Technology Commission and the State Planning Commission in Hueilongguan, a peasant-run hotel north of Beijing, to discuss the first draft of Chinese nuclear energy policy. The author of the present book, having no affiliation with any of the three kingdoms, was authorized by the State Science and Technology Commission to be the head of the drafting group. Over a hundred senior experts and technocrats from all ministries and institutes concerned were invited, and the meeting reached a consensus after intense discussion. The following policies were finally adopted by the meeting and submitted to the State Council for final approval:

1. The Pressurized Water Reactor should be adopted as the major reactor type for the first generation of Chinese nuclear power plants.
2. The unit capacity of each commercial power reactor should be in the range of 900 to 1,000 MWe.
3. The domestically designed 300-MWe prototype Pressurized Water Reactor should also be built in order to gain experience.
4. Foreign nuclear plant equipment should be imported together with technology transfer. A localization program should be planned in advance, and indigenous research and

development efforts should be strengthened and coordinated.

5. China should become self-reliant in its nuclear fuel supply, and the gas-centrifugal technique should be developed as the mainstream fuel process.

6. Reprocessing of spent fuel and recycling of uranium and plutonium should be developed. Research and development of final disposal of nuclear waste should be enhanced.

7. Nuclear safety regulations should be promulgated. An independent State Nuclear Safety Bureau should be established.

8. Nuclear power station sites should be carefully selected in advance.

9. Nuclear heat-production should be developed and a low-temperature heating prototype reactor should be built to gain experience.

10. Research work on advanced reactors such as fast breeder, high-temperature reactors, and fusion reactors should be continued. A small experimental fast breeder should be built by the late 1990s.

The three ministries were later coordinated by a special Office for Nuclear Power under the State Council, and the above-mentioned policies have been implemented. Chinese civil nuclear programs began to move forward after this meeting.

4.6.5. THE CURRENT CHINESE NUCLEAR PROGRAM AND PROSPECTS

The Chinese government has launched an ambitious nuclear program to develop both nuclear power and nuclear heat with a target of nine nuclear power reactors totaling 6 GWe in operation by 2000, and some 15 GWe by 2010. Demonstration nuclear reactors for district and industrial heating are also included.

The domestically designed 300-MWe PWR nuclear power station has been built in Qingshan,

70 miles south of Shanghai, and was scheduled to be commissioned by the end of 1990. The first unit of the commercial 2 x 900 MWe PWR nuclear power station in Daya Bay was to be completed in 1991. The first 5-megawatt thermal (MWt) low-temperature district heating reactor went critical and delivered heat to a local grid in November 1989. All the fuel elements used in these reactors except the first batch in the first commercial power plant were supplied by Chinese factories.

One special feature of the Chinese civil nuclear program is the active development of an "inherently safe reactor" for nuclear heating, which has been discussed in the world nuclear community for years. Because of the serious energy shortage and the environmental pollution encountered in the coal-dominant Chinese energy system, nuclear heat seems to be a reasonable solution for urban energy supply. These reactors must be inherently safe since they will be built adjacent to or even inside residential areas. Two types of heating reactors have been developed: the deep pool-type reactor for smaller heat grids (2-120 MWt each) and the low-pressure vessel-type reactor for larger heat grids (200-500 MWt each). Both have been demonstrated by domestic and some foreign experimental reactors.

An analysis of the potential district heating* market shows a tremendous potential demand for nuclear heating reactors of various sizes. Table 4.16 shows the market size for the cities north of Huang He (Yellow River), where the current Chinese regulation allows house heating in winter, amounting to 26.6 gigawatts thermal (GWt), which would require some 760 heating reactors of various sizes.

Feasibility studies for three advanced reactor types are under way. An experimental fast breeder reactor was planned to be built in the late nineties.

---

* Providing home heating in an urban district from a centralized heat source through a network of pipelines.

Table 4.16 District Heating Market in North China

Population size (in thousands)	Number of cities	Average population (in thousands)	Heat market (MWt)	Heating reactor market		
				Number of reactors needed	Unit size (MWt)	Proportion (%)
>2,000	4	3,773	6,000	30	200	22.6
1,000-2,000	10	1,289	5,000	50	100	18.8
500-1,000	19	745	5,600	80	70	21.0
200-500	47	311	6,000	200	30	22.6
<200	95	108	4,000	400	10	15.0
Total	175	383	26,600	760	35	100.0

SOURCE: See Lu, Yingzhong, *The Role and Prospects of Nuclear Heat in the Energy System of China*, article written for the Study of Nuclear Energy Strategies in China, sponsored by State Science and Technology Commission, May 1988.

A 10-MWt experimental HTGR for industrial heating is planned in cooperation with KWU of Germany. A small research facility for developing the fusion reactor has been placed in operation, and international cooperative projects have been carried out.

The state of the current Chinese nuclear energy program is shown in table 4.17 and figure 4.8. China now finally stands at the entrance to its nuclear era. It is a latecomer when nuclear power programs in most Western countries are already declining. However, China has to rely on its nuclear energy program to solve the unprecedented challenge of the energy demand of the next century. We will return to this subject in chapter 6, where the environmental issues of the future domestic and global energy system are considered.

4.6.6. ENVIRONMENTAL CONCERNS: RADIOACTIVE WASTE

The safety concerns in nuclear energy development have two major aspects: the safe operation of reactors and the safe disposal of the radioactive wastes

contained in the spent fuel discharged from the reactors. Chinese scientists have worked in both areas to assure the "absolute" safety of nuclear energy. The development of the inherently safe reactor mentioned above is a solution to the first challenge. Substantial progress has been achieved in building an inherently safe nuclear heating reactor. At the same time, research and development work on the reprocessing of spent fuel and the vitrification of high-level radioactive wastes has been carried out. Since the Chinese nuclear industry has certain experience in these technologies in connection with military applications, the safe disposal of radioactive wastes is believed to be realistic at the state-of-the-art level. This is the reason why the Chinese nuclear industry has repeatedly expressed its interest even in taking spent fuel from European countries and from Taiwan for reprocessing and final disposal.

The attitude of many Chinese environmentalists is somewhat different from that of their Western colleagues. Every kind of energy has its environmental impact. If one has to choose one evil over another, the more annoying one (in this case,

Fig. 4.9 Locations of Ongoing and Planned Nuclear Projects in China

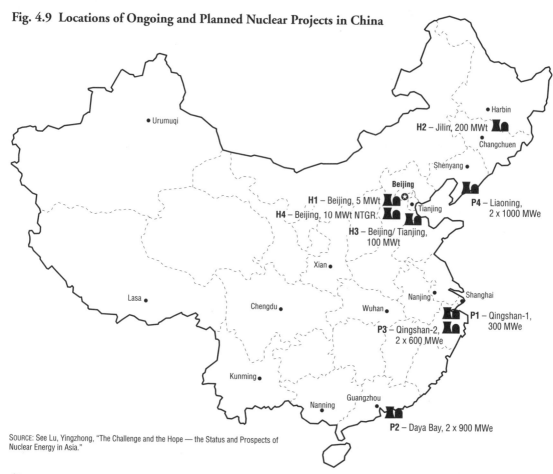

SOURCE: See Lu, Yingzhong, "The Challenge and the Hope — the Status and Prospects of Nuclear Energy in Asia."

Table 4.17 Nuclear Energy Program of the PRC

Location of reactors	Type	Capacity (MW)	Vendor	Status
1. Nuclear Power				
Qingshan 1	PWR	300	Domestic	Under construction, operation scheduled 1991
Daya Bay	PWR	2x900	Framatom (R), GEC (T)	Under construction, operation scheduled 1992
Qingshan 2	PWR	2x600	Domestic (cooperation with FRG)	Planned, negotiating with FRG
Liaoning	PWR	2x1,000	USSR	Planned, negotiating with USSR
Local	PWR	300	Domestic	Negotiating with provincial governments
2. Nuclear Heat				
Beijing	LTR	5	Domestic	In operation since November 1989
Jilin	LTR	200	Domestic	Planned
North China	POOL	100	Domestic	Negotiating
Beijing	HTGR	10	Domestic (cooperation with FRG)	Negotiating with FRG
3. Fast Breeder				
Beijing	FBR	2	Domestic	Beginning construction, scheduled operation by 2000

SOURCE: See Lu, Yingzhong, "The Challenge and the Hope — the Status and Prospects of Nuclear Energy in Asia," paper presented at the 1990 Annual Meeting of the American Nuclear Society, June 10-14, Nashville.

Note: R = reactor, T = turbine

coal) will be condemned. The Chinese public also prefers nuclear heat and electricity to suffering in a freezing house in the winter and to frequent black-outs. As a result, the Chinese response to the pre-vailing global anti-nuclear atmosphere is rather weak. Currently, the major constraint on the development of the Chinese nuclear program is still the lack of capital investment.

CHAPTER 5

FUELING THE FORGOTTEN MAJORITY
The Energy Situation in the Chinese Countryside
and Rural Energy Policy

5.1. THE RURAL ENERGY SITUATION
Before 1980, over 80 percent of the Chinese population was rural. However, very little commercial energy was supplied to the countryside. In 1979 rural areas consumed only 13.8 percent of the total commercial energy supply. When converted to per capita consumption, this figure accounts for only 4 percent of the energy used in urban areas. Even taking into account non-commercial energy, the per capita energy consumption in rural areas was less than 16 percent of that in urban regions. The per capita final energy utilized in the countryside was less than 8 percent of that used in cities.

The rural energy structure in 1979 is shown in table 5.1, and the energy flow diagram is shown in figure 5.1. Residential energy consumption accounted for about 80 percent of the total rural consumption, of which 85.6 percent was non-commercial biomass energy. The efficiency is low, the averages being 13.43 percent in rural residential and 29 percent in rural production. The situation is clearly shown in figure 5.2.

It was estimated that about 47 percent of rural households were short of fuel for more than three months of the year. The average basic energy need in rural regions was estimated to be about 4,500 kilocalories (kcal) effective energy per household per day, but the actual consumption averaged just 3,500 kcal, 22 percent less than the base line. The acute energy shortage affecting households has led to devastating deforestation and excessive collection of other plant materials. As a consequence, the ecological equilibrium has been seriously disrupted.

Energy supplies for rural production have also been insufficient. Only small amounts of petroleum products were allocated to rural regions, barely enough to maintain the operation of farm machinery, as shown in table 5.2. Only 56.3 percent of the minimum fuel demand was met. Less than 40 percent of the minimum oil supply demanded for agricultural production was supplied. Thus the total rural power shortage was estimated to be 37 percent. More than 46 percent of villages had no electricity at all in 1980. Only 20 to 40 percent of the total electricity demand for irrigation could be guaranteed during the busy season for irrigation. As a result, energy shortages seriously affected the economic development of Chinese rural regions.

Strangely enough, before 1980 no government agency was responsible to deal with the general energy problem in rural China. The critical energy situation of the majority of Chinese people seemed to be totally forgotten!

5.2 POTENTIAL RESOURCES AND TECHNOLOGIES AVAILABLE IN RURAL AREAS
The vastness of China's countryside and the lack of infrastructure makes the provision of commercial energy to the 800 million people living there extremely difficult. Since the energy shortage in Chinese cities has also been serious, very little surplus commercial energy could be allocated to the rural regions. Local energy resources in rural areas were therefore of great importance, especially renewable resources. Before detailing the formulation and implementation of the rural energy policy, the basic resources available for such a policy should be analyzed.

Table 5.1 Rural Energy Consumption Pattern, 1979

	Quantity (10⁴tce/10⁸kWh)	Energy (10⁴ tce)	Percentage (%)	Effective energy (10⁴ tce)	Efficiency (%)
Rural households	—	26,097.20	79.70	3,504.27	13.43
Agricultural wastes	23,406.00	11,368.72	—	—	—
Animal dung					
For biogas	100.88	61.25	68.34	2,815.33	12.58
For fuel	940.00	570.71	—	—	—
Firewood	18,160.00	10,377.14	—	—	—
Electricity	58.90	309.96	0.95	72.43	23.36
Kerosene	105.60	151.02	0.46	30.20	20.00
Coal	4,563.59	3,258.40	9.95	586.51	18.00
Rural production	—	1,965.20	6.00	572.08	29.00
Irrigation	131.00	689.44	2.10	136.90	19.86
Field work	—	—	—	—	—
Stationary work (diesel)	812.86	1,162.40	3.55	406.84	35.00
Transportation	—	—	—	—	—
Agricultural work (gasoline)	79.28	113.36	0.35	28.34	20.00
Side production	—	4,677.50	14.30	1,190.18	25.44
Kilns (coal)	3,581.65	2,557.30	7.81	769.17	30.00
Side products (electrical)	70.89	373.06	1.14	74.09	—
Village industry (electrical)	54.40	286.28	0.88	56.85	19.86
County industry (electrical)	277.60	1,460.86	4.47	290.17	—
Total		32,739.90	100.00	5,266.78	16.08

SOURCE: State Science and Technology Commission, *China's Technology Policy: Energy (Blue Paper No. 4)* (Beijing: State Science and Technology Commission, in press).

5.2.1. AGRICULTURAL RESIDUES

The production of agricultural waste (straw and stalks which could be burned) varied substantially among different regions. From table 5.3, local energy resources of twenty-nine provinces, agricultural waste is seen ranking first among all kinds of local energy resources. The per capita value of agricultural waste varies from 438.83 kilograms coal equivalent (kgce), the highest (in Jilin), to an almost negligible amount (in Tibet). In table 5.4, the amount of usable waste produced by various crops is estimated. Rice straw ranks first.

Agricultural residues are not only the most important household fuel in the Chinese countryside but also the major fodder and an indispensable organic fertilizer. As a result, the excessive burning of agricultural wastes as fuel has profoundly adverse impact on both agricultural production and husbandry.

5.2.2. FIREWOOD

Firewood in China is collected not only from woodlots but also from the wastes left after lumber harvesting, from scattered shrubs, and among "Four Sides" trees, that is, those planted along the sides of houses, roads, fields, and streams and rivers in ac-

Fig. 5.2 Rural Residential Energy Structure, 1979

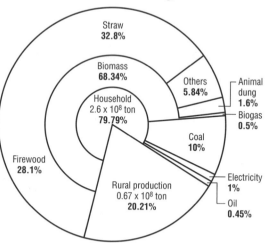

SOURCE: Institute for Agricultural Engineering Research and Design, *Report on China's Rural Energy Policy Issues.*

cordance with public policy. The supply potential of all these various sources of firewood in different regions is shown in table 5.5. In 1980, the area of woodlots for firewood amounted to 3.67 million hectares; of scattered forests, 15.63 million hectares; of shrubs, 29.57 million hectares. Four Sides trees were estimated to be 11.9 billion. According to table

Fig. 5.1 Energy Flow Diagram for Rural Regions, 1979
(Unit: 10^4 tce; Efficiency in percent)

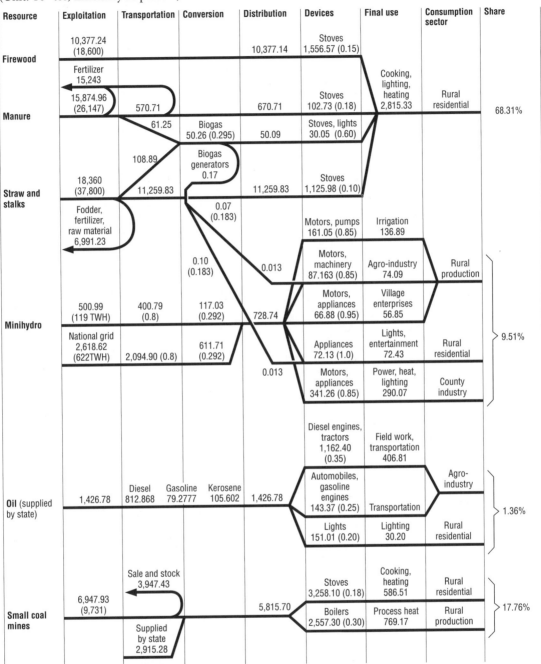

SOURCE: Institute for Agricultural Engineering Research and Design, *Report on China's Rural Energy Policy Issues.*
Note: Figures in parentheses under "Exploitation" denote gross quantity of energy source. All other figures in parentheses denote efficiency (%).

5.5, the rational annual supply of firewood would be 88.64 million tons, or an average per capita supply of 110 kilograms per year. Such a quantity of firewood could only meet two months' energy demand for rural households, or about 17 percent of the total residential consumption.

5.2.3. ANIMAL AND HUMAN WASTES

Both animal and human excrement are used as energy sources in rural China. The estimated total production of these wastes in 1983 amounted to 260 million tons, as shown in table 5.6. Dried animal dung may be directly used as fuel in stoves, but

Table 5.2 Diesel Fuel Demand in Rural Regions, 1979

	Farm machinery	Fishery machinery	Reclamation	Forestry machinery	Husbandry machinery	Village industry	Total
Capacity owned (10⁴ HP)	11,000	313	800	109	280	—	12,503
Supply (10⁴ ton)	450	100	547	27.5	16.8	163.86	812.36
Average annual work hours	204.5	1,597.4	342	1,260	300	—	—
Rational annual work hours	500	1,965	1,000	1,500	500	—	—
Availability, %	40.9	81.3	34.2	84	60	—	56.3

SOURCE: Institute for Agricultural Engineering Research and Design, *Report on China's Rural Energy Policy Issues* (Beijing: Institute for Agricultural Energy Reasearch and Development, 1982).

Table 5.3 Local Rural Energy Resources (Unit: Total=10⁴ Tce; /Capita=Kgce/per capita)

Province	Population (10⁴)	Agricultural wastes Total	Per capita	Manure Total	Per capita	Firewood Total	Per capita	Minihydropower Total	Per capita	Small coal mines Total	Per capita	Total Sum	Per capita
National Total	80,738.7	18,355.24	227.34	12,942.85	160.31	6,679.13	82.73	7,505.71	92.96	7,169.94	88.80	52,652.87	652.14
Beijing	374.6	111.02	296.37	56.00	149.49	10.11	26.99	9.47	25.28	96.39	257.31	282.99	755.44
Tianjing	360.1	85.51	237.46	31.50	87.48	11.26	31.27	0	0	0	0	128.27	356.21
Hebei	4,500.9	1,086.61	241.42	330.06	73.33	187.98	41.76	61.36	13.63	291.58	64.78	1,957.59	434.93
Shanxi	2,032.3	400.09	196.87	167.15	82.25	76.18	37.48	61.51	30.09	1,496.15	736.19	2,200.72	1,082.88
Neimonggu	1,312.3	371.58	283.15	221.87	169.07	327.42	249.50	40.73	31.04	192.99	147.06	1,154.59	879.82
Liaoning	2,228.9	721.75	323.81	653.00	292.97	165.78	74.38	49.15	22.05	165.29	74.16	1,754.97	787.37
Jilin	1,477.6	648.43	438.84	114.70	77.63	146.23	98.96	79.78	53.99	196.94	119.75	1,166.08	789.17
Helongjiang	1,854.0	612.84	330.55	179.99	97.08	407.19	219.62	76.62	41.33	182.96	98.58	1,459.40	787.16
Shanghai	428.3	114.76	267.94	109.90	256.60	0.08	0.19	0	0	0	0	224.74	524.73
Jiangsu	5,031.8	1,072.53	213.15	657.93	130.75	10.40	2.10	11.79	2.34	21.13	4.20	1,773.84	352.54
Zhejiang	3,314.5	763.10	230.23	991.00	298.99	280.44	84.61	273.23	82.43	9.28	2.80	2,317.05	699.06
Anhui	4,255.3	113.76	267.84	350.17	82.29	88.19	20.72	61.47	14.44	37.69	8.86	1,677.28	394.15
Fujian	2,128.5	347.50	163.26	513.59	241.29	370.57	174.10	378.27	177.72	95.11	44.68	1,705.04	801.15
Jiangxi	2,794.9	664.83	237.89	584.98	209.30	330.69	118.30	244.50	87.48	282.89	101.22	2,107.89	754.22
Shandong	6,537.5	1,375.35	210.38	484.72	74.14	177.79	27.20	22.63	3.46	386.94	59.19	2,447.34	374.37
Henan	6,542.7	1,539.59	235.31	494.72	75.61	364.36	55.69	108.51	16.58	946.96	144.74	3,454.14	527.93
Hubei	3,914.3	903.81	230.90	541.01	138.21	391.69	100.07	424.79	108.52	115.42	29.49	2,376.72	607.19
Hunan	4,615.8	956.31	207.18	1,528.19	331.08	337.68	73.16	436.37	94.54	666.98	144.50	3,925.53	850.46
Guangdong	3,079.4	699.66	227.21	828.10	268.92	341.77	110.99	421.74	136.96	130.43	42.36	2,421.70	786.44
Guangxi	4,751.5	906.27	190.73	649.39	136.67	335.87	70.69	244.39	51.43	129.21	27.19	2,265.13	476.71
Sechuan	8,621.8	1,801.97	209.00	1,277.51	148.17	678.28	78.67	618.66	71.76	627.37	72.76	5,003.76	580.36
Guizhou	2,404.3	303.52	126.24	416.47	173.21	269.95	112.28	268.81	111.80	347.54	144.55	1,606.29	668.08
Yunnan	2,765.8	456.92	165.20	753.66	272.49	595.84	215.43	943.04	340.96	331.67	119.92	3,081.13	1,114.01
Tibet	151.3	—	—	—	—	253.02	1,672.30	1,684.00	11,130.20	—	—	1,937.02	12,802.50
Shaanxi	2,395.3	671.11	280.18	224.25	93.62	326.14	136.16	165.14	68.94	154.58	64.53	1,541.22	643.43
Gansu	1,614.6	255.73	158.39	177.11	109.69	60.17	27.27	114.62	70.99	121.38	75.17	729.01	451.51
Qinghai	267.5	37.54	140.33	343.63	1284.60	67.63	252.82	210.50	768.92	11.29	42.21	670.59	2,506.88
Ningxia	284.3	79.95	281.22	35.05	123.29	1.77	6.22	2.42	8.56	23.48	82.59	142.67	501.83
Xingjiang	698.6	227.21	325.24	227.20	325.24	64.58	92.44	492.57	705.08	128.52	183.97	1,140.08	1,613.97

SOURCE: Institute for Agricultural Engineering Research and Design, *Report on China's Rural Energy Policy Issues.*

human excrement can only be used in biogas digesters for methane production. However, the biogas digester does not destroy the nutrients contained in the waste, and the sludge can still be used as fertilizer. Thus, the biogas system was considered an ideal technology for solving the rural energy problem. In the late 1970s, more than 5 million biogas pits were built, but the energy produced accounted for only one percent of the total rural energy consumed in the sixteen southern provinces suitable for biogas development. (The serious limitations of biogas development will be discussed later.)

Table 5.4 Production of Crop Residues, 1983

	Annual crop harvests (10⁶ ton)	Crop/ residue ratios	Total crop residue output (10⁶ ton)
Rice	168.9	1.0	169
Wheat	81.4	1.3	106
Corn	68.2	1.2	82
Other grains	39.5	1.3	51
Tubers	146.5	0.2	29
Oil crops	10.6	0.6	6
Sugar cane	31.1	0.2	6
Cotton	4.6	2.0	9
Total	—	—	458

SOURCE: V. Smil, *Energy in China's Modernaization, Advances and Limitations* (New York: M.E. Sharpe, Inc., 1988).

5.2.4. MINIHYDROPOWER

The potential exploitable minihydropower in China amounts to 71.3 GWe, of which only 11.3 percent was being used in 1982, as shown in table 5.7. About one-third of all the counties in China have more than 10 MWe of minihydropower potential. The development of minihydropower is shown in table 5.8. In 1980, 1,478 counties (more than 60 percent of the total number) had built minihydropower stations. Among them, 748 counties rely mainly on these power stations for their electricity supply. About 34 percent of the power consumed in agricultural production all over China was provided by minihydropower stations. The latter are therefore considered the most important means of rural electrification.

Table 5.5 Availability of Firewood, 1979

	Southern mountainous areas		Hills and plains areas		Northern mountainous areas	
	Area share	Production (kg/ha)	Area share	Production (kg/ha)	Area share	Production (kg/ha)
Firewood	1.0	7,500	1.0	7,500	1.0	3,750
Timber	0.5	750	0.7	750	0.2	600
Sheltered forests	0.2	375	0.5	375	0.2	375
Scattered trees	0.5	750	0.7	750	0.3	750
Shrubs	0.5	1200	0.7	1,200	0.3	1,200
"Four Sides" trees	1.0	2	1.0	2	1.0	2

SOURCE: Institute for Agricultural Engineering Research and Design, *Report on China's Rural Energy Policy Issues.*

Table 5.6 Output and Availability of Animal Dung, 1983 (Converted to dry material)

	Total head (Million)	Solid output (kg/head)	Total output (Million tons)	Collection rate (Percent)	Total collection (Million tons)
Cattle	78.1	800	62	30	19
Horses	12.2	900	11	30	3
Pigs	298.5	200	60	90	54
Sheep and goats	167.0	80	14	25	3
Total	—	—	147	—	79

SOURCE: V. Smil, *Energy in China's Modernization.*

Table 5.7 Small Hydropower Resources by Region, 1982

	Exploitable capacity		Exploited capacity		Exploited
	Gigawatts	% of national total	Gigawatts	% of national total	% of regional capability
Northeast	1.96	2.8	0.19	2.3	9.7
North	1.64	2.3	0.22	2.7	13.4
Northwest	9.36	13.1	0.48	5.9	5.1
East	9.42	13.2	1.95	24.2	20.7
South-central	15.54	21.8	3.42	42.3	22.0
Southwest	33.38	46.8	1.82	22.6	5.5
Total	71.30	100.00	8.08	100.00	11.3

SOURCE: V. Smil, *Energy in China's Modernization.*

Table 5.8 Small Hydropower Units in Rural Regions

Year	Number	Generating capacity (10^4kw)
1952	98	0.8
1957	544	2.0
1962	7,436	25.2
1968	82,387	228.4
1979	83,224	276.3
1980	80,319	304.1
1981	74,017	336.0
1982	66,256	353.0
1983	62,328	346.3
1984	60,062	361.5
1985	55,754	380.2
1986	54,136	387.9
1987	51,978	394.1

SOURCE: *China Statistical Yearbooks, 1980–1989.*

5.2.5. SMALL COAL MINES

Chinese coal and labor resources are both extremely abundant. There are no restrictions on small-scale mining. Policy is the only major factor influencing the development of small coal mines. The share of coal production from small coal mines has increased steadily and in recent years has exceeded that from the large state-owned mines. The new policy allows rural people to produce coal and sell it in local free markets, thus alleviating the energy shortage in certain rural regions. However, the supply of coal from local small coal mines is geographically limited to those regions abundant in coal resources, particularly northern China. As a consequence, most of rural China cannot benefit directly from small mines.

5.2.6. SOLAR RADIATION AND OTHER RENEWABLE RESOURCES

Solar radiation is an important energy source covering a vast area. In two-thirds of the total Chinese territory solar radiation intensity is higher than 140 kcal/cm^2 over 2,000 hours per year. The distribution of solar radiation is shown in figure 5.3. Vari-

Fig. 5.3 Solar Radiation Distribution in China, Kcal/m²/year

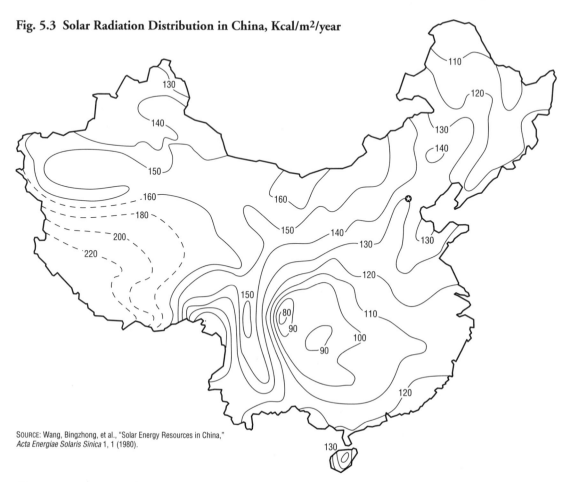

SOURCE: Wang, Bingzhong, et al., "Solar Energy Resources in China," *Acta Energiae Solaris Sinica* 1, 1 (1980).

---

ous solar devices have been developed and diffused according to local conditions. However, solar technologies are not mature enough for large-scale application in the near future, and solar energy cannot be considered a major factor at the present time.

Exploitable wind energy is concentrated in the southeast coastal belt, including the numerous islands; on the Tibet and Qinghai plateaus; and in northwest and northern China. The wind velocity averages more than 3 meters per second over 200 days a year in these regions. It is estimated that the exploitable wind energy in China amounts to some 100 GWe. The use of windmills for irrigation and rice husking has a long history in China, and modern wind power generation technology has already been commercialized. However, the location of wind

power stations is quite restricted, and the cost of wind power is relatively high. As a consequence, the application of wind energy in China is limited to isolated locations such as small islands, remote prairies, and high plateaus.

Geothermal resources are even more localized than solar and wind energy. However, geothermal power is also abundant if deep strata (up to 3 kilometers) conduction-dominated geothermal resources are considered. Tables 5.9-A and -B give the convection-dominated and conduction-dominated geothermal resources, respectively. The utilization of convection-type resources is limited by the temperature available. In agricultural production, however, low-temperature hot water could still have many applications, providing heat to greenhouses

Table 5.9.A. Geothermal Resources in China, Convection Type

Province	Number	Quantity (kgce/sec)	>80°C	80°-60°C	60°-40° C	40°-20°C
Zhejiang	6	0.12	0	1	3	2
Shandong	19	1.68	3	7	8	1
Hubei	32	3.77	1	4	7	20
Shanxi	10	14.26	0	1	2	7
Jiangsu	10	0.92	0	1	4	5
Neimonggu	44	0.23	0	2	1	41
Qinghai	30	1.41	3	5	8	14
Hebei	253	15.48	19	33	30	171
Tibet	293	98.17	41	73	90	89
Shaanxi	24	8.55	0	2	6	16
Henan	16	1.33	0	7	4	5
Anhui	12	0.47	0	3	4	5
Helongjiang	2	—	0	0	1	1
Guangxi	24	0.45	1	4	9	10
Ningxia	4	0.09	0	0	0	4
Gansu	23	2.24	0	0	4	19
Jilin	4	0.93	0	2	0	2
Jiangxi	96	1.98	1	15	36	44
Hunan	112	6.03	2	0	29	81
Yunnan	280	48.16	21	25	69	165
Beijing	20	1.11	0	1	14	5
Tianjing	192	11.74	2	0	40	150
Sechuan	264	6.73	9	18	96	141
Guizhou	64	1.8	0	0	21	43
Fujian	147	3.29	7	41	80	19
Liaoning	42	1.83	2	11	15	14
Guangdong	195	4.96	13	51	72	59
Taiwan	—	—	—	—	—	—
Xinjiang	7	0.28	0	0	3	4
Total	**2,225**	**237.68**	**125**	**307**	**656**	**1,137**

SOURCE: State Science and Technology Commission, *China's Technology Policy.*

and fish ponds. The technology for exploitation of deep-stratum geothermal resources needs to be developed, and its application is still far away.

5.3. FORMULATION AND IMPLEMENTATION OF RURAL ENERGY POLICY

5.3.1 GENERAL POLICY

According to the resources situation described, the explicit Chinese rural energy policy was that the rural energy supply should be "in line with local conditions, supplementing various energies mutually, utilizing resources comprehensively, and emphasizing economic benefits." More specifically, the following energy policies have been formulated and implemented:

1. Increasing biomass supply by planting more trees and grass
2. Developing and disseminating fuel-saving stoves
3. Developing and disseminating biogas digesters
4. Developing minihydropower stations
5. Increasing coal production from small coal mines
6. Developing small coal-fired power stations
7. Developing and disseminating solar, wind, and other renewable energy technologies
8. Promoting energy conservation in rural production processes and equipment

5.3.2. ESTABLISHMENT OF A RURAL ENERGY ADMINISTRATION SYSTEM

An administrative system has been set up in China for organizing research on rural energy policy and developing the use and the spread of technologies at various levels. Figure 5.4 shows the rural energy administration hierarchy. The designated tasks of this system are (1) implementation of the Guiding Principle on rural energy development; (2) working out rural energy policies, rules, and regulations; (3) making plans and putting them into effect; (4) organizing and coordinating scientific research and educational training on rural energy issues; (5) raising and allocating funds for rural energy development; and (6) disseminating new technologies and skills.

5.3.3 DEVELOPMENT OF RURAL ENERGY THROUGH DEMONSTRATIONS IN PILOT COUNTIES

After the formation of Chinese rural energy policies and the establishment of the administration system,

Table 5.9.B. Geothermal Resources in China, Conduction Type

Region	Exploitable resource (Mtce)
Songliao Basin	30.714
Depth > 3000 m	15.316
Depth < 3000 m	15.398
North China Plain (north)	48.068
Liaohe Delta	0.610
Central Hebei	13.408
Huanghua	4.619
Jiyang	9.954
Lingqing	10.145
Changxian	8.151
Chengning	1.181
North China Plain (south)	20.722
Kaifeng	2.159
Dongming	1.542
Zhoukou	1.021
Shengqiu	1.357
Hezai	5.403
Taikang	4.323
Linying	1.918
Danhao	1.306
Xixitai	1.693
North Jiangsu Plain	8.844
Yianfu	1.285
Jianhu	0.766
Dongtai	6.793
Jianghan Plain	9.484
Depth > 3000m	1.349
Depth < 3000m	8.135
Sechuan Basin	25.550
Shaangan'ning Basin	52.355
Depth > 3000m	2.565
Depth 2000 – 3000m	8.872
Depth 1000 – 2000m	40.918
Fengwei Basin	2.920
Total	**198.657**

SOURCE: State Science and Technology Commission, *China's Technology Policy.*

the implementation of these policies was carried out through demonstration by setting up (1) Rural Energy Demonstration Centers, (2) several hundred pilot counties for diffusing various energy technologies, and (3) eighteen pilot counties for comprehensive rural energy development.

In addition, more than a thousand energy service companies and demonstration stations and tens of thousands of rural project construction teams have been formed throughout the country. The out-

Fig. 5.4 Hierarchy of Rural Energy Administration

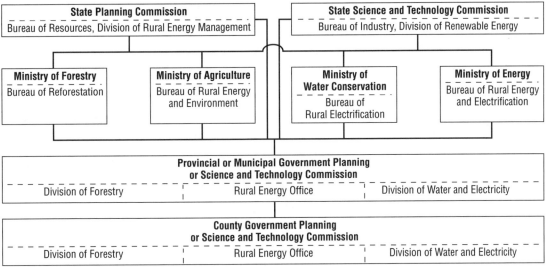

SOURCE: Qui, Daxiong, *Integrated Assessment of Rural Energy Technologies in Demonstrative County in China*, final report to Commission on the European Community, March 1989.

standing services of these organizations have played an important role in China, including material supply for rural energy projects, technical instruction and training, contracting for building projects, and even raising funds and arranging loans for many local projects.

5.3.3.1. RURAL ENERGY DEMONSTRATION CENTERS

Rural Energy Demonstration Centers have been set up for demonstration and development of new energy technologies — for example, a new-and-renewable energy village, a solar energy village, and the wind energy demonstration center.

5.3.3.2. PILOT COUNTIES FOR DIFFUSING SINGLE-ENERGY TECHNOLOGY

1. One hundred counties were selected in twenty-two provinces and autonomous regions to demonstrate development of minihydro-electricity in China. By the end of 1986, twelve pilot counties out of the hundred selected had met the targets of "preliminary rural electrification." By the end of 1986, 92 percent of all townships and 84 percent of all villages had been electrified to varying degrees, and 67 percent of peasant households had electricity.

2. Five hundred eighty-nine Pilot Counties were selected for testing and demonstrating improved woodstove technologies in over 90 percent of the peasant households, and 326 counties out of these 584 selected had already met the designated targets and were "checked

and accepted" by the Ministry of Agriculture by the end of 1987. At the beginning of 1988, the extensive spread of this technology had brought the number of peasant households with improved stoves up to more than 83.7 million, accounting for almost half of the country's peasant households.

3. Forty "sample counties" were selected to demonstrate biogas technology, and twenty experimental centers have been charged with developing a complete central biogas supply system. Twenty thousand peasant households used biogas supplied from these central biogas stations built in 1985. During the Sixth Five-Year Plan period (1981-1985), 2.5 million peasant households joined the ranks of biogas users in the countryside, bringing the number of digesters to 5 million. By 1987, biogas users further increased to a national total of some 6 million.

5.3.3.3. EIGHTEEN PILOT COUNTIES

Eighteen pilot counties were chosen for the demonstration of comprehensive rural energy development. As rural areas are richly endowed with various local renewable energy resources, comprehensive exploitation and utilization of various types of energy resources will provide a more effective solution to China's rural energy problem than merely relying on single-minded efforts to make use of only one type of energy resource or technology.

Comprehensive energy development implies that, in accordance with local energy resources available, all local biomass, hydropower, wind, and solar energy will be used with appropriate technologies developed for various purposes. Following the principle of maintaining ecological equilibrium in agricultural production, rural energy should be developed consistent with local economic development and environmental protection.

In 1983, the program of establishing pilot counties for comprehensive rural energy development was started. The first three counties were selected in 1983 and had already fulfilled their assigned experimental targets by 1986. Another three pilot counties were selected in 1986, and they fulfilled their respective experimental tasks in 1988. A third group of twelve pilot counties is being developed under the Seventh Five-Year Plan. These counties are located in different regions of China (see figure 5.5) in order to cover a variety of climate and agricultural conditions for the purpose of demonstration.

Nevertheless, integrated energy planning has not yet been applied in the experimental group of the first six counties. Although the research work for rural energy planning has been carried on for several years, the integrated rural energy planning framework has not been mature enough for practical use. The third group of twelve pilot counties is the first to use this sophisticated methodology in actual practice. The preliminary results are encouraging. We will return to the application of this methodology later in this chapter.

5.3.4. IMPLEMENTATION OF RURAL ENERGY POLICY AND RURAL ENERGY FORECAST

Since the Office of Rural Energy was established in 1980 to take responsibility for coordination and supervision of the implementation of Chinese rural energy policy, a series of surveys, research projects, and forecasts has been carried out. More reliable statistical data are now available. The forecasts and actual achievements in rural energy supply and demand in recent years may now be compared, and the effectiveness and relative merits of various policies can be evaluated.

A forecast of rural energy supply in both production and residential use for 1985 and 1990 as well as relevant investment requirements was made

Fig. 5.5 Pilot Counties for Integral Energy Planning

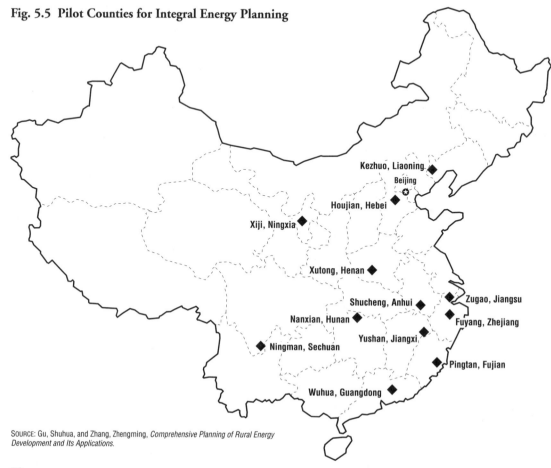

SOURCE: Gu, Shuhua, and Zhang, Zhengming, *Comprehensive Planning of Rural Energy Development and Its Applications.*

Table 5.10 Forecast of Rural Residential Energy Demand

	1979	1985	1990	Notes
Firewood				
Total energy (Mtce)	103.77	90.00	110.00	Transition to rational supply after 1979
Effective energy (Mtce)	15.56	14.40	17.60	Efficiency 16% after 1985
Households served (10^6)	62.00	60.00	72.00	
Agricultural wastes				
Total energy (Mtce)	112.60	111.00	113.00	Transition to rational supply after 1979
Effective energy (Mtce)	11.26	13.28	15.82	Efficiency: 1985, 12%; 1990, 14%
Households served (10^6)	47.00	56.00	67.00	
Biogas				
Digester totals (10^6)	3.46	12.00	20.00	6-month lifetime for each digester
Effective energy (Mtce)	1.96	6.79	11.31	Excess energy consumed by each household
Households served (10^6)	1.70	6.00	10.00	
Coal				
Total energy (Mtce)	32.58	35.49	39.21	Growth rate for small mines: 2.5%/year before 1985, 3% after 1985
Effective energy (Mtce)	5.87	6.39	7.84	Efficiency: 1985, 18%; 1990, 20%
Households served (10^6)	25.00	27.20	33.40	
Animal dung				
Total energy (Mtce)	5.70	6.00	6.31	Mainly used in pastoral areas
Effective energy (Mtce)	1.03	1.08	1.13	
Households served (10^6)	2.00	2.06	2.06	
Solar cookers				
Total number (10^3)	2.00	200.00	500.00	
Effective energy (ktce)	0.71	71.40	178.60	
Households served (10^3)	0.70	70.00	180.00	
Total				
Effective energy (Mtce)	35.67	42.01	53.88	
Households served (10^6)	137.70	151.36	184.66	
Percentage (%)	—	83.00	96.00	

SOURCE: Institute for Agricultural Engineering Research and Design, *Report on China's Rural Energy Policy Issues.*

in 1983 (see tables 5.10 through 5.12). The actual achievements in 1985 are shown in table 5.13.

In comparing these tables, the following observations can be made:

1. The number of fuel-saving stoves attained 80 million in 1985, or about four times the original forecast (20 million). The reason can be clearly seen from table 5.12. Fuel-saving stoves require the lowest specific state investment — 1.25 yuan per tce saved per year. This figure is about one-tenth that of a biogas digester, one-fifteenth that required for a firewood tree plantation, and one-twentieth that needed to develop a small coal mine. The dissemination of fuel-saving stoves is therefore proved by practice to be the most cost-effective measure in rural energy conservation.

2. The actual achieved number of biogas digesters in 1985 was only a third of the number forecast

Table 5.11 Forecast of Rural Energy Production Demand (10^6tce)

	Year		
	1979	1985	1990
Coal			
State supply	11.08	11.94	13.18
Local small mines	14.50	15.62	17.25
Total supply	25.58	27.56	30.43
Oil products	14.27	14.27	14.87
Electricity			
State grid	26.18	33.42	42.65
Minihydro	5.01	10.12	14.66
Biogas	0.01	0.02	0.05
Total supply	31.21	43.56	57.36
Wind energy	—	0.06	0.19
Total	**71.06**	**85.45**	**102.85**

SOURCE: Institute for Agricultural Engineering Research and Design, *Report on China's Rural Energy Policy Issues.*

Table 5.12 State Investment in Rural Energy Development

	1981 – 1985 (10^6 yuan)	1986 – 1990 (10^6 yuan)	Specific investment (yuan/tce/year)	Notes
Fuel-saving stoves	20.00	30.00	1.25	State subsidy 1 yuan per stove
Biogas				
Household digesters	180.30	273.8 0	15.03	State subsidy 17 yuan per digester
Power stations	2.19	8.33	128.80	State subsidy 570 yuan per station
Woodlots planted (number of trees)	460.00	670.00	20.00	State subsidy 90 yuan per hectare
Small coal mines	300.00	500.00	28.00	Investment 20 yuan per ton capacity
Minihydropower				
State investment	1,560.00	2,000.00	462.00	State subsidy 500 yuan per KWe
State loans	3,000.00	3,500.00	—	
Solar stoves	12.00	18.00	120.00	State subsidy 60 yuan per stove
Total	**5,543.49**	**7,000.13**	**—**	

SOURCE: Institute for Agricultural Engineering Research and Design, *Report on China's Rural Energy Policy Issues.*

Table 5.13 Actual Rural Energy Development, 1985

	1982 Forecast	Achieved, 1985	Notes
Fuel-saving stoves (10^6)	20	80	
Biogas			
Household digesters (10^6)	12	4.5	
Power stations	3,117	20	
Woodlots planted (10^6 ha)	6.3	6	
Small coal mines (10^6 t)	35.5	46.93	For residential use only
Minihydropower (TWh)	24	10.3	Different statistical criteria used
Solar stoves (10^3)	200	100	

in 1982, and the installed capacity of biogas power stations was only 0.6 percent of the forecast figure. The explanation is rather complicated; it is not simply because of the higher specific investment. The reasons and the prospects are given in detail in section 5.4.3.

3. The projected amount of woodlot planting has been fulfilled. This is a significant achievement since progress in afforestation will not only provide more fuel but also improve the environment in rural regions over the long term.

4. The actual achievement of minihydropower development exceeded the forecast figure. China had launched a very progressive rural electrification program, and it was successfully implemented. Both technical and economic problems in developing rural minihydropower were basically solved. The policy of "benefits to the investors" led to great success. Presently a more ambitious program is under way creating one hundred model counties using all types of electrification.

5. Although the actual number of solar stoves in place is only half of that forecasted, the prospects for solar energy are still very promising. The resource is abundant, and the only obstacle is the capital cost. Since the specific investment required for solar devices is steadily decreasing, the future market will undoubtedly grow. However, the amount of energy supplied by solar stoves is only a negligible fraction of the total energy demand.

6. The development of small local coal mines has been very rapid in recent years, hence the coal supply in rural regions has increased substantially. The actual coal supply in 1985 for households was 132 percent of the forecast value (table 5.13), and the residential coal supply in rural areas grew steadily until it matched the coal supply to urban households (table 5.14). However, due to transportation difficulties, coal is still not available in regions far from coal mines.

Table 5.14 Growth of Coal Supply

	1980	1981	1982	1983	1984	1985	1986	1987	1988
National total	8,267.1	8,635.3	8,897.9	9,331.5	9,987.9	10,536.2	11,058.5	11,530.4	12,169.2
Urban regions	4,194.1	4,446.3	4,616.9	4,919.5	5,458.9	5,843.2	6,227.4	6,317.5	6,486.9
Rural regions	4,073.0	4,189.0	4,281.0	4,412.0	4,529.0	4,693.0	4,831.1	5,212.9	5,682.4

SOURCES: *China's Energy Statistics Yearbook, 1989*, and Wu, Zongxin, et al., *China's Energy Demand by 2050.*

Table 5.15 Comparison of Improved and Traditional Stoves

	Simple cooking stove		Stove with brick bed (*kang*)*	
	Old style	Improved	Old style	Improved
Thermal efficiency for cooking (%)	10 – 12	25 – 40	7 – 10	20 – 30
Thermal intensity for cooking (kW)	1.5 – 2	2 – 3	2 – 2.5	2.5 – 4
Temperature of flue gas (°C)	200 – 300	100 – 150	300 – 400*	300 – 400*
Excess air ratio	> 3	1.5 – 3	> 2.5	1.5 – 2.4
Integral thermal efficiency (with bed) (%)			30 – 40	70 – 80
Temperature rise at bed surface (°C)			5 – 30	10 – 15
Rate of heat dissipation (°C/°C-hr)			0.15 – 0.2	< 0.1

*See section 5.4.1
SOURCE: Qiu, Daxiong, *Integrated Assessment of Rural Energy Technologies in Demonstrative County in China.*

5.4. THE EXPERIENCE OF CHINESE RURAL ENERGY POLICY

5.4.1. RURAL ENERGY POLICY EVALUATION
Chinese rural energy policy has achieved splendid successes in many areas since 1980, but the serious energy shortages affecting the 800 million people living in a vast region cannot be ended in only a few decades. Valuable experience has been gained and further progress is expected. Generally speaking, the guidelines of rural energy policy enumerated in paragraph 5.3.1 have proved appropriate and powerful. Localization, versatility, efficiency, and cost-effectiveness are the outstanding features of current Chinese rural energy development. Specifically, the development and dissemination of fuel-saving stoves, woodlot planting, minihydropower, small coal mines, biogas, and other renewable energies have produced invaluable technological and institutional experience. The highlights will be briefly discussed below.

5.4.2. DEVELOPMENT AND DISSEMINATION OF FUEL-SAVING STOVES
As mentioned above, the most successful program in Chinese rural energy development has been the development and dissemination of fuel-saving stoves. Most rural households in China used old-fashioned types of stoves before 1980, and the thermal efficiency for cooking was very low, averaging about 10 to 12 percent, as shown in table 5.15. The extremely

low efficiency is attributable to the inadequate design of the old stoves, which originated thousands of years ago and sustained few improvements over the centuries.

As shown in figure 5.6, the old-fashioned stoves in general have no grate, a very large combustion chamber which introduces a large volume of excess air during combustion, an inefficiently located chimney, and an unorganized gas flow path which results in incomplete combustion and the escape of a large amount of heat in high-temperature flue gas. When these stoves are connected with brick beds used for sleeping (*kang*), the gas channels in the beds are

Fig. 5.6 Traditional Stove

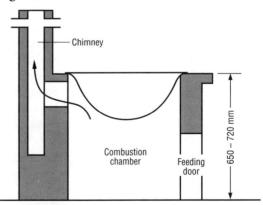

SOURCE: Qiu, Daxiong, et al., *Assessment and Innovation of Improved Firewood Stoves in China*, final report to Commission on the European Community, February 1990.

Fig. 5.7 Traditional Brick Bed

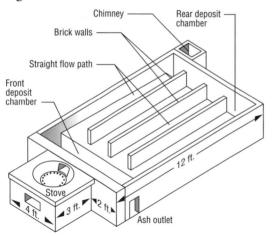

Note: Dimensions are approximate, for illustration only.
SOURCE: Qiu, Daxiong, et al., *Assessment and Innovation of Improved Firewood Stoves in China.*

Fig. 5.8 Improved Stove

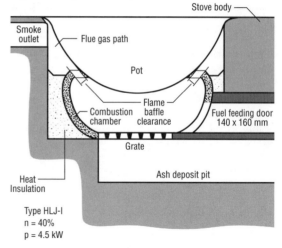

Type HLJ-I
n = 40%
p = 4.5 kW

SOURCE: Qiu, Daxiong, et al., *Assessment and Innovation of Improved Firewood Stoves in China.*

parallel to gas flow, resulting in very poor heat transfer performance (see figure 5.7). The improvements needed are therefore straightforward, as follows:

1. Grates should be added, and the size of fuel-feed openings should be reduced to improve the air flow path and diminish the excess air ratio.
2. The shape of the combustion chamber should be redesigned to promote more complete combustion.
3. A flame baffle should be added to direct the flame to the bottom of the cooking pan and enhance the transfer of useful heat.
4. The position of the chimney should be oriented to increase the draft.
5. For the brick bed, the arrangement of the partitions inside the gas flow channels should be changed to improve heat transfer performance.

The improved structure of the stove is shown in figure 5.8 and the performance in comparison with the old-style stove is shown in table 5.15.

Since the characteristics of biomass fuels and cooking customs differ from region to region and, in addition, local materials available for the construction of improved stoves vary, a number of different styles of improved stoves were developed in research institutes in different parts of China. Many of these designs have been tested, demonstrated, and accepted by the Ministry of Agriculture and collected in the Atlas of Outstanding Fuel-Saving Stoves, edited by the Institute for Agricultural Engineering Research and Design.

The dissemination of the fuel-saving stoves has been very successful. Over 83 million households,

Table 5.16 Fast-Growing Trees for Woodlot Planting in China

Species	Annual dry yield (tons/hectare)
Northeast	
Poplars (Populus sp.)	2 – 13
Willows (Salix sp.)	2 – 8
Birches (Betula sp.)	2 – 6
Northwest	
Narrow-leaved oleaster (Elaeagnus sp.)	6 – 9
Tamarisk (Tamarix ramosissima)	5 – 15
Saksaul (Haloxylon ammondendron)	5 – 7.5
North	
Acacias (Acacia sp.)	5 – 7.5
False indigo (Amorpha sp.)	5 – 7.5
Tamarisk (Tamarix ramosissima)	5 – 15
Poplars (Populus sp.)	2 – 8
Willows (Salix sp.)	2 – 8
South	
Acacias (Acacia sp.)	15 – 24
Eucalypts (Eucalyptus sp.)	15 – 22
Casuarina (Casuarina equisetifolia)	15 – 22
Leucaena (Leucaena leucocephala)	15 – 22
Mimosa (Mimosa sp.)	11 – 18
Tan oak (Lithocarpus thalassica)	20 – 24
Pines (Pinus sp.)	5 – 9

SOURCE: V. Smil, *Energy in China's Modernization.*

comprising about half the total rural population, had benefited from this project by 1988. The experience gained from this program therefore deserves more complete treatment, and it will be discussed fully in chapter 8.

Fig. 5.9 The Ups and Downs of the Chinese Biogas Program

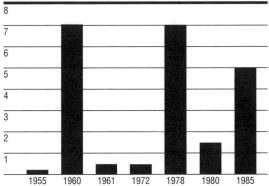

Digesters (millions)

SOURCE: Qui, Daxiong, et al., *Integrated Assessment of Rural Energy Technologies in Demonstrative County in China.*

5.4.3. INCREASE OF FIREWOOD SUPPLY BY AFFORESTATION

The consumption of firewood amounted to about a third of the total rural energy consumption in 1979. Thus, increasing the firewood supply was considered a strategic necessity in rural energy development. Deforestation over the past thousands of years has resulted in very light forest coverage in China (12.7 percent of the territory, or 121.6 million hectares, as surveyed in 1976, and still decreasing in recent years), and the result has been serious soil erosion and devastating floods in many regions.

A campaign of afforestation began in 1980. The new policy of advocating the private ownership of small woodlots and trees around houses was enthusiastically received by the peasants. About 6 million hectares of firewood was planted under the Sixth Five-Year Plan, corresponding to about a fifth of the previously barren hills and slopes available for afforestation. There are many varieties of fast-growing trees and shrubs suitable for firewood production in China (see table 5.16). It should be noted here that, when all the 30 million hectares of woodlots are in full production, the annual output will reach some 150 to 200 million tons of dry firewood — almost equal to the total firewood consumed today! With a sustained rational policy and reasonable support, this target seems to be attainable in the next two or three decades.

5.4.4. UPS AND DOWNS OF THE BIOGAS PROGRAM AND ITS PROSPECTS

The Chinese biogas program is known all over the world. The reported number of biogas digesters twice reached a peak of 7 million (in 1960 and 1979) but dropped again to less than 1 million and 1.5 mil-

lion, respectively (see figure 5.9.). This unexpected pattern led to controversies and doubts about the prospects of the biogas program in China. An in-depth analysis reveals a very complicated picture of this important rural energy technology.

The biogas program was based on Chinese technology and local resource conditions. First, over 99 percent of all the digesters are family size — each built by, operated by, and serving only one family. Both the raw materials and technical and management levels of the biogas digester are based on the conditions of the individual rural family. Second, the Chinese digester design is rather simple, using locally available raw material as much as possible; hence, the digester is inexpensive and easy to build (see figure 5.10). As a result, most rural families can afford to build a digester by themselves in a very short time, and this accounts for the rapid growth of the number of biogas digesters in a single year.

However, a third factor contributed to the "downs" in the biogas experience. The biogas technology is an alien "high" bio-technology contrasting with the natural low-level technology familiar to the Chinese rural household. Operation of the new digester requires knowledge about the appropriate nitrogen-to-carbon ratio in feedstock and the maintenance of its temperature within a certain range. Consequently, most peasant families were unable to properly manage or operate the digester, accounting for the failure of most of them after each surge in the biogas campaign. In short, the basic reason for the ups and downs of the Chinese biogas program is that the digester is easy to build and difficult to operate.

After 1980, more modest and careful steps were taken to develop biogas digesters steadily. The number of operating digesters reached 4.5 million again in 1985, and a target was set of 7.5 million by 1990. The biogas program is now considered a comprehensive energy-sanitation program in rural

Fig. 5.10 Chinese Household Biogas Digester

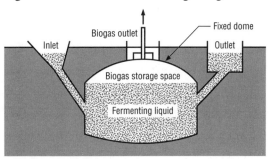

SOURCE: V. Smil, *Energy in China's Modernization.*

regions. Human and animal (mainly pig) excrement is the major feedstock for the household biogas digester. The fermentation process kills parasites and bacteria. The sludge from the digester is considered a better organic fertilizer than the raw wastes.

Although the contribution of biogas energy is only a rather small fraction of the total consumption (just 0.77 percent for 4.5 million digesters in 1985), the comprehensive effect is attractive. Development of the biogas program is therefore still a priority in Chinese rural energy development. However, due to the changing economic structure in the countryside under economic reform, more and more rural households have abandoned traditional pig-raising and turned to more profitable non-agricultural productive activities. The development of the household biogas digester may be replaced by centralized biogas stations at pig farms, and more and more families will rely on commercial energy sources for their cooking needs.

5.4.5. MINIHYDROPOWER STATIONS AND SMALL COAL-FIRED POWER PLANTS

Small hydropower stations are another well-known achievement in Chinese rural energy development. As shown in table 5.7, the small power stations in the countryside generated 4,168 GWe in 1989 and supplied about 13 percent of the total rural electricity needs. Since the term "small hydropower plant" covers a broad scope, two different sets of Chinese official statistics exist covering such plants, often leading to some confusion. One group of figures accounts for only the small hydropower plants located in rural areas and operated by rural administrations — 50,862 stations with a total capacity of 4,168 GWe by 1989, as noted above. Another set of statistics includes all those hydropower stations up to 12 MWe in capacity, a much higher figure of 63,000 stations producing 11.8 MWe in the same year. There are also two sets of rural electrification targets: one includes the county townships and the other does not. Obviously, the former figure is much higher. Due to the limited availability of data, both sets of figures are used in this chapter with appropriate notes.

According to the statistics including the townships, among the 2,291 counties (excluding Tibet and Taiwan), 99.4 percent had an electricity supply in 1986, but 0.6 percent, or fourteen counties, still had no electricity at all. Among the 203 million households in the electrified counties, only 70.2 percent had electricity in 1986. The average energy consumption (excluding industrial power consumption in county-owned factories) was 79.9 kWh per capita in 1986, of which residential consumption amounted to only 12.6 kWh, or one kWh per month per capita.

As to the sources of electricity supply, 77.8 percent of the total rural consumption (including that of the 2,277 county townships), or 133 TWh in 1986, was supplied by state-owned grids. Sixteen percent of the total (24.4 TWh) was supplied by small hydropower stations and 4.5 percent (7 TWh) by small coal-fired stations. The remaining 1.6 percent (2.2 TWh) was supplied by scattered diesel-generator units.

Presently a three-stage rural electrification program is in progress. In the preliminary stage, (1) 90 percent of all households in a given county will be provided with electricity and (2) the annual per capita consumption will reach 200 kWh, enough to meet the minimum energy requirements for rural residential and production use. In the second stage, basic electrification, (1) 95 percent of households in the county will be provided with electricity and (2) the annual per capita consumption will reach 400 kWh. For the comprehensive electrification stage, the last stage, the criteria are still under study. In principle, rural electrification is to reach the standard of the developed world, or about 1,000 kWh per capita per year.

The present target is for 85 to 90 percent of rural households to have electricity by the year 2000, implying that 90 percent of the counties will attain or exceed the level of the preliminary stage, among which 30 to 40 percent will meet the criteria of basic electrification. The total demand for electricity will then amount to 300 to 350 TWh, or about 250 percent of the consumption in 1986.

The supply of such an amount of electricity by 2000 will depend on various sources. Aside from the state-owned grids, which are expected to supply 70 to 75 percent of the total demand, small hydropower stations of about 25 GWe will be developed, to generate 65 to 70 TWh per year. Small coal-fired stations of about 5 GWe will be installed, which will supply 25 TWh of electricity. These small stations will be able to cover most regions where national grids are not readily accessible.

In 1983, the Chinese government selected 100 pilot counties for the demonstration of electrification based on minihydropower. Of these counties, 85 are located in the south and 15 in the north. The targets of the demonstration program by 1990 are:
1. Ninety percent of the households will have electricity for lighting, electric fans, electric

blankets, television, and other electric appliances. Electricity shall be available over 85 percent of the time during the year.

2. Over 20 percent of the total rural households will have electricity for cooking and water heating during the rainy season, or for six months a year.
3. A supply of electricity will be provided for processing of agricultural products, such as rice husking, flour milling, oil extraction, and so on.
4. Electricity will be supplied for irrigation, threshing, pig and chicken farms, dairies, and other agricultural enterprises.
5. An electricity supply will be available to meet the basic power demands of county- and village-owned industries.

The above criteria require an annual per capita electricity supply of over 200 kWh for each county. This program is so far being implemented very well. By the end of 1986, the total installed capacity in these 100 rural counties had increased from 1.47 GWe (1982) to 2.58 GWe (including plants under construction), and the available electricity had increased from 2.75 TWh to 4.53 TWh. In 46 of the 100 counties, 90 percent of all households had been electrified. Twelve counties had already attained their targets by 1986.

As a result of rural electrification, the value of aggregated industrial and agricultural products doubled. In the pilot counties, 2.1 million peasants entered the local factory labor force and hence promoted localized industrialization — a Chinese route for urbanization.

5.4.6. RENEWABLE ENERGY SOURCES AS SUPPLEMENTS

Solar, wind, and geothermal energy, in accordance with local conditions, are considered supplemental energy supplies for the Chinese countryside. Solar cookers have been disseminated in desert areas, where solar radiation is abundant and few other energy resources exist. Over 100,000 solar cookers were in use by 1985, mainly in Gansu and Qinghai provinces, which have intense solar radiation but little biomass. A survey of the solar cookers in various provinces and municipalities is shown in table 5.17. Chinese solar cooker designs use cheap materials and simple technology; among the most popular types are those using plastic film plated with aluminum, fiberglass plated with thin aluminum film, and cement baseplates covered with glass mirrors. In general, each cooker has a reflecting surface of two to

Table 5.17 Dissemination of Solar Stoves, End of 1987

Province and municipality	Number of stoves
National Total	103,188
Beijing	423
Tianjing	98
Hebei	17,657
Shanxi	73
Neimonggu	564
Liaoning	1,811
Dalian	96
Jilin	49
Helongjiang	943
Shanghai	17
Jiangsu	678
Zhejiang	70
Anhui	540
Fujian	34
Jiangxi	11
Shandong	1,645
Henan	128
Hubei	67
Wuhan	19
Hunan	11
Yunnan	123
Tibet	4,000
Shaanxi	144
Gansu	54,671
Qinghai	14,600
Ningxia	2310
Xingjiang	1,694
Qingdao	5
Hainan	500

SOURCE: Ren, Hongshen, et al., "A Review of Ten Years' Development of Solar cookers in China, " *New Energy* 11, 10 (1989).

three square meters, giving a peak output of about one kilowatt, barely sufficient for the cooking needs of one family of five people.

Solar water heaters are also installed widely in many counties, totaling 600,000 square meters of solar collection surface by 1987. Other solar energy applications, such as solar dryers for agricultural products, photovoltaic lighting and irrigation pumps, and solar-heated houses are all under development. Of course, greenhouses are also applications of solar energy, and they have been widely utilized in China for thousands of years.

The application of wind energy in rural regions is relatively limited. Most wind generators are used on islands and in pastoral areas. Chinese-designed wind generators are mostly small, with outputs of less than a kilowatt each. In 1985, about 1,500 wind generators were installed, with a total output of 3.4 MWe. In 1987, about 50,000 mini-wind generators were installed in the Neimonggu region alone, serving 18 percent of its rural herding families.

5.5. INTEGRAL ENERGY PLANNING IN RURAL CHINA

5.5.1. THE INTEGRAL EEE MODEL SYSTEM

Integral Energy-Economic-Ecological (EEE) planning in rural China began in 1981. A dynamic model was developed at INET sponsored jointly by SSTC and CEC during 1981-1984, based on the survey and data collected in Yucheng County of Shandong Province, in coordination with an agricultural development project sponsored by the World Bank. This model system took into consideration not only the balance of the energy supply and demand but also the ecological equilibrium and different scenarios of development of the rural economy. The factors under consideration are shown in figure 5.11, and the framework of the model system is shown in figure 5.12. This system consists of four interconnected submodels: the Forecasting Model (FORMOD), the Ecological Model (ECOMOD), the Non-Biomass Energy Model (NOEMOD), and the Energy-Economic-Ecological Optimization Model (EEEOM).

It was a difficult task for China to develop such a sophisticated mathematical model. The highly uncertain nature of rural production and ecological impacts made the modeling even more elusive. However, in-depth study gave a better picture of both the qualitative and quantitative relationships among these factors and may provide for much better understanding by policymakers. Appropriate mathematical tools such as stochastic simulation and multi-objective linear and non-linear programming helped the formulation of the model system. The algorithm for solving large-scale linear programming problems was also successfully developed. As a result, such an integral approach to rural energy-ecological planning is now being applied and disseminated to direct Chinese rural energy development.

5.5.2. APPLICATION OF INTEGRAL PLANNING IN TWELVE COUNTIES

As mentioned above, beginning in 1983, six counties in two groups of three were selected for the

Fig. 5.11 Variables in the Integral EEE Model System

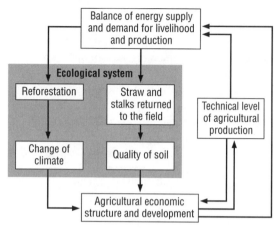

SOURCE: See Lu, Yingzhong, *A Methodology for Energy Supply and Demand Evaluation: A Dynamic Rural Energy Model and a Study of Energy Management and Conservation in Industry*, final report to commission on the European Community, October 1984.

Fig. 5.12 Structure of the Integral EEE Model System

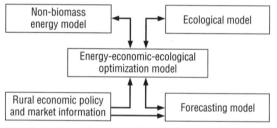

SOURCE: Lu, Yingzhong, *A Methodology for Energy Supply and Demand Evaluation*

demonstration of integral (or comprehensive) rural energy development. The three counties in the first group, Tongliang County in Sechuan Province, Yongchuen in Fujian, and Shancheng in Henan, had fulfilled the targets and had been checked and accepted in 1987. The progress of the other three counties is also very encouraging. On the basis of such a successful experience, the Ministry of Agriculture under the sponsorship of SSTC selected another twelve counties for more extensive and comprehensive experiments and demonstration for Chinese rural energy-economy development. The targets set for these twelve pilot counties include (1) formulation and implementation of a consistent set of rural energy-economic policies capable of promoting more rapid economic development on the basis of an adequate energy supply, (2) improvement of the comprehensive utilization of renewable energy and establishment of a favorable ecological cycle, (3) enhanced energy management and conservation and reduced energy intensity in rural industry, and (4) provision of a model of rural development for other countries having conditions similar to China's.

In directing the experimentation and demonstration efforts, the Ministry of Agriculture required all twelve counties to carry out integral energy-economy-ecology planning and asked INET, ITEESA, and IER to act as advisory groups providing methodology, training, and advice. This program began in 1986 and was approved by SSTC as one of the key national research programs of the Seventh Five-Year Plan (1986-1990). Since the twelve counties were distributed all over China (see figure 5.5), they represented different types of natural and socioeconomic conditions and hence could be considered models for most Chinese rural areas. By 1988 all these counties had finished their integral planning and had already made great progress in implementing many projects under the guidance of these plans. A brief description of the procedure, methodology, and outcome of the planning process is given below. (Interested readers are also referred to the bibliography at the end of this book, especially references 32 and 103.)

5.5.3. METHODOLOGY OF INTEGRATED RURAL ENERGY PLANNING

The tasks of rural energy planning at the county level are as follows:

1. Survey and analysis of present energy supply-demand balance
2. Objectives selection
3. Energy demand projection
4. Energy resource assessment and energy supply analysis
5. Technology assessment
6. Energy system optimization in connection with socio-economic and ecological considerations
7. Decisionmaking analysis
8. Policy analysis
9. Plan of implementation

Figure 5.13 shows the framework of rural energy planning (REP) at the county level. The methods for planning have been developed for each block of the whole framework, and the methods for integrated assessment of rural energy technologies have been developed in detail in this research project.

The procedure of integral REP includes the following steps:

1. The survey of the current status of rural energy supply and demand was carried out through available statistics and records (mainly com-

Fig. 5.13 Framework of Rural Energy Planning at the County Level

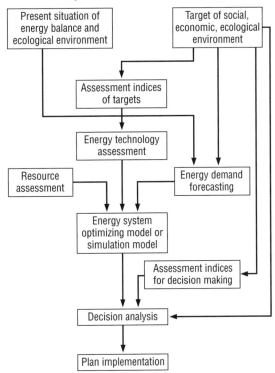

SOURCE: Qiu, Daxiong, *Integrated Assessment of Rural Energy Technologies in Demonstrative County in China.*

mercial energy). The data was collected and collated in the form of an energy flow diagram similar to figure 5.1 but more detailed. Carefully designed questionnaires and formats were provided to facilitate the survey and the subsequent analysis.

2. In order to simplify the energy planning and decisionmaking process, comprehensive energy demand-supply zonation was used to characterize the highly diversified rural energy situations in different regions. Energy sources and/or energy consumption data from many sample villages were normalized and listed in the form of a matrix with weighting factors attached to different parameters. The deviations among the data from different sample villages were then calculated, and these villages were grouped into various zones having distinct characteristics of respective energy shortage and resource availability levels. A zone map is shown in figure 5.14. It has proved very useful in rural energy planning in the pilot counties.

3. The forecast of rural energy demand was carried out by a regression model for residential energy demand and a sectoral analysis model

Fig. 5.14 Energy Zonation for Wuhua County

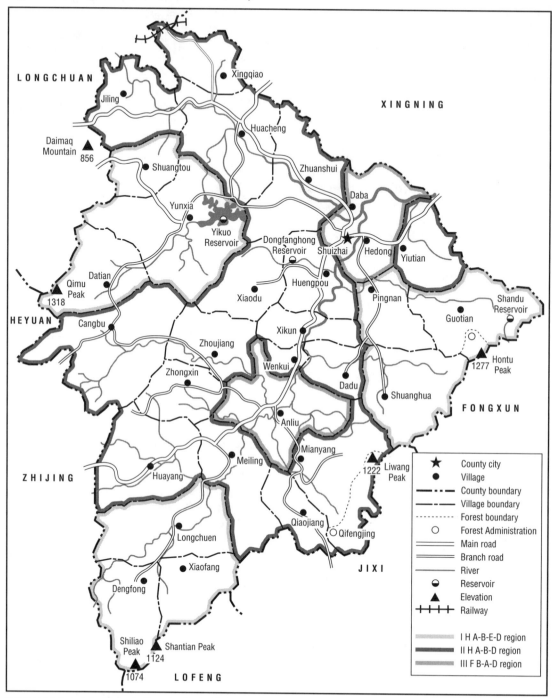

SOURCE: Institute for Agricultural Engineering Research and Design, *The Comprehensive Rural Energy Planning of Wuhua County* (Guangdong: Office of Rural Energy of Wuhua County, 1988).

for production energy demand. In the rural household energy model, population growth, income increase, and change of life style were considered. In sectoral analysis the energy conservation potential was taken into account.

4. The integrated assessment of rural energy

technologies was carried out through benefit matrices and constraint matrices weighted with factors representing the relative importance of each technology. These weighting factors may be adjusted by policymakers according to particular situations and conditions. With such

Fig. 5.15 Comprehensive Benefit Evaluation Procedure

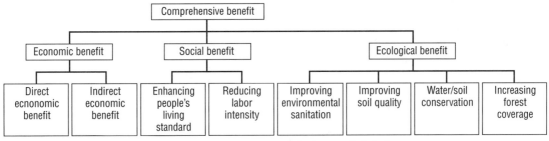

SOURCE: Gu, Shuhua, and Zhang, Zhengming, eds., *The Comprehensive Planning of Rural Energy Development and Its Applications*.

matrices, both economic and non-economic (for example, social and ecological) benefits may be taken into consideration, and hence comprehensive benefit assessment can be made, as shown in figure 5.15.

5. Several techniques for simulating and optimizing rural energy-economic systems have been tested in this program. In the pilot county of Shucheng, Anhui Province, the multi-objective linear programming model was used for rural energy-economic planning and decision-making. A framework for such a model is shown in figure 5.16.

The whole range of rural economic activities was divided into five sectors — the rural household, the township economy and public sector, agricultural production, rural industry, and township industry. Eighteen major industries were analyzed in detail. For the optimization of the energy system, three objectives were selected — the minimum energy cost, the minimum energy intensity,

Fig. 5.16 Framework of the Multi-objective Planning Model

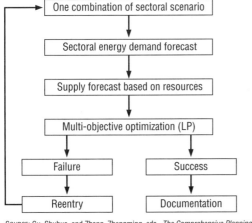

SOURCE: Gu, Shuhua, and Zhang, Zhengming, eds., *The Comprehensive Planning of Rural Energy Development and Its Applications*.

and the maximum output value. In the decision-making sub-model, the fuzzy criterion of satisfaction level was obtained by surveying experts.

The final result of such planning in Shucheng County was as follows:

A. Agricultural and industrial production will grow from 0.416 billion yuan in 1985 to 1.4 billion yuan in 2000, a 236 percent increase.

B. Energy consumption will be increased only 40 percent.

C. The proportion of agricultural waste used as fuel will decrease from 70 percent in 1985 to 45 percent in 2000. In addition, about 40,000 tons of dry grass, the amount burned as fuel in 1985, will no longer be consumed.

Appropriate policies have been formulated for attaining these targets, including energy conservation through dissemination of fuel-saving stoves and industrial energy savings. In addition, the afforestation program will increase the forest cover from 29.2 percent to 39 percent by 2000. As a result, the share of firewood in the rural energy supply will increase to 35.82 percent by 2000. Small hydropower generation will increase to 34 GWh by 2000.

6. An alternative approach to such planning uses a system dynamic simulation model (Dynamo) to correlate all relevant factors and evaluate various scenarios. (See figure 5.17.) This is a standard method, but the variables have to be carefully selected. In the planning of another pilot county, Xiji, a set of 9 state variables and 126 other variables were chosen, which included subsystems — rural energy, agricultural production, forests, husbandry, population, rural and township industry, and ecology. Ten different scenarios were input to this

Fig. 5.17 Energy-Population-Economy-Agricultural Flow in Xiji County

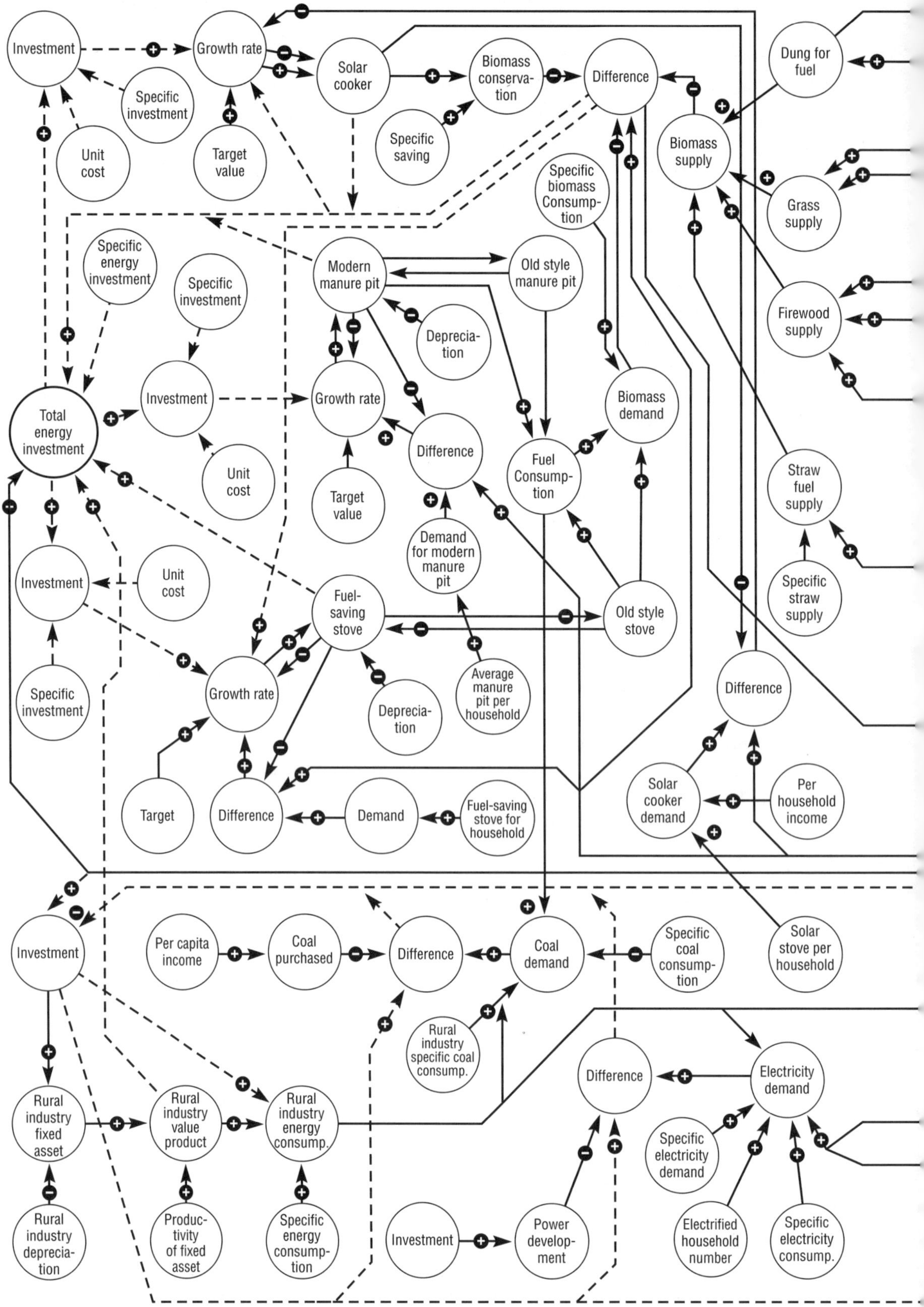

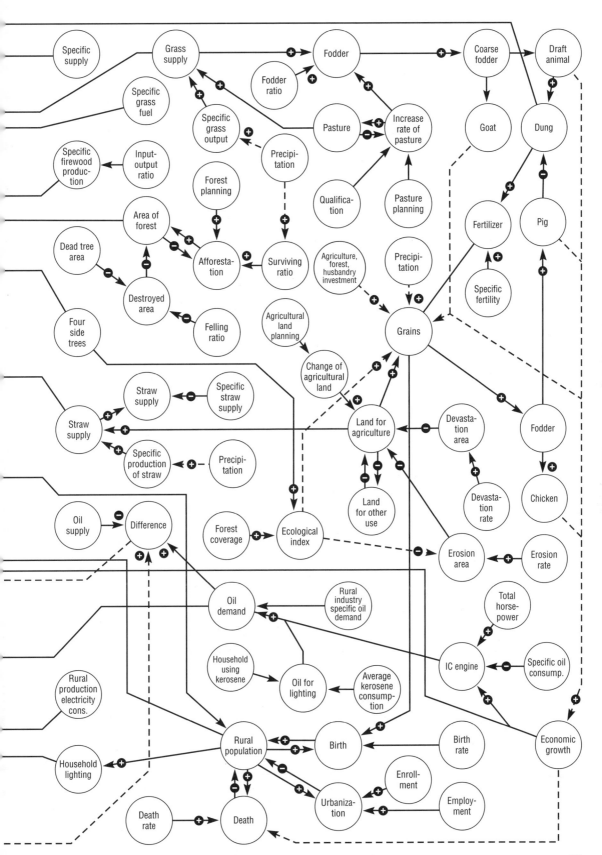

Table 5.18 Satisfactory Planning Results in Xiji County

	Year			
	1985	1990	1995	2000
Population planning				
Rural birth rate (%)	2.3	2	1.9	1.6
Rural population (10^4)	32.2	34.16	36.14	37.96
Urban birth rate (%)	2.3	2	1.9	1.6
Urban population (10^4)	1	1.33	1.69	2.07
Cumulative number of improved stoves	36,000	55,570	64,931	64,873
Cumulative number of improved biogas pits	100	50,280	85,578	91,136
Land utilization (10^4 mu)				
Agriculture	219.7	185.3	178.5	178.5
Forestry	94.8	122.8	128.4	128.4
Husbandry	129.5	149.5	153.5	153.5
Number of trees planted in "Four Sides" policy (10^4)	300	300	145	145
Specific firewood production (ton/10^4 trees)	10	15	15	15
Cumulative number of trees planted (10^4)	1,411	2,061.7	2,406.8	2,362.8
Specific grain production (ton/10^4 mu)	367	514	657	761.8
Specific straw and stalk production (ton/10^4 mu)	488	683	873	987
Specific firewood production in forests (ton/10^4 mu)	52.6	450	500	556
Specific grass production in pastures (ton/10^4 mu)	1300	1,993	2,544	1,949
Supply of commercial energy (tce/year)				
Coal	13,431	19,195	25,437	40,406
Petroleum products	3,855	4,464	5,541	6,899
Electricity	776.4	2,000	3,000	5,322
Supply of biomass fuels (tce/year)				
Firewood	10,885	24,779	35,940	42,200
Animal dung	33,600	46,600	47,000	37,900
Straw and stalks	13,630	12,380	11,430	8,800
Grass	22,100	30,800	33,000	31,900
Solar stove installation (per year)	210	1,000	2,000	1,000
Cumulative number of solar stoves	210	1,797	5,829	9,567
Investment in village enterprises (10^4 yuan/year)	69.6	214.2	93.1	93.1

SOURCE: Gu, Shuhua and Zhang, Zhengming, eds., *The Comprehensive Planning of Rural Energy Development and Its Applications* (Beijing: Beijing Press, 1990).

model and the final, satisfactory planning results shown in table 5.18 were obtained.

5.5.4. CONCLUDING COMMENTS

Chinese rural energy policy has made great progress since 1980. Aside from the successful dissemination of various rural energy technologies — such as fuel-saving stoves, minihydropower, and biogas — integral energy planning has been under way in pilot counties to provide comprehensive solutions to rural economic, energy, and ecological issues and lead to a brighter future for China's rural economy.

However, finding ways to provide enough fuel for 800 million people is not an easy task, nor can such a goal be realized in a few decades. A good beginning is just one step in the course of a ten-thousand-mile march. New situations emerging in Chinese rural regions, such as the accelerated local industrialization and the loss of control of population growth, will undoubtedly increase the rural energy demand substantially. However, since rural China is so populous and vast, the relief of the energy shortage will be a task of many decades. There is a very, very long way to go, even if rather striking achievements have already been gained.

It was estimated in 1989 that the shortage of electricity in the countryside still amounted to 40 TWh, and petroleum shortages had reached 50 percent. As a consequence, the implementation of successful rural energy policies are again and again emphasized, and more active measures are being taken to serve the formerly forgotten majority of the Chinese population.

CHAPTER 6

THE SWORD OF DAMOCLES

Energy-Environmental Issues of the PRC

The high pollution density, the high energy intensity, the coal-dominant energy mix in Chinese urban regions, and the vicious ecological cycle caused by rural energy shortages have resulted in serious environmental problems which already have become a constraint on further development of China's energy-economic system. Long-term energy development in China will have great impact on the global greenhouse effect. As a result, in the context of worldwide environmental protection, China's energy policy will have an important bearing on the world's future.

6.1. SHORT-TERM LOCAL ENERGY-ENVIRONMENTAL IMPACT

6.1.1. URBAN AIR POLLUTION
Coal is extensively used in cities as the major fuel for cooking and residential heating, and it is the major energy source for electricity, steam, and heat generation for urban industries. Over 700 million tons of raw coal was burned directly as a heat source in 1989, of which about 90 percent was consumed in cities. Alongside modern coal-fired power stations with flue gas cleaning equipment (unfortunately, most of them equipped with only fly ash precipitators), less than a quarter of the total, there are still tens of millions of small and medium-size boilers, furnaces, locomotives, and home cooking stoves which emit all kinds of pollutants into the urban atmosphere. Treatment of the flue gases from such a huge number of small, scattered coal-burning devices is impractical, and hence urban air pollution in China becomes worse and worse as the economy

grows. The air pollution conditions of the thirty largest cities in China are shown in figure 6.1, from which it can be seen that the concentrations of most of the pollutants are well above the usual allowable limits. The most serious photochemical smog incident occurred in Lanzhou in December 1977, where the concentration of several pollutants was comparable to that occurring in London in December 1952 (see table 6.1).

Such serious environmental impacts have already created constraints on expansion of the urban

Fig. 6.1 Air Pollution in Thirty Large Chinese Cities

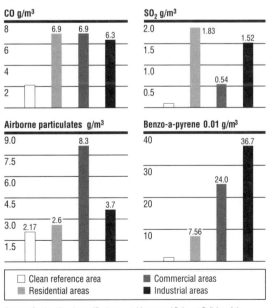

SOURCE: See Lu, Yingzhong, "Environmental Issues and Relevant Policies of the Energy System in the PRC," paper presented at the annual meeting of the Commission on the European Community Network on Energy in Developing Countries, May25 – 29, 1987, Brighton, England.

Table 6.1 Comparison of Smog in London and Lanzhou (in mg/m^3, average value of five days)

	Fly-ash	SO$_2$
London, December 1952	3.25	0.591
Lanzhou, December 1977	2.50	0.770

SOURCE: See Lu, Yingzhong, "Environmental Issues and Relevant Policies of the Energy System in the PRC."

energy system. A series of studies has been carried out, and relevant policies have been adopted which will be discussed below.

6.1.2. ACID RAIN

Acidic precipitations have been identified mostly in southwest China, due to both the high sulfur content of the local coal and the acidic nature of the soil. A recent map of acid rain distribution is given in figure 6.2, where it can be seen that the most affected region includes the province of Guizhou and southern Sechuan. Consequences of this acid precipitation have also been reported but have not yet been studied systematically. It is anticipated that the acid

rain resulting from the increasing use of coal in the future may reach unacceptable levels. This will impose another constraint on energy system expansion.

6.1.3. ENVIRONMENTAL IMPACT OF HYDROPOWER EXPLOITATION

Abundant hydropower resources are available in the PRC, and therefore first priority is given to their exploitation as one of the major sources of power generation. However, such development has proceeded rather slowly: only 6 percent of the exploitable resources have been developed during the past forty years. Besides the major constraint of the availability of capital investment, the environmental impact of hydropower development is also of much concern, sometimes dominating the decisionmaking on possible projects. Ecological effects are always of long-term nature and hence in most cases are overlooked, but the social consequences, particularly the rehabilitation of large numbers of local residents, are more acute and may produce prolonged disputes among the various parties involved. As mentioned before, the famous

Fig. 6.2 Acid Rain Distribution in China

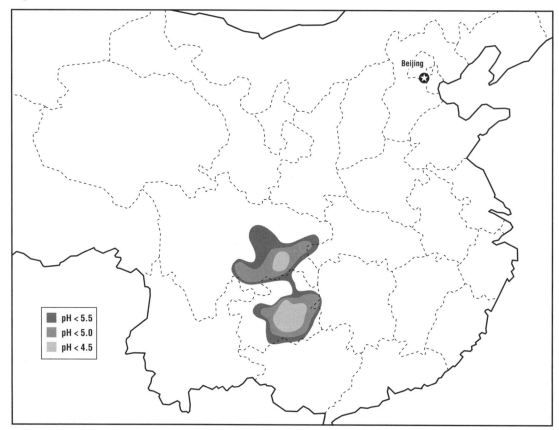

SOURCE: Zhao, D., et al., "Air Pollution and Acid Rain in China," *Ambio*, 1 (1985).

Shanxia (Three Gorges) hydropower station on the Yangtze River has been controversial for four decades since much of its environmental impact cannot be easily predicted. In this case the environmental concerns impose a major constraint on decision-making.

6.1.4. ECOLOGICAL DISEQUILIBRIUM IN RURAL REGIONS

The rural energy structure is quite different from the urban pattern, as shown in previous chapters. Further development of the rural energy system thus requires substantial changes in the energy supply and consumption patterns in rural areas — again under the major constraint of environmental factors.

6.2. A CASE STUDY OF URBAN AIR POLLUTION

Beijing, the capital of the PRC, is a typical northern Chinese city in many ways and was taken as an example for this analysis. In 1981 about 8 million people lived in Beijing, an area of some 350 square

Table 6.2 Energy Structure for Beijing, 1981

Energy source	Consumption (10^3tce)	Share (%)
Total	**21,480**	**100.00**
Coal	15,063	70.13
Fuel oil	3,604	16.78
Other oil products	2,410	11.21
LPG	295	1.38
Hydropower	108	0.50

SOURCE: See Lu, Yingzhong, "Environmental Issues and Relevant Policies of the Energy System in the PRC."

Table 6.3 Coal Consumption in Beijing, 1981

Sector	Consumption (10^3ton)	Share (%)
Industrial	1,259.3	72.12
Power generation	309.7	17.74
Coking	401.6	23.00
Metallurgy	102.6	5.87
Others	445.4	25.51
Agricultural	192.4	11.02
Transportation	13.1	0.75
Residential and Commercial	281.2	16.11
Residential	101.9	5.84
Commercial	58.2	0.33
Home heating	121.1	6.94

SOURCE: See Lu, Yingzhong, "Environmental Issues and Relevant Policies of the Energy System in the PRC."

kilometers, and consumed some 21.48 million tce of fuel. Coal constituted about 75 percent of the total energy consumed. The structure of the consumption is shown in table 6.2. The growth of energy consumption has been rapid (see figure 6.3); an average growth rate of around 8 percent was established between 1952 and 1981.

Of the 1,757 kilotons of coal consumed in Beijing in 1981, 71.6 percent was used in the industrial sector, 16 percent in households, and 10.9 percent in rural areas. A breakdown of coal consumption is shown in table 6.3.

Most of the small industries ("Others," table 6.3) used only low chimneys for flue-gas discharge into the atmosphere. In the residential sector, only 62.3 percent of homes had a clean gas fuel supply, and the remaining households continued to use coal briquets in small stoves. As a result, a total of 12,111 small and medium-size boilers, 9,154 teahouse boilers, 1,600 industrial furnaces, and about one million small stoves in households all together emitted several hundred thousand tons of pollutants into the urban atmosphere each year.

Concentration of pollutants in the atmosphere varied substantially from season to season, in particular between the home-heating season (November 15 to March 15 each year, as officially fixed) and the non-heating season. A summary of this survey is shown in table 6.4, and the monthly variations of the concentrations of several typical pollutants are shown in figure 6.4.

A diagram showing the expansion of the SO_2 pollution area is shown in figure 6.5. It has been

Fig. 6.3 Energy Consumption Structure in Beijing

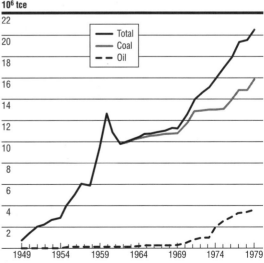

10^6 tce

SOURCE: See Lu, Yingzhong, "Environmental Issues and Relevant Policies of the Energy System in the PRC."

Table 6.4 Daily Average Concentrations of Various Pollutants in Beijing, 1981 (mg/m³)

Pollutant	Heating season		Non-heating season		Yearly average	
	Concentration	Frequency* (%)	Concentration	Frequency* (%)	Concentration	Frequency* (%)
SO₂	0.308	68.1	0.036	0	0.127	34.1
NOₓ	0.075	21.6	0.041	0	0.052	10.7
Fly ash	1.380	99.3	0.750	80.6	0.960	90.2
Carcinogens	3.290	88.2	0.756	22.0	1.600	55.4
Lead	0.626	34.6	0.362	13.3	0.450	24.4

* Frequency exceeding allowable limits.

Fig. 6.4 Monthly Variation of Pollutants

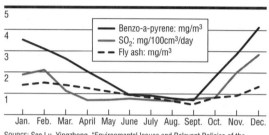

SOURCE: See Lu, Yingzhong, "Environmental Issues and Relevant Policies of the Energy System in the PRC."

predicted that energy consumption will double in the next two decades. Should there be no effective measures taken in time to reduce the pollution level, the situation will be intolerable in the near future.

It is very important to notice that air pollution is most serious in the heating season, which indicates that pollution is mainly caused by the heating boilers and small stoves used for home heating in

Fig. 6.5 Expansion of Air Pollution in Beijing

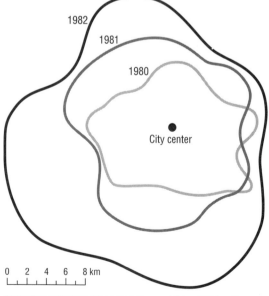

SOURCE: See Lu, Yingzhong, "Environmental Issues and Relevant Policies of the Energy System in the PRC."

winter. As a consequence, district-heating with clean heat sources such as co-generation plants and/or nuclear heating reactors is recommended as a priority for solving urban pollution issues in Beijing.

A more detailed analysis of the air pollution and the counter-measures taken in another northern city — Harbin — will be given in Part II to demonstrate the effectiveness of these measures.

6.3. LONG-TERM GLOBAL ENERGY-ENVIRONMENTAL IMPACTS

The global climate change due to the emission of carbon dioxide and other "greenhouse gases" has now become a focus of concern not only for the scientific community but also for responsible governments all over the world. Numerous studies have been carried out, in many countries and regions. However, the situations in the developing countries have not yet been studied thoroughly, in particular in the biggest one — the People's Republic of China, where over one-fifth of the world's population now lives, accounting for about one-eleventh of the

Fig. 6.6 World Carbon Emissions

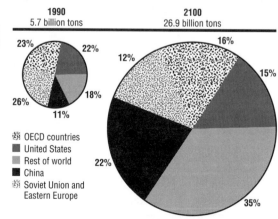

SOURCE: Alan Manne, et al., "Global CO₂ Emission Reduction — the Impacts of Rising Energy Costs," *Energy Journal* 12,1 (1991).

Fig. 6.7 Comparison of CO_2 Emissions from Major Developing Countries

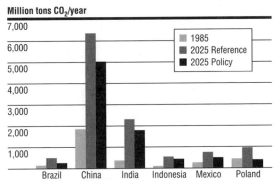

Million tons CO_2/year

SOURCE: David Jhirad, et al., *Greenhouse Gas Emissions and the Developing Countries: Strategic Options and the U.S.A.I.D. Response, A Report to Congress* (Washington: U.S. Agency for International Development, July 1990).

world's total energy consumption. Since the current growth rate of the Chinese economy is much greater than the world's average, the share of Chinese energy consumption in the global total will increase steadily. More and more recent work indicates the impact that the future Chinese energy system will have on global climate change. In figure 6.6 the outstanding share of CO_2 emissions in the world's total is seen, while in figure 6.7 it is noted that the emissions from the Chinese energy system by 2025 will be 2.8 times that from India and 13 times that from Brazil. As a result, the reduction of CO_2 emissions from China becomes a focus of all global energy-environmental studies.

Recently Manne and Richels carried out an economic analysis of the costs and penalties of CO_2 reduction in various regions in the world (see reference 132). It was demonstrated that the penalty for a 20 percent reduction in CO_2 emissions in the

twenty-first century would result in a 10 percent GDP loss in the case of China, as contrasted with a 3 to 4 percent loss in all other regions (see figure 6.8). As a consequence, the 20-percent-CO_2-reduction target is considered infeasible due to the particular energy situation in China. Only the relaxation of the CO_2 limit to three or four times the assumed original value might result in an acceptable cost for such an energy system (see figure 6.9). However, in the latter case, the assumed global target for the reduction of CO_2 emissions cannot be realized. The long-term energy policy of China has therefore a unique impact on the future world environment.

6.3.1. LONG-TERM ENERGY FORECAST FOR CHINA

6.3.1.1. POPULATION GROWTH

The current population of China has already exceeded one billion; it is now the greatest of any country in the world. Although rather strict population growth controls have been in place since the late seventies, the Chinese population is expected to steadily increase until the middle of the twenty-first century. Four scenarios have been suggested by Chinese researchers and have been adopted as the basis of the government's population policy. The assumptions of these scenarios are as follows:

Scenario 1:
The average fertility of Chinese females will decrease steadily from 2.63 percent (that is, 2.63 births per 100 females per year) in 1982 to 1.70 percent by 1990 and 1.5 percent by 1995, and thereafter it will be kept at 1.5 percent.

Scenario 2:
The same as Scenario 1 before 2001, but after 2001 fertility will return to and be kept at 2.0 percent,

Fig. 6.8 Economic Cost of CO_2 Reduction in Different Countries

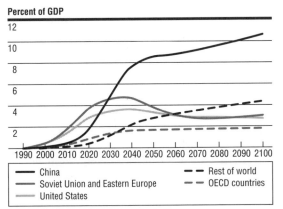

Percent of GDP

SOURCE: Alan Manne, et al., "Global CO_2 Emission Reduction — the Impacts of Rising Energy Costs."

Fig. 6.9 Penalty from Relaxation of CO_2 Limit on the PRC

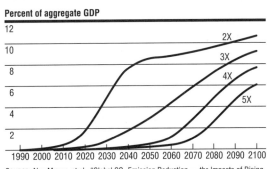

Percent of aggregate GDP

SOURCE: Alan Manne, et al., "Global CO_2 Emission Reduction — the Impacts of Rising Energy Costs."

Table 6.5 Scenarios for Population Growth in the PRC (10^6)

Year	Scenario 1	Scenario 2	Scenario 3	Scenario 4
1983	1,022.07	1,022.07	1,022.07	1,022.07
1989	1,095.56	1,095.56	1,100.10	1,101.63
1995	1,147.99	1,147.99	1,179.35	1,207.88
2001	1,191.21	1,191.21	1,254.04	1,307.73
2007	1,218.68	1,247.35	1,309.60	1,385.78
2013	1,233.57	1,288.35	1,353.35	1,454.25
2019	1,234.37	1,312.92	1,392.14	1,530.74
2025	1,221.10	1,323.77	1,424.52	1,609.14
2031	1,192.55	1,328.81	1,441.57	1,672.32
2037	1,148.47	1,324.11	1,441.58	1,718.55
2043	1,091.68	1,306.09	1,431.36	1,761.73
2049	1,026.19	1,278.07	1,416.53	1,809.33
2055	956.37	1,248.54	1,397.58	1,855.70
2061	887.64	1,223.79	1,376.16	1,898.15
2067	823.27	1,203.22	1,355.48	1,942.48
2073	763.88	1,184.05	1,337.29	1,993.67
2079	709.39	1,167.92	1,320.55	2,048.59

SOURCE: Wu, Zongxin, et al., *China's Energy Demand by 2050.*

Table 6.6 Scenarios of Chinese Economic Growth (%)

Scenario	Growth rate (Synthetic factors)	Elasticity of capital	Elasticity of labor	Average growth rate
High	3.5	0.4	0.6	5.5
Medium	3.4	0.4	0.6	4.7
Low	2.5	0.4	0.6	3.9

SOURCE: Wu, Zongxin, et al., *China's Energy Demand by 2050.*

Table 6.7 Forecast for Per Capita GNP (in 1984 US dollars)

Scenario	Year 2000	2030	2050
High	800–1,000	5,000	14,500
Medium	800–1,000	4,000	10,000
Low	800–1,000	3,100	6,700

SOURCE: Wu, Zongxin, et al., *China's Energy Demand by 2050.*

that is, in the next century the policy of allowing two children in each family will be adopted.

Scenario 3:
The average fertility will decrease slowly from the 1982 value of 2.63 percent to 2.0 percent in 1990, which will be maintained thereafter.

Scenario 4:
The average fertility rate will be kept at the 1984 level of 2.40 percent indefinitely.

The results of these scenarios are shown in table 6.5. Scenarios 1 and 2 have been recommended to the government as two ideal scenarios, in which the total population will attain its maximum by 2019, at 1,234,370,000, or by 2031, at 1,238,810,000, respectively, and then decline. However, the development of events indicates that the first two scenarios are unrealistic and that the third scenario is more likely. The present forecast is therefore based on Scenario 3, which gives the peak population of 1,441,580,000 by 2037, increasing very slowly in the next century, but always staying above 1.3 billion. It is noted in particular that during the next four decades the Chinese population will have a net increase of more than 400 million, presenting a formidable challenge to all planners and decisionmakers.

6.3.1.2. ECONOMIC GROWTH

The target for Chinese economic growth has been established as the quadrupling of the gross national product by the year 2000, based on the figures of 1980. However, no official target has yet been declared beyond that point, except a more or less vague suggestion that the per capita income of Chinese people will match that of the "low limit of the developed countries" after another fifty years or so. Based on analysis of the history of development of various newly industrialized and less developed countries — for example, Brazil, South Korea, Greece, Spain, and Italy — three scenarios have been proposed. (The estimated economic growth and the per capita GNP of these scenarios up to 2050 are listed in tables 6.6 and 6.7, respectively.) It is believed that the second scenario is the most likely one.

The high-growth scenario is considered possible when comparing the relevant factors with those of Japan and South Korea during their take-off period, 1960 to 1975. However, taking into account the probable influence of some non-economic factors, the scenario of medium growth is considered more feasible. In the following analysis, therefore, the medium-growth scenario has been adopted.

6.3.1.3. STRUCTURAL CHANGE IN THE NATIONAL ECONOMY

In order to predict possible changes in the structure of the Chinese national economy during a period as long as sixty years, a comparison with some typical countries at different development levels has been made and the trends of structural change analyzed. It is concluded therefrom that (1) the agricultural sector's share of China's economy will decrease

Table 6.8 Forecast of Structural Changes in the Chinese Economy

GDP/Capita (In 1984 US dollars)	Sectoral Share (%)			
	Agriculture	Industry	Service	Transportation
246	36	54	16.6	3.4
2,000–3,000	10	45	39.0	6.0
4,000–5,000	8	40	46.0	6.0
10,000–15,000	4	36	54.0	6.0

SOURCE: Wu, Zongxin, et al., *China's Energy Demand by 2050.*

Table 6.9 Forecast of Chinese Industrial Energy Demand

	Year		
	2020	2030	2050
GDP per capita (1980 US$)	2,000–2,500	3,000–4,000	8,000–10,000
Population (million)	1,393	1,441	1,416
Share of value added in GDP (%)	45	40	36
Value added (10^9 US$)	1.25–1.57	1.73–2.31	4.08–5.09
Energy intensity (kgoe/US$)	0.43	0.32	0.2
Energy demand (10^9 tce)	7.68–9.64	7.91–10.65	11.66–14.54

SOURCE: Wu, Zongxin, et al., *China's Energy Demand by 2050.*

steadily from its present value of 36 percent to 3 to 5 percent, (2) the service sector share will increase steadily from its present value of 20 percent to around 60 percent, and (3) the industrial sector share will decrease from the present value of 54 percent to 36 percent. A forecast of the changes in the economic structure of China based on the above analysis is given in table 6.8.

6.3.1.4. ENERGY DEMAND FORECAST

Sectoral analysis is carried out in forecasting the future energy demand of the Chinese economy. The final energy demand of each sector is determined first, and then the primary energy demand is calculated by incorporating the losses in exploitation, conversion, and distribution.

1. Industrial Energy Demand

The energy intensity of Chinese industry is compared with that in different developed countries, and the causes of the obvious discrepancy are identified: First, the large number of less energy-efficient small and medium-size industries contribute about 70 percent of the total value of products in China, the small industries accounting for over 50 percent. Second, coal is extensively used in the industrial sector and in power generation, which causes low efficiency as well as high pollution. Third, the large proportion of obsolete equipment and processes results in additional waste of energy. With more detailed analyses of various energy-intensive industries

and their respective energy conservation potentials, a conservative assumption has been made that the energy intensity of Chinese industry in 2050 will approach that of the developed countries in 1985, allowing for a lag of sixty years. However, this assumption still requires an annual energy conservation rate of 3.5 percent during the period 1980 to 2020, 3.0 percent from 2020 to 2030, and 2.3 percent from 2030 to 2050. The industrial energy demand forecast under such assumptions is shown in table 6.9.

2. Agricultural Energy Demand

The future share of China's agricultural sector in total GDP will decrease substantially, as seen above. However, since the present mechanization and electrification levels of Chinese agriculture are now very low, with modernization this sector will require more input of commercial energy than it consumed before. As a result, the absolute increase in the commercial energy supply will be high, as shown in table 6.10. The elasticities of both electricity and petroleum products are seen to be much higher than in the industrial sector.

3. Transportation Energy Demand

Since the transportation sector is an oil gobbler in most developed countries, future energy consumption in this sector deserves particular attention in this forecast. However, transportation modes and intensity depend on many factors, including the structure of the economy, the size and natural con-

Table 6.10 Forecast of Energy Demand in Agriculture Sector

	Year			
	2000	2015	2030	2050
Growth rate of value added (%)	4.00	3.00	2.00	2.00
Elasticity of electricity (%)	1.00	0.90	0.80	0.80
Elasticity of petroleum (%)	1.00	0.80	0.65	0.50
Growth rate of electricity consumption (%)	4.00	2.70	1.60	1.60
Growth rate of petroleum consumption (%)	4.00	2.40	1.30	1.00
Electricity demand (TWh)	51.00	76.00	96.40	132.40
Petroleum demand (10^6 ton)	12.78	18.24	22.14	27.02

SOURCE: Wu, Zongxin, et al., *China's Energy Demand by 2050.*

Table 6.11 Forecast of Transportation Energy Demand

	Scenario	Year		
		2020	2030	2050
Population (billions)		1.39	1.44	1.42
GNP per capita (US$)	High	2,500	4,000	9,000
	Low	2,000	3,000	8,000
Freight traffic: Total (10^9 ton-km)	High	10,700	17,800	39,600
	Low	8,600	13,400	35,000
Energy intensity (kgoe/10^3 ton-km)	High	12.4	12	11.3
	Low	10.3	9.7	9.3
Energy demand (10^6toe)	High	132.68	213.6	447.48
	Low	88.58	129.98	325.5
Passenger traffic: Total (10^9 man-km)	High	2,970	4,944	11,000
	Low	2,370	3,698	9,790
Energy intensity (kgoe/10^3 man-km)	High	20	19.4	18.3
	Low	16.7	15.9	14.4
Energy demand (10^6toe)	High	59.4	95.8	201.3
	Low	39.6	58.8	14
Total energy demand (10^6toe)	High	192.08	310.4	648.78
	Low	128.18	188.78	466.5

SOURCE: Wu, Zongxin, et al., *China's Energy Demand by 2050.*

Table 6.12 Forecast of Energy Demand in the Service Sector

	Year		
	2020	2030	2050
GDP (10^9 US$)	2,780–3,480	4,320–5,670	11,300–14,100
Share of service sector in GDP (%)	39	46	54
Value added (10^9 US$)	1,080–1,350	1,990–2,650	6,100–7,610
Energy intensity (kgoe/US$)	0.087	0.067	0.05
Energy demand (10^6 tce)	134–168	190–244	436–543

SOURCE: Wu, Zongxin, et al., *China's Energy Demand by 2050.*

ditions of the territory, life styles, and technological development. Very careful analysis is therefore needed in estimating future traffic levels as well as the intensities of various modes of transportation. The final results of such an analysis are summarized in table 6.11.

4. Energy Demand in the Service Sector

The present production level and energy consumption of the Chinese service sector (excluding transportation services) are rather low. Besides, this sector has long been disregarded in national statistics since in socialist economic theory it is considered non-productive and hence a parasite on the productive sectors. The situation has changed very much since the recent economic reform; more and more attention has been paid to the development of the service sector. As a result, the growth of this sector will be the fastest among all sectors in the coming decades, and the total sectoral energy demand will skyrocket as well. The energy demand forecast for this sector is shown in table 6.12.

5. Residential Energy Demand

The improvement of the standard of living in both urban and rural areas will require substantial increases in the energy supply. In the cities, the increasing number of households with central heating and a hot water supply, and the popularization of electric appliances, will result in rapidly increasing demand for electricity and fossil fuels. Since the oil supply will decline in the next century and the prospects for natural gas in China are quite uncertain, coal gasification seems to be indispensable in meeting the clean energy requirements of urban areas. The results of a study on this issue are summarized in table 6.13.

Residential energy demand in the Chinese countryside presents a quite different picture. In the year 1985, about 76 percent of rural residential energy came from noncommercial sources, mainly agricultural wastes (straw and stalks). Only 72.64 million tce of commercial fuel was supplied to rural regions, averaging less than 100 kilograms per capita per year. However, due to the declining availability of biomass fuels and the ecological equilibrium

Table 6.13 Forecast of Urban Residential Energy Demand/Supply

	Year 2020	Year 2030	Year 2050
Total energy demand, 10^6 tce	226	357	584
Shares by uses (%)			
Home heating	36	36	37
Cooking	16	14	11
Hot water	40	39	36
Lighting and electrical appliances	8	11	16
Shares by kinds (%)			
Coal	55	49	42
Gas	32	32	31
Electricity	8	11	16
Heat	5	8	11

SOURCE: Wu, Zongxin, et al., *China's Energy Demand by 2050*.

consideration, the consumption of noncommercial fuels in rural regions will decrease and the supply of commercial energy will increase substantially in the coming decades. On the other hand, since the rural population will decrease (due to rapid urbanization), the total energy demand will eventually decrease even though the per capita consumption increases. The results of our forecast are shown in table 6.14.

The total energy demand of the residential sector is summarized in table 6.15, in which the demand for commercial energy is shown to almost double from 2020 to 2050, while the consumption

Table 6.14 Forecast of Rural Residential Energy Demand

	Year 2020	Year 2030	Year 2050
Per capita useful energy consumption (kcal/man-day)	1,600	2,400	3,800
Rural population (million)	890	720	430
Energy efficiency (%)	25	28	30
Share of biomass (%)	45	40	30
Electrification (%)	85	90	95
Non-commercial energy demand (10^6 tce)	134	129	85
Fuel wood (10^6 ton)	90	90	90
Agricultural wastes (10^6 ton)	173	153	67
Others (10^6 tce)	1.4	1.2	1
Commercial energy demand (10^6 tce)	163	193	199
Coal (10^6 ton)	215	257	368
Petroleum (10^6 ton)	2	2	2
Electricity (TWh)	53	52	41
Total energy demand (10^6 tce)	297	322	284

SOURCE: Wu, Zongxin, et al., *China's Energy Demand by 2050*.

95

Table 6.15 Forecast of Residential Energy Demand

	Year		
	2020	2030	2050
Total residential energy demand (10^6 tce)	523	679	868
Commercial (10^6 tce)	389	550	783
Non-commercial (10^6 tce)	134	129	85
Per capita energy demand (kgce/man-year)	375	471	613
Per capita commercial energy (kgce/man-year)	279	382	553
Per capita electricity consumption (kW/man-year)	146	261	553
Energy structure: Share of commercial energy (%)	74	81	90
Share of non-commercial energy (%)	26	19	10

SOURCE: Wu, Zongxin, et al., *China's Energy Demand by 2050.*

Table 6.16 Forecast of Total and Sectoral Energy Demands

	Year				OECD, 1985
	2020		2050		
	Energy demand (10^6tce)	%	Energy demand (10^6tce)	%	%
Final energy demand: Industry	7.69–9.64	36.3	11.66–14.54	26.7	26.3
Agriculture	0.30–0.40	1.5	0.50–0.60	1.1	1.1
Transportation	1.83–2.74	9.6	6.67–9.27	16.2	20.9
Services	1.34–1.68	6.3	4.36–5.43	10.0	8.4
Residential	3.70–4.08	16.3	7.43–8.22	16.0	13.5
Total	14.85–18.54	70.0	30.6–38.06	70.0	70.5
Conversion and distribution losses	6.37–7.95	30.0	13.12–16.31	30.0	29.5
Total demand	**21.21–26.49**	**100.0**	**43.74–54.37**	**100.0**	**100.0**

SOURCE: Wu, Zongxin, et al., *China's Energy Demand by 2050.*

of electricity triples. However, compared with the most developed countries, the standard of per capita electricity consumption in China will still be low, even by 2050. The dominant role of coal in the urban residential energy structure will give rise to increasingly serious environmental pollution if no technological solution is found in the near future.

6. Total Energy Demand Forecast

A summary of all the above sectoral forecasts is presented in table 6.16, in which the losses of conversion and distribution are added to obtain the total energy demand. A comparison of the projected Chinese sectoral energy structure in 2020 and 2050 with the 1985 figures of OECD countries is also shown in this table. The projected Chinese energy structure by 2025 is quite similar to the OECD structure, while the 2030 structure is different. The coincidence of the 2050 structure demonstrates the adequacy of this approach and the validity of the assumptions.

6.3.1.5. ENERGY SUPPLY FORECAST

1. Availability of Energy Resources

Most conventional energy resources are abundant in the PRC. In table 6.17 the proven reserves and

the potential resources of these fuels are summarized. It is noted that only coal is really abundant on a per capita basis, and all the others are quite limited in view of the future huge demand. In particular, the indispensable oil resources seem to be inadequate to meet future demand.

The oil supply will therefore be the most critical issue in the long-term energy supply. The rapid depletion of China's oil resources will result in the decline of production soon after the turn of the century, as predicted in 1984. More recent work gives the peak production and the timing of various scenarios (table 6.18).

It is seen in this table that the peak production is a function of the coefficients of confidence, that is, the lowest production (200 million tons annually) is most likely to be realized but the highest production (300 million tons) is least likely. However, under any conditions, maximum production will not exceed 300 million tons per year, and the peak time will be around 2020/2030.

Hydropower resources are relatively more abundant — amounting to 1,800 kWh per capita, 3.8 times the per capita energy consumption today.

Table 6.17 Energy Resources of the PRC

	Proven reserves		Potential resources	
	Total	Per capita*	Total	Per capita*
Coal	769.2 Gton	719 ton	>3,200 Gton	2,994 ton
Oil	5.5 Gton	5.2 ton	60 Gton	56 ton
Natural gas	1,000 Gm³	936 m³	33,000 Gm³	30,882 m³
Hydropower	—	—	19 TWh/yr	1,778 KWh/yr
Uranium**	10 kton	0.01 kg	—	—

* Based on 1987 population
** Based on official published figures of the uranium supply available for 15 GWe nuclear power plants.
SOURCE: See Lu, Yingzhong, "Long-Term Energy Demand and the CO₂ Issues in the PRC," paper presented at the Twelfth International Conference of the Intrernational Association of Energy Economists, New Delhi, January 4–6, 1990.

Table 6.18 Forecast of Petroleum Production

	Scenario 1	Scenario 2	Scenario 3	Scenario 4
Production in 2000 (Mt)	175	185	180	200
Peak production (Mt)	200	225	240	300
Peak time (Year)	2010/20	2010/20	2010/30	2020/30
Resource requirement: final proven reserves (Mt)	46,450	50,340	60,130	70,820
Ratio of final proven to potential reserves	0.59–0.76	0.64–0.82	0.76–0.98	0.91–1.15
Confidence level	0.94	0.72	0.39	0.11

SOURCE: Wu, Zongxin, et al., *China's Energy Demand by 2050.*

However, considering the tremendous increase in electricity demand expected by 2050, hydropower can only provide some 20 percent of the total power it will be necessary to generate; thus its share in total energy supply will remain almost the same as it is today. Other energy sources for power production are therefore needed on a mammoth scale.

Chinese coal resources seem unlimited, but there are other restrictions on utilization, as mentioned in previous chapters. The geographical distribution of coal resources is highly uneven. As a consequence, transportation will be the first serious restriction. As mentioned before, it is estimated that about 4 billion tons of raw coal will have to be transported from the Shanxi/Shaanxi/Inner Mongolia region all the way to the east coast of China — a task whose technical feasibility will be in question. The second, more knotty problem with the use of such huge amounts of coal is the environmental impact. The best option is therefore to develop alternative energy sources to replace coal as much as possible, and the list of possibilities includes both nuclear and solar energy.

2. Structure of the Primary Energy Supply
Taking into account all the resource-limitation, transportation, and environmental-quality constraints and also considering possible technological advances in the early part of the next century, a rational primary energy mix for the future Chinese energy system is suggested in table 6.19. It should

be pointed out that nuclear energy is assigned a prominent role since it is the only available alternative to coal that can be readily developed on a multi-GWe scale. However, other new energy sources are also assigned important roles, and solar energy will occupy a prominent place. The share of new and renewable energy is seen to be larger than that of oil by 2050, that is, 4.8 percent versus 3.2 percent, or 250 tce versus 166 tce in absolute volume.

However, a much greater challenge will be encountered in the development of nuclear power. As shown in table 6.19, in order to replace a sizable amount of coal — 10.70 percent, 20.7 percent, or 30.7 percent of the total primary energy supply — the annual growth rate of nuclear power would have to reach 4.82 percent, 7.16 percent, or 8.58 percent, respectively, from 2020 to 2050. The total installed capacity of nuclear power would then be 150 percent, 280 percent, or 418 percent of total world nuclear capacity in 1987! Some new, inherently safe and economical reactor designs will have to be developed in order to implement such an ambitious program if there is no other choice in China's energy future.

6.3.2. CHINA'S CONTRIBUTION TO GLOBAL CO₂ EMISSIONS

The quantity of CO_2 emissions from China's future energy system is out of proportion to its energy share

Table 6.19 Scenarios of the Structure of Primary Energy

	Unit	Year 2000	2020	2050		
Total	**Mtce**	**1,500**	**2,400**	**5,200**		
Oil	Mt	200	250	116		
	Mtce	286	358	166		
	%	19.1	14.9	3.2		
Natural gas	Gm³	40	100	200		
	Mtce	53	133	266		
	%	3.5	5.5	5.1		
Hydropower	GWe	83	174	263		
	TWh	291	609	921		
	Mtce	100	210	320		
	%	6.7	8.8	6.2		
New energy	Mtce	0	10	250		
	%	0	0.4	4.8		
				Case A	Case B	Case C
Coal	Mt	1,470	2,280	5,100	4,370	3,640
	Mtce	1,051	1,626	3,640	3,120	2,600
	%	70.1	67.8	70	60	50
Nuclear	GWe	5	30	291	563	835
	TWh	30	180	1,750	3,378	5,008
	Mtce	10	63	558	1,078	1,598
	%	0.7	2.6	10.7	20.7	30.7

SOURCE: Wu, Zongxin, et al., *China's Energy Demand by 2050*.

because of the high percentage of coal consumed. On the same energy output basis, coal will emit about 120 percent more CO_2 than natural gas and 50 percent more than oil. Using the forecast of global carbon emission made by Edmond, et al. (see reference 11), the share of Chinese CO_2 emissions has been calculated and is summarized in table 6.20. This share will exceed that of the population in 2050 except in the high-nuclear Case C. The three nuclear options will reduce this share by 3.43 percent, 6.63 percent, or even as much as 9.83 percent (Case C), respectively. The decision and the effort to create an ambitious Chinese nuclear program can be justified in the context of global environmental protection alone.

6.4. LONG-TERM ENERGY POLICY ISSUES IN CHINA

In view of the above long-term energy demand forecast and the reanalysis of the relevant supply strategies, a series of long-term policy considerations on the future of the Chinese energy system has been identified. Detailed analysis has been carried out elsewhere, but some conclusions will be summarized as follows:

1. Control of population growth, especially in rural areas. According to the most optimistic estimates, China will add roughly the population of one Malaysia, one East Germany, one Czechoslovakia, or one Australia per year in this decade; it will create additional population of the size of one United States plus one Japan within the next six decades, that is, in the period from now to 2050. The pressure of population growth and the people's desire for a better life will always drive the anxious Chinese decisionmakers to take the risk of overheating the economic growth of this huge country.

2. Rationalization of economic policies, in particular, to continue on to thorough economic reform. Only successful economic reform can give the energy industry new impetus for large-scale energy development and eliminate China's chronic energy shortages.

3. Emphasis on energy conservation. The forecast is based on a long-term elasticity of around

Table 6.20 Chinese Contribution to Global CO$_2$ Emissions

			2050			
	2000	**2025**	Case 0	Case A	Case B	Case C
Global						
Carbon emissions (10^9 ton)	7.200	10.300	14.500	14.500	14.500	14.500
China						
Proportion of world population (%)	19.170	20.910	19.920	19.920	19.920	19.920
Carbon emissions (10^9 ton)	1.131	1.717	3.952	3.455	2.991	2.627
Proportion of world carbon emissions (%)	15.710	16.670	27.260	23.830	20.630	17.430

SOURCE: See Lu, Yingzhong, "Long-Term Energy Demand and the CO$_2$ Issues in the PRC."

0.50 to 0.55, which implies very great energy conservation efforts. Not only should energy-saving equipment and processes be utilized, but also a less energy-intensive economic structure and life style should be pursued.

4. Better use of conventional energy resources and development of alternative energies. The rational and clean use of coal, of course, will be one of the most important policy issues in the PRC. On the other hand, the depletion of domestic oil resources will require a large-scale transition to synthetic liquid fuels. The important role that nuclear energy might play in China's future energy system has been emphasized by many experts and recognized by the Ministry of Energy, though there still exist some obstacles in both the safety and the economic aspects of this option.

5. Pursuit of long-term integrated planning. Long-term planning integrating energy, economic, environmental, and social development is indispensable for a fast-growing economy and energy system. A number of critical issues still need to be studied, such as the availability of the huge amounts of capital investment required, the technology options, the tremendous manpower and other resource requirements, and management strategies. The global issue of climate change presents a new challenge to Chinese decisionmakers which also requires an integrated effort in a global context.

PART II

SOME CASE STUDIES ON CRITICAL ENERGY ISSUES

CHAPTER 7

THE SCIENTIFIC TOOL FOR INTEGRAL ENERGY PLANNING
A National Energy-Economy Model for China

7.1. FRAMEWORK FOR A MEDIUM-/LONG-TERM NATIONAL ENERGY-ECONOMIC MODEL SYSTEM

In order to meet the Four Modernizations targets proposed in 1980, during the Sixth Five-Year Plan a medium-/long-term energy-economic model system was developed for China to forecast energy supply and demand by the year 2000 and beyond. This work was jointly carried out by INET/ITEESA of Tsinghua University and ISE of Tianjing University under the sponsorship of the State Science and Technology Commission. The model system was applied in a research project, "China by 2000," sponsored by the State Council in 1985, and the outcomes also provided the basis for the formulation of Chinese official energy planning and policies. (For details of this case study, see reference 10, pp. 395-459.)

The framework of this Energy-Economic Model System is shown in figure 7.1. A Macro-Economic Model (MEM) generates several consistent sets of macro-economic parameters relevant to energy demand for scenarios of economic development conforming with the national development targets, the economic development.

An Energy Demand Model (EDM) generates the energy demand both of final energy and of primary energy for each scenario of economic development.

The national energy demand thus generated in EDM is broken down by the Regional Energy Demand Model (REDM) into the energy de-

Fig. 7.1 Energy-Economic Model System

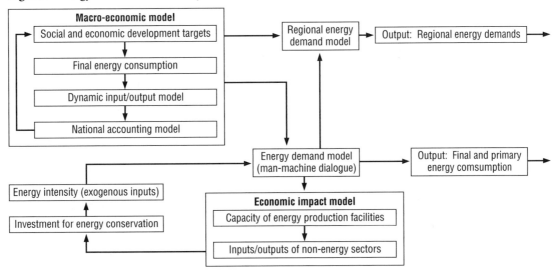

103

mands in each province and municipality, providing the basic parameters for regional energy production optimization.

A model entitled Economic Impact Model (EIM-1) guarantees the consistency of the financial need of the energy sector within the whole economy. One particular factor is considered in this model, that is, energy conservation, its investments and benefits. Different energy conservation levels and associated investment needs are given exogenously, and the net effects are calculated and compared to identify the best solution.

Both the national and regional energy demands are then put into the Energy Supply Model System, which consists of five sub-models as shown in figure 7.2.

The Energy Supply Strategic Model (ESSM) determines the rational structure of the future energy system, forecasts the development of various energy technologies, and estimates the energy flow among different regions.

The Energy Supply Distribution and Planning Model (ESDPM) belongs to the second level of planning models, providing information on the distribution and production levels of energy supply industries in various regions.

The third-level model of energy supply planning is the Energy Supply Bases Development Model (ESBDM), which optimizes the scale and time schedule of the development of each of the major energy bases.

One Energy Import/Export Model (EI/OM) accounts for the balance of energy demand and supply through energy import/export.

Finally, the Economic Impact Model (EIM-2) evaluates the social, political, economic, and technological impact of the supply strategy under consideration.

Such a comprehensive integral energy-economy model system has been applied to forecasts of the Chinese energy system to the year 2000, and the results are very encouraging.

7.2. MODEL FOR ENERGY DEMAND EVALUATION

7.2.1. MACRO-ECONOMIC MODEL (MEM)
The Macro-Economic Model consists of the Dynamic Input/Output Economic Sub-Model (DIDESM) as the core, the Final Consumption Sub-Model (FCSM), and the National Accounting

Sub-Model (NASM). In this model, a set of time-dependent consumption equations describe the change of the energy consumption preference and the change of consumption structure as a function of increasing per capita income. The evaluated consumption level will be the input to the DIOESM to generate a consistent set of the activities of each economic sector, using the Leontief input/output equation:

$$(I - A)X = F,$$
$$F = C + IV + EX - IM,$$

in which,

X = Vector for total output
A = Matrix for I/O coefficients
I = Unit matrix
F = Vector for final production
C = Vector for final consumption
IV = Vector for accumulation
EX = Vector for export, and
IM = Vector for import.

The time-dependent behavior of the vector for accumulation is included in this model, which accounts for the multi-period investment and the lead-time of major projects. As a result, DIOESM guarantees the consistency and the equilibrium of all economic sectors during the entire planning period.

However, since in DIOESM only the equilibrium of material products is taken into consideration, a National Accounting Sub-Model is developed on the basis of DIOESM outputs to take care of the financial equilibrium of the entire national income over a prolonged period. This sub-model simulates the primary and secondary distribution of national income as well as the final use of funds and checks for financial equilibrium to determine the validity of the scenario under consideration.

Fig. 7.2 Regional Energy Supply Model

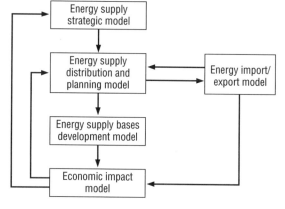

The final outputs of the above three sub-models are the following macro-economic parameters: total value of social production, total value of industrial and agricultural production, national income, the amounts of annual consumption and accumulation, per capita consumption, detailed sectoral value products, multi-period sectoral investments, and so on. All these values should be mutually consistent. In addition, this model provides the equilibrium of an energy-intensive product mix within each sector.

The consistency of input/output coefficients is difficult to guarantee since the changes in these coefficients are not simply the direct effects of material inputs. Two criteria are adopted in assessing the exogenously given forecast on technological progress — first, the technological feasibility evaluated by comparing with the progress of more advanced countries, and, second, the financial feasibility of accommodating this progress by evaluating the effi-

ciency of investment for innovation and consumption. The latter evaluation will be generated in another model, the EIM-1.

7.2.2. ENERGY DEMAND MODEL (EDM)

The core of this model system is the EDM, based on very detailed accounting of final energy consumption in six sectors and eighty-five subsectors, excluding the energy sector, as shown in table 7.1. Such a division conforms with Chinese practice of planning and statistics, as well as with the availability of data.

An energy flow diagram is used to convert the final energy into the primary energy needs as shown in figure 7.3. The procedures of calculation are as follows:

Step 1. Calculate the final energy demand for each subsector from the activity levels input

Fig. 7.3 Energy Accounting Flow Diagram Used for Modeling

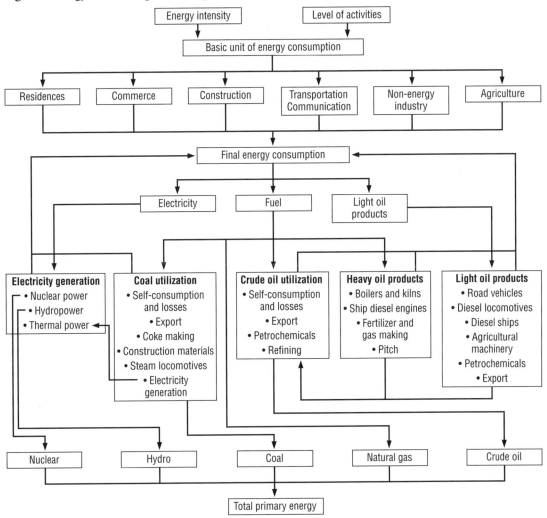

Table 7.1 Basic Units for Energy Consumption Accounting

Sector and accounting unit	Activity level	Index of energy consumption	Form of final energy consumption
Agriculture			
Planting			
Irrigation	Area irrigated with pump	Energy/hectare	Electricity, diesel
Agricultural machinery	hp X operating hours/year	g (oil)/hp-hr	Diesel
Rural Industry			
Metallurgy	Weighted value product	Energy intensity	Electricity, fuels
Chemicals	Same	Same	Same
Machine building	Same	Same	Same
Construction materials	Same	Same	Same
Food processing	Same	Same	Same
Textiles	Same	Same	Same
Energy Industry			
Coal			
Mining	Output/year	Self- and electricity consumption	Electricity, coal
Washing	Throughput/year	Washing loss, electricity consumption	Electricity, coal
Coke production	Washed coal used	Coking loss, electricity consumption	Electricity, coal
Oil and Gas			
Exploitation	Output/year	Self- and electricity consumption	Crude oil, electricity
Refining	Throughput/year	Fuel oil and electricity consumption	Fuel oil, electricity
Electricity			
Thermal	Annual generation	Coal consumption/ kWh, self-consumption	Electricity
Hydro	Annual generation	Self-consumption	Electricity
Transmission, Distribution	Annual generation	Line loss	Electricity
Non-energy Industries			
Ferrous metals			
Pig iron	Annual output	Specific energy intensity	Electricity, oil, fuels
Steel	Same	Same	Same
Steel products	Same	Same	Same
Non-ferrous metals			
Copper	Annual output	Specific energy intensity	Electricity, oil, fuels
Aluminum	Same	Same	Same
Lead, zinc	Same	Same	Same
Chemicals			
Sulfuric acid	Annual output	Specific energy intensity	Electricity, oil, fuels
Caustic soda	Same	Same	Same
Soda ash	Same	Same	Same
Syn. NH_3 (large)	Same	Same	Same
Syn. NH_3 (medium)	Same	Same	Same
Syn. NH_3 (small)	Same	Same	Same
Pesticides	Same	Same	Same
Ethylene	Same	Same	Same
Calcium carbide	Same	Same	Same
Carbon black	Same	Same	Same
Machine building			
Agricultural machines	Sector value produced	Specific energy intensity	Electricity, oil, fuels
Industrial equipment	Same	Same	Same
Transportation equipment	Same	Same	Same
Electronics	Same	Same	Same
Household utensils	Same	Same	Same
Construction materials			
Cement	Output/year	Specific energy intensity	Electricity, oil, fuels
Brick	Same	Same	Same
Tile	Same	Same	Same
Plate glass	Same	Same	Same

Table 7.1 Basic Units for Energy Consumption Accounting (Continued)

Sector and accounting unit	Activity level	Index of energy consumption	Form of final energy consumption
Forestry			
Lumbering	Output/year	Specific energy intensity	Electricity, oil, fuels
Processing	Same	Same	Same
Food processing			
Salt (sea and lake)	Output/year	Specific energy intensity	Electricity, oil, fuels
Salt (mines)	Same	Same	Same
Sugar	Same	Same	Same
Wine	Same	Same	Same
Beer	Same	Same	Same
Ethanol	Same	Same	Same
Textiles			
Synthetic fibers	Output/year	Specific energy intensity	Electricity, oil, fuels
Artificial fibers	Same	Same	Same
Yarn	Same	Same	Same
Cloth	Same	Same	Same
Paper and cardboard making	Output/year	Specific energy intensity	Electricity, oil, fuels
Other industries	Output/year	Specific energy intensity	Electricity, oil, fuels
Transportation and communications			
Railway			
Steam locomotive	Freight volume	Coal consumption/ 10,000 ton-km	Coal
Diesel locomotive	Same	Oil consumption/ 10,000 ton-km	Diesel
Electric locomotive	Same	Electricity consumption/ 10,000 ton-km	Electricity
Road			
Gasoline truck	Freight volume	Oil consumption/ 100 ton-km	Gasoline
Diesel truck	Same	Diesel consumption/ 100 ton-km	Diesel
Waterway			
River shipping	Freight volume	Oil cons./ 10,000 ton-nautical mile	Diesel, fuel oil
Coastal shipping	Same	Same	Same
Ocean shipping	Same	Same	Same
Air transport	Freight volume	Oil consumption/ 10,000 ton-km	Kerosene, gasoline
Pipeline transport	Freight volume	Energy consumption/ 10,000 ton-km	Crude oil, electricity
Communications	Sector value produced	Specific energy consumption	Electricity, oil, fuels
Construction	Sector value produced	Specific energy consumption	Electricity, oil, fuels
Commerce	Sector value produced	Specific energy consumption	Electricity, oil, fuels
Urban residential			
District heating	Area heated	Standard of house heating	Coal
Centralized heating	Same	Same	Same
Decentralized heating	Same	Same	Same
Cooking (coal)	Number of households	Standard for cooking energy	Coal
Cooking (gas)	Same	Same	LPG, coal gas
Water supply	Urban pop. water quota	Specific electricity consumption	Electricity
Non-industrial power	Social consumption	Specific electricity consumption	Electricity
Urban lighting	Urban population	Per capita electricity consumption	Electricity
Mass transportation	Number of vehicles	Oil consumption/ 100 km	Light oil products
Taxis	Same	Same	Same
Institution vehicles	Same	Same	Same
Rural residential			
Cooking	Rural population	Specific consumption X share of commercial energy	Coal
House heating	Same	Same	Same
Lighting	Same	Level of electrification	Electricity, kerosene

from MEM in seven energy forms: coal, crude oil, fuel oil, light oil products, natural gas, electricity, and coke.

Step 2. Aggregate the final energy consumption according to six sectors, which are the basic units in Chinese official statistics.

Step 3. Aggregate the final energy consumption according to seven energy forms and calculate the crude oil demand for all kinds of oil products. The self-consumption of oil products by the oil industry itself is considered in this calculation.

Step 4. Calculate the self-consumption of their own products by the energy industries, including the mutual supply of energy — for example, the coal and oil consumption in the power generating sector, the electricity consumption in coal and oil industries, and so on.

Step 5. Add the energy consumption of non-energy and energy sectors from steps 2 and 4 to obtain the total national consumption.

Step 6. Subtract the electricity and light oil products consumed from the total national energy consumption to obtain the total fuel consumption.

Step 7. Obtain the forecast of national gas production from exogenous sources.

Step 8. Subtract the production of crude oil, natural gas, hydropower, nuclear energy, and energy imports from the sum of total national energy consumption and energy exports, all calculated in tons of coal equivalent, to obtain the demand of coal production.

The outputs of this model thus include (1) the demand of every kind of primary energy; (2) the flow and the uses of coal, crude oil, and all kinds of oil products; (3) the final energy consumption of each sector and subsector of the seven energy forms; and (4) the estimate of energy conservation:

$$S_A = Y_t \left(E_0/Y_0 - E_t/Y_t \right)$$

in which,

S_A = Energy conservation;

E_0, Y_0 = Energy conservation and value production at the beginning of the planning period; and

E_t, Y_t = Energy consumption and value production at the end of the planning period.

7.2.3. ECONOMIC IMPACT MODEL 1 (EIM-1)

In order to estimate the upper limit of specific investment for energy conservation and provide an

estimate of possible reduction of energy intensity within the planning period, the Economic Impact Model 1 is designed to give the comprehensive specific investment for energy production. It is considered economically reasonable for energy conservation projects provided that the specific investment for conservation is less than the comprehensive specific investment for energy production. The latter should take into consideration all direct and indirect investments for units of additional capacity of energy production facilities, including not only the expansion of the infrastructure but also the relevant expansion of the capacity of other sectors. Two submodels are designed to account for the direct and indirect investments, respectively. The total direct investment of year t is estimated in the Energy Sector Expansion Submodel as follows:

$$J_e(t) = \sum_{e \in E} \sum_{\tau = t}^{t + \lambda} f_e(t, \tau) \, Z_e(t);$$

in which,

$f_e(t, \tau)$ —the t year specific investment of the facilities producing the eth energy sources scheduled to operate in year τ,

$Z_e(t)$ — the newly added capacity of the eth energy source in year τ; and

λ_e — the construction period of the eth energy source.

The total indirect investment of year t in the Non-Energy Sector Expansion Sub-Model is estimated as follows:

$$Y_j(t) = \sum_{e \in E} a_{je} X_e(t) + \sum_{\tau = t}^{t + \lambda_e} f_{je}(t, \tau) \, Z_e(t)$$

in which,

$X_e(t)$ — the production capacity of energy source e in year t.

a_{je} — the input/output coefficient for energy source e.

$f_{je}(t, \tau)$ — the coefficient of investment matrix: from jth sector for eth energy source.

From the solution of the above model, the indirect investment is found to be:

$$J_n(t) = \sum_{i \in N} \sum_{\tau = t}^{t + \lambda_i} f_i(t, \tau) \, Z_i(\tau).$$

Then the total investment

$$J(t) = J_e(t) + J_n(t)$$

could be used to set the upper limit of energy conservation investment. The effect of energy conservation will be reflected in the reduction of sectoral energy intensity.

7.3. MODEL FOR OPTIMIZING THE NATIONAL ENERGY SUPPLY SYSTEM

A model system for multi-regional energy supply

Fig. 7.4 Regional Energy Production Sub-Models

A. Coal sub-model

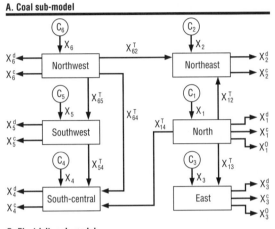

B. Electricity sub-model

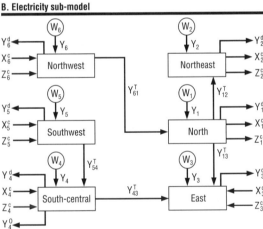

A. Coal sub-model

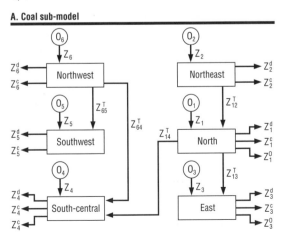

optimization has been designed to provide an optimum solution to meet the regional energy demand generated in the Energy Demand Model.

7.3.1. ENERGY SUPPLY STRATEGY MODEL (ESSM)

The structure of the future energy supply system, the development of energy supply technology, and the direction of energy flow between regions are given by this Energy Supply Strategy Model. The methodology of analogy and comparative analysis is adopted to select a set of rational macro-indices, such as the structure and the technology level of the future energy supply system. However, in order to rationalize the regional supply level of different kinds of energy, the resources, consumption, and economic development of each region must be taken into consideration. To this end, a linear programming model is designed to estimate the best combination of various variables. Three major energy sources, coal, oil, and electricity, are evaluated by this model as shown in the block diagrams in figures 7.4-A, -B, and -C. The equilibrium of energy flow is considered as a set of constraints to the minimizing problem:

$$\min F = \sum_{i=1}^{6} [(I^c_i/TC + P^c_i)X_i + (I^w_i/TW + P^w_i)Y_i$$
$$+ (I^c_i/TO + P^o_i)Z_i + (r^c_i/TE + V^c_i)X^e_i +$$
$$(r^o_i/TE + V^o_i)Z^e_i] + t^c_{12}X^T_{12} + t^c_{13}X^T_{13}$$
$$+ t^c_{14}X^T_{14} + t^c_{54}X^T_{54} + t^c_{62}X^T_{62} +$$
$$t^c_{64}X^T_{64} + t^c_{65}X^T_{65} + t^w_{12}Y^T_{12} +$$
$$t^w_{13}Y^T_{13} + t^w_{43}Y^T_{43} + t^w_{54}Y^T_{54} +$$
$$t^w_{61}Y^T_{61} + t^o_{12}Z^T_{12} + t^o_{13}Z^T_{13} +$$
$$t^o_{14}Z^T_{14} + t^o_{64}Z^T_{64} + t^o_{65}Z^T_{65}$$
$$+ q^c_1X^o_1 + q^c_3X^o_3 + q^w_4Y^o_4 + \sum_{i=1}^{4} q^o_iZ^o_i$$

in which:

X_i, Y_i, Z_i — the production of coal, electricity, and oil, respectively;

X^T, Y^T, Z^T — the transport of coal, electricity, and oil, respectively;

X^o, Y^o, Z^o — the export of coal, electricity, and oil, respectively;

I, r — specific investment for energy source and electricity, respectively;

P, V — operation cost for energy source and electricity, respectively;

TC, TW, TO, TE — depreciation time of coal mines, hydropower plants, oil fields, and thermal power plants, respectively;

q_i, $t_{i,j}$ — cost for export and transport of unit energy, respectively; and

i, j = 1 – 6 — regions for energy supply analysis.
Subject to:

1. 18 constraints of energy resources

2. 25 constraints of energy demands

3. 18 constraints of the equilibrium of supply and demand

4. 6 constraints of the policy of limiting oil burning in power generation

Fig. 7.5 Procedures for Multi-Objective Programming

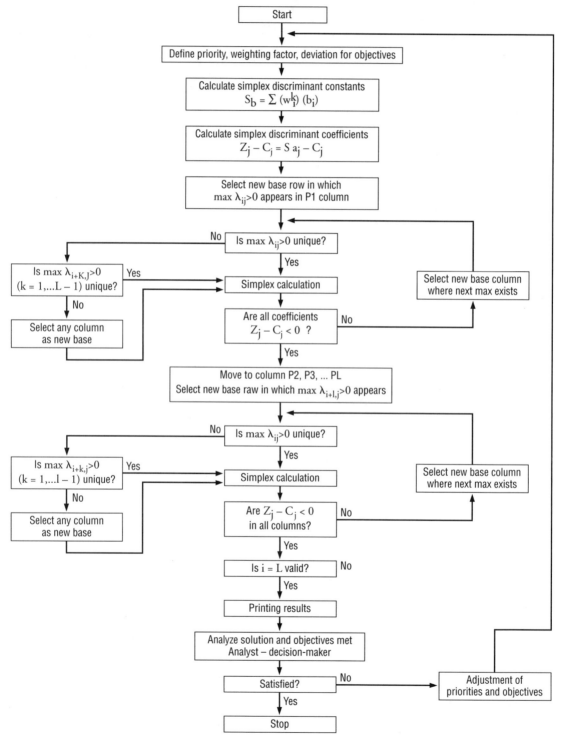

7.3.2. ENERGY SUPPLY DISTRIBUTION AND PLANNING MODEL (ESDPM)

Based on the top-level strategic decisions made from the foregoing model, the present model will give the distribution of the energy supply industries and the costs. Multi-objective programming is adopted for this purpose, which is shown schematically in figure 7.5.

The equations used in coal production programming include the constraints on the following objectives for each province or municipality:

1. Domestic coal demand objective
2. Export objective
3. State investment objective
4. Transportation objective
5. Production objective of state-owned mines
6. Production objective of local government-owned mines
7. Production objective of village-owned mines
8. Lower limit of production of state-owned mines
9. Upper limit of production of state-owned mines
10. Upper limit of local government-owned and village-owned mines
11. Non-negative constraints on all variables

Six levels of objective functions are defined in the following order:

1. Production of each category of coal mines should be within the limits set by equations (8), (9), and (10)
2. Total production should match the sum of domestic demand and export
3. State investment should not exceed the available budget
4. Throughput of coal transportation should not exceed the maximum possible capacity of each major railway
5. Minimum total cost of coal production and transportation should be attained
6. Minimum waste of coal resources should be achieved

Similar programming constraints and objectives are designed for the oil and power sectors.

7.3.3. ENERGY SUPPLY FACILITY DEVELOPMENT MODEL (ESFDM)

The Energy Supply Facility Development Model gives the concrete plan of the exploitation of various energy supply facilities within each province (or region). Integer programming is adopted to find the optimized major energy facility development plan with maximum output and minimum investment.

7.3.4. ECONOMIC IMPACT MODEL 2 (EIM-2)

This model gives the impact of energy planning on economic and social systems. Three submodels are developed for evaluating the impacts on various aspects of the national and energy economies.

7.3.4.1. SUBMODEL OF THE RELATIONSHIP BETWEEN ENERGY INVESTMENT AND ECONOMIC GROWTH

The mutual relationship of the growth of the national economy, the investment in various sectors, and the energy supply and consumption are expressed in the following set of equations:

$$g = \{1 + \eta(t) \, [\gamma_r \quad \alpha_t (1 + P)^t - \epsilon_0 \ (\alpha_t - \alpha_{e,t})$$
$$(1 + P_e)^t] - 1\}^{1/t} \text{, or}$$

$$g = \{1 + \epsilon_0 \ (1 + \ P_e)^t \, / \, B_j - 1)\}^{1/t} - 1$$

in which,

g — Average growth rate of national economy during the planning period;

r_o — Total investment in base year;

E_o — Energy investment in base year;

α_t — Expected efficiency of investment in non-energy sector;

$\alpha_{e,t}$ — Expected efficiency of investment in energy sector;

P — Average increase rate of total investment;

P_e — Average increase rate of energy investment;

$\eta(t)$ — Lead time of energy investment;

B — Elasticity of energy consumption;

D_0 — Specific energy consumption of national economy in base year;

J — Specific investment of energy sector (104 yuan/tce);

t — Years in planning period.

The results of the calculation based on historical data and a set of assumptions are shown in figure 7.6. It is noted that:

1. With B = 0.5, J = 0.08 (corresponding to 800 yuan/tce), P = 0.07 and α = 0.75, the annual growth rate of economy g will be maintained at 7 percent when the increase rate of energy investment P_e remains 5.5 percent.
2. If the expected efficiency of investment increases to α = 1.0, the growth of the economy will attain 8 percent when P_e = 9 percent, that is, a higher growth rate can be maintained.

Fig.7.6 Relationship between Economic Growth and Energy Investment

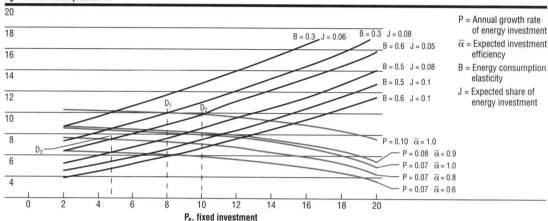

Total industrial and
agricultural value product: %

P = Annual growth rate of energy investment

$\bar{\alpha}$ = Expected investment efficiency

B = Energy consumption elasticity

J = Expected share of energy investment

P_e, fixed investment

7.3.4.2. ENERGY RESOURCE EXPLOITATION EVALUATION MODEL

The shadow prices of various energy products in different regions are calculated as the solution of the dual problem of the linear programming model in section 7.3.1. The results are listed in table 7.2. These figures represent the shadow prices of various energy sources in each region.

Several conclusions can be drawn from table 7.2, as follows:

1. Energy-intensive industries should be located in regions with low energy shadow prices.
2. The specific investment of energy consumption measures in various regions should be correlated to the respective shadow prices.

3. The adjustment of the prices of energy products should be referred to the respective shadow prices.
4. Shadow prices should be considered in the exploitation of energy resources in different regions.

7.3.4.3. EVALUATION MODEL FOR LOCAL SMALL COAL MINES

Since local small coal mines now produce more coal than state-owned large mines, in-depth analysis should be carried out in long-term coal exploitation planning. Small coal mines require much smaller specific investment and shorter lead time. However, the life span of the small mines is also much shorter,

Table 7.2 Shadow Prices of Energy in Various Regions

	North	Northeast	East	South-central	Southwest	Northeast
Coal	26.400	40.500	41.900	39.700	45.100	32.900
Electricity	0.023	0.027	0.027	0.027	0.021	0.025
Crude oil	128.500	116.900	138.800	139.800	152.000	122.200

Table 7.3 Energy Forecasts by the Year 2000 from Various Sources

Author	Total (10^9 tce)	Composition (%)				
		Coal	Oil	Natural gas	Hydropower	Nuclear
INET (1985)	1.455	67.42	20.17	4.57	6.67	1.17
IER (1984)	1.469	66.87	23.36	3.17	6.60	—
World Bank (1984)	1.428	78.71	14.01	0.91	6.37	—
J. Woodard (1980)	1.416	67.09	15.14	13.51	4.39	0.24
Ministry of Energy (1990)*	1.430	72.93	16.98	2.79	6.66	0.69

*Quoted from the speech made by the Chinese minister of energy, Huang Yicheng, in the International Conference on Energy and Electricity Development, October 23, 1990, Beijing. Published in the People's Daily, Overseas Edition, October 24, 1990, page 1.

Fig.7.7 Rate of Decommissioning Small Coal Mines

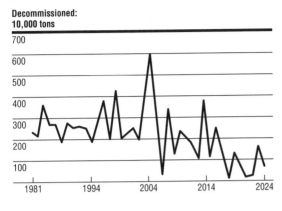

Fig.7.8 Additional Capacity of Small Mines for Maintaining Current Production

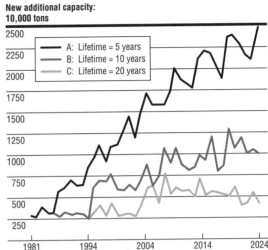

and the recovery rate of coal is rather low. This model is based on the depreciation curve shown in figure 7.7, derived from the 1983 statistics for local government-owned small mines (total annual capacity of 178.9 million tons). An estimate of the new capability required for maintaining the current level of the output from the small mines is shown in figure 7.8, in which three different life spans are assumed. It is noted that unless the average service life of the small mines exceeds fifteen to twenty years, new additional capacity will have to increase steadily in the coming decades.

7.4. APPLICATION OF THE NATIONAL ENERGY-ECONOMIC MODEL SYSTEM

The Medium-/Long-Term National Energy-Economic Model System has been used since 1983 in forecasting energy demand/supply for the year 2000.

The predicted energy demand compares very well with the results from other sources, as shown in table 7.3. The forecast of energy supply has already been shown in table 6.19 and discussed in chapter 6. Regional distribution of coal and electricity production have been evaluated, the transportation of coal between regions has been shown in table 2.5, and the associated policy implications have been addressed in chapter 2. It is noted that the flow of coal will be mainly from northern China to all other regions except the northwest and southwest, amounting to about 400 million tons by 2000. Electricity, on the other hand, will be transmitted from four regions — north, northwest, southwest, and south — to three regions — northeast, east, and central. These results have been extensively utilized in the formulation of Chinese official energy policy.

CHAPTER 8

SUCCESSFULLY FUELING NINETY MILLION RURAL HOUSEHOLDS

The Dissemination of Improved Woodstoves

8.1 BACKGROUND

During the period 1983-1988, 99.16 million fuel-saving woodstoves were installed in Chinese rural households. The huge scale of the improved-stove program reflects both the government's commitment to this energy technology and the extremely low thermal efficiency of biomass, which was formerly being burned as cooking fuel. A case study has been conducted to summarize the experience of this massive effort. A summary will be given in this chapter. (For more details of the case study, see reference 152.)

Some 220 million tons of straw and other crop residues and 170 million tons of firewood were being consumed annually in rural China at such a low conversion efficiency as to provide only 3,500 to 3,700 kilocalories of useful energy per day per capita — some 20 percent less than the minimum daily requirement.

The acute energy shortage led to serious consequences. In some villages as much as a quarter of the available labor time was used for collecting fuel. Instead of being plowed under, nearly 70 percent of crop residues were used for cooking, and the consequent reduction in organic content of the soil (an average decline from 9 percent to 2 percent) has decreased the fertility of China's northeast plains.

While the relationship between biomass utilization and environmental degradation is complex, it is widely believed that the excessive burning of biomass as fuel exacerbates the massive scale of soil erosion and seriously damages the environment.

The rapidly growing energy demand in the countryside has resulted from the expanding rural economy following the economic reforms that began in 1979. Demand is currently being met by substantial increases in the supply of commercial fuel; rural consumption of commercial energy rose from 99.5 million tons coal equivalent (Mtce) in 1980 to 193.3 Mtce in 1985. But consumption of biomass is still rising (from 230 Mtce in 1980 to 233.7 Mtce in 1985).

The government has tackled the rural energy shortage through many programs. In addition to the well-known biogas and minihydropower programs, the government has also promoted afforestation and the dissemination of improved woodstoves. Of the country's 2,300 counties, 684 have already won the title of "Demonstration Counties for Improved Stoves" by having over 90 percent of their households adopt the new stoves. This is in fact the most successful rural energy program in China.

8.2. FOUR TYPICAL COUNTIES

In order to study the issues and experiences of the successful dissemination of improved stoves in China, a case study has been carried out in four typical counties. From among ten potential candidates, four were finally selected for the survey, that is, Zunhua County of Hebei Province, Wuhua County of Guangdong Province, Huangpi County of Hubei Province, and Jiangjin County of Sechuan Province, covering both northern and southern parts of China. As is shown in figure 8.1, they are models of diverse types. For instance, Zunhua County of Hebei Province, about 200 kilometers east of Beijing, has a topography characterized by hills and plains, with an annual mean temperature of 10.4° C. Winter there is long and cold, and woodstoves are used for home heating. These are called "stoves connected to *kang* [heated brick bed]" (used for sleeping). Before the dissemination of improved woodstoves, the peasants suffered from severe shortages of cooking fuel. Besides firewood and crop residues, coal was also widely used for cooking. The energy situation in this county basically reflects the general situation in rural areas of northern China. Although the other three counties in the study are well located in southern China, they represent different topographies, resources, ecological environments, and various levels of economic development. Table 8.1 shows the basic features of the counties.

The four counties selected were all assigned experimental counties for the diffusion of improved woodstoves after 1983. The stoves are of different types, developed to suit local conditions. Three out of the four counties, Zunhua, Wuhua, and Jiangjin counties, started the program only in 1986, sponsored by the Bureau of Energy and Environmental Protection of the Ministry of Agriculture, but by 1988 all of them had already fulfilled the requirements spelled out in the contracts after acceptance tests. The fourth county, Huangpi, was among the first ones chosen for experiments in 1983 and had already fulfilled the planned target by 1985. Thus, in the current survey on Huangpi County, particu-

lar attention was given to finding out the actual performance of those stoves disseminated and whether farmers had stuck to them in the intervening three years.

The basic features of the four counties surveyed are shown in tables 8.2 through 8.4.

8.3. CONSEQUENCES OF RURAL FUEL SHORTAGES

The severe shortage of cooking fuel not only has affected farmers' daily lives, but also has had serious consequences for economic and social development as well as ecology in these counties.

1. Farmers could not prepare adequate meals. In 1985, before the improved stoves were disseminated, Jiangjin County suffered severe shortages of cooking fuel. Farmers in some villages could cook only one meal a day in summer and had to eat the other two meals cold. Some households were even forced to cut up the legs of their wooden beds and burn them as fuel.

Fig. 8.1 Location of Four Survey Counties

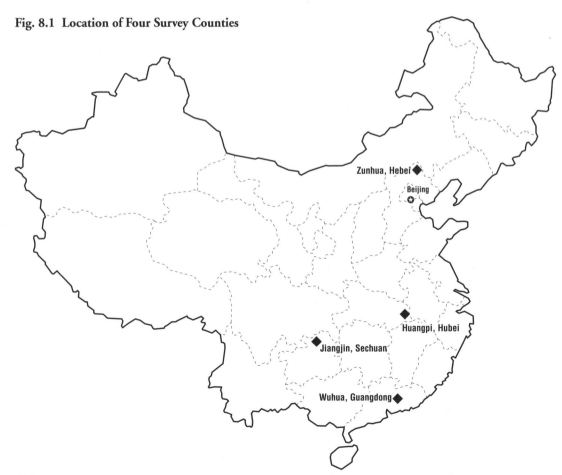

Table 8.1 Characteristics of Four Typical Counties for Field Survey

	Topography	Proximity to major city	Local energy resource	Economic development	Feature of local model stove
Zunhua, Hebei	Plain and hills	Medium, about 200 km	Medium, straw and firewood	Medium level	Stove with brick bed
Wuhua, Guangdong	Mountains	Far, about 400 km	Rich in grass	Medium level	Stove burning biomass
Huangpi, Hubei	Plain	Near, about 50 km	Shortage,straw	Well developed	Stove burning biomass
Jiangjin, Sechuan	Hills and mountains	Medium, about 120 km	Medium, straw, firewood and coal	Medium level	Stove burning biomass

Table 8.2 Economic and Social Status in 1985

	Zunhua	Wuhua	Huangpi	Jiangjin
Total population (1,000)	580	903	952.1	1,388.6
Farm population (1,000)	544	822	863.1	1,214.9
Number of farm households (1,000)	136	149	197.2	313.8
Total area (1,000 *mu*)	2,280	4,791	3,395.3	4,720.5
Total arable land (1,000 *mu*)	880	498	935.4	1,135.0
Existing forests (1,000 *mu*)	648	786	510.9	1,138.0
Land suitable for forests (1,000 *mu*)	938	3,656	906.1	1,175.0
Number of draft animals (1,000 head)	35.8	63.4	53.2	48.0
Agricultural output value (100 million yuan)	2.95	1.63	2.85	3.69
Industrial output value (100 million yuan)	2.41	0.71	2.70	2.74
Farmers' per capita net (yuan)	532	259	461	395

Table 8.3 Residential Energy Consumption Mix, 1985

	Zunhua Consumption (1,000 tce)	%	Wuhua Consumption (1,000 tce)	%	Jiangjin Consumption (1,000 tce)	%
Crop residue	113.00	47.06	31.5	37.2	338.9	44.0
Firewood	41.30	17.13	85.3	15.9	130.9	17.0
Grass	36.50	15.15	168.7	—	11.7	1.5
Animal dung	0.40	0.16	0.4	2.1	0.6	0.1
Coal	47.00	19.51	69.4	37.3	285	37.0
Oil	0.40	0.18	12.6	5.2	0.4	0.1
Electricity	2 .00	0.81	4.0	2.3	2.7	0.3
Total	240.60	100.00	374.3	100.0	770.2	100.0
Per capita energy consumption (kgce)	442.90		425.4		643.0	
Overall conversion rate (%)	12.62		10.8		10.2	
Per household effective energy (kcal/day)	4,284.00		3,524.0		4,746.0	

Table 8.4 Energy Shortages in Rural Households before Improved Stoves

County	Number of households (1,000)	Percentage of population suffering energy shortage	Less than 3 months	3-6 months	Over 6 months
Zunhua	136	85.0	18.0	56.0	11.0
Wuhua	149	75.4	15.5	47.2	12.7
Huangpi	197	76.0	19.8	20.3	35.9
Jiangjin	314	91.1	13.1	54.4	23.6

2. Large quantities of crop stalks were used as fuel and therefore could not be returned to the fields as organic fertilizer, resulting in serious loss of organic content in the soil as well as nitrogen and phosphate constituents. In Huangpi County, as crop residues were not plowed into the fields, the soil became compacted, causing degradation and subjecting fine crop varieties to diseases. In this county the area of arable land with soil containing less than 2 percent organic matter reached 21,500 hectares, 34.5 percent of its total acreage. The crop yields from the deteriorated soil were only a third to two-thirds of those grown on fertile soil.

3. Farmers used not only crop stalks, tree branches, and wood residues as fuel but also burned large amounts of useful timber; as a result, the volume of felled trees exceeded their growth rate, seriously damaging forest resources. The forest coverage of Wuhua County dropped dramatically, from 53.4 percent in 1957 to 16.4 percent in 1985. Such a situation has also affected afforestation efforts. In Huangpi County, trees have been planted on 68,700 hectares of land since 1949, but only 24,133 hectares of trees have survived, only 35.1 percent of the total reforested area. A local saying is, "Trees were planted every year but no trees can be seen."

4. Since even the roots of trees and the grass were dug up and used as fuel, serious soil erosion has resulted. The Nieshui River in Huangpi County has washed away as much as 6 billion tons of silt since the 1950s, averaging 16 million tons a year. In 1985, the area of land in Wuhua County affected by erosion reached 875.8 square kilometers. Since 1960, the riverbeds of Wuhua and Qinjiang have risen by 90 centimeters and 54.3 centimeters, respectively, due to silt accumulation.

5. A large proportion of the labor force was needed to collect fuel. For instance, in Donjige Village of Zunhua County, before using the improved stoves the villagers would spend fifteen days at a time cutting firewood in distant mountains, each household harvesting about 500 kilograms of wood, barely enough for two to three months. Some of the farmers in Huangpi Township of Jiangjin County had to walk as far as 25 kilometers to gather firewood or to buy coal. In the eight years preceding 1985, nine people from Sanhe Village who were gathering firewood or carrying coal home fell to their deaths from the steep hills.

8.4 DIFFUSION OF IMPROVED STOVES IN CHINA

Since 1949, the Chinese government has attempted several times to disseminate improved woodstoves in the vast rural area, but poor management, inadequate measures, and lack of comprehensive planning always brought failure. In the 1980s, rural China faced more serious energy shortages and increasing deterioration of the environment. Replacing the old-fashioned woodstoves used in over 90 percent of farm households came to be considered the most important and cost-effective measure to mitigate energy problems. After carefully studying the historical experience, the Chinese government drew up a comprehensive plan for disseminating improved stoves all over China and carried out some reforms, particularly in dissemination methods. The central government and provinces selected several groups of counties which had both the administrative and the technical capability to implement the dissemination program. The state and provinces provided the necessary financial subsidies to carry out tests and demonstrations, to gain experience and training, so as to promote and stimulate the all-out national campaign of "improving stoves to save firewood."

Table 8.5 Dissemination of Improved Stoves in China

Year	Number of pilot counties	Number of households starting to use improved stoves in each year (million)		Total number of households using improved stoves by end of year (million)	
		Total	Disseminated by pilot counties	Total	Disseminated by pilot counties
1983	90	6.641	2.615	6.641	2.615
1984	200	20.719	11.034	27.360	13.649
1985	100	17.876	8.368	45.236	22.017
1986	97	18.420	9.896	63.638	31.933
1987	101	18.034	8.924	81.672	40.837
1988	96	17.491	10.009	99.163	50.846
Total	684	NA	NA	99.163	50.846

Starting in 1983, the Bureau of Environmental Protection and Energy under the Ministry of Agriculture selected about 100 pilot counties annually to sign technical contracts for dissemination of improved woodstoves over a three-year period. The government subsidized rural households that wanted to build the improved stoves by providing technology, key components, raw materials, and some cash. The peasants themselves provided labor and locally available materials. By 1988, all together 684 counties had carried out the project, in six groups, of which 415 counties successfully fulfilled the requirements of the contracts and passed the acceptance tests. As shown in table 8.5, a total of 50.85 million farm households benefited from the improved stoves, saving both firewood and labor time. In addition, all the provinces and municipalities have also taken up stove-dissemination programs at the local level. Thus the total number of improved stoves all over China reached 99.16 million, half of China's farm households. It should be concluded that the program and its implementation have achieved outstanding success.

8.5. DISSEMINATION POLICIES FOR IMPROVED STOVES

The general rural energy policy states that energy development should be "in line with local conditions, mutually supplementing various energies, comprehensively utilizing them, and attaching importance to economic returns as far as the energy construction in rural regions is concerned" and that it should "place equal emphasis on energy exploitation and conservation and give priority to conservation in the near term." In accordance with this policy, the national stove dissemination program required replacement of the old-style stoves used by 200 million farmers by state-of-the-art improved stoves of much higher efficiency. It is estimated that an annual saving of about 200 million tons of biomass fuel will thus be achieved, or about one-third of the total fuel used for cooking by all farmers.

In carrying out the distribution program, the policy of "Self-building, Self-managing, Self-using" was also implemented, which implies that farmers' enthusiasm and initiative should be stimulated and relied on through demonstration and training.

While implementing the program in provinces, municipalities, and counties, specific policies were drawn up according to local conditions. For instance, in Wuhua County of Guangdong Province, the following goals were stipulated:

1. To incorporate dissemination of improved stoves with poverty-relief and reforestation programs. Some of the townships have made it a rule that only those farm households using improved stoves are allowed to cut firewood in the mountains at preferential prices.
2. To help poor households by providing them with factory-made castings of stoves.
3. To draw up regulations concerning rewards and punishments:
   — The county will give an award of 300 to 500 yuan to those townships which have satisfactorily fulfilled their task of stove improvement.
   — Cadres in villages must take the lead in improving their own stoves. Otherwise, they will be punished by bonus reduction at the end of the year.
   — Skilled workers who still build old-fashioned stoves will be fined 50 yuan plus suspension of their operating licenses. For those who satisfactorily conduct the assigned work of improving stoves, a reward is offered.

In Jiangjin County, the following policies were implemented:
1. First priority is given to supplying materials for improved stoves to concerned enterprises and township enterprises under the jurisdiction of the county. Tax deductions are offered according to relevant achievements.
2. Improved woodstoves must be installed in every new house. The township government will only give approval for using the land to build houses with improved woodstoves.

The above policies have greatly facilitated the dissemination of improved stoves in the rural regions.

8.6. ORGANIZATIONAL SYSTEM FOR STOVE DISSEMINATION

Effective organization plays a vital role in the distribution of the improved stoves. The organizational system is shown in figure 8.2.

8.7. STOVE RESEARCH AND MANUFACTURING

A good stove model should be firewood-saving, safe, hygienic, convenient, and inexpensive. This is why the selection of a good stove model is key to an effective stove dissemination program. Once the right stove model is selected, fewer mistakes are likely during implementation. As a result, from the central government down through the provinces, municipalities, and pilot counties, each party paid great attention to research and manufacturing of improved stoves, investing considerable amounts of money, time, and manpower in the research and development work. Research on factory-based manufacturing of woodstoves has begun, responding to the new need to raise the commercialized share of the stoves in the dissemination program. Engaged in the research are national scientific research institutes, provincial and municipal research institutes and units, and even rural energy offices and groups in counties. The research work is mainly conducted at the following levels:

1. Scientific research institutes at the national level. Scientific research on improved woodstoves is undertaken by the energy conservation division of the Energy Center under the Chinese Academy of Agricultural Engineering Research and Planning (CAAERP). Begun in 1983, the research project was completed in 1984 with a total investment of 50,000 yuan, having successfully developed the Firewood Stove Model NG-I (hardwood stove) and Model NG-II (softwood stove), which are suitable for use in most parts of China. This tech-

nology has now been transferred to many counties, with satisfactory results.

2. Provincial and municipal research units. The provinces and municipalities, as the assistant parties in the dissemination project, have also played active roles in research and development in order to compensate for the counties' limited technical and scientific strength, funds, and experimental equipment.

3. County offices. Convenience for the users is one of the principles in the selection of ideal stove models. China's vast territory contains diverse life styles region by region. Some counties have invented local stove models suited to their own needs and customs, and they have been warmly welcomed by the local farmers. For example, in Zunhua County, local people are used to heating their brick beds by flue gas from the cooking stoves. Therefore, the cooking pot must be set deep enough into the fire chamber so that its edge is lower than the top of the stove and water is prevented from overflowing onto the floor or bed. For these reasons the stove model needed is unique and has been developed locally to meet people's requirements.

4. Counties and State scientific research institutions jointly. For instance, in 1980 Wuhua County set up a cooperative research group for improved woodstoves comprising technical personnel from the Energy Center of CAAERP, the Office of Rural Energy in Wuhua County, and the Biogas

Fig. 8.2 Organization for Diffusion of Improved Stoves

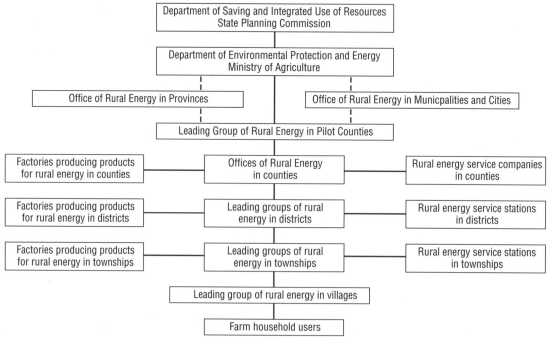

Research Institute in Guangdong Province. After a half-year of research and repeated experiments, by the end of 1986 the WH-Model improved woodstove had been successfully developed.

8.8. PROPAGANDA AND TRAINING IN THE DISSEMINATION PROGRAM

8.8.1 PROPAGANDA AND EDUCATION

Chinese farmers have been using their old-style stoves for thousands of years. Thus, the dissemination of improved stoves is in fact a revolution, which requires a lot of propaganda and mobilization of the public. The propaganda is mainly conducted in the following ways:

1. **Meetings to improve the public's understanding of the significance of energy savings.** In 1984, the State Planning Commission, State Economic Commission, State Science and Technology Commission, and the Ministry of Agriculture jointly sponsored the National Working Meeting of Biogas and Rural Improving Pilot Counties, which was attended by more than 500 people responsible for rural energy policy in the State Planning Commission, State Economic Commission, State Science and Technology Commission; agricultural bureaus of twenty-nine provinces, municipalities, and autonomous regions; magistrates in charge of stove improvement in the pilot counties; magistrates in charge of the biogas pilot counties; officials from various ministries of the central government; experts from related institutions; and the media. State leaders and Minister of Agriculture He Kang delivered important speeches at the meeting, specifically emphasizing the significance of the use of improved woodstoves and their contribution to rural economic development.

2. **Establishment of pilot units at all levels to demonstrate the benefits of the new stoves to the public.** Actually, pilot counties for improved stoves are found all over the country. They have successfully disseminated improved woodstoves and gained obvious economic benefits in a short time, exerting a great influence over the nearby areas through demonstrations. Similarly, within each pilot county one or two townships have been chosen as demonstration townships. Generally speaking, the pilot counties have implemented the dissemination project in three stages: (1) in the first year, setting up pilot townships; (2) in the second year, extending the project; and (3) in the third year,

completing the project. Within each township, one or two pilot villages have been established for demonstration purposes. The villages will in turn set up pilot households, which are most likely to be those of the village cadres.

3. **Propagandizing improved woodstoves through farmers' own experiences.** In the case of Jiangjin County, some households were at first reluctant to accept the improved stoves because of the deep-rooted tradition of using their old-fashioned stoves. In order to convince the public, a group of farm households which had already adopted improved stoves were organized to tell their stories about the benefits of using the new stoves. Their words were also broadcast on radio and posted on bulletin boards. The stark contrast the farmers reported between the situation before and after the adoption of improved stoves convinced the public. After listening to the stories, many people went to visit the model households in order to see with their own eyes and even try the stoves. Back home, they followed suit and improved their own stoves. This way, stove improvement became a conscious action of the farmers themselves instead of an administrative fiat.

8.8.2. TRAINING

Technical training has been emphasized by the leaders at all levels in the dissemination of improved stoves. As a result, a number of technical personnel have been trained, and 420,000 farmers received training across the country in 1988. In the pilot counties alone, a million farmers have attended the training courses over the past six years. A technical contingent has been sent to the pilot counties to help improve the stoves as well as to transfer the technology to other locales. This has played an important role in the national campaign to disseminate the new stoves.

8.9. ACCEPTABILITY TEST

In order to guarantee the quality of the dissemination programs, the Department of Environmental Protection and Energy under the Ministry of Agriculture has set up standards for improved woodstoves, including testing methods for stoves. This department is also responsible for conducting the acceptability test in the pilot counties which have completed their projects.

1. **Standards of acceptability for pilot counties.** The number of households using improved woodstoves must be over 90 percent of all farm

households in a county. Over 90 percent of the stoves must have a thermal efficiency of more than 18 percent (14 percent for stoves connected to brick beds). Random sampling is adopted during the test. A boiling test must be conducted in thirty households, and at least 200 users must be investigated. Among the total number of tested stoves, 90 percent must meet the standards for the county to pass the acceptability test.

In order to further improve the quality of improved woodstoves and ensure their installation, a new standard for the acceptability test was added to the original one in 1988, that over 50 percent of the improved stoves must use commercially produced components, and the stove performance must be kept at the same level for three years after passing the acceptability test.

2. Testing method for improved woodstoves. A unified and rational testing method is indispensable for further research, production, and dissemination of the new stoves. In 1982, at the request of the Ministry of Agriculture, the Office of Rural Energy Engineering Research and Planning organized a standards-drafting group. After a series of investigations, researches, experiments, tests and verification, and discussion and revision, the State Bureau of Standards issued the "Testing Method of Firewood Stoves for Civil Use and of Heat Performance of Firewood Stoves" (National Standards: GB 4643-84). This testing method can evaluate the actual performance of the stoves. It is also clear-cut and easy to understand for anyone with a middle school education. The test uses simple equipment and instruments. Anyone can quickly master this method after brief training.

8.10. DEVELOPMENT OF THE RURAL ENERGY INDUSTRY FOR IMPROVED STOVES

A rural energy industry has been newly established along with the ongoing reforms in the rural eco-

nomic system and State investment system as well as with the construction and development of rural energy sources. It plays an important role in the dissemination of the improved stoves.

8.10.1. DEVELOPMENT STAGES AND SCALE

Since 1980, China's rural energy industry has gone through several developmental stages — from small-scale to large-scale, from operational to productive, and from products only for rural energy to diversified goods. As a result, the rural energy industry has grown into a production and service system which integrates production, procurement of supplies, marketing, construction, management, and maintenance of rural energy commodities. At the county level, a service network has been established in which the county rural energy service companies serve as the focus, township service stations as the liaison, and the contracting teams as the basis. By 1988, 940 enterprises and 2,230 rural energy service companies had been established under the administration of the Ministry of Agriculture, totalling 110 million yuan of fixed assets, 120 million yuan of circulating funds, 530 million yuan of turnover, 50 million yuan of profit, and 50,000 staff members, including 7,000 technicians and 130,000 workers in the construction teams.

8.10.2. BUSINESS SCOPE

According to the classification of industries, China's rural energy industry belongs to the secondary and tertiary industries level. It includes factories producing goods needed for the construction of rural energy projects, such as raw materials, equipment, tools, lights, stoves, gas piping, and accessories. It also includes the factories for processing and producing commercial fuels; the contracting teams specializing in building biogas pits and manufacturing of improved stoves, as well as their management and maintenance; and the service units providing necessary supplies, facilities, components and technical information.

8.10.3. THE RURAL ENERGY INDUSTRY SYSTEM AND DISSEMINATION OF IMPROVED STOVES

The industrial system of rural energy has played a vital role in the dissemination process insofar as it has (1) ensured the material supplies for the dissemination project by offering an integrated service of production, procurement of supplies, and marketing; (2) provided part of the funds needed for the dissemination projects, such as stove-improving subsidies to poor households; (3) guaranteed the

Table 8.6 Cost of Improved Stoves

| County | Raw material | | Labor | | Total (yuan) |
	Cost (yuan)	Proportion (%)	Cost (yuan)	Proportion (%)	
Zunhua	20.00	70	8.50	30	28.50
Wuhua	40.30	69	18.00	31	58.30
Huangpi	45.00	90	5.00	10	50.00
Jiangjin	66.80	77	19.90	23	86.70
Average	32.03	71	12.85	29	44.88

commercialization of stove components so as to further improve the quality of the new stoves; (4) offered services in stove building, improvement, and repair through contracted management; (5) introduced competition into rural energy service companies, factories, and construction teams to stimulate the enthusiasm of the staff and invigorate the enterprises. Four main types of management are presently used in rural industry: contracting, leasing, joint operation, and "leadership" operation (with one person responsible for the whole factory). Economic means instead of administrative means is used to strengthen the rural energy industry as well as to attract technical personnel.

8.11. FINANCING IMPROVED WOODSTOVES

8.11.1. COST OF STOVES
Differences in the prices of raw materials and labor have resulted in radical differences in the cost of the improved stoves in the four pilot counties, as shown in table 8.6.

It should be noted that the cost of raw materials accounts for approximately 71 percent of the total cost of the stoves and that of labor only 29 percent.

8.11.2. FUNDS FOR THE DISSEMINATION PROJECT
There are three main sources of funds in China's improved stove project (see tables 8.7 and 8.8), that is, (1) funds provided by the state, (2) funds provided by provinces and municipalities, and (3) funds allocated by counties and collected by districts, townships, and the public.

8.12. FUNDAMENTAL EXPERIENCES IN THE DISSEMINATION PROJECTS
1. **Successful reforms have been carried out in the system of dissemination in the selected pilot counties.** The State exerts its control over the project only through the technical contracts in which the duties and responsibilities of the pilot counties are explicitly set forth. The local governments in pilot counties are the authorities responsible for the projects, under the technical guidance of the provincial and municipal offices of rural energy. The county governments then assign the task to townships through a post-responsibility system and prescribe appraisal criteria with planned supplies of materials and funds. The county Offices of Rural Energy are responsible for the operation of the sys-

Table 8.7 State Funding for Stove Dissemination Project

Year	Number of counties	Number of households adopting improved stoves within the year (million)	Total (1,000 yuan)	State financial aid Average per county (1,000 yuan)	State financial aid Average per household (yuan)
1983	90	2.615	8,200	91.11	3.14
1984	200	11.034	8,290	41.45	0.75
1985	100	8.368	6,300	63.00	0.75
1986	97	9.896	2,400	25.00	0.24
1987	101	8.924	2,575	25.00	0.29
1988	96	10.009	2,400	25.00	0.24
Total	**684**	**50.846**	**30,165**	**44.10**	**0.59**

Table 8.8 Source and Allocation of Funds in Jiangjing County, Sechuan Province (1,000 yuan)

Source of funds	Amount 1986	Amount 1987	Amount 1988	1986 R	1986 T	1986 P	1986 B	1987 R	1987 T	1987 P	1987 B	1988 R	1988 T	1988 P	1988 B
State	11	14		2	3	4	2	2	3	2	7	—	—	—	—
County	18.2	5	15	1	8	2	7	1	1	1	2	2	4	2	7
Township	50	40	24	7	20	8	15	5	10	5	20	1	7	2	14
Farmer	2,100	2,352	2,227	1	40	1	2,060	1	40	1	2,312	1	26	1	2,201
Total	**2,179**	**2,411**	**2,266**	**10**	**71**	**14**	**2,084**	**8**	**54**	**8**	**2,341**	**3**	**37**	**4**	**2,222**

Note: R = Research, T = Training, P = Propaganda, and B = Building Stoves.

tem, and they have established a technical contingent to offer technical guidance to households.

2. The excellent technological and economic performance of the improved stoves is welcomed by the farmers. The pilot counties must first choose some stove models with excellent performance suitable to the local farmers' life style and the fuel available. Such choices are based on three criteria — fuel-saving ability, convenience, and hygiene. After the appropriate models have been chosen, a stove-improvement technical contingent is organized composed of farmers, serving farmers, and enjoying trust and satisfaction from farmers. In order to ensure quality control in the improved stoves, standards and testing methods have been established. The testing methods are easy to master and can precisely evaluate the technical performance of the stoves.

3. The industrial system of rural energy has played an important role. In pilot counties, rural energy service companies and/or stations have been set up under the principles of "Self-management, Self-responsible-for-benefit-and-loss, Self-accumulation, Self-improvement, and Self-perfection." All these policies strengthen local economic power, improve service, and contribute to furthering the dissemination of improved woodstoves.

8.13. ANALYSIS OF RESULTS

Compared to biogas and minihydroelectric power, the improved woodstove is better received by farmers due to the smaller investment and the immediate benefits. The benefits of improved stoves can be summarized as follows:

8.13.1. ENERGY CONSERVATION BENEFITS

Although the efficiencies of different types of the new stoves vary widely, the energy savings are remarkable with all of them.

1. Higher Thermal Efficiency

The thermal efficiency of the traditional Chinese stove is around 10 percent. The average thermal efficiency of improved woodstoves, measured by the boiling test in four pilot counties, is around 20 percent, as shown in table 8.9.

2. Large Amount of Biomass Saved

The saving of fuel with the improved stove is generally 30 to 50 percent over the traditional woodstove. Based on a survey of twelve households made by the Office of Rural Energy in Jiangjin County using on-site testing of actual performance in the kitchen, the results are encouraging (see table 8.10). The new stoves can save up to 46.7 percent of the firewood required by the old-fashioned stoves.

Table 8.9 Comparison of Thermal Efficiencies of Stoves

	Zunhua	Wuhua	Huangpi	Jiangjin
Average thermal efficiency of improved wood stove (temperature increase section), %	18.5	30.9	27.44	27.32
Average thermal efficiency of old-fashioned wood stove (temperature increase section), %	9.6	8.3	10.00	14.22
Average increase of thermal efficiency, %	92.7	272.3	174.40	92.10

Table 8.10 Performance Test of Improved and Old-fashioned Stoves

	Improved stove					Old-fashioned stove				
Number of people	3	4	5	6	Total	3	4	5	6	Total
Houses surveyed	1	2	2	1	6	1	2	2	1	6
Number of pigs*	3	9	8	3	23	3	6	6	3	18
Test items:										
Rice cooked, kg	11.4	29.25	36.55	19.15	96.35	10	28.9	43	25.25	107.4
Vegetable, kg	9.25	40	36.05	26.25	111.55	7.85	53.45	30.45	27.5	119.25
Green feed, kg.*	0	296.5	87.15	105.5	489.15	0	414	175.5	131.9	721.4
Concentrated feed, kg*	0	20.5	0	9	29.5	0	28.5	22.75	0	51.25
Water, kg	170.65	476.15	347.05	220.75	1,214.6	209.85	660	693.4	309.5	1,872.25
Test time, min.	437	1,718	1,480	1,559	5,194	533	2,554	3,940	1,316	8,343
Fuel consumed, kg	25.8	118.95	99.35	82.1	326.2	68.5	187.85	230.35	118.85	578.35
Percentage of fuel conserved, in % of consumption in old-style stoves	62.3	36.7	56.8	30.9	43.6					

*In Chinese rural families, pig raising is an important side-production activity. As a result, a considerable portion of household energy is used for cooking the food for the pigs.

Using the same method, two households with stoves connected to brick beds in Zhulian Township of Tong Yuan County were compared. The test showed that a new stove linked with a heatable brick bed can save about 34 percent of the biomass fuel used by a traditional stove.

8.13.2. SOCIAL BENEFITS
1. Improved Hygienic Conditions
As chimneys and grates have been installed in improved stoves, the combustion of firewood can be greatly enhanced. As a result, smoke can be reduced, and hygiene conditions in rural kitchens are substantially improved. Therefore, these stoves are well received by women in rural areas.

Due to the improved kitchen hygiene, the incidence of some diseases has notably decreased. Based on a survey by the public health department of Huangpi County, the incidence of ophthalmological and respiratory tract infections in rural areas of the county was reduced by more than 30 percent and 20 percent, respectively, after dissemination of the new stoves.

2. Improved Social Order
Before the arrival of the improved stove, poor farmers had to exert great effort to get enough firewood for cooking and heating. As a result, illegal cutting of trees and stealing of coal often occurred. After dissemination of the new stoves, such incidents were remarkably reduced. Thus the improved stoves played an active part in maintaining social order. For instance, farmers in Xiaba Township, Jiangjin County, had been stealing coal from the trains and cutting trees along the highways and railways. After the dissemination of improved stoves, coal-stealing and deforestation were reduced year by year.

3. Saved Cooking Time
Much time can be saved in cooking with the new woodstoves. From the survey conducted by the Rural Energy Resources Office of Jiangjin County (see table 8.10), it was reported that each household saved an average 87 minutes per day over that needed in cooking with the old stove, 53 labor-days per year. If these labor-days are utilized in sideline agricultural production, greater economic benefit can be created.

4. Reduced Fuel Collection
Since the improved stoves can save a lot of firewood, the work spent to collect firewood can be reduced, too. According to the statistics, an average household can save about 38 days of work per year. For instance, the Fifth Economic Cooperative in Xinhua Village, Jiangjin County, comprises 31 households

and 135 people. Before 1986, the cooperatives had to purchase 23 tons of coal each year in addition to all the agricultural wastes and firewood they used as fuel. Since April 1987, 29 households have installed the new stoves, and they have become completely self-sufficient using biomass as fuel. Coal is no longer used. Twenty-seven of the households have even destroyed their old coal stoves. In addition, this economic cooperative saved 1,178 labor-days every year, averaging 40.6 labor-days each household per year previously used to collect fuel. The savings of coal amounts to 2,294 yuan RMB.

8.13.3. ECOLOGICAL BENEFITS
In recent years, ecological disruption has been better controlled in most areas where improved woodstoves have been installed.

1. Protecting Reforestation
In rural areas where improved woodstoves have been disseminated, the critical cooking fuel problem is basically solved. Farmers need not collect large amounts of firewood or dig sod to burn. Forest resources are thus protected and reforestation can be carried out more smoothly. The rate of forest coverage has increased year by year. For instance, forest coverage increased from 28.3 percent in 1985 to 29.6 percent in 1987 in Zunhua, Hebei Province. Since 1986, the planting of forest and fruit trees in Wuhua County, Guangdong Province, has reached 1 million mu (66.7 thousand hectares); and at the same time, other natural vegetation has been restored. Unused land has been gradually covered by grass.

The rate of forest coverage in Huangpi, Hubei Province, was 14.7 percent in 1980, constituting 242,000 cubic meters of wood. By 1985 forest coverage had increased to 17.6 percent, and the total accumulated amount of wood was 318,700 cubic meters. In Jiangjin, Sechuan Province, the rate of forest coverage had been reduced from 23.39 percent to 8.9 percent over the twenty-seven years between 1951 and 1977. Since the beginning of dissemination of the improved stoves in 1980, the county government has emphasized forest plantation, and the forest coverage rose to 19.5 percent in 1988.

2. Enhancing Soil Fertility
Since less agricultural waste was burned for fuel after the availability of improved stoves, more organic matter could be returned to the soil. As a result, the organic content of the soil has been increased and soil fertility enhanced. According to a survey conducted by the Agricultural Department of Huangpi County, the organic content in the soil increased from 3.62 percent in 1982 to 4.78 percent in 1985.

8.13.4. ECONOMIC BENEFITS

The economic benefit of improved woodstoves is greater than biogas and small hydropower stations. It is characterized by quick return with much less investment.

1. Financial Analysis

Detailed financial analysis has been conducted on the improved stove of the Zunhua 86-II type used by one farm household in Zunhua County, in Hebei Province. The result is shown in table 8.11. The total cost of building the stove amounted to 22.5 yuan. The maintenance cost is estimated at 1 yuan per year and the savings of fuel at 80 yuan per year. Thus, the payback period for this type of improved stove is as short as 104 days!

Similar analyses in Jiangjing County are shown in tables 8.12 through 8.14. Improved stoves which are renovated from existing, old-style stoves have short lifetimes (three years compared to ten for the ready-built improved stoves), but the investment and maintenance costs are both lower. As a result, there is much more annual net profit (199.3 yuan per stove, as against 130.65 yuan for a new stove, as shown in table 8.14).

2. Input and Output Analysis

Starting in 1983, China began to expand the improved stove project and has cumulatively disseminated them to 99.16 million households. What has been the economic outcome of this progress? From table 8.15 it can be seen that all investment was returned within one year. As a result, such a program could be self-financing. From table 8.16, it can be seen that the investment in the improved stoves could be recouped within one year. This is an important reason for the rapid dissemination of the stoves.

3. Indirect Economic Benefits

A. Some of the agricultural waste saved with use of the new stoves became raw materials for developing handicraft industries in rural areas. The income of farm households was therefore increased and the rural market economy diversified. For example, in Baiyieshu Village of Huangpi County, the straw that would have been burned in the past for fuel was used to weave straw bags and ropes, and 103 households in this village thus created an annual revenue of 100,000 yuan.

B. The labor saved from collecting fuel was used to develop agriculture and a courtyard economy, and hence the income of rural households was further increased. For instance, farmer Cao Neng Zhu's household of the No. 2 Cooperative of Meiwan Village, Jiangjin

Table 8.11 Materials and Labor for Building Stoves in Zunhua County

	Quantity	Cost (yuan)
Brick (pieces)	80	8
Lime (kg)	25	1.8
Hemp (kg)	1	1
Sand (m³)	0.1	0.7
Grate	1	2.5
Skilled labor (labor-day)	1	5
Labor (labor-day)	1	3.5

Table 8.12 Cost of Improved Stoves in Jiangjin County

	Newly built improved stove	Improved stove renovated from existing stove
Cost/expenses (yuan/per unit)		
Materials cost	61.85	8.2
Labor cost	17.5	3.5
Total	79.35	11.7
Cost for annual maintenance (yuan/per unit)	2	1
Period of usefulness (years)	10	3

Table 8.13 Annual Savings from Improved Stoves in Jiangjin

	Newly built improved stove	Improved stove renovated from existing stove
Annual saved firewood (kg)	1,200	1,200
Market price for firewood (yuan/kg)	0.06	0.06
Annual cost of firewood (yuan)	72	72
Annual saved labor (labor-days)	40	40
Cost for labor (yuan/labor-day)	3.5	3.5
Annual saved labor cost (yuan)	140	140

Table 8.14 Total Profit from Improved Stoves in Jiangjin

	Newly built improved stove	Improved stove renovated from existing stove	Total
Total improved wood stoves (1,000)	50	229	279
Investment (1,000 yuan)	3,967.5	2,679.3	6,646.8
Annual saved fuel cost (1,000 yuan)	3,600	16,488	20,088
Annual saved labor cost (1,000 yuan)	7,000	32,060	39,060
Annual maintenance cost (1,000 yuan)	100	229	329
Annual net profit (1,000 yuan)	6,532.5	45,639.7	52,172.2

County, formerly had to use one full day per week to collect firewood. After using the new stove, the household supply of biomass fuel was basically sufficient, and the farmer could use half of his work time to raise ducks and thus create an additional annual income of more than 400 yuan. In Minhe Village of this same county, the surplus labor force enthusiastically took part in developing the courtyard economy of silkworm breeding. In 1988, this village became one of the key silk cocoon production villages in the whole county.

C. Most of the crop residue formerly used for fuel was now returned to fields as fertilizer. As a result, agricultural production increased. Farmer Li Zhugao of the No. 4 Cooperative of Longfeng Village, Jiangjin County, built an improved stove in 1986. He then was able to use surplus stalks as basic fertilizer in his orange orchard. The output of oranges was increased about 14 percent for two years in succession, and the quality of oranges was also better than before. In Huangpi County, farmers used the

straw saved to cultivate mushrooms, and the residue was put into a biogas digester. Eventually the slurry was used as fertilizer or to feed pigs or fish. In this way, a benign ecological cycle from agriculture was established.

8.14. STUDY OF PROSPECTS FOR DISSEMINATION OF IMPROVED STOVES

Remarkable benefits in economy, ecology, and energy have been gained from the improved woodstove in China. It is therefore necessary to sum up the experience and lessons of what has been done in the past few years and, further, to study the future development and strategy for the dissemination of the new stoves. Since the dissemination program is implemented at the county level, Zunhua County of Hebei Province has been taken as an example. A system dynamic model is used to simulate and study quantitatively the press of disseminating the improved stove. In this study, policies and measures implemented and their effective-

Table 8.15 Disseminating Improved Stoves in China

Item / Year	1983	1984	1985	1986	1987	1988	Total
Investment in building stoves (1,000 yuan)	282,243	880,558	759,730	782,085	766,445	743,368	4,214,429
Total number of stoves disseminated this year* (1,000)	6,441	20,719	17,876	18,402	18,034	17,491	99,163
Accumulated number of stoves disseminated by year end (1,000)	6,641	27,360	45,236	63,638	81,672	99,163	
Average cost for improved wood stoves** (yuan/per unit)	42.5	42.5	42.5	42.5	42.5	42.5	
Average usage of firewood per year (kg/per unit)	2,000	2,000	2,000	2,000	2,000	2,000	
Average saved firewood per year (kg/per unit)	1,000	1,000	1,000	1,000	1,000	1,000	
Average price for firewood (yuan/kg)	0.06	0.06	0.06	0.06	0.06	0.06	
Average saved labor per year (labor-day/per unit)	40	40	40	40	40	40	
Average price for labor force (yuan/labor-day)	3.5	3.5	3.5	3.5	3.5	3.5	
Average cost of maintenance per year (yuan/per unit)	1.5	1.5	1.5	1.5	1.5	1.5	
Average service life (years)	6	6	6	6	6	6	

* On the basis of improved stove for each household.
** The funds used for disseminating improved stoves, and the ratio of investment by the county, the local government, and the farmers was 1:8:140. By the end of 1988, the accumulated investment by the county was 30.165 million yuan, 241.32 million yuan by local government, and 4,223.1 million yuan by local people. These funds were basically used for building and improving stoves, and the average cost for each improved wood stove was 42.5 yuan.

Table 8.16 Total Profit from Improved Stoves Disseminated in China (million yuan)

Item / Year	1983	1984	1985	1986	1987	1988	Total
Total annual value of saved firewood	398.460	1,641.600	2,714.160	3,818.280	4,900.320	5,949.780	19,422.6000
Total annual value of saved labor	929.740	3,830.400	6,333.040	8,909.320	11,434.000	13,882.820	45,319.3200
Total annual investment in improved stoves	282.243	880.558	759.730	782.085	766.445	743.368	421.4429
Total annual cost of maintenance	9.962	41.040	67.854	95.457	122.508	148.745	485.5660
Total annual profit	**1,035.995**	**4,550.402**	**8,219.616**	**11,850.060**	**15,445.370**	**18,940.490**	**60,041.9300**

Fig. 8.3 System Flow Diagram of Improved Stoves in Zunhua County

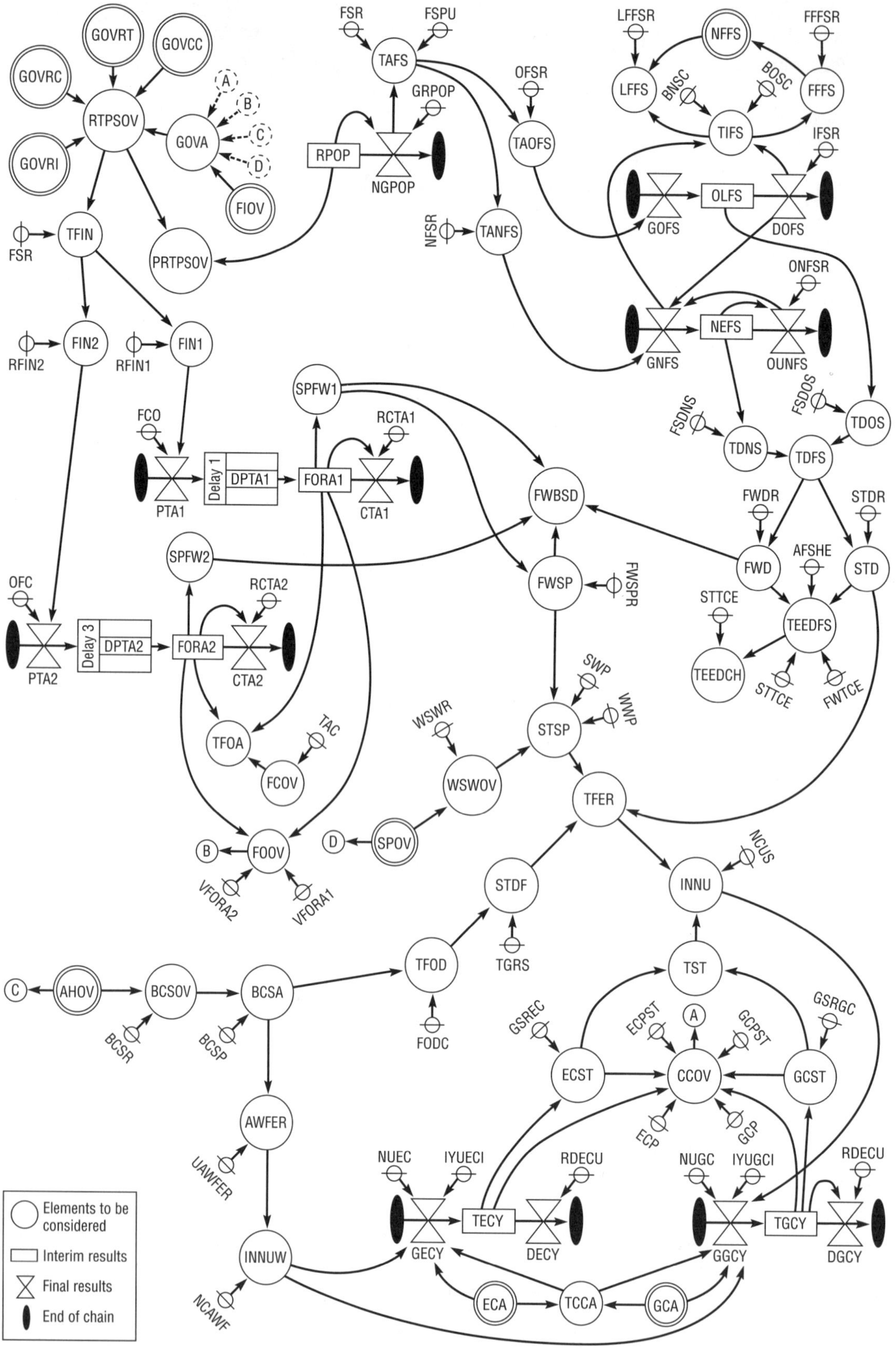

Acronyms for Main Variables Used in Figure 8.3

AHOV	Animal husbandry output value		NGPOP	Net increase of rural population
AWFER	Animal manure output		OLSF	Total number of old-fashioned stoves
BCSA	Large animals and sheep and goats in stock		OUNFS	Number of worn-out improved stoves
BCSOV	Output value of large animals and sheep and goats		PTA1	Firewood afforestation area
			PTA2	Afforestation area of other tree species
CCOV	Crop cultivation output value		RPOP	Total rural population
CTA1	Cutting area of firewood forest		RTPSOV	Rural total social product output value
CTA2	Cutting area of other tree species		SPOV	Sideline production output value
DCCY	Yearly output decrease of cash crop		SPW1	Firewood supply from firewood forest
DGCY	Yearly output decrease of grain crop		SPW2	Firewood supply from other tree species
DOFS	Number of old-fashioned stoves reduced		STD	Primary straw demand
DPTA1	Delayed variables of order 1		STDF	Straw demand in fodder for large animals and sheep
DPTA2	Delayed variables of order 2		STSP	Straw demand from side production
ECA	Cash crop area		TAFS	Total stove number for increased population
ECST	Economic (cash) crop straw ourput			
FCOV	Forestry coverage percentage		TCCA	Total crop area sown
FFFS	Users' investment in improved stove construction each year		TDFS	Total primary energy demand of firewood, crop straw
FIN1	Firewood forest investment		TDNS	Total primary energy demand of firewood, crop straw for improved stoves
FIN2	Investment in other tree species		TDOS	Total primary energy demand of firewood, crop straw for old-fashioned stoves
FIOV	Fishery output value			
FOOV	Forestry output value			
FORA1	Firewood forest growing area		TECY	Total ourput of cash crop
FORA2	Growing area of other tree species		TEEDCH	End use for cooking and heating
FWBSD	Gap between firewood supply and demand		TEEDFS	End use for stoves
			TFCY	Total grain crop yield
FWD	Primary firewood demand		TFER	Total amount of straw for field fertilizer
FWSP	Firewood demand for processing of side production		TFIN	Total forestry investment
			TFOA	Total forestry area
GCA	Grain crop area		TFOD	Large animal and sheep and goats fodder demand
GCST	Grain crop straw output			
GECY	Yearly output increase of cash crop		TGFS	Total stove number for increased population
GGCY	Yearly output increase of grain crop			
GNFS	Increase of improved firewood stoves		TGNFS	Total number of new stoves for increased population
GOFS	Number of newly built old-fashioned stoves			
			TGOFS	Total number of old-fashioned stoves for increased population
GOVA	Gross output value of agriculture			
GOVCC	Gross output value of commerce and catering trade		TIFS	Total investment in improved stove construction each year
GOVRC	Gross output value of rural construction		TST	Total straw output
GOVRI	Gross output value of rural industry			
GOVRT	Gross output value of rural transportation			
INNU	Increase of nutrients through straw returning to fields			
NEFS	Total number of improved stoves			
NFFS	State investment in improved stove construction each year			

ness are analyzed. In doing so, the future development of improved stoves can be studied with the aim of formulating dissemination programs and concrete policies.

8.14.1. A SYSTEM DYNAMICS MODEL AND THE STUDY TOPICS

The improved woodstove, as a device for cooking in farm households, is not a complicated technology in itself. However, improvement and dissemination of such stoves are not only closely associated with fuel consumption in hundreds of thousands of families in rural areas but are also connected to rural population control, rural economic development, and the environment. Meanwhile, sizable funds must be provided and adequate methods worked out for the dissemination of the new stove. Hence the objective of establishing a system dynamic simulated model is to study the various factors which influence the diffusion.

Figure 8.3 gives the causal diagram in disseminating improved stoves in the system dynamic simulation for Zunhua County. It is clear in this figure that the number of stoves is positively connected with the growth of population. Financial resources are also a constraint in terms of the growth rate of the economy. The crop residues and firewood used in improved stoves can alternatively be used as livestock feed and as raw materials for sideline production. On top of this, the use of crop wastes and firewood is closely associated with development of forests and timber production. Therefore, the rational use of straw, crop residues, and wood as fuel is related to rural economic growth and the improvement of the local ecology. Through this model, the following aspects can be studied in detail:

— Methodology of the dissemination of improved woodstoves
— Cost of building improved stoves and the sources of funds
— Development of timber production and the growth of forests as well as the improvement of natural environment

The dissemination of improved woodstoves in Zunhua County was started in 1986, and 1985 was therefore set as the base year. The study will cover fifteen years, up to the year 2000. Both positive and negative outcomes from the stove program will be observed and studied. Several options for disseminating the new stoves have been proposed for comparison and selection. Figure 8.3 is the system flow chart of this model.

Table 8.17 Benefits from the Dissemination of Improved Stoves

Year	TRSPOV (10^6 yuan)	New stoves (1,000)	Stove investment (1,000 yuan)	Forest coverage (%)
1985	753.3	—	—	28.3
1986	884.7	147.24	4,277.61	28.8
1987	1,041.0	222.59	2,620.01	29.4
1988	1,227.0	262.01	1,796.88	29.5
1989	1,415.0	283.50	3,791.06	29.7
1990	1,602.0	296.04	1,193.97	29.9
1991	1,791.0	304.13	1,101.30	30.1
1992	1,980.0	310.01	1,046.75	30.3
1993	2,169.0	314.81	1,045.76	30.4
1994	2,360.0	319.10	1,051.43	30.6
1995	2,550.0	323.14	1,060.51	30.9
1996	2,742.0	327.10	1,060.51	31.1
1997	2,934.0	331.03	1,071.37	31.8
1998	3,126.0	334.96	1,083.19	32.1
1999	3,320.0	338.93	1,095.57	32.5
2000	3,514.0	342.94	1,108.31	32.8

Note: TRSPOV = Total Rural Social Product Output Value.

Table 8.18 Supply and Demand for Straw and Stalks

Year	Yield (1,000 ton)	Fuel (1,000 ton)	Raw material (1,000 ton)	Fodder (1,000 ton)
1985	742.84	317.85	1.70	88.43
1986	763.79	267.48	4.80	110.06
1987	785.11	243.57	5.21	142.03
1988	807.23	232.91	6.73	165.20
1989	831.75	228.89	8.23	198.37
1990	857.47	228.20	9.74	231.54
1991	884.41	229.20	11.24	264.71
1992	912.59	231.05	12.74	297.88
1993	942.03	233.35	14.23	331.05
1994	972.77	235.89	15.72	364.22
1995	1,004.84	238.56	17.21	397.39
1996	1,038.27	241.32	18.69	430.55
1997	1,073.11	244.14	20.17	463.72
1998	1,109.38	247.01	21.65	496.89
1999	1,147.13	249.91	23.13	530.06
2000	1,186.39	252.86	24.61	563.23

Some calculation results of the simulation model of Zunhua County are shown in tables 8.17 and 8.18. The number of new stoves built will be more than doubled (see table 8.17). The ecological benefit is obvious too; for example, forest coverage will increase from 28.3 percent in 1985 to 32.8 percent in 2000, a high figure in China. The straw used as fodder and raw materials will increase so much that the rural total products will be quadrupled from 1986 to 2000, as shown in table 8.18, while that consumed as fuel will decrease. These figures show a bright future resulting from the dissemination of the improved stoves.

8.15. POLICY RECOMMENDATIONS

The improved stove dissemination program in China is considered a vital part of a long-term strategic rural energy development program. After the next ten years' efforts, from 1990 to 2000, the new stoves will be made available to the remaining half of China's farm households. It should be emphasized here that various measures must be taken to ensure that the existing improved stoves maintain good performance so as to consolidate the program's achievements. Some concrete measures are as follows:

1. The State should continue to select new pilot counties in a planned way and implement supporting policies to provide funds and materials for the construction of improved stoves in the nation's economic development program. Zero-interest or low-interest loans should be made available to the farmers willing to build the improved stoves. Taxes on the rural energy industry engaged in the manufacture and marketing of improved stoves and spare parts should be reduced or eliminated for a period of time.

2. A system should be developed to provide equipment and technical services for the new stoves. Manufacturing capacity should be developed step by step to produce more stoves of better performance and their spare parts.

3. Research on improved woodstoves should be pursued, and technical staff should be organized to disseminate new techniques and assist in stove-building. The commercial production of improved stoves should be standardized and encouraged.

4. Testing standards and methods should be improved and perfected. A comprehensive standards system should be set up for evaluating the performance of the improved stoves.

CHAPTER 9

ENERGY AUDITS AND CONSERVATION RECOMMENDATIONS IN FIVE DEMONSTRATION PLANTS

9.1. SELECTION OF DEMONSTRATION PLANTS

In order to gain more experience in energy conservation in a variety of different industrial subsectors, three energy-intensive subsectors, one high economic output subsector, and one energy-producing subsector were selected as representative of industry for this energy conservation research project. (For more details of this case study, see references 59, 60, 138, 161, 171, and 201.)

An analysis of the current status of the energy intensity of various industrial subsectors was made to identify the representative sectors and choose a demonstration plant in each sector for the study.

The shares of the output value and the energy consumption of different subsectors in industry are listed in table 9.1. It is noted that the machine building, textile, chemical, and food processing industries are relatively high output sectors, and the chemical, metallurgical, building materials, and machine building industries consume more energy than the others. Table 9.2 illustrates the energy intensities of the various subsectors, indicating that the building materials, paper-making, metallurgical, and chemical industries are the most energy intensive. Accordingly, due in part to the availability of data, the building materials, chemicals, paper-pulp, textiles, and refinery industry sectors have been selected as the five representatives. The next step is to identify the representative product and demonstration plant in each subsector.

The building materials industry is an important raw-materials producing sector. The major products are cement, plate glass, and brick, making up 65 percent of the total output value and 90 per-

cent of total energy consumption of this sector. Cement and cement products make up 35 percent of the sectoral energy consumption; plate glass, 3.5 percent; and brick, 53 percent. Because of the availability of data, cement was selected as the typical product of the sector for this study. Two hundred million tons of cement were produced in China in

Table 9.1 Shares of Output Value and Energy Consumption of Various Industrial Subsectors in China, 1987

	Share of net output value, %	Share of energy consumption, %
Coal mining and dressing	2.92	5.84
Petroleum and natural gas extraction	5.00	2.97
Food, beverages, and tobacco	10.64	4.93
Textiles	9.23	4.52
Paper making	1.80	2.52
Power and heat generation	4.52	5.05
Petroleum processing	3.72	2.31
Coke, gas, and coal products	0.17	1.33
Chemicals	6.64	16.39
Medical and pharmaceutical industry	1.66	0.97
Chemical fibers	1.15	1.17
Building materials	6.11	15.37
Smelting and pressing of ferrous metals	6.51	15.12
Smelting and pressing of nonferrous metals	1.76	2.64
Machine building, electric equipment, and electronics	20.96	7.44

Table 9.2 Energy Intensities of Industrial Subsectors in China, 1987

	Energy intensity kgce/yuan
Coal mining and dressing	3.36
Petroleum and natural gas extraction	0.94
Food, beverages, and tobacco	0.78
Textiles	0.83
Paper making	2.36
Power and heat generation	1.88
Petroleum processing	1.04
Coke, gas, and coal products	12.85
Chemicals	4.16
Medical and pharmaceutical industry	0.98
Chemical fibers	1.72
Building materials	4.34
Smelting and pressing of ferrous metals	3.92
Smelting and pressing of nonferrous metals	2.53
Machine building, electric equipment, and electronics	0.60

Table 9.3 Energy Consumption for Cement Clinker Production

	Energy consumption (kcal/kg clinker)
Wet Process	
China	1,400
Advanced technology level	1,250-1,300
Dry Process	
With long-length kiln	900-1,000
With preheater	750-800

1988, of which 20 percent came from large and medium-size plants and 80 percent from small plants. Of the fifty-nine large and medium-size plants in China, six contributed an annual production of more than a million tons and the remaining fifty-three medium-size plants annually produced 500,000 to a million tons. About 5,000 small-scale plants annually produced 10,000 to 20,000 tons.

Technology in the Chinese cement industry is backward. Most of the plants were based on technology of the 1940s and 1950s, only a few operating at 1960s and 1970s levels. More than 60 percent of the large and medium-size cement plants were using the wet process for making cement, which has a high specific energy consumption. Table 9.3 lists the energy consumption of different processes in cement production. Based on this analysis, one of the medium-size plants using the wet process, the Datong Cement Mill, was selected as a demonstration plant to represent the situation of most large- and medium-scale plants using the wet process in China.

The Chinese chemicals industry is a multi-subsector, multi-product, energy-intensive sector. More than 40,000 varieties of products are made, including synthetic ammonia, soda, calcium carbide, and sulfuric acid. In 1987 the output of synthetic ammonia was 19.4 million tons, caustic soda 2.74 million tons, calcium carbide 2.41 million tons, and sulfuric acid 9.83 million tons. These products consumed 70 to 80 percent of the total energy used by the chemicals industry. The energy consumed in

synthetic ammonia production alone accounted for more than 40 percent. Therefore, chemical fertilizer was selected as the typical product of the chemical industry for this project.

The proportion of ammonia production in fertilizer plants of different sizes are as follows: 22 percent from large plants, 23 percent from medium-size plants, and 55 percent from small plants. The raw materials used in these plants are coal, oil, and natural gas, coal making up 65 percent of the total.

Large-scale ammonia plants have adopted more advanced technologies. These plants were imported in the 1970s and use natural gas as the raw material. Their specific energy consumption is substantially lower than for older plants. Among sixty-five medium-size chemical fertilizer plants, thirty-four used coal and coke as raw material and twenty-two used oil and natural gas. The energy consumption per unit product of different size plants and the comparable levels in advanced countries are listed in table 9.4. Based on the above analysis, one of the medium-size plants using coal as raw material, the Shijiazhuang chemical fertilizer plant, was selected as the demonstration chemical plant for this study.

The pulp- and paper-making industry is also an energy-intensive one. In 1987, the more than 10,000 paper/pulp mills in China produced 11.41 million tons of paper. One hundred eighty-nine large mills, with an annual output of more than 10,000 tons of paper, contributed 40 percent of the total paper production in China. At most Chinese mills, the technology of paper-making remains at 1940s-50s levels, and only a few use 1960s-70s technologies. The Qiqihar mill, a large paper/pulp plant, was selected for this study.

Refining is an important subsector of the petroleum industry. China has thirty-seven oil refineries, with a total annual throughput of more than 100 million tons of crude oil. Twenty-eight large refineries, each with an annual throughput of more than a million tons, account for 95 percent of the

Table 9.4 Unit Energy Consumption of Ammonia Production by Different Processes and Plant Sizes

| | Unit energy consumption (million kcal/ton ammonia) | | | | |
| | Domestic | | Abroad | | |
	Average (A)	Advanced (B)	Advanced (C)	A/B	A/C
Large plant					
Oil	9.81	9.81	8.50	1.00	1.15
Natural gas	9.70	9.70	7.00	1.00	1.40
Medium plant					
Coal	16.16	14.41	12.03	1.12	1.34
Coke	15.32	13.54	—	1.13	—
Oil	15.13	13.61	9.72	1.11	1.56
Natural gas	12.38	11.36	9.82	1.09	1.26
Average	15.64				

national production. In view of the prominent role of large refineries in China, the Beijing Dongfanghong refinery, the biggest one in China, was chosen as the demonstration plant for this study.

China's textile industry has a high economic output. It includes a number of subsectors, such as cotton, wool, and linen textiles; chemical fibers; printing and dyeing; textile machine manufacture; and knitting. Cotton textile manufacture is the backbone of the industry, making up 55.3 percent of total output value in 1987. Table 9.5 shows the 1980 energy consumption of various textiles subsectors. Table 9.6 shows the unit energy consumption in cotton textile manufacture and the comparison with levels in technologically more advanced countries. Due to the different levels of process mechanization and automation, electricity consumption in foreign textile plants is much higher than in Chinese factories. But labor input in Chinese textile plants is much higher, estimated at 250 times that in Europe.

There are more than 3,000 cotton textile plants in China. From the 100 large plants, Beijing No. 2 Cotton Textile Plant was selected for this study.

9.2. PRELIMINARY ENERGY AUDIT

9.2.1. DATONG CEMENT MILL

This plant is located in the town of Kouquan, Datong City, Shanxi Province, and covers an area of 1.446 square kilometers. It was built in 1954 with equipment supplied by the German Democratic Republic and began operating in 1957. The mill was enlarged in 1959 and now consists of six main workshops — mining, raw materials, sintering, grinding, packing, and a special vertical kiln work-

Table 9.5 Energy Consumption by Subsectors in Textile Industry

	Energy consumption Mtce	Ratio %
Textiles (Total)	16.60	100.00
Chemical fibers	4.58	27.60
Printing and dyeing	2.74	16.50
Textile-machine building	0.35	2.20
Cotton textiles and others	8.89	53.70

Table 9.6 Unit Electricity Consumption in Cotton Textiles

	Cotton yarn kWh/ton	Cotton cloth kWh/km
Unit overall productive energy consumption		
Domestic (1984)	1,900	220
Abroad (1980)	3,040	340

shop. In addition, it has three auxiliary workshops — machine repair, power, and water and heating control. There are 2,508 employees in this mill, among which 1,507 are workers.

Either of two basic processes — wet or dry — may be used in making cement. Datong Cement Mill uses the wet process in four rotary kilns, which produced 680,000 tons of cement in 1986. Overall unit energy consumption was 226.6 kgce per ton clinker and 225.17 kgce per ton cement, and unit electricity consumption was 107.9 kWh per ton. Both unit energy figures are a little higher than the average indexes in the cement industry in China.

Total energy consumption in the mill was 152,000 tce in 1986. Figure 9.1 is an energy flow diagram of the mill in that year. Seventy-five percent of the energy was consumed by the four rotary kilns; the average heat consumption was 1,628.4

Fig. 9.1 Energy Flow Diagram of Datong Cement Mill in 1986

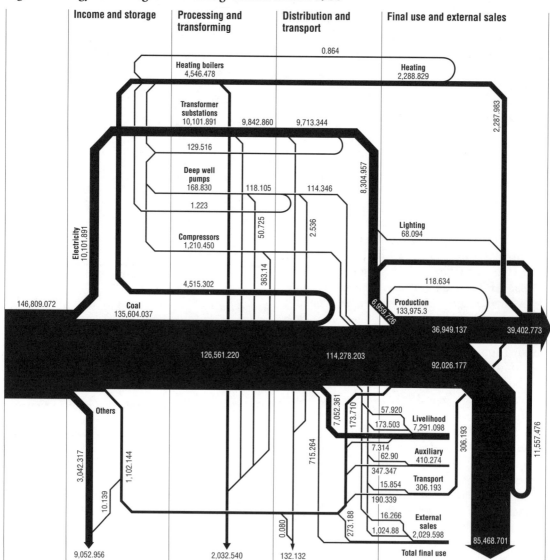

kcal/kg clinker, which is higher than the average national energy consumption level, 1,330 kcal/kg clinker. The accountable efficiency of these kilns was only 26.38 percent, as shown in table 9.7, much lower than that of advanced kilns. Overall energy consumption per unit cement production in this mill is 15 percent higher than the average in similar mills in China and 80 percent higher than that in technologically advanced mills. After a detailed analysis of the energy consumed in various processes, the following energy conservation recommendations can be made:

1. Change from wet process to dry process. The energy consumed in evaporating water amounts to 486.3 kcal/kg clinker (see table

9.10), corresponding to 29.52 percent of the total energy consumed, or 110 percent of the effective energy used for production. Additional energy is needed to draw water from deep wells (figure 9.1). The most important conservation measure would therefore be conversion to use of the dry process, although replacement of major equipment would be required.

2. Improve insulation of the kiln body to reduce heat radiation loss. Heat loss from the surface of the kiln accounts for the second-largest waste of energy input, that is, about 14.07 percent of the total energy consumption, or 53 percent of the effective energy (see table 9.7). Better insulation would dramatically reduce this loss.

Table 9.7 Energy Balance of Cement Kilns at Datong Cement Plant

	kcal/kg	%
Heat input		
Chemical heat of fuel	1,560.30	95.82
Physical heat in fuel	3.00	0.18
Physical heat in dry raw material	10.20	0.63
Physical heat in liquid material	24.50	1.50
Heating of primary air	7.60	0.47
Heating of secondary air	11.30	0.69
Heating of draining air	4.30	0.26
Heat brought in by ash	7.20	0.44
Heat input total	**1,628.40**	**99.99**
Heat output		
Heat for producing clinker	418.62	26.38
Heating for water and steam	468.30	29.52
Physical heat absorbed by clinker	94.70	5.97
Heat emitted from kiln surface	223.30	14.07
Heat brought in by ash	33.40	2.11
Chemical energy loss due to incomplete combustion	26.60	1.68
Physical heat loss due to incomplete combustion	76.14	4.80
Heat brought out by waste gas	241.20	15.20
Steam for heating water and coal powder	4.40	0.28
Heat output total	**1,586.60**	**100.00**
Excess heat	41.8	2.63

3. Utilize heat contained in the flue gases to preheat the feed. Heat wasted in the escape of hot flue gas amounts to 223.3 kcal/kg clinker, or 57.6 percent of the effective energy. One conservation measure already adopted in the Datong mill is the incorporation of moving heat-resistant steel chains as heat storage in the flue gas channel inside the kiln; the absorbed heat is used to preheat the feed. It is expected that 35 percent of the waste heat in flue gas can be recovered with this measure.

4. Decrease the temperature of clinker formation to reduce the heat loss in hot clinker. It has been found that the addition of small amounts of tailing and cinders can reduce the formation temperature of the clinker.

5. Increase the primary air feed speed and the thickness of the coal layer to enhance combustion.

Other conservation measures in the operation of powder mills and energy management in general have also been recommended.

9.2.2. SHIJIAZHUANG CHEMICAL FERTILIZER PLANT

This medium-size plant was built in 1957, using coal as raw material. Its annual production capacity for synthetic ammonia in 1988 was 133,000 tons. There are 3,796 employees in this plant, including 500 technicians.

The total energy consumption in the plant in 1988 was 404,000 tce, of which 73.7 percent was coal and coke. Electricity consumption was 263.5 GWh that year. The energy consumed in manufacturing various products is listed in table 9.8. Ammonia was the major product, accounting for 75.7 percent of the total energy used. The specific energy consumption of ammonia was 16.36 Gcal per ton NH_3, nearly the same as the average for medium-size fertilizer plants in China. The details of energy consumption by processes and energy sources are listed in table 9.9.

Due to poor management, the gap between the specific energy consumption of NH_3 in this plant and that in technologically advanced Chinese plants was 100 percent. Even the best record of the specific energy consumption of NH_3 in China is 30 percent higher than for technologically advanced factories elsewhere in the world. Thus, great potential for energy conservation exists in this fertilizer plant.

The following recommendations have been made by the audit team:

1. Improve the gasification process. Energy consumed in the gasification process accounts for about 62 percent of total consumption (table 9.12). The observed efficiency of the gasifier is only 55 to 60 percent, and the effective carbon utilization is also 55 to 60 percent. To increase the efficiency of the gasifier (a) the residue carbon in slag (about 16 percent by weight) should be utilized as boiler fuel, (b) superheated steam should replace saturated steam to increase the steam decomposition rate and the thermal efficiency, and (c) the newly designed, high-efficiency water gas generator should be adopted.

2. Adopt the pressurized conversion process to replace the atmospheric conversion process in order to reduce the compressor power need (about 20 percent).

3. Reduce steam consumption in the conversion process by increasing conversion pressure, improving the heat recovery system, and controlling the conversion temperature to attain a better reaction equilibrium.

Table 9.8 Energy Consumption in Shijiazhuang Fertilizer Plant, 1988
(Energy consumed in water and air supply not included)

	Electricity (kWh)	Steam (ton)	By-products (ton)	Coke and coal (ton)	Fuel oil (ton)	Others (ton)
Ammonia						
Consumption, total	2×10^8	348,381.0	−22,313.0	238,717.0	—	−1,201.0
Unit consumption, Kgce/t	608.0	271.0	−16.0	1,392.0	—	−32.0
Unit electricity consumption	1,643.0	—	—	—	—	—
Urea						
Consumption, total	14,264,545.0	162,334.0	—	—	—	—
Unit consumption, Kgce/t	54.0	211.0	—	—	—	—
Nitramine						
Consumption, total	618,871.0	60,379.0	—	—	—	—
Unit consumption, Kgce/t	3.0	104.0	—	—	—	—
Granulated $(NH_4)_2CO_3$						
Consumption, total	2,640,592.0	29,630.0	—	—	—	—
Unit consumption, Kgce/t	43.0	167.0	—	—	—	—
Nitric acid						
Consumption, total	11,893,532.0	—	−120,162.0	—	—	—
Unit consumption, Kgce/t	52.0	—	−131.0	—	—	—
Nitrate						
Consumption, total	4,271,234.0	114,763.0	—	—	—	—
Unit consumption, Kgce/t	59.0	548.0	—	—	—	—
Sodium carbonate, total						
Unit consumption	3,344,176.0	12,628.0	—	—	—	1,201.0
Unit consumption, Kgce/t	97.0	126.0	—	—	—	304.0
Composite fertilizer consumption	49,369.0	259.0	—	—	—	—
Catalyst consumption	60,913.0	2,258.0	—	—	—	—
Total products						
Consumption	2.34×10^8	730,645.0	−142,474.0	238,717.0	—	—
Convert to standard coal, tce	94,734.3	88,968.8	−13,510.3	184,503.3	226.0	−79.2
Auxiliary losses						
Consumption	28,986,970.0	146,894.0	—	725.0	—	—
Convert to standard coal, tce	11,710.7	20,411.4	—	561.0	—	—
Total (including losses)						
Consumption	**2.63×10^8**	**877,539.0**	**−142,474.0**	**239,442.0**	**—**	**—**
Convert to standard coal, tce	**106,445.0**	**109,380.2**	**−13,510.3**	**185,064.3**	**226.0**	**−79.2**

4. Optimize the heat exchange network of the whole plant.
5. Use the radical flow ammonia reactor to reduce the pressure drop across the catalyst bed.
6. Integrate power generation with steam generation by installing high-pressure boilers and back-pressure steam turbines. The return period of the capital investment of this innovation is estimated to be as short as three years.
7. Optimize process operating conditions.
8. Utilize waste gas comprehensively to produce oxalic acid.
9. Increase plant capacity to benefit from scale effect.

9.2.3. QIQIHAR PAPER MILL

This plant was built in 1952 and is one of the thirty-two key paper mills in China. The output of paper in 1988 was 76,000 tons, of which 98 percent was newspaper. Total output value was 104 million yuan. The mill has 5,300 workers, of which 160 are technicians, and nine main workshops: log workshop, wood preparation, mechanical pulp, chemical pulp, paper-making, and caustic soda recovery. In addition, there are four supplementary workshops including a captive power plant, a machine shop, and a water supply station. The mill processes pine and poplar wood.

Table 9.9 Process Energy Consumption for Ammonia Production, 1988

	Coal (kg/ton)	Electricity (kWh/ton)	Steam (kg/ton)	Underground water (ton/ton)	Recycled water (ton/ton)	Soft water (ton/ton)	De-oxygenated water (ton/ton)	Conversion to coal equivalent (kg/t)	Total energy consumption (kcal/t)
Gasification	1,392	61	−44	8.6	49	0.960	2.855	1,449	1,014
Sulfur removal	—	39	28	—	—	—	—	18	13
Compression	—	1,028.5	—	—	151	—	—	435	305
Synthesis	—	50.2	−148	21	—	—	0.187	15	11
Blowing (system I)	—	10.5	—	—	25	—	—	36	25
Atmospheric conversion (system I)	—	10	1,264	34.7	—	1.489	—	139	97
Water scrubbing (system I)	—	329.6	—	—	—	—	—	133	93
Copper scrubbing (system I)	—	54	454	16	—	—	—	71	49
Purification (system II)	—	83	4,013	—	264	4.582	—	480	336
Average (systems I and II)	1,392	1,506	2,465	60	319	3.675	3.042	2,337	1,636
Energy conversion factor	—	0.404	0.1022	0.2	0.13	0.354	9.900	—	—

Table 9.10 Energy Consumption in Qiqihar Paper Mill, 1985

	Qiqihar Mill consumption	Domestic average	Domestic advanced level
Electricity consumed in mechanical pulping, kWh/t	1,337	1,249	1,102
Coal consumed in mechanical pulping, tce/t	0.19	0.126	0.076
Water consumed in mechanical pulping, t/t	40	29.5	16
Electricity consumed in chemical pulping, kWh/t	262	371	199
Coal consumed in chemical pulping, tce/t	0.52	0.758	0.241
Water consumed in chemical pulping, t/t	370	293	131
Electricity consumed in producing newsprint, kWh/t	771	527	396
Coal consumed in producing newsprint, tce/t	0.40	0.384	0.279
Water consumed in producing newsprint, t/t	240	121	54

The Qiqihar Mill's total energy consumption in 1988 was 1,996,000 tce. The overall specific energy consumption was 2.707 tce per ton paper, higher than the average in the Chinese paper industry. In table 9.10 the specific energy consumption for various products is compared with the values for average and technologically advanced plants in China. A more detailed comparison by products and processes is given in table 9.11.

Coal and oil are the main fuels used in the mill, of which 90 percent is used for power and steam generation. The remaining fuel oil is used in the caustic soda recovery oven and the limestone rotary kiln.

Of the electricity generated in the captive power station, 80 percent is used in the mechanical pulp, paper-making, and water supply workshops, 47 percent of which is used for mechanically processing pulp. More than 65 percent of the steam generated is used for mechanical and chemical pulp- and paper-making.

Several important issues were identified during the auditing, which may be briefly described as follows:

1. The specific fuel consumption in the power plant was high, and the self-consumption was 29 percent. Steam was extracted from the back-pressure turbine at nine atmospheres and then throttled down to four atmospheres to meet the process needs. A new back-pressure turbine with five atmospheres back pressure should be installed to increase the power output and decrease the exhaust loss.

2. Heat loss in the piping system was high, amounting to about 8.2 percent of the total heat supply. Better insulation is therefore recommended to reduce the heat losses.

Table 9.11 Major Technical Indices in Key Chinese Paper Mills, 1986

	Yalujiang Paper Mill	Jilin Paper Mill	Shixian Paper Mill	Qiqihar Paper Mill	Nanping Paper Mill	Jiangxi Paper Mill	Yueyang Paper Mill	Guangzhou Paper Mill	Yibin Paper Mill
Paper and paperboard output (ton)	46,857	148,035	53,739	75,394	94,737	44,614	48,241	112,703	49,363
Newsprint output (ton)	24,019	49,566	28,842	46,324	93,838	28,000	9,492	97,061	37,655
Gross output value (1,000 yuan)	51,150	167,500	99,200	87,730	108,000	48,020	66,730	102,090	53,670
Soda recovery									
Total amount (ton)	6,075	44,805	—	4,611	22,607	3,189	5,718	—	4,625
Recovery rate (%)	42.6	—	83.8	70.1	81.6	51.7	—	—	—
Self-sufficient rate (%)	47.7	—	—	—	97.3	—	—	—	—
Power stations									
Electricity generated (10^3 kWh)	—	24,060	—	124,750	128,010	10,940	81,480	184,340	45,470
Coal consumed (G/kWh)	—	—	—	576	465	500	444	580	572
Integrated Specific energy consumed/year (10^3 tce)	73	181	162	163	187	93	99	182	79
Energy consumed (tce/10^3 yuan)	1.42	1.08	1.26	1.86	1.73	1.93	1.49	1.78	1.48
Electricity consumed for newsprint (kWh/t)	449	491	429	651	621	577	646	533	424
Coal consumed for newsprint (kg/t)	428	320	—	398	427	558	340	274	360

Table 9.12 Overall Energy Consumption in Dongfanghong Refinery, 1978-1988

	1978	1979	1980	1981	1982	1983	1984	1985	1986	1987	1988
Total energy consumed, 10^4 toe	54.34	54.02	50.23	44.68	40.65	38.3	40.4	39.59	42.33	39.37	40.6
Refined crude oil, 10^4 ton	600.7	586.46	591.06	533.46	533.53	563.83	589.59	589.67	617.79	638.5	643.22
Specific energy consumed, 10^4kcal/ton	91.32	91.88	84.87	83.69	76.18	67.92	68.54	67.14	68.52	61.52	63.11
Energy factor	3.19	3.21	3.24	3.3	3.49	3.55	3.67	3.68	4.04	3.75	3.99
Normal specific energy consumed, 10^4kcal/ton	79.92	81.12	81.3	86.7	83.71	63.9	66.18	66.2	72.77	61.66	71.88
Specific consumption of energy medium											
Fuel, kg/ton	32.39	32.48	30.88	28.68	24.95	22.09	20.88	18.33	18.37	16.8	17.56
Steam, ton/ton	0.41	0.46	0.43	0.47	0.41	0.35	0.4	0.35	0.35	0.29	0.28
Electricity, kWh/ton	44.7	44.7	42.6	45.23	44.09	39.58	30.88	40.67	44.33	34.07	27.35
Catalytically burned coke, kg/ton	11.5	11.74	10.56	9.57	8.44	8.71	9.51	11.47	12.4	12.7	12.67
Fresh water, ton/ton	1.67	1.52	1.63	2.01	1.57	1.5	0.96	0.99	1.08	1.01	0.51
Circulating water, ton/ton	20.05	19.68	17.32	17.07	17.09	16.52	17.3	19.09	20.54	19.06	17.35

3. Bark, sawdust, and black liquor were not utilized. The former two wastes amounted to 12,000 cubic meters each year, 3,700 tce annually. A new wood waste boiler should be developed to utilize bark and sawdust for power generation and steam production. (Presently China has no domestically designed wood boiler, and the shortage of foreign currency prohibits the import of such equipment.) The black liquor disposed of by the plant is equivalent to 4,400 tce per year. The lack of a domestically made boiler is also a problem in this case.

Other energy conservation recommendations covering pulp-making, paper-making, energy measurement, and energy management have been made.

9.2.4. BEIJING DONGFANGHONG REFINERY

This refinery was built in 1967 and put into operation in September 1969. Its annual throughput is 7 million tons. The refinery has fourteen sets of refining equipment, which are capable of producing

Table 9.13 Specific Energy Consumption of Process Units, 1978-1988 (10^4kcal/ton)

	1978	1979	1980	1981	1982	1983	1984	1985	1986	1987	1988
Distillation Unit No.1	27.15	26.30	25.82	24.70	—	—	25.19	19.77	19.50	25.69	20.49
Distillation Unit No.2	27.30	24.98	23.28	19.23	16.40	14.77	14.42	13.95	13.69	13.32	13.06
Distillation Unit No.3	26.48	24.15	22.37	20.01	15.93	13.88	13.22	13.16	13.15	12.99	13.30
Catalytic Cracking Unit No.1	98.61	92.04	87.40	78.01	73.91	71.76	72.22	69.62	73.55	73.94	71.50
Catalytic Cracking Unit No.2	—	—	—	—	—	125.92	64.33	89.68	79.76	71.44	75.06
Platforming	251.95	249.60	216.26	241.39	208.46	197.87	150.97	146.91	139.34	133.45	137.56
Furfural refining	58.03	53.45	45.42	44.33	42.98	40.02	46.72	45.54	51.86	51.05	51.94
Ketone-benzol de-waxing	149.69	151.70	159.14	161.13	162.46	156.54	143.69	141.39	138.15	128.58	114.76
Paraffin hydro-refining	—	—	—	—	—	37.28	49.22	49.34	45.67	42.94	45.13
Lubricating oil hydro-refining	39.58	36.68	37.64	35.31	25.70	21.20	21.27	21.27	20.86	18.00	16.81
Propane de-asphalting	84.07	85.52	81.29	80.45	71.57	70.36	75.46	71.09	65.60	36.55	22.80
Molecular sieve de-waxing	271.18	307.79	323.85	289.07	288.84	271.28	308.14	310.41	261.66	312.15	306.94
Wax refining	37.49	35.96	38.49	52.54	51.14	43.34	18.22	5.79	—	—	—
Wax molding	97.60	86.77	91.69	79.12	76.34	59.86	21.01	8.41	9.54	5.51	4.81

gasoline, kerosene, diesel fuel, lubricants, heavy oil, paraffin, LPG, benzene, and other raw materials for the petro-chemical sector.

The refinery processed 6.43 million tons of crude oil in 1988. Self-consumption amounted to roughly 7 to 8 percent of the processed crude oil; 406,000 tons of oil were consumed in 1988. Tables 9.12 and 9.13 show the basic data, the structure of energy consumption by sources and by sectors from 1978 to 1988. Overall specific energy consumption in 1988 was 71.88 kgce per ton crude oil, nearly the same as the average level in China but 30 percent higher than in advanced plants in the rest of the world.

Since this refinery had already taken a number of effective energy conservation measures since 1980 and the comparable specific energy consumption had dropped from 91.32 kilograms oil per ton in 1978 to 71.88 kilograms oil per ton in 1988, more in-depth analysis was needed to identify means of further energy conservation. A mathematical model has been worked out to modify the complex steam system of the whole plant, and the optimal operational modes are listed in table 9.14. The economic benefit of this model is very attractive. The payback periods for the two options are both within 1.2 years, with an optimistic estimate as short as 0.6 years.

Other recommendations have also been made, including retrofitting the distillation units and the catalytic cracking units, setting up a waste heat generating unit (using the organic vapor cycle), and the installation of combined cycle generating units to make full use of the combustible off-gas.

9.2.5 BEIJING NO. 2 COTTON TEXTILE PLANT
This plant was built in 1954 and put into operation in 1955. After 1980, some imported advanced equipment was installed. Presently this plant has 145,000 spindles and 2,520 looms. It produced 24,000 tons of cotton yarn and 68.75 million meters of cotton cloth in 1987. The overall output value was 195 million yuan, and the net profit gained in foreign exchange was $42 million.

The plant has seven workshops: clearing, pre-spinning, spun yarn, bobbin twist thread, preparation, weaving, and rearranging. There are also three auxiliary workshops — power supply, maintenance, and measuring instruments.

Overall energy consumption in this plant was 3,987,000 tce in 1988, of which electricity was 71.19 GWh (263,000 tce) and steam was 1.004 million tons (109,000 tce). Electricity accounted for 66 percent of the total energy consumed. Three indexes are used for comparing the energy consumption level among various textile plants — that is, (a) basic energy consumed per unit product, which denotes the energy directly used in production; (b) overall energy consumed per unit product, which denotes the energy both directly and indirectly used in production; and (c) plant overall energy consumed per unit product, which denotes total energy used in the plant in both production and non-production. Table 9.15 shows these three indexes of energy consumption in Beijing No. 2 Cotton Textile Plant from 1983 to 1988 for three major products. Table 9.16 gives the details of the consumption by products and by energy sources in 1987.

This textile plant has already adopted a number of effective conservation measures since 1980. Among them are (1) adoption of new energy-saving motors for spinning frames, which achieved an en-

Table 9.14 Optimal Alternative Operational Modes for Energy Conservation

Item and values of objective function	No limit on investment		Limit of 3 million yuan		Present circumstances	
	Min. AEC	Min. ACC	Min. AEC	Min. ACC	Min. AEC	Min. ACC
Waste heat boiler in FCC No.1,						
ton/hr	20	—	—	—	—	—
kg/cm^2	35	35	—	—	—	—
Waste heat boiler in FCC No.2,						
ton/hr	11	11	—	—	—	—
kg/cm^2	8	8	—	—	—	—
Boiler House No.1, ton/hr	130	130	130	130	130	130
Boiler House No.2, ton/hr	65.4	110.8	65.4	110.8	90.8	90.8
CHP 15 kg/cm^2, ton/hr	0	30	0	13.8	7.5	30
CHP 8 kg/cm^2, ton/hr	27.1	13.7	35.1	59.3	106.9	65.4
Turbine B35/16, Mw	2.4	2.4	—	1.6	—	—
Turbine B15/10, Mw	0.1	0.7	—	—	—	—
Turbine B8/4.5, Mw	—	—	—	—	—	—
Turbine B8/3.5 in old section, Mw	3.2	3.2	—	3.2	—	—
Turbine B8/3.5 in new section, Mw	1.3	1.3	—	1.3	—	—
Air compressor in FCC No.1, drive unit	turbine	turbine	turbine	turbine	turbine	turbine
Gas compressor in FCC No.1, drive unit	turbine	electricity	electricity	turbine	turbine	turbine
Air compressor in FCC No.2, drive unit	turbine	turbine	turbine	turbine	turbine	turbine
Gas compressor in FCC No.2, drive unit	turbine	electricity	electricity	turbine	turbine	turbine
Steam heaters in KBD and in PD, kg/cm	15	15	15	15	8	8
Steam stripping, kg/cm^2	3	3	3	3	8	8
Steam pumps, kg/cm^2	15	15	15	15	8	8
Steam injectors, kg/cm^2	15	15	15	15	15	15
Steam pipeline of 15 kg/cm^2	set up	set up	set up	set up	—	—
Steam pipeline of 3 kg/cm^2 in old section	set up	set up	—	set up	—	—
Steam pipeline of 4 kg/cm^2	—	—	—	—	—	—
Steam pipeline of 3 kg/cm^2 in new section	set up	set up	—	set up	—	—
Annual energy consumption, 10^9 kcal	1,241.3	1,401	1,430.2	1,573.6	1,803.8	1,831
Annual decrease in ACC, %	31.2	23.5	20.7	14.1	—	—
Annual calculated cost, 10^6 yuan	14.2	12.94	18.23	15.58	20.54	20.38
Decrease in ACC, %	30.9	36.5	11.2	23.6	—	—
Annual capital investment, 10^6 yuan	6.79	6.46	3	3	—	—
Operating costs, 10^6 yuan	13.52	12.3	17.93	15.28	20.54	20.38
Payback period, years	1	0.8	1.2	0.6	—	—

Note: AEC = Annual Energy Consumption; ACC = Annual Calculated Cost; FCC = Fluidized Catalytic Cracking; CHP = Combined Heat & Power Plant; KBD = Ketone-Benzol De-waxing Unit; PD = Propane De-asphalting Unit.

ergy saving of 4 percent, or 600 MWh annually; (2) use of ball bearings in the mechanical drive device, which saved about 400 MWh per year; (3) control of shock load in operation and adoption of belt pulley spring bumpers in the looms; and (4) conversion to a new transformer, which saved 244 MWh per year.

Further recommendations for energy conservation include adoption of (1) a frequency conversion device for motor speed control; (2) a new dryer for the sizing machine, which can improve the heat efficiency from 25 percent to 40 percent; (3) new,

highly efficient dust removal equipment to replace obsolete types; (4) a closed-circuit air conditioning system for temperature and humidity control; (5) a computer system for material and energy management and control; and (6) other short-term measures, such as the adoption of high-efficiency air compressors, energy-saving lamps, and high-efficiency motors.

As mentioned above, specific energy consumption in textile plants in China is in general lower than that in advanced foreign textile plants due to the lower level of process mechanization and

Table 9.15 Specific Energy Consumption in Beijing No. 2 Cotton Textile Plant

	1983	1984	1985	1986	1987	1988
Cotton yarn						
Specific direct energy consumption, tce/ton	0.9435	0.9603	0.9672	0.9285	0.9285	0.8891
Specific enterprise energy consumption, tce/ton	0.9818	0.9995	1.0136	0.9792	0.9804	0.9617
Cotton cloth						
Specific direct energy consumption, tce/km	0.1514	0.1521	0.1509	0.1492	0.1528	0.1539
Specific enterprise energy consumption, tce/km	0.1576	0.1585	0.1583	0.1571	0.1616	0.1685
Yarn						
Specific direct energy consumption, tce/ton	3.3216	3.1481	3.1807	3.1671	3.2306	3.3140
Specific enterprise energy consumption, tce/ton	3.4449	3.2660	3.3197	3.3242	3.3931	3.5808
Total output						
Total output value, 10^4 yuan	20,613.4	20,017	20,111.6	19,598.4	19,507.7	18,697.5
Total general enterprise energy consumption, tce	40,643.1	39,773	39,682.5	39,507.7	4,0842.8	39,865.7
Specific general enterprise energy consumption, tce/10^4 yuan	1.97	1.98	1.97	2.01	2.09	2.13

Table 9.16 Production Energy Consumption for Textile Products

Product and output	Electricity (10^4kwh)	Steam (ton)	Coal (ton)	Coke (ton)	Gasoline (ton)	Diesel oil (ton)	Specific energy consumed (tce/ton yarn)
Cotton yarn, 211,108 t							
Productive energy consumed	3,789.03	38,498.52	16.5000	3.84	62.7700	13.28	
Productive energy consumed per unit product	0.1795	1.8236	7.8200	1.82	0.0030	6.29	
Production energy consumed per unit product, converted to tce/ton yarn	0.7252	0.1969	5.5800	1.78	0.0044	9.88	0.9282
Cotton cloth, 68,752 km							
Production energy consumed	1,299.16	47,981.09	9.0400	2.10	34.4100	7.28	
Production energy consumed per unit product	0.0189	0.6979	1.3100	0.30	5.0000	1.06	
Production energy consumed per unit product, converted to tce/ton yarn	0.0764	0.0754	0.9300	0.29	7.3500	1.66	0.1528
Yarn produced in 30,000 spindles shop, 2,564.6 t							
Production energy consumed	1,668.93	13,826.99	6.2600	1.46	23.8200	5.04	
Production energy consumed per unit product	0.6508	5.3915	0.0024	5.69	0.0093	0.002	
Production energy consumed per unit product, converted to tce/ton yarn	2.6292	0.5823	0.0017	5.52	0.0137	0.0031	3.2306

automation, but labor used in Chinese plants is much higher. Beijing No. 2 Cotton Textile Plant has imported a production line with highly automated technology, but it consumes ten times as much electricity as the original production line. In the Chinese situation, it is very difficult to disseminate such technologically advanced, highly energy-intensive technology. It is therefore especially important to analyze potential energy conservation under the current conditions of Chinese textile technology.

9.3. GENERAL ANALYSIS OF ENERGY CONSERVATION POTENTIAL IN CHINESE INDUSTRIES

The preliminary energy audits of the five demonstration plants noted that although the energy consumption structures in various industry sectors differ from one another, some common features exist. Three major types of energy — process heat, steam, and electricity — are used in all sectors. Several common energy conservation measures can thus be identified. Generally speaking, industrial energy conservation can be realized in four areas: technical processes, energy-utilizing devices, energy management, and energy systems.

1. Technical Processes

The backwardness of technical processes in the five typical plants is the main factor contributing to high energy intensity. In Datong Cement Mill the technology being used is the wet process, which is more energy intensive than the dry process. Traditional stone milling technology is still in use for mechanical pulp-making in the Qiqihar Paper Mill. These technologies are far behind the modern standard. Shijiazhuang Fertilizer Plant produces synthetic ammonia from coal instead of natural gas, and this is the major cause of its high energy intensity. The Dongfanghong Refinery was built in the 1950s, and many technical processes need to be updated and improved. Backwardness of technology is therefore a general problem in Chinese industry.

2. Energy Utilization

Poor performance of energy-utilizing devices is another major cause of energy intensiveness. Pumps, compressors, and ventilators consume some 40 percent of the electricity used in each of the five plants, but their efficiency is generally 10 to 20 percent lower than that of more advanced devices. The operational efficiency of boilers and steam pipe systems is relatively low. For instance, the 15-cubic meter compressor in Beijing No. 2 Textile Plant is equipped with a 130-kilowatt motor, but a more advanced compressor of the same capacity needs only a 65-kilowatt motor. The efficiency of the large high-pressure boiler used in the Qiqihar Paper Mill is only 80 percent, compared with 90 percent in more advanced models. Sealing and insulation in steam pipeline systems are often in bad condition, resulting in serious leakage and heat loss. It is estimated that the potential energy savings in this respect would amount to about 20 percent in Chinese paper mills. The insulation of industrial furnaces for process heat is usually inadequate, so the efficiency is quite low. For instance, the efficiency of the No. 3 Rotary Kiln in Datong Cement Mill is only 26 percent, according to the heat balance test. Among the reasons for such low efficiency are (1) high heat loss from the surface of the kiln due to poor insulation (as high as 384.4 kcal/kg clinker compared to the average value of 176.6 kcal/kg clinker), (2) high rate of air leakage into the kiln (as high as 17.7 percent, compared to the average of 10 percent in China and only 4 percent for advanced technology), and (3) imperfect combustion.

3. Energy Management

China has recently made some progress in energy management in industrial plants. Many plants have been certified as "qualified unit[s] of the first (or second) class of measurements." First or second class of measurement implies that a practice of routine monitoring has been established for 90 percent or 80 percent, respectively, of measuring instruments in the plant. All five of the demonstration plants have won these titles, but there are still many deficiencies in energy management. It is necessary to implement strict regulations in order to eliminate all loopholes. A comprehensive energy management system should be introduced into the large and medium-size enterprises with first- or second-class measurement levels, such as using energy balance tables, energy flow diagrams, and energy management information systems in microcomputers.

4. Energy Systems

An energy system consists of many subsystems, such as fuel supply, fuel storage, energy conservation, and secondary energy supply systems — steam supply, electricity supply, compressed air, water supply, and so on. A series of problems must be solved for each system to fit the parameters required, to improve the system design, and to optimize the system performance, among other things.

Potential energy conservation in this respect is quite high. In Qiqihar Paper Mill, steam is provided by cogeneration. It is extracted from a turbine at a pressure of 0.88 MPa, but the technological processes need steam at only 0.49 MPa; hence, the extracted steam needs to be throttled down to reduce pressure and temperature. Energy loss is therefore very high, simply because the parameters of output and need do not match well. Another example is in Dongfanghong Oil Refinery. The three steam pipeline systems maintain pressures of 3.43 MPa, 1.47 MPa, and 0.98 MPa, respectively. The whole network operates inefficiently. In the chemical fertilizer plant, gas exhausted from the synthetic ammonia process contains 200 cubic meters of hydrogen per ton of ammonia. If the exhaust gas could be recovered, then the annual ammonia production could be increased by 4 percent.

9.4 ENERGY CONSERVATION MEASURES
1. Energy Savings from Technological Innovation

Methods of energy saving are closely connected to technical reform of processes themselves. If the complete replacement of an energy-intensive process is not feasible, partial improvement may still achieve some savings. For example, in cement plants, the dry process is much more efficient than the wet process, but large amounts of investment are needed to convert from the wet process to the dry process. However, there are several ways to improve the efficiency of the wet process kiln. If the water content in the raw materials for the wet process can be reduced from 33 percent to 28 percent, a savings of about 5 percent of the total energy consumption will result. Similarly, if the water content of pulp in the paper making process could be reduced, then substantial amounts of electricity and water could be saved.

2. Energy Savings in Equipment and Apparatus Improvement

a. Industrial Furnaces

According to the heat balance analysis, 15 to 70 percent of the heat from furnaces is carried away by waste gas, and 20 to 50 percent of the heat is lost from surface heat transfer. Decrease of the heat loss from furnaces could be achieved by improving the gas circulation, installing heat recovery apparatus, and improving thermal insulation of kilns.

b. Boilers

Improving the internal structure and the operation of boilers is an effective measure for energy savings in some plants. For instance, the design efficiency of the boiler in Qiqihar Paper Mill was 89.4 percent, but the operation efficiency was only 80 percent, so efficiency can be increased from 80 to 89.4 percent by improving the operating conditions. In some other paper mills, the efficiency of boilers was raised from 60 percent to 75 percent simply by installing air preheaters.

c. Steam Pipelines

Energy savings from improving the thermal insulation of pipelines is simple and effective. The steam pipeline network in one plant was moved from underground to overhead and its insulation improved in 1986. As a result, 20 tons of heavy oil has been saved annually.

d. Ventilator Pumps and Motors

It is estimated that technical changes and rational matching of the complete sets of equipment could save 10 to 20 percent of electrical energy used.

3. Energy Conservation Management

Energy management in a plant means systematically monitoring and controlling the energy flow in the plant from the fuel input to the end-use. Establishment of an energy management information system using small computers is an effective measure.

Such a system differs from the on-line automation systems for automatic control of plants which have been installed in most technologically advanced countries. Automation systems are difficult to set up in most existing Chinese plants at the present stage. Installation of an energy management information system is, on the other hand, more realistic and useful under Chinese conditions. Such a system was set up in a cable factory in 1986, and it increased the speed of energy data analysis by a factor of sixteen. Management was improved, and energy savings amounted to some 6 percent of the total energy consumption in 1987.

4. Energy Conservation by Optimizing the System

Optimizing the system is one of the most important modern energy conservation techniques. For instance, the steam system of Dongfanghong Refinery is a very complex one. An optimization model has been developed, in which the objective function is minimizing the integrated energy consumption. Steam loss was reduced by 31 percent, and the payback period of the investment was only one year.

In conclusion, the preliminary energy audit in five demonstration plants confirmed that the potential of energy conservation in Chinese enterprises is rather high. Besides the specific recommendations made for these plants, various common measures for energy saving can also be applied to all industrial plants.

CHAPTER 10

ENVIRONMENTAL IMPACT OF ENERGY USE IN HARBIN

10.1. BACKGROUND

Harbin is a large center of heavy industry in northeast China. Heating is needed up to half the year, and coal is the main fuel. For this reason, Harbin was selected as a typical city for this case study focusing on the assessment of the impact of energy consumption on the environment. (For more details on this study, see reference 119.)

A preliminary survey of present conditions identified the main characteristics and existing issues for the economy, energy system, and environment in Harbin, such as the typical heavy industry structure; the low output rate of fixed capital; the "overheating" of the economic growth rate; the dominance of coal in the energy structure; energy shortages, especially in electricity supply; serious air pollution caused by heating in winter; and the pollution of the Song Hua River, peaking in spring due to the surface run-off containing pollutants from melting snow.

A long-term socioeconomic development strategy and targets by the year 2000 have been proposed and several alternative scenarios of future economic growth, energy supply and demand, and environmental quality have been generated under the guidance of the municipal planning authorities.

An integral model system, consisting of a socioeconomic development system dynamic model, an energy forecasting model, an energy-environment system multi-objective programming model, an air pollution dispersion model, and a unified transport model for toxic substances in the water system are used for the comprehensive assessment of the economy-energy relationship, the investment allocation, and the impact of energy supply scenarios on the environment. In particular, the environmental impact of the Low-Temperature Nuclear Heating Reactor project, the large-scale Yilan Mine-Mouth Gas Works project, and the natural gas pipeline project have been analyzed in detail.

The results from running the model system show that even though capital-intensive urban energy projects may dramatically reduce the contribution of the residential sector to air pollution concentration, the overall air quality in the year 2000 can only be improved marginally over the level of 1985 because of a kind of "environmental pollution shifting." This is due to the substantial increase of final energy consumption in the industrial sector, which is the biggest energy consumer in Harbin. Since the industrial sector will continue to be fueled with coal, the additional contribution to air pollution from this sector will much more than make up for the reduction of the pollutants emitted from the household sector. Therefore the next phase of the study on the energy-environmental issues in Harbin should be focused on the clean utilization of coal by the industrial sector.

10.2. INTEGRATED PLANNING FOR THE ECONOMY-ENERGY-ENVIRONMENT IN HARBIN TO THE YEAR 2000

10.2.1. DEVELOPMENT TARGETS

Since the development of Harbin is an issue concerning a large-scale socioeconomic-environmental system, the formulation of long-term development planning should be based on correct assumptions in strategy and policy.

During the period 1985-1987, the municipal planning authorities submitted a proposal, "Socioeconomic Development Strategy for the Year 2000

Table 10.1 Socioeconomic Development Targets for Harbin by 2000

	1985	2000	
		Scenario A	Scenario B
Total social product, 10^8 yuan	105.40	320.0	380
Gross national product, 10^8 yuan	53.30	169.5	147
National income, 10^8 yuan	43.50	110.0	130
Gross output value of agriculture and industry, 10^8 yuan	78.10	251.1	294
Urban population, 10^4	262.55	308.0	308
Living standard:			
Gasification rate, %	36.30	85.0	
District heating rate, %	10.50	77.4	
Living space per capita, square meters	3.98	8.0	
Gross national product per capita, yuan	1,400	3,600	
Consumption level per capita, yuan/year	678	1,700	
Environmental quality grade standard:*			
Urban area	II-III	I-II	
Scenic areas	II	I	

*The air pollution quality grades in China are as follows (mg/m³ air, daily average):
Suspended particles: I - 0.15;   II - 0.30;   III - 0.50
Fly ash: I - 0.05;   II - 0.15;   III - 0.25
Sulfur dioxide: I - 0.05;   II - 0.15;   III - 0.25

in Harbin," in which the main socioeconomic development targets were outlined as the two scenarios shown in table 10.1.

10.2.2. STRATEGIC FACTORS IN INTEGRATED PLANNING

In order to realize these ambitious targets, the following strategic factors were assumed:

1. Comprehensive equilibrium, including materials, finance, market, labor, and foreign trade
2. Coordinated and consistent development patterns in economy, energy, and environment
3. Reasonable growth rates of and ratios between consumption and accumulation over the planning period
4. "Tilted" allocation of limited investment among various industrial branches to direct the adjustment of industry structure
5. Full use of the advantage of the existing industrial base in Harbin (For example, machinery and power equipment manufacturing, food processing, chemicals, textiles, medicines, and building materials industries should contribute more to the national economy.)

10.2.3. INTEGRAL MODEL SYSTEM

In order to achieve the socioeconomic, living-standards, and environmental targets, several scenarios have been considered in planning which put varying emphasis on certain strategic factors mentioned above. The problem to be solved is therefore a multi-

Fig. 10.1 Energy-Economic-Environmental Model System

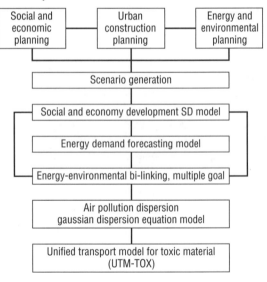

objective and multi-criterion decision problem for the large-scale socioeconomic system of Harbin. As a consequence, an integral model system was designed for this purpose (see figure 10.1).

10.3. PLANNING SCENARIOS

10.3.1. SOCIOECONOMIC SCENARIOS

The socioeconomic development scenarios can be

Table 10.2 Socioeconomic Scenarios

	1985	1990	1992	1995	2000
Total social product, 10^8 yuan	A, B, C: 105.4	A: 175.6	B: 204.2 C: 175.5	A: 250.90	A: 380.0 B: 320.0 C: 320.0
Growth rate of total social product, %/year	A, B, C: 10.7	B: 9.91 C: 7.56	A: 7.4	A: 8.90 B: 5.94 C: 7.97	—
Gross output value of industry, 10^8 yuan	A, B, C: 76.3	A: 131.1	B: 153.5 C: 130.3	A: 190.80	A: 299.0 B: 250.0 C: 250.0
Living space per capita, sq.m/capita	A, B, C: —	A: 6.0 B: 6.0 C: 6.0	—	—	A: 8.0 B: 8.0 C: 8.0

classified as shown in table 10.2. Three scenarios (A, B, and C) are designed to attain certain targets of total social product by 2000.

Scenario A is called the "Economic Benefit-Oriented Scenario," which implies a higher average growth rate strategy resulting in a total social product of 38.6 billion yuan in the year 2000. Both scenarios B and C imply a lower growth rate strategy in which the annual growth rate between 1985 and 2000 will average 7.77 percent as compared with 9.02 percent in scenario A. However, the growth rates of scenarios B and C up to 1992 are different. The term of the current municipal government expires in 1992. Scenario B pursues a higher growth rate than scenario C up to 1992 to identify the influences on future development.

Of course, some other scenarios may also be considered, such as the "Energy Saving-Oriented Scenario."

10.3.2. SYSTEM DYNAMIC SIMULATION RESULTS

The System Dynamic Model gives detailed information for each scenario on industrial structure, investment allocation, and other elements. For the most realistic scenario (C) mentioned above, the growth of social product during the period 1985-2000 is shown in figure 10.2. The structural change of the economy and in particular of industry is shown in figures 10.3 and 10.4.

This scenario aims at a total social product of 31.9 billion yuan by the year 2000, which is about three times as much as that in 1985. The economic structure changes very little from 1985 to 2000 (see figure 10.3); however, the detailed structure of each

Fig. 10.2 Growth of Total Social Product

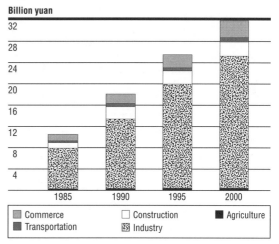

Fig. 10.3 Change in Economic Structure

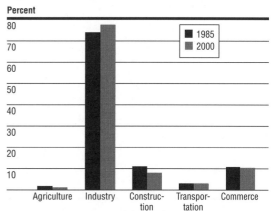

sector changes a bit more. In the industrial sector, the shares of textiles, power generation, medicines, and building materials will increase while those of food

Fig. 10.4 Change in Industrial Structure

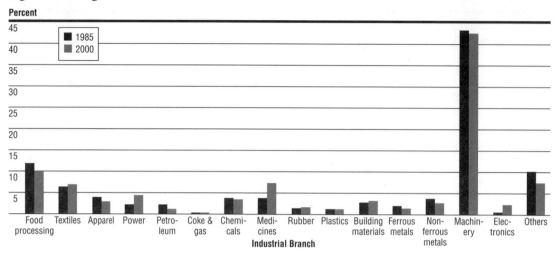

processing, apparel, petroleum, metallurgy, and machine building decrease. Much more change will be
identified in the product mix of each subsector, which

**Table 10.3 Industrial Investment Allocation,
Harbin, 2000**

Branch	Investment 10⁸ yuan	%
Food processing	12.50	7.2
Textiles	8.10	4.6
Apparel	1.65	0.9
Power generation	34.80	19.8
Petroleum	1.64	0.7
Coke and gas production	2.56	1.5
Chemicals	6.79	3.9
Medicines	3.89	2.2
Rubber	1.00	0.6
Plastics	1.86	1.1
Building materials	12.20	6.9
Ferrous metallurgy	2.16	1.2
Non-ferrous metallurgy	7.30	4.2
Machinery and electric equipment	72.80	41.3
Electronics	2.10	1.2
Others	11.10	6.3

**Table 10.4 Energy Conservation Ratio
of Elasticity** (Percent/year)

Sector and branch	1985	1990	1995	2000
Agriculture	3.26	1.0	1.0	1.0
Industry	0	0	0.7	0.6
Transport and communication	8.00	1.0	3.9	1.0
Construction	—	—	—	—
Commercial	4.00	4.0	3.0	3.0
Services	−7.00	−8.0	−6.0	−4.0

is oriented toward higher value-added products. In
order to realize such adjustments of the structure of
the industrial sector, the System Dynamic Model also
gives the "tilted" allocation scenario of investment
shown in table 10.3. The branches assuming a higher
growth rate acquire a sizable amount of investment,
although these figures could not be compared directly
due to the radical differences among the specific investments in the subsectors.

10.4. ENERGY DEMAND FORECASTING

10.4.1 FORECASTING PROCESS
Once the annual output values by branch for the
planning year are given by the System Dynamic
Model, the energy demand forecast can be made by
branch and by form of energy. The techno-economic
parameters such as the annual energy conservation
rate over time and the final energy consumption per
unit of output value used in the forecasting is shown
in table 10.4 (for electricity). The results are shown
in table 10.5 and figures 10.5 and 10.6.

10.4.2. FORECAST ANALYSIS
1. **Relationship between the Economy and
Energy Demand**
The relationship between economic trends and energy demand can be described by energy intensity,
energy conservation rate, and energy elasticity
(summarized in tables 10.6 and 10.7).

If the total social product in 2000 attains 31.9
billion yuan (over three times its value in 1985), the
final energy demand in 2000 will be 10.72 million
tce (about 2.4 times the 1985 figure). The required

Fig. 10.5 Energy Demand Forecast by Sectors in Harbin

10⁶ tce

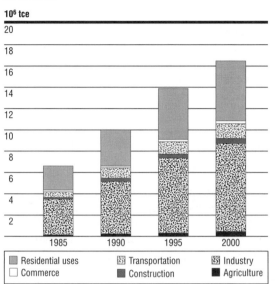

Fig. 10.6 Energy Forecast by Sources in Harbin

10⁶ tce

Legend Fig 10.5:
- Residential uses
- Commerce
- Transportation
- Construction
- Industry
- Agriculture

Legend Fig 10.6:
- Electricity
- Nuclear heat
- Gas
- Light oil
- Fuel oil
- Coal

final energy and electricity intensity should therefore decrease, respectively, from 4.2 tce/10,000 yuan and 2,100 kWh/10,000 yuan in 1985, to 3.36 tce/10,000 yuan and 1780 kWh/10,000 yuan in 2000. As a consequence, great effort has to be made to increase energy conservation in order to keep the average annual conservation rate at 1.48 percent and 1.10 percent for energy and electricity, respectively. Also, it can be determined from these tables that the expected energy conservation potential was greater during 1985-1990 due to the low management level. The conservation rate is expected to increase, however, during 1995-2000 because of scientific and technological progress and the potential investment effect.

In summary, the consistent relationship between the economy and energy can be characterized by

appropriate energy elasticity, whose value is seen to be 0.79 for energy and 0.84 for electricity from 1985 to 2000, and which is anticipated to assume a higher value during 1990-1995, when the energy conservation rate will be lower (see table 10.6).

2. Energy Composition

Since there will be no fundamental change in the whole economic structure between 1985 and 2000 (see figure 10.4), it is also expected that the energy composition by sectors will basically remain the same up to the year 2000, as shown in figure 10.7.

3. Energy Conservation Analysis

One set of key techno-economic parameters used in the Energy Demand Forecasting Model is energy intensity. These parameters can be deter-

Table 10.5 Energy Demand Forecasting for Harbin (10⁴ tce)

Branch	1985	1990	1995	2000
Industry	341.4	500.4	703.4	829.6
Agriculture	11.6	20.0	30.2	35.4
Transportation and communication	63.5	95.1	123.1	139.4
Construction	14.1	31.4	36.5	42.6
Commercial	9.9	13.4	19.0	24.6
Services	93.5	140.7	179.9	230.7
Residential	133.4	200.4	290.5	329.6
Urban	106.0	162.3	244.0	280.2
Rural	26.7	38.1	46.5	49.4
Total	**667.4**	**1,001.4**	**1,382.6**	**1,631.9**

Table 10.6 Energy Conservation Analysis for Harbin

	1985	1990	1995	2000
Total social product, 10⁸ yuan	105.1	179.6	256.0	318.8
Final energy demand, 10³ tce	441.0	660.3	912.2	1,071.6
Electricity demand, 10⁸ kWh	22.20	32.36	47.61	56.64
Energy intensity, tce/10⁴ yuan	4.20	3.68	3.56	3.36
Energy conservation rate, %/year	2.61	0.66	1.15	—
Electricity intensity, kWh/10⁴ yuan	2,100	1,802	1,860	1,780
Electricity conservation rate, %/year	3.04	−0.66	0.88	—

151

Fig. 10.7 Change in Energy Structure

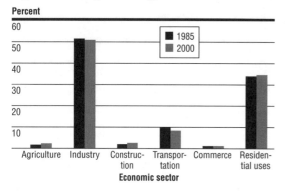

Percent

mined through detailed consideration of energy conservation rates. A comparison of energy and electricity intensity for each industrial branch between 1985 and 2000 can be made from figures 10.8 and 10.9, respectively.

Energy conservation is an indispensable measure in all branches, and much more effort must be made to conserve electricity since the acute shortage of power is expected to continue to be a major constraint up to 2000. For energy-intensive areas such as coking and gas works, chemicals, building materials, and non-ferrous metallurgy, more emphasis should be put on the adoption of advanced energy-saving technologies and better management.

Finally, it should be recalled that even when all these conservation measures are realized, there will still be an immense amount of final energy demand by 2000 — an increment of about 10 million tce between 1985 and 2000, of which the 7 million tce of coal demand will also present difficulties for transportation and increase environmental pollution.

10.5. ENERGY SUPPLY ASSESSMENT

10.5.1. OBJECTIVES AND KEY ISSUES OF ENERGY SUPPLY SYSTEM PLANNING

In an integrated energy planning framework, energy supply is a core issue closely associated with both economic development and environmental protection. Based on the current economy, energy supply, and environment in Harbin, the requirements for an energy supply system should be, first, to meet the energy demands of all economic sectors and all branches in the industrial sector. Since the energy demand forecast is based on certain socioeconomic development scenarios (as mentioned above), energy supply may be considered the guarantee of the realization of socioeconomic objectives. Second, the requirements of improved air quality

Fig. 10.8 Energy Intensity Change

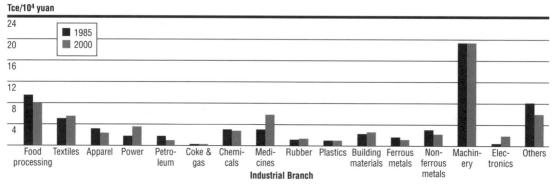

Tce/10^4 yuan

Fig. 10.9 Electricity Intensity Change

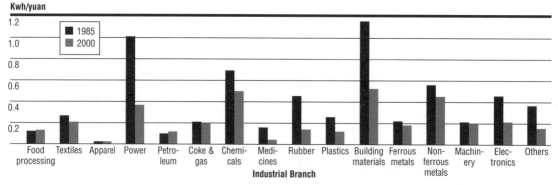

Kwh/yuan

Table 10.7   Energy and Electricity Elasticity for Harbin

	1985-1990	1990-1995	1995-2000	1985-2000
Growth rate of social product, %/year	11.31	7.35	4.50	7.68
Rate of energy increase, %/year	8.40	6.68	3.27	6.10
Energy elasticity	0.74	0.91	0.72	0.79
Rate of electricity increase, %/year	7.83	8.03	3.53	6.45
Electricity elasticity	0.69	1.09	0.78	0.84

must be met, as measured by SO_2 and trisodium phosphate (TSP) ground concentration levels graded according to the National Standard. Third, the available amount of energy capital investment affordable in the economic system may not be exceeded. If the amount of investment is not explicitly given by the economic model, an objective of minimizing energy capital investment should be included in the analysis.

Since these objectives have been proposed as goals by planning authorities or by preceding models, a multiple-objective programming model rather than a linear programming model is preferred. In this case the objective functions will refer to the minimization of the deviation between the objective value and the calculated one.

The Energy Supply Model proposes to deal with the following key issues:

1. Achieving an energy demand and supply balance, particularly for electricity
2. Creating an urban energy system for the residential sector, that is, district heating, gas supply, and fuel substitution
3. Estimating the necessary energy investment, which will send a very important message to government policymakers about the financial feasibility of a particular scenario
4. Determining the space distribution of energy consumption, especially the coal consumption distribution, which will provide information on the pollutant emission sources and the resultant air pollution
5. Assessing large-scale energy projects, such as the Low Temperature Nuclear Heating Reactor and Yilan Mine-Mouth Gas Works

10.5.2. ENERGY SUPPLY SCENARIO

Two major energy projects in the urban residential sector which can have the most profound potential impact on the reduction of air-borne pollutants have been studied in detail and the resultant improvements in air quality evaluated against the investment increment.

Table 10.8   Development Plan for District Heating

	1985	1990	1995	2000
Capacity of district heating* network, 10^6 kcal/h	915.3	2,544.9	3,644.3	4,194.3
Floor space heated, 10^4 m²	345	1,201	2,171	2,807
Total floor space in districts, 10^4 m²	2,492	3,076	3,676	4,276
Proportion of floor space covered by district heating network, %	13.9	39	59.6	66

*Including the capacity for process heating

1. Urban District Heating System

Coal-fueled, decentralized space-heating devices accounted for 35.4 percent of the SO_2 concentration and 39.3 percent of the TSP concentration in Harbin in 1985. Thus, urban district heating is a key issue associated with urban energy supply and the reduction of air pollution in Harbin.* Based on the socio-economic development scenario and urban building construction planning, the urban district heating development is summarized in table 10.8. Coal consumption in industrial process heating is another major pollution emission source whose environmental effect should not be neglected. Unfortunately, it has not been emphasized as much as the issue of home heating, hence it is not included in this study. However, we have identified this issue and proposed appropriate research for the near future. The development trend of process heating is shown in table 10.9.

Considering the advantage of power equipment manufacture capability and the existing district heating system in Harbin, three candidates for district heating sources have been considered and compared: a cogeneration coal-fired power plant, a district heating coal-fired boiler station, and a Low-Temperature Nuclear Heating Reactor (LTNHR). Two scenarios, "nuclear heating" and "conventional

---

*District heating connects many buildings and homes in urban districts through a network of hot water or steam pipelines. It is more efficient and clean than heating individual spaces with scattered small boilers or stoves. District heating has been used for centuries in Europe and some United States cities.

Table 10.9 Trend of Industrial Process Heating in Harbin (10^4 tce)

Type of heating	1985				2000		
	Useful energy	Final energy	%		Useful energy	Final energy	%
Co-generation	27	31.8	14.7		60.0	70.6	12.5
Coal-fired	111	185	85.3		297.6	496	87.5
Gas	0	0	0		17.4	—	—
Total	138	216.8	100.0		375	566.6	—

Table 10.10 Nuclear Versus Conventional District Heating in Harbin

	1985			2000							
	Conventional			Conventional				Nuclear			
	DH area (10^3 m²)	DH ratio (%)	Coal-fired (10^3 tce)	DH area (10^3 m²)	DH ratio (%)	Coal-fired (10^3 tce)	Invest-ment (10^8 yuan)	DH area (10^3 m²)	DH ratio (%)	Coal-fired (10^3 tce)	Invest-ment (10^8 yuan)
Co-generation	230	9.3	—	930	21.7	—	1.54	930	21.7	—	1.54
District boilers	115	4.6	5.6	1,506	35.2	65.0	3.48	1,206	28.2	52.2	2.73
Small boilers	1,476	—	83.0	1,370	—	77.0	—	770	—	43.3	—
Small stoves	671	—	24.5	471	—	17.2	—	471	—	17.2	—
Nuclear heating	—	—	—	—	—	—	—	899	21.0	—	4.85
Total	2,476.5	13.9	112.5	4,276	57	159.2	5.02	4,276	71.0	112.7	9.12

heating," were chosen. The results of comparisons are listed in table 10.10.

It can be seen that the nuclear heating scenario will substitute for 465,000 tce of coal per year by increasing 4,100,000 yuan of investment over the conventional heating scenario (not including fuel inventory costs for the nuclear heating reactor, which will be "rented" from the government company). The improvement of air quality made possible by the nuclear option is attractive, and further financial analysis on the availability of the necessary additional investment should be made to evaluate its feasibility.

3. Urban Gas Supply System

Small coal-fired stoves used for cooking and water heating accounted for 43.1 percent of the SO_2 concentration and 45.6 percent of TSP concentration in Harbin in 1985. According to socioeconomic development planning, the number of households in Harbin will increase from 600,000 in 1985 to 850,000 in 2000. If the capacity of the municipal gas supply remains the same as in 1985, then the number of small coal-fired stoves for cooking and water heating will more than double — from 237,000 in 1985 to 487,000 in 2000. These additional stoves will burn about 480,000 tce of coal,

Table 10.11 Comparison of Gas Supply Scenarios

	1985		Scenarios for 2000								
			Yilan gas			Natural gas			Coke oven gas		
	NH (10^3)	GR (%)	NH (10^3)	GR (%)	Investment (10^8 yuan)	NH (10^3)	GR (%)	Investment (10^8 yuan)	NH (10^3)	GR (%)	Investment (10^8 yuan)
LPG	31.8	53.0	20.5	24.0	—	8.0	9.4	—	22.5	26.4	—
Coke oven gas	2.7	4.5	—	—	—	—	—	—	—	—	—
High quality gas	1.8	3.0	1.8	2.1	—	1.8	2.1	—	1.8	2.1	
Yilan coal gas	—	—	50.0	58.8	6*	—	—	—	—	—	—
Natural gas	—	—	—	—	—	66.7	78.5	2.2	—	—	—
New coke oven gas	—	—	—	—	—	—	—	—	48.8	56.5	3.7
Small stoves	23.7	—	12.7	—	—	8.5	—	—	12.8	—	—
Total	60.0	69.5	85.0	85.0	6	85.0	90.0	2.2**	85.0	85.0	3.7

NH = Number of Households; GR = Gasification Rate.
 * Of total investment, 12x10^8 yuan, half of the gas produced is for industrial use.
** An additional 1.6x10^8 yuan investment is needed for providing gas for industrial use.

Table 10.12 SO$_2$ Ground Concentration in Harbin, 1985 (mg/m^3)

Pollution source	Dao Wai District	Dao Li District	Nan Gang District	Dong Li District	Xiang Fang District	Tai Ping District	Sun Island	Capitol Building
Industry	0.023	0.011	0.012	0.016	0.024	0.027	0.009	0.03
%	6.87	9.85	10	20	32	18.5	8.9	31.3
Transport	0.002	0.002	0.003	<.001	0.002	0.003	<.001	0.001
%	0.56	1.34	2.61	1.11	2.7	1.8	0.7	1.1
Scattered boilers	0.034	0.01	0.011	0.011	0.012	0.017	0.008	0.019
%	9.78	8.41	9.12	13.7	16.8	11.7	8.5	19.2
Small stoves	0.195	0.019	0.049	0.034	0.019	0.077	0.013	0.026
%	57.9	17	40.1	43.4	26.4	52.8	13.1	27.4
Cooking	0.083	0.071	0.046	0.016	0.014	0.02	0.019	0.019
%	24.5	62	37.2	20.8	19.3	14	8.6	20
Energy industry	<.001	0.001	0.001	<.001	0.002	0.002	<.001	<.001
%	0.18	1.26	0.96	1	2.4	1.12	0.8	0.9
District heating	<.001	<.001	<.001	<.001	<.001	<.001	0.059	<.001
%	0.02	0.056	0.022	0.01	0.015	0.02	59.3	0.02
Total	**0.339**	**0.114**	**0.122**	**0.076**	**0.073**	**0.0146**	**0.098**	**0.095**
%	**100**	**100**	**100**	**100**	**100**	**100**	**100**	**100**

emitting a total of twice as much SO$_2$ and TSP as in 1985. This is a serious problem faced by the decisionmakers in the municipal government, and it has been given the highest priority on their agenda.

Three options of gas supply technology have been considered in this study. The first is the gasification of the low-quality coal in the nearby Yilan coal mine by installing an advanced Lurgi gasifier. A 260-kilometer-long gas pipeline would be constructed to transport 1.5 million cubic meters of gas per day to Harbin. The second option is to transport the natural gas from the Shong Liao Basin (30 to 100 kilometers distant) to the city. A third proposal is to increase the coke-oven gas production in Harbin. The results of comparison are shown in table 10.11.

The comparison of the three scenarios is not based simply on financial issues. The natural gas option seems to be the most attractive idea. However, the extent of resources and the availability of natural gas remain uncertain. Besides, natural gas is a valuable raw material for the high value-adding petrochemical industry, which will also be a development target pursued by the municipal decisionmakers. Low-quality coal is abundant in Yilan, but gasification technology is not only still expensive but difficult to operate. The third option, increasing the gas output of coke ovens, uses the least desirable but the most mature means. Further study is needed before the final decision is made. However, the environmental implications of these scenarios can be identified in this study.

10.6. ENVIRONMENTAL IMPACT OF ENERGY SUPPLY SCENARIOS

There are many perspectives from which the environmental impact of increasing the energy supply may be assessed. In this study the focus is the ground concentration distribution of SO$_2$ and the pollution contribution from different economic sectors and various districts in Harbin by the year 2000, as well as the comparative analysis for the scenarios described above (00, 01, 10, 11).

1. Scenario option 10:
A. Nuclear heating — 10 million square meters of space heating area will be supplied by LTNHR in Dao Li district.
B. No Yilan Gas Works — The urban gas demand will be mainly supplied by natural gas.

2. Scenario option 00:
A. No nuclear heating — Some decentralized heating boilers and small stoves will be replaced by conventional district heating.
B. No Yilan Gas Works.

3. Scenario option 01:
A. No nuclear heating.
B. Yilan Gas Works — 1.5 million cubic meters per day gas supply capacity, of which 0.75 million will go to 450,000 households, 0.45 million to industry, and 0.30 million to public services.

4. Scenario option 11:
A. Nuclear heating.
B. Yilan Gas Works.

155

Table 10.13 SO$_2$ Ground Concentration in Harbin, 2000 Forecast (mg/m^3)

Pollution source	Dao Wai District	Dao Li District	Nan Gang District	Dong Li District	Xiang Fang District	Tai Ping District	Sun Island	Capitol Building
Industry	0.085	0.046	0.051	0.075	0.065	0.067	0.035	0.16
%	37.4	50.5	53.1	28.5	67	59	49.6	66
Transport	0.003	0.002	0.005	0.001	0.003	0.004	0.001	0.002
%	1.3	2.2	5.2	0.9	2.7	3	1.9	4.8
Scattered boilers	0.023	0.004	0.006	0.009	0.011	0.015	0.005	0.016
%	10.1	4.4	6.3	8.03	10	11.1	9.4	8
Small stoves	0.058	0.004	0.014	0.01	0.006	0.023	0.003	0.008
%	25.6	4.4	14.6	8.9	5.5	17	5.7	4
Cooking	0.049	0.028	0.014	0.011	0.012	0.014	0.004	0.007
%	21.6	30.1	14.6	9.8	10.9	10.4	7.5	3.5
Energy industry	0.005	0.003	0.003	0.004	0.012	0.01	0.002	0.005
%	2.2	3.3	3.1	3.6	10.9	7.4	3.8	2.5
District heating	0.004	0.004	0.003	0.002	0.001	0.002	0.003	0.002
%	1.8	4.4	3.1	1	0.9	1.5	5.7	1
Total	**0.227**	**0.091**	**0.096**	**0.112**	**0.11**	**0.135**	**0.053**	**0.2**
%	**100**	**100**	**100**	**100**	**100**	**100**	**100**	**100**

According to the spatial distribution of coal consumption calculated with the Energy Flow Optimization Model (EFOM) for each scenario option (00, 10, 01, and 11), the Air Pollution Dispersion Model is used to calculate the intensity and distribution of SO$_2$ pollutant emission sources as well as the resultant SO$_2$ pollution ground concentration distribution. Tables 10.12 and 10.13 list the background data of the spatial distribution of SO$_2$ in 1985 and the calculated results of scenario 11 (with both nuclear heat and Yilan coal gas works). A more detailed comparison of all these four options is shown in figure 10.10.

Fig. 10.10 Distribution of SO$_2$

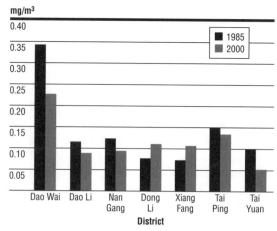

10.6.1. DISTRIBUTION OF SO$_2$ BY 2000

From tables 10.12 and 10.13, a comparison of the spatial distribution of SO$_2$ ground concentration between 1985 and 2000 is seen and the following conclusions may be drawn:

1. In most districts (for example Dao Wai, Dao Li, Nan Gang, and Tai Ping), the air quality in 2000 will be somewhat improved. This will result from the great effort made in developing a district heating system and an urban gasification program. Very impressive achievement appears in Dao Wai District, currently the most seriously polluted area in Harbin. In the winter of 1985, the SO$_2$ concentration observed in this area was 0.339 mg/m^3, worse than Grade III of the National Standard. In the year 2000, the pollution will decrease to 0.24 mg/m^3 if all the previously described measures are realized. In Sun Island, a well-known scenic spot on the Song Hua River, the air quality clearly will be ameliorated, with the reduction of SO$_2$ concentration from 0.098 mg/m^3 in 1985 to less than 0.05 mg/m^3 in 2000, between Grades I and II of the National Standard.

2. On the other hand, however, the improvement of air quality will be only marginal in some other districts. The reason is the rapid population increase and the industrial coal consumption in these areas (addressed in more detail in the next section).

3. There will be two cases in which the air quality will be worsened even if all the above-mentioned environmental improvement measures have been adopted. These are the Dao Li and Xiang Fang districts, where the SO$_2$ concentra-

Fig. 10.11 Air Pollution Isoline Diagram of Harbin, Winter 1985 (SO_2 in mg/m^3)

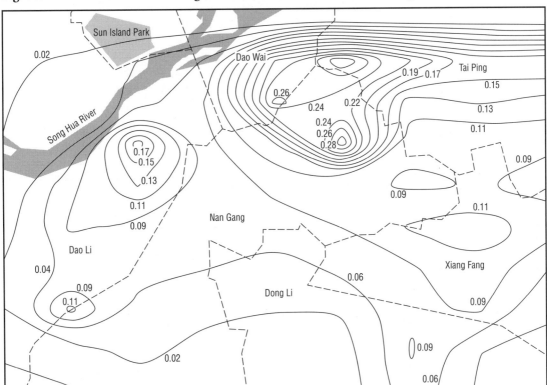

Fig. 10.12 Air Pollution Isoline Diagram of Harbin, Winter 2000 (SO_2 in mg/m^3)

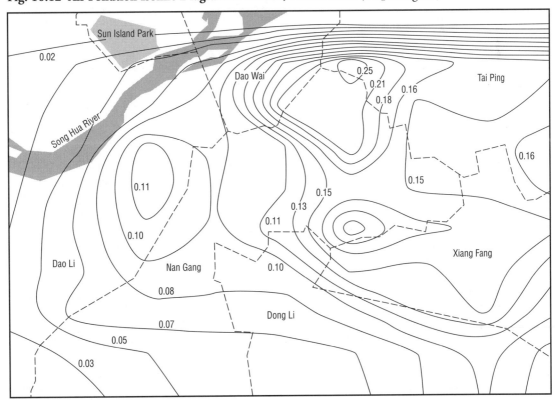

tion will increase from 0.076 and 0.073 mg/m^3 in 1985 to more than 0.115 mg/m^3 in 2000. The increase of industrial coal consumption in these two districts is the major cause of the additional pollution.

The differences in the pollution levels in all these regions can be found by comparing the isoline diagrams of Harbin for the years 1985 and 2000 (figures 10.11 and 10.12).

10.6.2. CONTRIBUTION TO SO$_2$ CONCENTRATION BY SECTORS

Comparing the contribution shares of various coal-consuming sectors in 1985 and 2000 (figures 10.13 and 10.14), a very striking picture is presented and the direction of future efforts can be visualized. The most substantial change in the pollution sources in all these districts is the abrupt increase of pollution from the industrial sector and the obvious reduction of pollution from the scattered boilers, small heating stoves, and cooking stoves. Pollution from industry will increase from 7 to 32 percent in 1985, to 35 to 65 percent in 2000 for various districts, while the maximum share of SO$_2$ pollution from small heating and cooking stoves will decrease from some 60 percent in 1985 to 25 to 30 percent in 2000.

The effect of the planned district heating program is therefore obvious, and the necessity of a parallel program to reduce industrial SO$_2$ from increased coal consumption is addressed. Further study is proposed to find the final solution of the air pollution problem produced by both residential and industrial sectors.

10.7 CONCLUSION

From the results obtained above, the following conclusions can be drawn:

10.7.1. ECONOMIC STRATEGY

Harbin is one of the major production bases for the manufacture of heavy machinery and electrical power equipment in China. The advantage of this heavy industrial base should be fully exploited to make greater contributions to the national economy.

On the other hand, however, Harbin's industrial structure is capital-, energy-, and raw material-intensive, and there exist certain disadvantages. Two particular conditions must be mentioned.
1. There is a lower output rate per unit fixed

assets. Hence the payback of capital investment is slower than for light industry.
2. At present the growth rate of the economy has slowed. If it is desirable to speed up economic growth, serious shortages of funds, energy, and raw material supply will be encountered, as has indeed happened in the past few years.

As a consequence, economic development in Harbin should be economic benefit-oriented and energy savings-oriented rather than growth speed-oriented. Economic growth should not depend simply on the expansion of capacity by increasing investment, but should also depend on the improvement of the economic system through the adjustment of industrial structure and raising of the STM level.

In particular, the following are recommended:

1. The growth rate of total social product should be kept at an average of 9 percent annually from 1985 to 2000, rather than the high value of 11 percent attained in 1987. With such a moderate growth rate, the total social product will reach 38.6 billion yuan by the year 2000, a more reasonable target.

   An alternative option, allowing for a growth rate of 7.77 percent and a total social product of 32.0 billion yuan by 2000, is considered more conservative and feasible.
2. The investment rate, which is defined as the ratio of investment to national income, should be decreased from the too-high figure of 44 percent to around 36 percent, on average, between 1988 and 2000.
3. The industrial product structure should be adjusted so that some higher value-added and lower energy-consuming branches, such as the textile, apparel, medicine, and electronic instruments industries, may contribute a greater share by 2000. The machinery and power equipment manufacturing industries will retain their dominant positions.
4. In order to direct the adjustment of industry structure, the allocation of limited investment among various industrial branches should be "tilted" to favor the most profitable sector with the least pollution.
5. Part of the investment budget for fixed assets should be shifted to the budget for scientific technology and management development. It is estimated that a 0.25 increase in the scientific, technical, and managerial (STM) level will substitute for about 5 billion yuan of total industrial investment.

Fig. 10.13 District Contribution to SO₂ Concentration, 1985

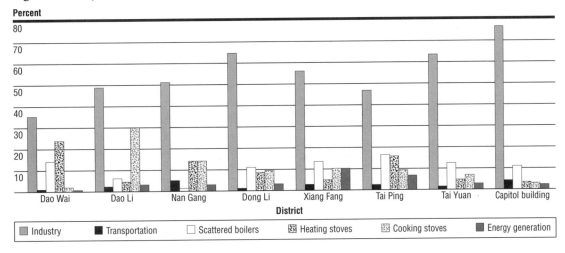

Fig. 10.14 Projected District Contribution to SO₂ Concentration, 2000

10.7.2. ENERGY STRATEGY
The main features and problems of energy development in Harbin are as follows:

1. Socioeconomic development in Harbin is suffering because of energy shortages, especially of electricity. The statistics show that during 1981-1985 the electrical consumption elasticity was only 0.58, much less than the normal value of 1.1 to 1.4.
2. The dominance of coal in final consumption causes heavy transportation burdens and serious air pollution.
3. The final energy consumption in the industrial sector amounts to 57 percent of total final energy consumption. By contrast, household energy consumption accounts for only 15.7 percent.
4. A great amount of coal is needed for space heating. Seasonal energy consumption aggra-

vates the shortage of energy as well as air quality degradation.
5. Investment funds are particularly short in energy infrastructure construction, such as for electric power systems, district heating systems, and urban gas systems.

In the framework of integrated development planning, energy strategy would play a key role, and it may strongly influence the economy and environmental development. The strategy of energy development can be summarized as follows:

1. Both energy exploitation and energy conservation should be emphasized in order to reverse the long-term energy shortage as rapidly as possible.
2. Improvement of energy composition by sectors and fuel substitution efforts should aim at increasing the share of energy consumption in

159

the residential sector by supplying clean and high-quality forms of energy such as electricity, heat, and gas in order to reduce direct burning of coal in final use and improving both living standards and the environment.

3. The municipal energy planning authority should make decisions on certain large-scale energy projects (electric power plants, the Low-Temperature Nuclear Heating Reactor, Yilan Mine-Mouth Gas Works, and the natural gas pipeline), which have proved to be economically and financially feasible.

4. According to energy demand forecasting, a great amount of coal will continue to be consumed in the future, mainly in the industrial sector. As a consequence, clean utilization of coal and appropriate siting of energy-intensive enterprises should be emphasized in order to reduce air pollution in urban areas.

In particular, the following scenario is recommended:

1. Energy demand:
The total final energy demand in 2000 will be around 16.3 million tce, of which 10.7 million is for production sectors, including industrial, agricultural, transportation, and commercial, about 2.4 times that in 1985. The total final electricity demand in 2000 will be 71.67 x 108 kWh and 1,194 MW. In 1985 it was 27 x 108 kWh and 490 MW.

2. Energy intensity:
The required final energy and electricity intensity should be 3.36 tce/104 yuan and 1,780 kWh/104 yuan by the year 2000, respectively. In comparison, these figures were 4.2 and 2,100 in 1985.

3. Energy conservation:
The corresponding average energy conservation rate will be around 1.48 percent annually and 1.10 percent annually for energy and electricity, respectively.

4. Energy consumption elasticity:
To keep a rational relationship between the economy and energy, the proper energy consumption elasticity of total social product value will average 0.79 for energy and 0.84 for electricity from 1985 to 2000.

5. Energy supply planning:
A. Electrical power: In the Harbin region, the total electricity supply will increase from 2.836 TWh in 1985 to 7.106 TWh in 2000. The total installed capacity will increase from 500 MW in 1985 to 1,314 MW in 2000. The municipal government and the enterprises in Harbin will provide up to 814 million yuan of investment. The total capacity of utility-owned

power plants in Harbin will be expanded to 2,225 MW, which will require 3.5 billion yuan of investment.

B. District heating: Dao Li and Dao Wai districts are the most densely populated and densely urban areas. These two districts are presently the most seriously polluted parts of the Harbin area in winter. The municipal government is interested in building two 200-MWt Low-Temperature Nuclear Heating Reactors in those districts if necessary funds can be collected.

C. Urban gas supply: Small coal-fired stoves for cooking and water heating accounted for 43.1 percent of SO_2 concentration and 45.6 percent of TSP concentration in Harbin in 1985. Therefore the municipal government has given high priority to the development of urban gas supply. Three different technical approaches — coal gasification, natural gas, and coke-oven gas — are under consideration, the choice to be determined according to the resource and investment availability.

10.7.3. ENVIRONMENTAL STRATEGY
The present situation and existing problems of air and water pollution in Harbin can be summarized as follows:

1. Pollutant Emission Intensities
Pollutant emission intensities per unit of energy consumption and per unit GNP in Harbin are much higher than in most parts of China. The annual pollutant emission of dust (TSP), SO_2, and NO_x were 217,000, 48,000, and 45,000 tons, respectively, in 1986. With a 9 percent annual rate of increase of TSP and SO_2 emissions during 1980-1986, the estimated pollutant emission would be 281,000 tons of TSP and 62,400 tons of SO_2 by the year 2000, if no further environmental control measures are taken.

2. Source of Pollutant Emissions
The industrial and residential sectors produce the major part of SO_2 and dust (TSP) emissions. Coal combustion was responsible for 60 percent of the total dust emissions and 87 percent of total SO2 emissions in Harbin in 1986.

3. Distribution of SO_2 and TSP Ground Concentration
The average ground concentration of SO_2 and TSP in Harbin in winter 1986 were 0.082 mg/m^3 (higher than Grade II) and 0.473 mg/m^3 (higher than Grade III) in Dao Wai, while the lowest concentrations of SO_2 and TSP were 0.075 mg/m^3 (Grade II) and 0.24

mg/m^3 (between Grades I and II) in Dong Li and Xiang Fang districts.

4. SO$_2$ Pollution by Energy Consumer Branches

Industry and small stoves for home heating, cooking, and water heating contribute 17.4 percent and 43.1 percent to SO$_2$ concentration, respectively. The shares of TSP are similar.

It is clear, therefore, that the development of a district heating and gas pipeline network as discussed above would be the most effective measure for environmental protection.

Those combined options will improve the air quality somewhat. In particular, significant improvement will be realized in Dao Wai district, the most heavily polluted area. The SO$_2$ concentration will decrease to about 0.24 mg/m^3, as compared with 0.339 mg/m^3 in 1985. In Tai Yang Dao (Sun Island), air quality will improve from having contained 0.098 mg. SO$_2$ per cubic meter (Grade II-III) in 1985 to having only 0.05 mg. per cubic meter (Grade I-II) in 2000.

The share of SO$_2$ concentration contributed by the industrial sector, however, will increase dramatically — for instance, in Xiang Fang, from 32 percent in 1985 to 65 percent in 2000. As a result, industry will become a dominant pollution source by 2000. On the positive side, the pollution contribution of small stoves and cooking devices will decrease from maximum value, about 60 percent in 1985, to only 25 to 30 percent by 2000.

This explains the marginal overall improvement of air quality in Harbin by 2000. It is obvious, therefore, that the next important task will be the introduction of clean coal technology in the industrial sector.

CHAPTER 11

A TWENTY-FIRST CENTURY PERSPECTIVE ON THE ELECTRICITY SYSTEM OF CHINA

11.1. TRENDS IN ELECTRICITY CONSUMPTION

11.1.1. DEVELOPMENT OF THE POWER SECTOR AND CAUSES OF POWER SHORTAGES

The Chinese economy has grown very rapidly during the past four decades, but the growth rate of the electricity supply has been even greater. The final energy and electricity consumption by sectors and per capita is shown in table 11.1; the population share served with electricity, in table 11.2. (For more details of this case study, see reference 67.)

Although China's electric power industry has gained new achievements since 1980, when economic reforms began, the electricity shortage remains acute and has become the bottleneck for economic development. The reasons for the shortage of electricity can be summarized as follows:

1. Overheated Economic Growth

China's national economy has grown much faster than its electricity supply. In 1988, the GNP grew by 10.8 percent and the gross industrial product grew by 14.8 percent, whereas electricity generation only increased 9.6 percent. The elasticity was 0.88 over GNP and 0.63 over industrial growth in 1988. By contrast, this elasticity was 1.08 during the period 1980-1982.

2. Small Investment in Electricity Generation

Normally, investment in the energy sector as a share of the total investment in fixed assets of state-owned enterprises in China was kept at about 23 percent before 1979. But for a long period afterwards it was much lower. For instance, in 1986-1988 the percentage dropped to 8.6. The share of investment in

Table 11.1 Energy and Electricity Consumption in China

Year	Final energy consumption (10^6 toe)	Final energy per capita (toe/cap)	Final energy per GNP (toe/10^6USD)	Electricity consumption, TWh				Electricity consumption per capita (KWh/cap)	Electricity consumption per unit GNP (KWh/USD)
				Industrial	Residential	Other	Total		
1970	191.71	0.231	2,357.0	92.0	5.0	8.2	105.2	126.7	1.29
1972	244.73	0.281	2,607.3	112.5	6.5	19.0	138.0	158.3	1.47
1975	299.85	0.324	2,587.9	137.6	7.8	30.5	175.8	190.3	1.52
1978	378.81	0.394	2,438.3	184.0	10.3	37.5	231.8	240.8	1.49
1980	402.56	0.408	2,233.8	216.8	10.5	49.1	276.3	280.0	1.53
1982	415.18	0.409	2,027.7	234.0	12.1	55.7	301.8	297.1	1.47
1985	515.10	0.490	1,765.5	288.0	22.3	71.1	381.3	363.0	1.31
1987	581.04	0.538	1,656.4	364.5	28.7	69.3	462.4	427.9	1.32
1988	624.64	0.570	1,607.0	398.5	34.3	75.9	508.7	464.1	1.31

Table 11.2 Share of the Population Served with Electricity

Year	Urban (%)	Rural (%)
1980	100	68
1982	100	70
1985	100	73
1987	100	75
1988	100	76

Table 11.3 Tax and Profit Rate Change in Power Sector

	1962	1986
Generating cost, yuan/GWh	32.2	47.1
Tax rate, %	5	25
Prices, yuan/GWh	78.3	75.3
Profit rate, %	15	5.53

the power sector is a fraction of the investment in the energy sector. It dropped substantially in the same period. During 1981-1985, the power sector's share of total investment was only 4.3 percent, much lower than the normal share of 7 to 10 percent.

3. Disproportionate Growth of Coal and Transportation Sectors

During 1986-1988, primary energy production grew by 3.8 percent, coal by 4 percent, and transportation capacity by 3 percent, while electricity generation increased by 9 percent annually. This uneven growth pattern led directly to dramatic reductions in power generation, whose growth rate decreased from 11.1 percent during January-August 1988 to 4.2 percent during September-December 1988. In January-February 1989, the growth rate dropped even further, to 2.6 percent.

4. Weak Self-Financing and Expansion Capacity

It can be seen clearly from table 11.3 that the power industry has become a highly taxed sector, second only to tobacco, brewery, and cosmetics industries. As a result its profit rate fell from 15 percent in 1962 to 4.73 percent in 1988, below the national average of 10.7 percent. It is now very difficult to raise funds from society and banks for the power sector.

5. Changes in Electricity Investment

During the recent economic reforms, to encourage the participation of local governments and enterprises, the central government decreased its direct investment from 75 percent to 46.8 percent in 1980 and to

Table 11.4 Increase of Power-Generating and -Consuming Equipment (GWe)

	1985	1988	Increase	Annual growth rate (%)
Capacity of power generating equipment	87.06	112.9	25.84	9.05
Capacity of power consuming equipment	212.58	289.95	77.37	10.90
Ratio of consuming to generating equipment	2.44	2.57		

25.1 percent in 1985. However, localities' considerations of their own short-term interests and emphasis on local benefits made the municipalities and enterprises unwilling to invest in the electricity sector.

Other factors also contribute to the power sector bottleneck, including low electrical efficiency and poor management.

11.1.2 DRIVING FORCES OF THE POWER SECTOR

11.1.2.1 INDUSTRIAL SECTOR

The driving forces of electricity consumption in industry are as follows:

1. High ratio of power-consuming equipment to power-generating equipment. The rapid growth of manufacturing industries, especially consumer goods production, has resulted in substantial increases in the capacity of power-consuming equipment (see table 11.4).

Since the load demand is far more than the power generating capacity, it is inevitable that in peak load hours the power supply will have to be cut back, without advance warning. It is estimated that about 20 percent of industrial equipment was idle due to power shortages in 1988.

2. Increasing electricity intensity of products. Electricity intensity has increased for various reasons — among them, changes in production conditions, such as the adoption of water injection in oil fields; the rise of the mechanization level; the deep processing of crude oil; and improvement of the working environment, for example, by ventilating and air conditioning in textile plants.

11.1.2.2. RESIDENTIAL AND SERVICE SECTORS

Due to the industry-oriented energy policy in China, the share of residential and service-sector electrical consumption decreased continuously after 1949. The share was 24 percent in 1949, 10 to 15 percent under the First Five-Year Plan, 6.6 to 8.8 percent under the Second Five-Year Plan, and in 1966 and

Table 11.5 Electricity Consumption in Residential and Service Sectors

Subsector	1986		1987	
	GWh	%	GWh	%
Running water supply	5,372	14.86	5,798	14.44
Transport, mail and tele-communications services	556	1.54	655	1.63
Shops, restaurants, and other services	4,121	11.40	4,945	12.32
Others: utilities, lighting, traffic, offices, etc.	12,682	35.07	14,290	35.60
Urban households	13,426	37.13	14,457	36.01
Total	36,157	100.00	40,145	100.00

Table 11.6 Electricity Consumption of Residential Sector, 1986

	Electricity per capita (kWh)	Share of total consumption (%)
China		
Rural	16.0	2.2
Urban	57.6	3.0
Total	23.0	5.2
Developed countries	1,000 - 3,000	22 - 40

1967 it dropped to an extremely low figure, around 5 percent. However, during the recent economic reform, the government decided to place more emphasis on improving the people's standard of living. Thus, the residential and service-sector electrical consumption increased to 8.04 percent in 1986, to 36.157 TWh, as compared with 16.602 TWh in 1980.

Electricity consumption in households and the service sector can be divided into five categories (see table 11.5). Urban households account for only 36 to 37 percent of consumption in this sector. In 1986 the national electricity consumption attained 442.9 TWh, of which urban and rural household consumption was only 23.15 TWh, corresponding to a share of 5.2 percent, or just 23 kWh per capita. A comparison of Chinese household consumption with that of developed countries is shown in table 11.6. Rural Chinese consume less than a third of the electricity used by urban residents.

In addition to the improvement in people's living standards, the following driving forces are also important explanations for the dramatic increase of urban electricity consumption during the past ten years.

1. Urbanization
Since the reforms of 1978, all of China's cities, large, medium, and small, have expanded rapidly. Large numbers of surplus rural laborers rushed into cities and towns, resulting in rapid urbanization.

Allowing 50 kWh per person for residential power consumption, plus 60 kWh per person in urban power consumption per year, it is estimated that an additional amount of about 19.555 TWh of electricity was consumed between 1980 and 1986 due to urbanization.

2. Development of the "third sector"
With the progress of economic reform, the "third sector" (services) of the economy developed with an annual growth rate of 12.6 percent — more rapid than the primary (agricultural) and the secondary (industrial) sectors. For example, the newly opened commercial, restaurant, and service units, usually equipped with refrigerators, air conditioners, and electric heaters, increased by 39.5 percent per year during 1980-1986. Even more electricity-intensive is the development of luxury hotels for tourists. From 1980 to 1986, the number of such hotels increased from 230 to 964, the number of beds from 6,000 to 33,200. Considering a demand of 3,500 kWh per bed-year, the power consumed in these hotels increased from 266 TWh in 1980 to 1,162 TWh in 1986.

3. Modernization
This trend mainly refers to the development of modern office buildings, office automation, modern information processing techniques, telecommunications, education, cultural life, and broadcasting. For example, the number of telephones in city centers increased from 2.539 million in 1983 to 4.436 million in 1986, an annual rate of 20.4 percent.

4. Rapid popularization of electric home appliances
With the improvement of living standards, the greatest part of Chinese family income is spent on the purchase of electric appliances. Table 11.7 shows the rapid popularization and the power consumed in households. However, it should be noted that this is not the major driving force of consumption.

11.1.2.3 AGRICULTURAL SECTOR
With the expansion of China's electrical grid and the proliferation of small thermal power plants and minihydropower stations, electricity consumption in rural areas has increased rapidly.

However, due to the rural electricity shortage, a gap of about 20 TWh existed between supply and

Table 11.7 Electricity Consumption in Households

Year	Population, millions Urban	Rural	Total	Growth (%)	Appliances per 100 urban households Electric fans	Television sets	Refrigerators	Energy consumed per capita Energy (tce)	Electricity (GWh)
1980	191.4	795.7	987.1	1.2	—	57.65	0.08	0.097	10.7
1982	211.3	804.6	1,015.9	1.4	53.17	73.31	0.67	0.108	11.9
1984	331.4	707.4	1,038.8	1.1	66.41	87.42	3.22	0.123	15.4
1985	384.5	666.0	1,050.5	1.1	73.91	84.07	6.58	0.127	21.3
1986	441.0	624.3	1,065.3	1.4	90.08	92.83	12.71	0.128	23.5
1987	503.6	577.1	1,080.7	1.4	103.90	99.40	19.91	0.133	26.5

demand in 1985. Commonly, the power supply for agriculture was squeezed by industrial demand once the load exceeded the supply. As a result, the electricity supply in rural areas is highly unreliable.

Rural power shortages can have adverse consequences. In 1985, 31.8 percent of the 11.5 billion tons of diesel oil allocated for operation of farm machinery was consumed by rural industry for power generation (total 2 GWe) at low efficiency and high cost. A sizable fraction of irrigation had to be performed by diesel engines substituting for electric motors. This is quite inconsistent with the current oil conservation policy.

The main driving forces for the increasing electricity consumption in rural areas are the following:

1. Rapid growth of the rural economy. It was reported that during the Sixth Five-Year Plan the gross agricultural product increased by 11.7 percent

per year. The power supply grew just 3.7 percent per year, lagging far behind economic growth.

2. Structural change from agricultural production alone to diversified economic structure. Production values of village and town industries in 1986 exceeded the production value of agriculture for the first time, which led to a dramatic increase in demand for electricity.

11.1.3 ELECTRICITY CONSERVATION

Since the 1980s, China has taken many administrative, regulatory, technological, and economic measures to promote energy conservation. In the State Council and in each province, municipality, and seventeen major energy-consuming departments, at least one of the highest officials is assigned the responsibility for energy conservation. This is intended to guarantee electricity savings.

Table 11.8 shows the electricity consumption intensities for several important products. It is noted that the improvements in the energy-intensity of these products have been relatively small, less than 5 percent in all cases.

11.1.4 FORECAST OF ELECTRICITY DEMAND

The forecast of electricity demand is shown in table 11.9.

The method of sectoral activity analysis is employed in the forecast. The total demand is the sum of demand of all sectors.

Table 11.8 Electricity Consumption Intensity of Manufacture of Some Products

Year	Steel kWh/T	Aluminum kWh/T	Ammonia kWh/T
1980	647	15,432	1,441
1982	643	16,108	1,434
1983	635	15,633	1,406
1984	619	15,456	1,352
1985	626	15,047	1,385

Table 11.9 Final Energy and Electricity Demand Forecast

Year	Final energy consumption (10^6 toe)	Final energy per capita (toe/cap)	Final energy per unit GNP (toe/10^6USD)	Electricity consumption, TWh Industrial	Residential	Other	Total	Electricity consumption per capita (kWh/cap)	Electricity consumption per unit GNP (kWh/USD)
1990	660.17	0.586	1,533.40	452.2	43.9	89.6	585.8	520.2	1.36
1995	795.01	0.658	1,347.80	599.1	66.3	123.9	789.3	653.4	1.34
2000	947.15	0.741	1,199.80	816.5	104.0	185.9	1,106.4	865.7	1.40
2010	1,246.88	0.910	993.63	1,277.1	205.6	321.1	1,803.8	1,316.6	1.44
2015	1,454.88	1.029	929.18	1,602.6	286.8	423.2	2,312.5	1,651.8	1.48

Table 11.10 Electricity Generation in China by 2010

	Hydropower %	Hydropower TWh	Coal-fired %	Coal-fired TWh	Oil-fired %	Oil-fired TWh	Natural-gas fired %	Natural-gas fired TWh	Thermal total %	Thermal total TWh	Nuclear power %	Nuclear power TWh	Total TWh
					Thermal power								
1970	17.7	20.5	—	—	—	—	—	—	82.3	95.4	0	0	115.9
1972	18.9	28.8	—	—	—	—	—	—	81.1	123.6	0	0	152.4
1974	24.5	41.4	53.9	91.0	20.8	35.0	0.8	1.3	75.5	127.4	0	0	168.8
1975	24.3	47.6	52.5	102.8	21.8	42.7	1.4	2.7	75.7	148.2	0	0	195.8
1976	22.5	45.6	52.6	106.8	23.1	46.9	1.9	3.8	77.5	157.5	0	0	303.1
1978	17.4	44.6	60.9	156.2	20.0	51.4	1.7	4.4	82.6	212.0	0	0	256.6
1979	17.8	50.1	61.5	173.5	18.9	53.4	1.8	5.1	82.2	231.9	0	0	282.0
1980	19.4	58.2	60.5	182.0	18.0	54.0	2.1	6.4	80.6	242.4	0	0	300.6
1982	22.7	74.4	59.7	195.7	15.5	50.8	2.1	6.8	77.3	253.3	0	0	327.7
1985	22.5	92.4	63.8	262.0	11.0	45.0	2.7	11.2	77.5	318.3	0	0	410.7
1987	20.1	100.2	67.1	333.5	9.2	45.6	3.6	18.0	79.9	397.1	0	0	497.3
1988	20.0	109.2	68.7	374.7	8.8	47.9	2.4	13.2	80.0	435.9	0	0	545.1

The basic assumptions for each sector are as follows:

For the industrial sector:

1. The industrial share of GNP, which is higher than normal for developed economies, will decrease to 50 percent, and the share of manufacture in the industrial sector will also decrease, to 70 percent.
2. Specific consumption per unit GNP in industry is very high; thus, great potential for electricity conservation exists.
3. With the development of mechanization, automation, and electric heating, the share of electricity in final energy consumption will increase.
4. Per capita major industrial products increase with the growth of per capita income.

For the agricultural sector:

The forecast is made by each subsector: irrigation, agricultural operation, preliminary processing of agricultural products. The results are then summed to get the total demand.

For the transportation sector:

The forecast is made considering the scenarios of future population, GNP per capita, volume of goods and passengers transported, mix of transportation devices by energy and electricity intensity.

For the service sector:

The energy consumption in the service sector can be characterized as follows:

1. Services have low energy intensity.
2. The share of electricity in total energy consumption is greater than that of any other sector.
3. The energy consumption elasticity is very low, namely, 0.5.

For the residential sector:

Total demand is the sum of demand for (1) space heating, (2) cooking, (3) water heating, and (4) lighting and electric appliances.

11.2. TRENDS IN ELECTRICITY SUPPLY

11.2.1 PAST TRENDS OF ELECTRICITY GENERATION

The structure of electricity generation and installed capacity is shown in tables 11.10 and 11.11. The structure of power plants used to supply electricity by installed capacity, age, and scale is shown in tables 11.12 and 11.13, respectively. The following comments may be made:

1. Coal-fired power stations constituted over 60 percent of the installed generation capacity and accounted for 68 percent of the total generation, and the shares were increasing. The number of oil-fired power plants was reduced by policy. However, although their greater importance and benefits were emphasized over and over again, hydropower plants maintained an almost constant share.
2. Although newly built power stations occupied a significant position in the power plant structure (80 percent were less than twenty years old, among which 60 percent were less than ten years old), the scale of power plants still remains relatively small (55 percent generate less than 200 MWe, of which 25 percent produce less than 50 MWe). Most of

Table 11.11 Trends of Installed Capacity in China by 2010

	Hydropower %	Hydropower GW	Coal-fired %	Coal-fired GW	Oil-fired %	Oil-fired GW	Diesel-fired %	Diesel-fired GW	Gas-fired %	Gas-fired GW	Thermal total %	Thermal total GW	Nuclear power %	Nuclear power GW	Total capacity GW
1970	26.2	6.23	—	—	—	—	—	—	—	—	73.8	17.54	0	0	23.77
1972	29.5	8.70	—	—	—	—	—	—	—	—	70.5	20.80	0	0	29.50
1975	30.9	13.43	48.3	20.98	20.1	8.71	0.2	0.09	0.5	0.22	69.1	29.98	0	0	43.41
1978	30.3	17.28	51.9	29.65	17.1	9.77	0.2	0.11	0.5	0.29	69.7	39.84	0	0	57.12
1979	30.3	19.11	52.8	33.27	16.2	10.21	0.2	0.13	0.5	0.31	69.7	43.91	0	0	63.02
1980	30.8	20.32	50.7	30.04	17.7	10.46	0.2	0.13	0.5	0.30	69.2	45.55	0	0	65.87
1982	31.7	22.96	52.1	33.69	15.5	10.04	0.2	0.14	0.5	0.30	68.3	49.40	0	0	72.36
1985	30.4	26.42	57.1	45.47	11.8	9.36	0.2	0.17	0.6	0.47	69.6	60.63	0	0	87.05
1986	29.4	27.54	60.5	52.00	9.3	8.01	0.2	0.19	0.6	0.52	70.6	66.28	0	0	93.82
1987	29.2	30.19	—	—	—	—	—	—	—	—	70.7	72.71	0	0	102.90
1988	28.3	32.70	60.3	62.34	10.3	10.68	0.2	0.23	0.9	0.91	71.7	82.80	0	0	115.50

the larger plants have only 200-Mwe units, while the largest capacity of any single unit was only 300 MWe.

11.2.2 DEVELOPMENT OF POWER GRIDS

There are eleven regional power grids in China, with a total capacity of 87.39 gigavolt-amperes (GVA), over 220 kilovolts. The voltage levels adopted are generally 220/110/35/10 KV. The capacity of each regional grid is shown in table 11.14, and the coverage is shown in figure 11.1.

During the 1980s, China increased the rate of expansion of its power grids. The first 500-KV AC transmission line was put into operation at the end of 1981 to connect Hubei and Henan provincial power grids. The construction of the first super-high voltage 500-KV DC transmission line (from

Gezhouba to Shanghai) began in 1985. This line was scheduled to be put into operation at the end of 1990. The length of transmission lines is listed in table 11.15. The inter-provincial grids have been established for northern, eastern, central, and northeastern China with the mainframe of 500-KV or 220-KV transmission lines.

11.2.3 ELECTRICITY DEVELOPMENT POLICY

According to the situation and distribution of primary energy resources and the energy development strategy with electricity as the nucleus, the policy for power industry development has been formulated as follows:

1. Construction of thermal power plants
According to resources policy, thermal power plants are to be based on coal, and no oil-fired power plants

Table 11.12 Age of Chinese Power Plants

Power source	Built before 1960 Capacity (MW)	Built before 1960 Number	Built 1960-1970 Capacity (MW)	Built 1960-1970 Number	Built 1971-1980 Capacity (MW)	Built 1971-1980 Number	Built 1980-1988 Capacity (MW)
Hydro	3,106.8	65	3,717.9	90	9,496.4	211	9,296.3
Thermal	1,031.7	395	8,159.8	294	24,355.7	477	34,434.4
Total	**4,138.5**	**460**	**11,877.7**	**384**	**33,852.1**	**688**	**43,730.7**

Table 11.13 Scale of Chinese Power Plants

Type	50 MW Total MW	50 MW Number	50-200 MW Total MW	50-200 MW Number	200 MW Total MW	200 MW Number	Total Total MW	Total Number
Hydro	6,398.2	363	11,909.1	133	3,690.0	14	21,997.3	510
Thermal	15,817.9	1,172	29,565.0	382	27,640.0	118	73,022.9	1,672
Diesel	284.5	33	0	0	0	0	284.5	33
Gas	908.7	44	0	0	0	0	908.7	44
Other	18.0	3	0	0	0	0	18.0	3
Total	**23,427.3**	**1,615**	**41,474.1**	**515**	**31,330.0**	**132**	**96,231.4**	**2,262**

Table 11.14 Chinese Power Grids

Region	Installed capacity (10⁴ kW)			Generation (10⁸ kWh)		
	Total	Hydro	Thermal	Total	Hydro	Thermal
Northeast	1,320.7	291.6	1,029.1	665.6	112.4	553.2
North	1,247.9	75.7	1,172.2	694.1	12.5	681.6
East	1,414.4	188.9	1,225.5	761.9	43.9	718.0
Central	1,364.1	524.6	839.5	664.1	223.6	440.5
Northwest	585.2	249.4	335.8	301.2	106.6	194.6
Southwest	577.7	277.5	299.9	275.0	116.8	158.2
South	443.8	215.6	228.2	210.6	78.4	132.2
Shangdong	463.3	4.7	458.6	298.0	0.5	297.5
Fujian	182.0	94.5	87.5	70.4	35.5	34.9
Yunnan	156.8	82.5	74.3	72.6	39.3	33.3
East of Northeast	142.4	14.7	127.7	86.2	6.4	79.8
Xingjiang	129.7	37.2	92.5	42.9	9.4	33.5

will be built. All of the large and medium-size thermal power-generating units commissioned during the Sixth Five-Year Plan were coal-fired; their total capacity was 10.620 GWe. At the same time, some of the existing oil-fired units which had been originally designed for burning coal were reconverted to use coal.

To speed up the expansion of electricity generation and increase energy savings, large high-temperature, high-pressure units were installed in the new thermal plants. By the end of 1984, the aggregate capacity of the large units (100-megawatt and above) accounted for 47.7 percent of total installed

Fig. 11.1 Coverage of Chinese Power Grids

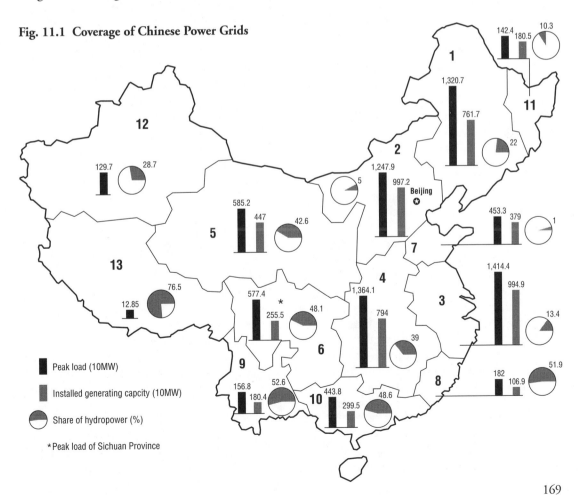

169

Table 11.15 Recent Development of Transmission Lines in China (km)

Year	Total (35 KV and above)	500 KV	330 KV	220 KV	110 KV
1978			535	22,672	57,418
1985	346,646	2,539	1,278	46,056	84,504
1986	369,491	3,269	1,695	49,419	89,229
1987	394,162	4,477	2,530	54,477	95,585
1988		5,677	2,786	62,145	101,474

capacity, and this share will increase greatly as more and more 300-MW and 600-MW units under construction are put into operation.

2. Building of hydropower stations near load centers

Since 1980, the construction of hydropower plants has been accelerated. However, the total hydropower installed capacity together with those under construction was still less than 10 percent of China's total exploitable hydropower potential. Because most hydropower resources were located in the far west of China, remote from major load centers, the investment for capital construction is proportionally high and the construction period long. China has focused on step-exploitation of some river sections with favorable site conditions and superior economic indexes.

3. Development of nuclear power plants

Due to the shortage of coal and hydropower potential in northeast and eastern China, and in Guangdong Province, along with the limited coal transport capacity, building of nuclear power plants in these areas is urgently needed. Two commercial nuclear plants, Daya Bay of Guangdong Province (1,800 MW) and Qingshan of Zhejiang Province (300 MW), are under construction, and more are planned.

4. Diversification of power generation

In areas far from the major power grids, small hydro, wind, and geothermal power plants have been built in accordance with local energy resource conditions.

5. Development of power transmission networks

Super-high voltage DC and AC transmission systems have been developed in step with the development of the power industry, especially the expansion of power networks and the construction of large thermal and hydropower plants. Transmission of 500-KV and 330-KV AC and DC has been developed and lines are being constructed according to local situations.

6. Investment in electric power

With the progress of economic reform, local governments and enterprises will play more and more

significant roles in investment in the power sector. In order to alleviate the present acute shortage of electricity, the central government has taken a number of measures to attract capital to the power sector. The official principles of the reform of the electric administration system are: "Separate government functions from enterprise activities, recognize each province as an individual unit, interconnect the provincial grids, diversify the sources of capital for electricity development in accordance with the local conditions and network situations." The most effective measure is to raise the electricity tariff and allow the local governments and enterprises to collect capital for power sector development by any means appropriate to their situations.

11.2.4 FUTURE OF ELECTRICITY GENERATION

With an eye on China's energy resources, the basic policy for development of the electric power industry is as follows: To accelerate the construction of both hydropower and thermal power plants, to appropriately develop nuclear power plants, to enhance power network construction, and in the meantime to upgrade existing power equipment.

The plan for future electricity generation up to 2010 is shown in tables 11.16 and 11.17. Detailed arrangements have been made for implementing the plan according to the distribution of resources.

Since China is well endowed with coal resources, coal-fired power plants will continue to be the mainstay. A number of large power stations, each with a capacity of 1,200 to 2,400 MW, will be built. A few mine-mouth power plants may be of even greater capacity where conditions are especially favorable. More emphasis will be put on the construction of large mine-mouth power plants in coal-rich provinces such as Shanxi, Anhui, Shandong, and the Inner Mongolia Autonomous Region. Mine-mouth power plants with an aggregate capacity of about 10,000 MW will be built according to the pace of the exploitation of each of the five huge open-cast coal mines — Pingshuo, Zhunger, Yuanbaoshan, Huolinhe, and Yimin. The coal used for electricity generation is estimated to be one-third of the total coal output by the year 2000.

In hydropower development, China will concentrate its efforts on continuous step-exploitation of some river sections with abundant hydropower potential and favorable site conditions for comprehensive utilization, such as the upper and middle reaches of the Changjiang (Yangtze River) and its tributaries, the upper reaches of the Huanghe (Yellow River), and the Hongshuihe Basin.

Table 11.16 Planned Electricity Generation by 2010

	Hydro-generated		Thermal-generated		Nuclear-generated		Total
	%	TWh	%	TWh	%	TWh	TWh
1990	20.2	128.8	79.8	507.9	0	0	636.7
1995	20.9	179.5	77.8	667.0	1.2	10.5	857.0
2000	20.0	240.0	77.5	930.0	2.5	30.0	1,200.0
2010	20.2	394.0	74.7	1,457.0	5.1	99.0	1,950.0

Table 11.17 Planned Installed Capacity in China by 2010

	Hydro		Thermal		Nuclear		Total
	%	GW	%	GW	%	GW	GW
1990	29.6	39.03	70.1	92.34	0.2	0.30	131.67
1995	30.6	54.38	68.2	121.28	1.2	2.10	177.76
2000	31.1	74.70	66.4	159.30	2.5	6.00	240.00
2010	29.1	113.50	66.3	248.57	4.6	18.00	390.00

Due to the shortage of coal deposits and hydropower resources in the coastal economically developed region, more nuclear power units will be built. Within this century, nuclear plants having a total capacity of 10,000 MW will be constructed.

Since major hydropower and coal reserves are concentrated in southwestern, northwestern, and northern China, more long-distance transmission lines will be built to alleviate the severe power shortages in the coastal provinces. In addition, some large power plants will also be built at harbors and railway junctions near load centers. In the areas far from power grids, in accordance with local resources, small hydro, thermal, wind, geothermal, and tidal power plants will be built to meet the electricity demands of the vast rural areas and scattered small cities and towns. It is predicted that the hydropower plants will supply a fourth of the electricity requirements of rural regions.

11.3. INSTITUTIONAL FRAMEWORK

11.3.1 STRUCTURE OF UTILITIES

At present all large and medium-size power plants in operation are state owned. The Chinese power industry has three levels: national electricity utilities, local electricity utilities, and adaptive power plants owned by other industries. In 1986, the capacity shares of the power plants rated of 500 KW and over were, for the three levels, 76.9 percent, 14.4 percent, and 8.7 percent, respectively. Although the proportion of adaptive power plants is rather small, such plants account for a quarter of the total power plants of 500-KW capacity and over. In 1986, electricity generated by those adaptive power plants reached 32.27 TWh, and their capacity was 7.5 gigawatts. Since 1988, the role of the central government in electricity investment has become less significant, and adaptive power plant construction has been encouraged. As a consequence, power generation and installed capacity of these plants have increased rapidly.

11.3.2 INSTITUTIONS AND THE DECISIONMAKING PROCESS

Since 1978, China has conducted a series of economic and political reforms, among which institutional reform has been outstanding and effective. Since reform began, China has changed the institutional structure repeatedly, searching for what is most suitable for its economy. Of course, every new type of institution made some progress, but each had its weaknesses and brought forth new problems. Here we give a brief description of the present institutions and the decisionmaking process in the energy field.

The Ministry of Energy is described in figure 11.2. When a decision is to be made, the responsible department will consult with other concerned ministries and state bureaus to create a proposal. The proposal will be presented to the State Planning Commission. Once approved by this commission, the proposal can be decided upon and executed. If the proposal is considered important enough, it needs to be submitted to the State Council. After being approved by the responsible vice-premier, or even the premier himself, the decision can be made final.

11.4. KEY ISSUES IN THE CHINESE POWER INDUSTRY

11.4.1 FINANCIAL SITUATION OF UTILITIES

China has been suffering a profound, chronic electricity shortage. The government has had to implement load shedding even though thermal power plants were operating more than 6,000 hours a year. This situation resulted in part from insufficient investment in the power sector.

Generally speaking, in the past the proportion of investment in the power sector declined vis-à-vis gross capital formation. From 1957 to 1960, the period of the Great Leap Forward, the electricity shortage was extremely severe, and the percentage of investment in electric power was later increased to 7.4 percent of gross capital formation. By 1961 the power shortage had been somewhat alleviated, but in 1963 the investment again declined, to 4.1 percent, causing severe power shortages again in 1965. Electricity investment was gradually increased again. Though during the period from 1966 to 1969 the electrical share was 7 to 8 percent, this time the alleviation of electricity shortages did not appear, due to the abnormal political and economic situa-

tion. In 1971 the share of investment in electricity fell again (to 5.4 percent), and once again there were severe shortages. In the years thereafter, the share of electricity investment remained approximately between 5 and 6 percent, and therefore power shortages have continued. After 1976, investment began to rise again, reaching 7.5 percent in 1978. Unfortunately, in 1980, when the situation appeared to have improved just slightly, electricity investment was again suddenly cut.

During the Sixth Five-Year Plan period (1981-1985), the growth rate of gross fixed capital investment in the Chinese economy attained 27.8 percent, but in the power sector it was only 17.8 percent. As a result, power shortages became ever more acute. Such an imbalance in growth rates between the power industry and other industries has resulted from inconsistency and arbitrariness in policymaking. That was also the reason why the gap between electricity supply and demand widened over such a long period of time. The situation continued to worsen.

This reflects a weakness in Chinese economic reform. Decentralization of some decisionmaking was one of the main features of reform. It was ex-

Fig. 11.2 Organization of the Ministry of Energy, 1989

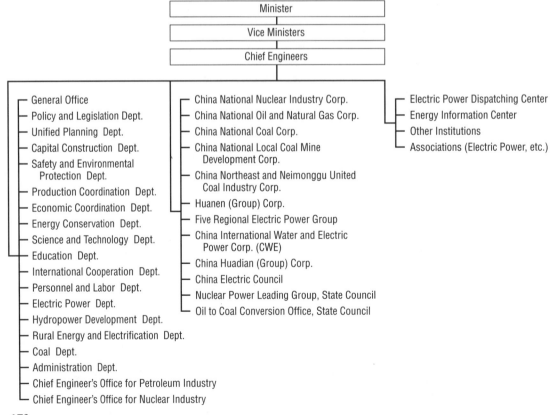

pected that decentralization would activate the initiative of enterprises and hence the workers' enthusiasm. This proved to be problematic in practice. Since the price of electricity was still tightly controlled by the government and kept consistently low to avoid inflation, the relaxation of government control of investment resulted in a new imbalance between the unprofitable power industries and the more profitable light industries.

From the point of view of the national economy, the power industry was of first importance. However, the power sector is capital intensive, with long lead-times and low return rates, so it is not attractive to small, local, and private investors. Local investors were eager to fund light industries, which are smaller in scale, quicker to construct, higher in profit, and shorter in payback periods. Such investors preferred to enjoy power supplied by the finances of others at low returns on capital investment. Thus the gap between power supply and demand continued to widen.

Since 1986, China has tried again to reform irrational profit distribution and to shape the investment pattern to contribute toward a sound industrial structure. The new policy stated: "Those who need electricity must invest in power plants, and those who invest in the power sector may decide the allocation of electricity." The new policy of raising capital through multiple channels for power plant construction seemed to be effective and began to mitigate the power shortage.

At present the electricity sector gets its capital from the following sources:

1. State-budget capital, mostly transferred from grants into the form of bank loans
2. Local electricity construction funds, mainly collected from the raising of electricity tariffs by 0.02 yuan RMB per kWh
3. Foreign funds, managed by the official investment institution (Huaneng International Electricity Development Corporation, HIEDC) and several other organizations
4. Funds from the Substituting Coal for Oil Project, managed by Huaneng Electricity Generation Corporation (HEGO)
5. Funds collected from "selling electricity capacity" to local industries which badly need power (most of the capacity is sold at the "market price" of 2,500 RMB per kilowatt)
6. Electricity Construction Bonds issued by provincial power authorities, power grid authorities, and local governments

7. Subsidies provided by the central government for mini-thermal and minihydropower plants, mainly for rural electrification

11.4.2 PRICING POLICY

The institutional reform of the Chinese economy at present includes the introduction of a "Planned Commodity Economy" on the basis of public ownership. Since June 1989, the dominant role of the planned economy has once more been emphasized. According to this new policy, the prices of major commodities will be controlled by the government. Therefore, pricing and adjustment of electricity tariffs must be approved by planning authorities.

Since the foundation of the People's Republic of China, the electricity and heat tariffs have experienced a series of adjustments and "reforms" in compliance with the nation's economic policy under various conditions. During the early stages of economic restoration before 1952, tariffs were quite diversified, differing even from district to district within the same city. The policy at that time was to keep the current tariff basically unchanged for the sake of political stability and economic recovery. Historical experience has shown that this policy played an active role in stabilizing the economy and improving the standard of living.

After 1953, the central government placed controls on electricity pricing and tariff adjustment and pursued a nationwide rate schedule by which an energy charge, capacity charge, and power factor charge have been imposed on large industrial customers. Thirty-odd years later, the rate schedule has been adjusted to some extent. For instance, the industrial and residential rates in some areas have been lowered and allowed to be influenced by economies of scale. In northeast China, where electric rates were comparatively lower than in other regions, they have been raised slightly due to the increased number of thermal power plants. In order to promote agricultural development and modernization, electricity rates were subsidized by the government. After the 1960s, some subsidies have also been given to ten electricity-intensive industries (such as aluminum alloy manufacturing) to accelerate their growth. In the meantime, the dual-level tariff and power factor charge system have been further improved.

The existing tariff structure thus formed can be classified either by the electrical metering system, such as flat rates and dual-level rates, or by the usage of electricity, such as for lighting or power. Tariffs can further be classified by the capacity of the transformer and the inlet voltage level, which usually differ among various power-consuming sectors. In addition, there are also wholesale and retail rates.

The current multi-level electricity tariffs are as follows:

1. Lighting and residential service, defined as the electricity used for lighting, cooking, space heating, household and medical electric appliances, air conditioning and water heating for households, is supplied at low voltage with single-phase lines. For consumers in this category, single-phase kWh meters are installed and customers are billed monthly.

Rate Schedule I. Residential Tariff
(unit: RMB/kWh)

Region	Up to 1 KV	1KV and over
Northeast China	0.09	0.088
Other regions	0.15 – 0.20	0.145 – 0.195

2. Agricultural production service, defined as the electricity used for drainage, irrigation, and processing agricultural products within villages and towns in rural areas, state-owned farms and pastures, is usually supplied at low or medium voltage with three-phase lines. For customers in this category, the government has provided subsidies to promote agricultural production. In addition, special subsidies have been granted for the construction of deep wells and high head pumping.

The agricultural production tariff, in the form of a flat rate, is basically the same throughout the country. It can be subdivided into retail and wholesale rates and also varies with the voltage supplied.

Rate Schedule II. Agricultural Tariff
(unit: RMB/kWh)

Type of service	Up to 1 KV	1 – 10 KV	35 KV and over
Retail service	0.06	0.058	0.055
Wholesale service	—	0.035	0.030
High-head pump or deep well			
51 – 100m.	—	0.04	—
101 – 300m.	—	0.03	—
Over 300m.	—	0.02	—

3. Small industry and non-industrial service is defined for industrial customers with transformer capacity less than 320 kilovolt-amperes (KVA) or research institutions with transformer capacity over 3 KVA for electric motors, electric furnaces, or electrochemical use. For customers with a power factor below 0.95, an additional charge is levied. The tariff in this category is basically a flat rate, except in northeast China and a few other areas, as shown in the following table.

Rate Schedule III. Light Industry or Non-industrial Tariff (unit: RMB/kWh)

Region	Up to 1 KV	1 – 10 KV	35 KV and over
Northeast China	0.07	0.065	0.06
Other regions	0.085	0.083	0.08

4. Large industry service, defined as serving industrial customers which have transformer capacity over 320 KVA, where the power is used for motor-driving, electric furnaces, electrolysis, electrochemical processes, and so

Table 11.18 Financial Situation of Chinese Power Industry

	Fixed assets	Revenue (10⁹ RMB)	Profits	Sale cost (RMB/MWh)	Average	Electricity rate (RMB/MWh) Industrial	Agricultural	Residential
1955	2.7	0.6	0.3	33.9	74.44	—	—	—
1960	8.4	3.4	2.1	26.4	66.70	—	—	—
1965	12.4	3.5	1.7	28.7	65.71	—	—	—
1970	17.2	5.9	2.5	27.5	65.70	—	—	—
1975	27.5	9.9	3.7	31.2	66.09	63.42	58.74	156.95
1980	43.7	15.2	4.8	32.8	65.47	61.88	53.96	161.20
1981	46.4	15.7	4.5	33.5	65.86	61.96	54.74	160.93
1982	51.5	16.9	5.2	35.6	66.13	62.94	53.68	160.10
1983	56.8	18.6	5.4	37.5	67.16	64.11	54.50	161.23
1984	62.1	20.5	5.2	39.7	68.96	65.40	54.76	160.71

on. This service is supplied mostly at high distribution network voltage or even at the grid voltage, that is, 110 KV or 220 KV. For customers in this category, a dual-level tariff includes an energy charge, a demand charge, and a power factor charge. The rates are at about the same level throughout the country, except in northeast China, where they are lower.

Rate Schedule IV. Large Industry Tariff
(unit: RMB/kWh)

Part I: Fixed Charge (RMB/KVA/month)			
Transformer capacity	Maximum demand	1 – 10 KV	35 KV and over
3.5	5.0	0.035	0.030
4.0	6.0	0.058	0.055

Part II: Energy Charge (RMB/kWh)		
	1 – 10 KV	35 KV and over
Aluminum, calcium carbide industry	0.038	0.035
Electric furnace, electrolysis	0.048	0.048

Some historical financial data are listed in table 11.18, and from it the following can be pointed out:

During all the years from 1955 to 1984 the electricity price was kept at the very low level of 0.07 RMB/kWh. The rates were established according to the average cost within the grid, without relation to the load time and type — that is, whether the power consumption was at the peak-load time or not. This kind of tariff has stifled supply and encouraged waste, thus also contributing to the acute shortage of electricity.

Since 1986 the central government has no longer been the sole investor in electric power, and local governments and enterprises have assumed an important role in power sector investment. A new electricity pricing policy was needed consistent with the new conditions. Therefore, in 1987 the State Council issued a regulation implementing multiple price levels for electricity. The rate for electricity generated by the old power plants remains unchanged, but for the new power plants rates will be determined according to the current actual cost. As a consequence, the new tariff is much higher than the old one.

In 1988, the tariff was increased by some 50 percent (0.02 RMB/kWh) for most industrial customers in order to increase the power-plant construction funds, and the preferential electricity rates for some industries were canceled. But electricity prices in China are still relatively low. In 1989, a feasibility study was carried out in which the experts suggested increases of another 0.03 RMB/kWh, taking into consideration the possible influence of electricity prices on inflation.

11.4.3 PERFORMANCE OF THE CHINESE POWER SYSTEM

Generally speaking, the Chinese power system is not performing well. This results from the grave shortage of electricity. Many generating units with low thermal efficiency which should have been decommissioned are still in use. Working hours of existing thermal power units are abnormally long, and operation at reduced frequency is common. Such a

Table 11.19 System Losses and Efficiency in the Chinese Power Industry

	Transmission distribution losses (%)	Self-consumption, average (%)	Thermal efficiency, average (kcal/kWh)	Plant utilization (hours/year)		
				Hydropower stations	Thermal stations	Average
1970	9.22	6.54	3,241	3,790	6,100	5,526
1972	9.43	6.68	3,248	3,700	6,536	5,746
1975	10.21	6.23	3,150	4,147	5,631	5,197
1978	9.64	6.61	3,038	2,941	6,018	5,149
1980	8.93	6.44	2,891	3,293	5,775	5,078
1982	8.64	6.32	2,828	3,708	5,542	5,007
1985	8.18	6.42	2,786	3,853	5,893	5,308
1987	8.48	6.66	2,779	3,771	6,011	5,392
1988	8.18	6.69	2,779	3,710	5,907	5,313
1990	8.00	—	2,716	3,300	5,500	5,000
1995	7.80	—	2,625	3,300	5,500	5,000
2000	7.50	—	2,485	3,300	5,500	5,000
2010	7.50	—	2,401	3,300	5,500	5,000

situation will continue for an extended period of time. For example, in the northeast grid, there were 263 line-hours of forced outage per day in 1988, and the percentage of operating time at abnormally low frequency rose to 24.9 percent in August 1988.

Transmission and distribution losses, annual total hours of operation, and thermal efficiency of power plants are shown in table 11.19.

11.4.4 ABSORBING FOREIGN FUNDS AND INCREASING DOMESTIC CAPABILITY

Since China adopted the "open door policy" after 1979, foreign funds have been welcome, especially in the power sector, where (as we have seen) investment is badly needed. From 1979 on, the electricity sector was one of the major sectors receiving preferential loans, as well as grants and export credits from many foreign governments and international financing organizations. During the past ten years, the power industry has signed contracts for loans, grants, and export credits with the World Bank, Japan Overseas Economic Cooperation Foundation, Kuwait Arabian Development Foundation, some United Nations organizations, and the governments of Canada, France, Norway, Australia, England, and Finland, among others. The total amount of such aid amounted to $4.4 billion for twenty-four thermal and hydropower projects, as well as for transmission and distribution systems with a total installed capacity of 17 GW.

Loans from the World Bank are the main source of foreign funds in the power sector. Electric power projects under construction with foreign loans include the Lubuge hydropower station in Yunnan, the Yantan hydropower station in Guangxi, the Shuikou hydropower station in Fujian, the Beilungang thermal power plant in Zhejiang, the Wujin thermal power plant in Shanghai, the Yanshi thermal power plant, and the Xuzhou-Shanghai 500-KV transmission and distribution system. Some foreign companies have invested directly in projects; the nuclear power station in Guangdong is a joint venture of Hong Kong Nuclear Power Investment Incorporation, Limited, and Guangdong Nuclear Power Investment Incorporation, Limited. In addition, China imports some 200-GW and 500-GW thermal power plant equipment from the Soviet Union and East European countries through open accounts, barter trade, and loans.

In order to solve the problem of the acute shortage of electricity, installed capacity and annual electricity generation must reach 240 to 260 GW and 1,200 to 1,300 TWh, respectively, by 2000.

Accordingly, China needs to add 12 GW of installed capacity each year throughout the nineties, making a good outlook for China's electric equipment manufacturers. On the other hand, the need for electric equipment is also attractive to the international market, which is now depressed. Large capital goods producers in industrialized countries hope to gain a sizable share of the Chinese market, and many loans and bilateral trade arrangements are based on selling power equipment to China. The amount of imported power-generating equipment has increased rapidly in recent years. To take the Seventh Five-Year Plan as an example, since 1986 the purchasing of power plant units with a rated capacity of 14 to 15 GW has been arranged, and many more are being negotiated.

But problems always exist. The shortage of foreign exchange is also severe in China, and the ability to pay debts sets a limit on foreign loans. Additionally, foreign equipment is always more expensive than domestic products. In view of this fact, China expects to take some measures to increase domestic manufacturing capacity and to increase the local share of capital goods supplied to the power sector in the following ways:

First, power generating units are as much as possible to be supplied by major domestic power equipment manufacturers. Large amounts have been invested in importing foreign technologies to manufacture large generating units, and a great deal of money has been spent on technical innovation in domestic power plant equipment manufacturing. For example, the manufacturers in Harbin, one of the major Chinese industrial centers, are now able to produce four 600-MW generating units annually. The government has drawn up some policies to promote the growth of the domestic power equipment industry, such as requiring new power plants to use domestic products where possible.

Second, the importing of power equipment will be encouraged where domestic products are not available. China will not limit the import of foreign equipment, since the government has realized that to preserve backwardness by protectionism is harmful to the development of domestic industry. Competition will stimulate the determination of Chinese manufacturers. However, importing equipment is necessary to cope with the present acute shortage of electricity. China needs every source of investment. Considering the shortage of foreign exchange deposits and China's limited capacity to repay debts, some adjustment has been made to the policy of importing equipment, including (1) trying to import advanced technologies and management in connection with the imported equipment, (2) establishing joint ventures in equipment manufacturing with foreign companies, (3) importing large forged components and other critical parts rather than complete units, (4) importing the major plant components and procuring the balance of the equipment domestically, and (5) digesting and absorbing the technology from the advanced equipment after import.

Third, efforts will be made to give full play to the strengths of domestic industries. The competition among products is in fact based on quality, performance, price, and service. Foreign equipment has the advantage of performance and quality, but domestic products will have the advantage of price and service. The strategy of the domestic power equipment industry is to work intensively to overcome the weakness of quality in local products and at the same time to give great attention to the reduction of cost and the improvement of service.

Fourth, competition will be encouraged among domestic manufacturers in conformity with the general economic reform policy of combining the centrally planned economic system with the market economy and "breaking the iron rice bowl." At the same time, China seeks to foster coordination among the major manufacturers, such as by allocating work according to the respective strengths of different factories.

Generally speaking, currently the most critical obstacles for development of China's power-equipment manufacturing are the shortage of capital investment and the lack of key materials, while the long-term weakness in such manufacturing is the backwardness of technology and shortage of qualified professionals.

11.4.5 RURAL ELECTRIFICATION AND REGIONAL DEVELOPMENT POLICIES

11.4.5.1 RURAL ELECTRIFICATION

Although the growth rate of electricity consumption in China's rural areas is higher than the national average, the electrification level in the countryside remains low. About 30 percent of rural households are still not served with electricity. The rural residential energy supply continues to depend mainly on biomass. In order to accelerate the pace of rural electrification and meet the rural residential and agricultural electricity demand, the following policies have been adopted:

1. For the rural areas nearby, electricity will be supplied from the power grids. For areas far from power grids, electricity will be supplied by mini-thermal and minihydropower plants according to the local conditions. Research and experimentation on alternative and renewable energy sources such as solar, wind, geothermal, and biogas power generation are encouraged, and these new energy sources will be popularized gradually after they are proven economically and technically mature.

2. Reasonable plans should be made for rural electric grids. For counties with power loads over 10 MW, construction of local grids surrounding the transforming substations should be considered.

3. Larger fluctuations in rural voltage will be tolerated, allowing for a normal deviation of +7.5 percent and -10.0 percent. However, the rural electric grid must have appropriate voltage and reactive power compensation devices, and the reactive power compensation device must be set up to balance the local loads.

4. The backward two-wire/one-ground rural electric circuit must be upgraded to a three-wire system. Unreliable electric circuits and those interfering with communication lines must be rebuilt.

5. In order to reduce the rural power line loss, the local grid voltage must be increased and the grid layout must be improved, in addition to improving administration. Obsolete and inferior transformers must be upgraded.

11.4.5.2 REGIONAL POWER DEVELOPMENT

In order to improve the mismatching of the geographical distribution of economic centers and energy sources, policies for regional power development have been worked out. Integrated regional energy-economic planning will be carried out to adjust industrial distribution. The main measures are as follows:

1. Appropriate energy-economy zoning will be worked out according to the local energy resources and the relationship among energy production, consumption, and reasonable energy transportation. The barriers between different economic sectors and administrative jurisdictions must be removed.

2. Planning and construction of regional power generation bases will emphasize appropriateness to local resource conditions. Examples are the

thermal power bases in Shaanxi Province, in the Jiangsu-Shandong-Anhui triangle, in northeast China (including eastern Inner Mongolia), and in Guizhou; the hydropower system in central China, in northwest China (along the upper reaches of the Huanghe River), in southern China (Hongshuihe River valley), and the hydropower base of southwest China (along the upper reaches and branches of the Yangtze River in Yunnan, Guizhou, and Sechuan provinces); and the oil production base of Xinjiang Autonomous Region.

3. The industrial distribution layout will be adjusted according to the distribution of energy resources. The locations of energy production and consumption must be coordinated. New energy-intensive enterprises must built near energy production centers and not in the areas already severely short of energy.

4. More large-scale hydropower stations with capacities of over 1 GW are to be constructed at favorable sites, such as the upper and middle reaches of the Yangtze River and the upper reaches of the Huanghe, Hongshuihe, and Nanchang rivers. Capital should be raised from local governments and enterprises to construct medium-size hydropower stations with lower capital investment, a shorter construction period, and higher profits.

5. Electricity will be planned to flow from the west to the east.

11.4.6 EFFECTS OF ENVIRONMENTAL POLICIES ON THE ELECTRICITY SECTOR

The energy sector, including the electricity industry, is a major contributor to environmental pollution. Atmospheric pollution from thermal power plants presents a major problem. Since many power plants burn coal with low heat value and high ash content and use wet-type or mechanical-type dust collectors having an average efficiency of only around 80 percent, the emission of fly ash is a serious problem. The sulfur content of coal burned by power plants varies from 0.2 percent to 6 percent. Coal with sulfur content in excess of 2 percent is used for about 25 percent of the installed capacity. Some coal mines in Sechuan, Guangxi, Shandong, Hunan, Shaanxi, and Guizhou provinces produce coal with sulfur content as high as 3 to 6 percent, and sulfur dioxide pollution is very serious from power plants burning high-sulfur coal. At present sulfur dioxide pollution abatement relies mainly on high chimneys. For power plants built in recent years, chimneys 160

to 240 meters high have been generally used.

Much attention has been focused on the environmental pollution problem. In 1981, the State Council issued an order requesting all levels of government "to regard the protection of the environment and natural resources as a major task in comprehensive planning and to establish the goals, requirements, and measures of environmental protection as a part of social development plan."

The sixth article of the State Environmental Protection Regulation of China states:

In the projects of engineering construction, reconstruction, and expansion, reports on environmental impact must be submitted to the State Environmental Protection Bureau and other concerned authorities. Only after the examination and approval of this report will the design work be allowed to begin. Features for preventing pollution and other public hazards must be designed, constructed, and operated simultaneously with the core part of these projects. The emission of any hazardous material must comply with the State Regulation Standards.

In May 1981 the State government issued Environmental Protection Regulation of Capital Construction Projects and the Outline of the Report on Environmental Impact, in which the detailed requirements for the pre-assessment of the projects were mandated. In May 1989 the above measures and regulations were reappraised, and five new regulations were issued, that is, the "Responsibility System for the Goals of Environmental Protection," the "Quantitative Examination System of Integral Control of the Urban Environment," the "License for Pollutant Emissions," "Concentration Control of Pollution," and the "Regulation of Pollution Control within a Definite Time." These regulations and laws on environmental protection have profound effects on the power sector.

In order to reduce the environmental pollution caused by particulates emitted from power plants, many old-type wet scrubbers, which were extensively used until the 1970s, have been converted into an improved new type of scrubber, in which inlet Venturi sections or inlet screens composed of inclined tubes were added. Another new type of electrostatic precipitator with wide-spaced electrode plates, cross-positioned channel plates, and secondary electrodes has been developed and successfully put into operation. A number of power plants were selected to install and test the performance of bag filters on a commercial scale. As for flue gas desulfurization, several processes of bench-scale tests as well as pilot plant tests have been conducted. For example, with the two 350-MW units of the newly commissioned Luo Huang Power Plant in Chongqing, desulfurization devices imported from Japan have been installed.

Owing to the progress made in pollution control as mentioned above, although the annual coal consumption in Chinese power plants increased 50 percent from 1985 to 1988 (that is, 70 million tons), the total amount of ash released into the atmosphere in the same period increased by only 15.1 percent (0.5 million tons). In this period, China spent 1.15 billion RMB on 2,917 projects to control the pollution from existing plants.

China plans to take the following measures to protect the environment:

1. Greater efforts to promote further energy conservation. Energy waste exacerbates environmental pollution. The development of high-parameter large units is being emphasized. Installation of small-scale industrial boilers and small generating units will be strictly limited. Cogeneration and district heating will be actively developed.

2. Construction of mine-mouth power plants in collaboration with the development of large coal mines. Pollution sources must be located far from populous urban areas. The utilization and the reduction of waste water and ash must be taken into account in power plant construction.

3. Popularization of electric scrubbers and dry scrubbing technology to reduce the pollutants as well as the secondary pollution of waste water.

4. Use of depleted coal mines for ash storage, which will help in restoration of the environment.

5. Improvement of coal dressing and decreasing ash content in commodity coal to alleviate the burden of transportation and reduce atmospheric pollution from power plants.

6. Banning of dumping of ash in rivers.

CHAPTER 12

A COMPARISON OF ENERGY CONSUMPTION, SUPPLY, AND POLICY

In India and the People's Republic of China

12.1. SIMILARITIES AND DIFFERENCES BETWEEN THE CHINESE AND INDIAN ECONOMIES

India and the People's Republic of China are the two largest developing countries in the world. Their populations combined constitute more than a third of the total world population. They consume at present about one-eighth of the global commercial energy, leaving aside the consumption of a comparable amount of traditional fuels. It is expected that their share of world energy demand will increase rapidly in the coming decades and that their proportion of worldwide CO_2 emissions will rise disproportionately, due to the extremely large share of coal in their primary energy systems. It is therefore very important from the global point of view to study the energy future and relevant policies of these two giants. (For details of this case study, see references 118 and 78.)

National characteristics must also be considered in comparing these countries. On the one hand, the similarities between India and China are striking; hence, much can be learned by each country from the other's successes and failures in energy policy and development. Both countries are heavily populated and are in the process of development, and both have long cultural histories and hence rather rigid social structures and conservative traditions. Both of them have undergone revolution and independence movements in modern times, and accordingly their citizens express strong patriotic sentiments and a preference for self-reliance. Also, interestingly enough, even though China and India have radically different ideological outlooks, both have adopted economies of mixed public and private ownership, and the public-owned enterprises are predominant particularly in the energy and heavy industry sectors.

On the other hand, although the per capita national incomes of these two countries are quite similar, a great discrepancy of per capita energy consumption (as much as 250 percent) is observed. This fact has naturally raised the question (in particular from the higher consumption side) of the causes of such a great difference and the effectiveness of the respective energy policies. At the same time, the notably different economic growth rates and the radically dissimilar social distribution patterns attract the interest of one country to learn more from the other.

The general economic and energy data of the two countries are shown in table 12.1. The most striking figures are their respective demographic numbers: 1,045,000,000 (China) and 754,000,000 (India) in 1985. Considering the different population growth rates of China and India (1.24 percent and 2.0 percent, respectively), it is estimated their populations will approach each other at the turn of this century. By 2000 the population of China is expected to reach 1,257,000,000, and India 1,004,000,000, according to the current growth rates. With China's present population control policy (aimed at less than 1,500,000,000 in the middle of the twenty-first century), India's population will surpass China's around 2018 (at 1,386,000,000) should India maintain its current growth rate. Though India is trying to decrease its growth rate, its population will eventually exceed that of China, sometime around the middle of the next century. Thus in the long run India will face a more serious

Table 12.1 General Information on China and India

	China	India
Population (millions)	1,045	754
Proportion of urbanized population (percent)	20	25
GDP (in current U.S. dollars, billions)	321	204
Per capita GDP (U.S. dollars)		
At 1980 exchange rate	456	238
At 1985 exchange rate	310	270
Sectoral shares in GDP (percent)		
Agriculture	33	34
Industry	47	26
Manufacturing	37	17
Services	20	34
Transportation	—	6
Gross domestic capital formation in GDP (percent)	38	25
Total commercial energy requirement (Mtoe)	534	144
Non-commercial energy consumption (Mtoe, estimated)	200	175
Per capita commercial energy consumption (toe)	0.511	0.193
Commercial energy requirement/GDP (kgoe/US dollars)	1.66	0.72
Primary energy shares in commercial energy requirement (percent)		
Coal	5.8	52.6
Crude oil	17.1	29.8
Natural gas	2.3	3.1
Hydropower	4.8	13.5
Nuclear	0	1
Composition of final energy consumption by sectors (percent)		
Agriculture	7.5	7.2
Industry	61.5	57.6
Transportation	5	22.7
Service and residential	24	12.5

The data used in this chapter are based on the ITEESA/TERI joint survey conducted in 1985, which sometimes may differ from those used in the Appendix and other chapters.

energy challenge than China's, simply because of its greater momentum of population increase.

The present proportions of urbanization in the two countries are roughly the same, that is, 20 percent for China and 25 percent for India. However, with the recent economic reform in China, even though there has been temporary stagnation due to the political environment, China has greatly accelerated the growth of local industry and commerce in rural regions and hence turned hundreds of millions of peasants into workers and merchants. Such development will surely increase the proportion of urbanization in China, and it may soon surpass that

in India. From the viewpoint of growth in energy demand, China has already felt the pressure from the transformation of its rural economy. Such a trend will also appear in India sooner or later.

The per capita GDP of these two countries is roughly comparable in terms of U.S. dollar value, that is, $310 (China) versus $270 (India). Since the pricing systems in these two countries are entirely different, it is very difficult to compare any factors simply in monetary terms. Roughly speaking, the prices of raw materials, agricultural products, and commodities of subsistence such as food and energy products are cheaper in China than in India. However, prices of industrial products are not always lower in China. The difference in subsidies from the respective governments makes the comparison even more difficult. However, the per capita production in physical terms is higher on the Chinese side. In the next section some examples will be given in this regard. (The data used in this chapter are based on the ITEESA/TERI joint survey conducted in 1985, which sometimes may differ from those used in the appendix and in other chapters.)

Though the apparent similarities of these two economies are numerous, radical differences nevertheless predominate in many important areas. The structures of the two economies differ in the relative proportions of the industrial and service sectors. The proportion of domestic capital formation in GDP is much higher in China than in India. The per capita energy consumption in the two countries presents the most important and controversial difference. Each Chinese consumes almost two and half times as much commercial energy as each Indian does, while the ratio of energy consumption per unit GDP in the two countries amounts to 230 percent. The discrepancies in the shares of energy consumption in the service and residential sectors are obvious. The share of oil and hydropower in the energy structure is much higher in India, even though there are few domestic oil reserves.

One of the major objectives of this study is to explain these discrepancies.

12.2. COMPARISON OF ECONOMIC GROWTH AND ENERGY CONSUMPTION IN CHINA AND INDIA

12.2.1 ENERGY CONSUMPTION ELASTICITY
The per capita economic growth rate of China is much higher than that of India. The average growth rates from 1970 to 1986 are 5.40 and 1.75 percent

Fig. 12.1 Economic Growth of China and India

GDP US$ per capita

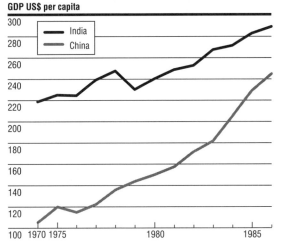

Fig. 12.2 Energy Consumption Rates of China and India

Million toe

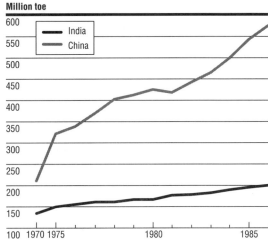

for China and India, respectively, and the difference in growth of per capita energy consumption is also impressive, that is, 3.40 percent versus 1.24 percent. The extremely low growth rate for energy consumption in India is partly due to the higher growth rate of its population, that is, 2 percent per year compared to 1.24. These differences are clearly seen in figures 12.1, 12.2, and 12.3. However, the elasticities of both per capita and total energy consumption of these two countries differ in a reversed order. As seen in table 12.2, the elasticities in India are greater than those in China (the total elasticity is 0.869 in India and 0.710 in China). Here the Indian economy seems more energy intensive per unit increment of its GDP.

Both countries have adopted the policy of reliance on domestic supplies of primary energy, so production has increased very rapidly in recent decades (see figure 12.4). Energy production in India, however, is increasing much more slowly than in China.

12.2.2 PER CAPITA PRODUCTION AND ENERGY CONSUMPTION

The obvious differences in per capita production in physical terms may partly account for the different per capita energy consumption in these two countries. In table 12.3 the per capita outputs of a number of widely diversified products of the two countries are given and their ratios calculated.

In China, two to three times as much of the most energy-intensive products — such as iron, steel, cement, petro- and heavy chemicals and fertilizers — are consumed per capita as compared with India. Further documentary and on-site surveys have been carried out in these energy-intensive industrial

Fig. 12.3 Per Capita Energy Consumption in China and India

Toe per capita

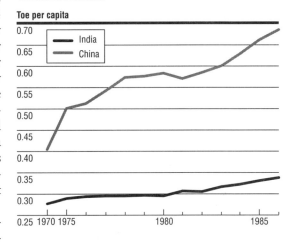

subsectors to find out the possible differences of energy intensity per unit product. These surveys found no substantial differences, and in most cases the energy intensities are even lower in China. Hence the higher per capita energy consumption in China is partially attributed to the larger quantity of industrial products shared by the Chinese people. These results will be discussed in more detail below.

12.2.3 ENERGY CONSUMPTION STRUCTURE

The commercial energy consumption structures of China and India resemble each other in their high percentage of coal consumption, 76.1 and 55.7 percent, respectively, in 1986 (see table 12.4). However, India consumes more oil and utilizes more hydropower than China. This fact results in higher efficiency in India's commercial energy utilization. The trends of the changing proportions of various

183

Table 12.2 Economic Growth and Energy Consumption of China and India

	China				India					Total energy consumption elasticity	
	GDP per capita	Energy consumption per capita		Per capita energy consumption elasticity	GDP per capita	Energy consumption per capita		Per capita energy consumption elasticity		China	India
	(US$)	Growth rate (%)	toe	Growth rate (%)		US$	Growth rate (%)	toe	Growth rate (%)		
1970	105.2	—	0.403	—		218.5	—	0.277	—	—	—	—
1975	120.2	2.71	0.500	4.41	1.63	225.7	0.65	0.289	0.84	1.21	1.35	1.06
1976	115.3	−4.05	0.513	2.64	−0.65	224.0	−0.73	0.293	1.59	−2.18	1.51	2.55
1977	122.7	6.35	0.542	5.57	0.88	237.1	5.84	0.293	−0.17	−0.03	0.90	0.25
1978	135.9	10.77	0.572	5.48	0.51	247.2	4.24	0.295	0.61	0.14	0.56	0.44
1979	143.5	5.63	0.577	0.86	0.15	230.0	−6.93	0.296	0.41	−0.06	0.31	−0.55
1980	150.8	5.10	0.584	1.21	0.24	239.5	4.10	0.295	−0.44	−0.11	0.38	0.29
1981	156.2	3.54	0.570	−2.37	−0.67	248.4	3.71	0.305	3.67	0.99	−0.20	1.00
1982	170.7	9.27	0.584	2.42	0.26	252.0	1.46	0.304	−0.56	−0.38	0.36	0.44
1983	181.3	6.21	0.601	3.03	0.49	266.0	5.55	0.315	3.62	0.65	0.56	0.75
1984	203.8	12.43	0.629	4.54	0.31	270.4	1.66	0.320	1.75	1.08	0.44	1.02
1985	228.3	12.00	0.663	5.51	0.46	281.5	4.12	0.330	3.00	0.73	0.50	0.82
1986	243.9	6.85	0.688	3.72	0.54	288.2	2.37	0.337	2.21	0.93	0.60	0.97
Average	—	5.40	—	3.40	0.63	—	1.75	—	1.24	0.71	0.71	0.87

energy sources are very interesting (see figures 12.5A and 12.5B). In China, the relative share of every kind of energy except coal has turned downward since 1983, while in India natural gas shows a great rising momentum. However, the share of traditional/noncommercial energy consumption is much larger in India (table 12.1). The ratio of noncommercial to commercial energy is 121.5 percent in India and 37.5 percent in China. Two conclusions may therefore be drawn: first, the total energy consumption, including both commercial and noncommercial energy, in India is almost 2.2 times its commercial energy consumption, while this figure is 1.38 in China; thus the difference in specific energy consumptions of the two countries is reduced from 2.65 to 2.00. Second, taking into consideration the very low value of noncommercial energy, the overall efficiency of energy utilization is lower in India.

The proportion of oil used is larger in India and remained almost constant (around 30 percent) from 1970 to 1986. However, the proportion of oil used varies in China and attained its maximum value in the year 1977-1978 (around 22.6 percent). Since China relies solely on its indigenous oil supply, this trend implies that China is already facing shortages in its oil supply. (In references 5 and 7 more detailed analysis has been given, and the major outcomes are listed in table 12.5.) The maximum annual production of Chinese crude oil will not exceed some 240 million tons (or 4.6 million

Fig. 12.4 Energy Production of China and India

Million toe

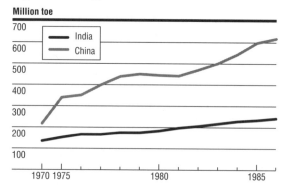

barrels per day) with a 39 percent confidence, which will require some 400 billion barrels proven reserves (table 12.5). In India, along with the exploitation of indigenous resources, an oil import policy has been adopted which eliminates the gap between oil demand and supply. It is expected that China will necessarily become an oil importer sooner or later.

12.3. ENERGY INVESTMENT
One similarity between the two countries lies in governmental efforts emphasizing the development of indigenous energy industries. Most of the major energy enterprises are state- or public-owned, and financial investments in them are part of govern-

Table 12.3 Major Products Per Capita

	China	India	Ratio
Chemical fibers, kg	0.91	0.21	4.40
Yarn, kg	3.38	2.01	1.68
Cloth, m	14.67	9.33	1.57
Silk, kg	0.04	—	—
Paper and paperboard, kg	9.11	1.50	6.07
Sugar, kg	4.32	8.63	0.50
Salt, kg	14.20	13.09	1.08
Television sets, number	0.0016	0.0003	5.33
Coal, kg	834	205	4.07
Chemical fertilizer, kg	12.65	7.33	1.73
Chemical pesticides, kg	0.20	0.065	3.08
Plastics, kg	1.32	0.23	5.74
Motor vehicles, number	0.00042	0.00015	2.80
Tractors, number	0.00083	0.00011	7.55
Crude oil, kg	120	56.91	2.11
Natural gas, m^3	14.90	10.80	1.38
Electricity, kWh	293.0	255.5	1.54
Pig iron, kg	43.83	13.28	3.30
Steel, kg	46.79	16.11	2.90
Steel finished products, kg	36.93	12.71	2.91
Cement, kg	145.95	42.44	3.44
Timber, m^3	0.061	—	—
Sulfuric acid, kg	6.76	2.73	2.48
Soda ash, kg	2.01	0.83	2.42
Caustic acid, kg	2.35	0.71	3.31
Grain, kg	362.80	199.56	1.82
Cotton, kg	3.97	1.94	2.05
Oil-bearing crops, kg	15.10	14.79	1.02
Sugarcane, kg	57.80	227.70	0.25
Tea, kg	0.41	0.86	0.48

ment budgets. Such an arrangement guarantees the priority of energy investment in both countries. However, there is an obvious discrepancy in energy investment as a share of total industrial investment in both countries (see table 12.6). In India this amounted to 27.8 percent during 1980-1985 and 30.5 percent during the 1985-1990 period, or about 50 percent more than the share of the energy budget in China. The proportion of investment in the Indian power sector is also much higher than the comparable Chinese figure, 62.5 percent and 48.5 percent, respectively. Combining these figures shows that investment in the power sector in India amounts to 19 percent of total industrial investment, as against the Chinese share of 9.9 percent, or roughly a ratio of 2 to 1. This fact may explain in part the reason for the more severe chronic shortage of electric power in China. However, considering the much larger proportion of gross capital formation in GDP for China (38 percent compared to 25 percent), the shares of energy investment in GDP are roughly comparable in the two countries. As a result, the development of energy industries in both countries is rapid, and the growth rates of energy production are high.

However, the comparison of investment in monetary terms alone does not give a true picture of energy growth. Differences in efficient utilization of capital investment both in quantity and in timing would result in different installed capacity and energy output even with exactly the same amount of financial input. No data is readily available currently for the evaluation of the aggregated effectiveness of capital investment in both countries.

Table 12.4 Energy Consumption by Sources (%)

	China					India				
	Coal	Oil	Natural gas	Hydro	Nuclear	Coal	Oil	Natural gas	Hydro	Nuclear
1970	80.9	14.7	0.9	3.5	0	57.9	30.4	0.6	10.1	1.0
1975	71.9	21.1	2.5	4.5	0	58.7	29.1	0.9	10.4	0.8
1976	69.9	23.0	2.8	4.3	0	58.8	29.0	1.1	10.2	1.0
1977	70.3	22.6	3.1	4.0	0	58.3	29.1	1.1	10.8	0.6
1978	70.7	22.7	3.2	3.4	0	54.3	31.0	1.2	12.8	0.8
1979	71.3	21.8	3.3	3.6	0	54.5	31.4	1.3	11.9	0.8
1980	72.5	20.7	3.1	4.0	0	55.2	30.7	1.5	11.8	0.8
1981	72.2	20.0	2.8	4.5	0	54.7	31.3	1.8	11.5	0.7
1982	73.9	18.8	2.5	4.8	0	53.4	32.8	2.3	11.0	0.5
1983	74.2	18.1	2.4	5.3	0	56.6	29.9	2.4	10.3	0.7
1984	75.3	17.4	2.4	4.9	0	54.9	31.2	2.7	10.5	0.8
1985	75.9	17.0	2.3	4.8	0	56.7	30.5	2.7	9.2	0.9
1986	76.1	17.0	2.2	4.7	0	55.7	30.3	4.1	9.1	0.8

Fig. 12.5A Primary Energy Consumption in China

Percent

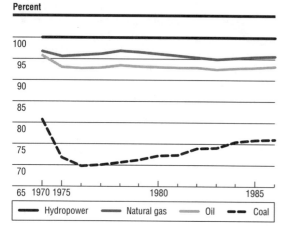

- ▬▬ Hydropower ▬▬ Natural gas ▬▬ Oil ▬ ▬ Coal

Fig. 12.5B Primary Energy Consumption in India

Percent

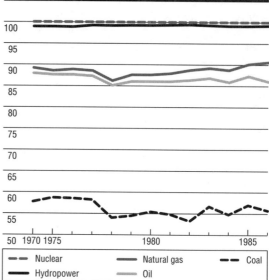

- ▬ ▬ Nuclear ▬▬ Natural gas ▬ ▬ Coal
- ▬▬ Hydropower ▬▬ Oil

12.4. ENERGY IMPORT AND EXPORT

Both China and India have pursued a policy of self-reliance in energy and have made great progress. Presently China is a net energy exporter, but India remains an energy importer. As seen in table 12.7, the energy import share in India was reduced from 13.19 percent in 1980 to 8.9 percent in 1986, while the export share in China increased from 4.6 percent in 1980 to 7.3 percent in 1985. However, Chinese oil exports dropped in 1986 (see figure 12.6).

The extremely high ratio of oil imports to total exports placed a heavy burden on Indian foreign exchange balance and had an adverse effect on the acquisition of other valuable import commodities and technologies. As a consequence of the successful implementation of Indian energy policy, oil imports dropped steadily after 1980 (figure 12.7). In the case of China, the revenue earned from crude oil exports reached a level of about one-quarter of total annual export income. In fact, China badly needs oil to fuel its domestic industry and transportation, and the export policy is simply based on the need to obtain hard currency. Should other Chi-

Table 12.5 Resource Constraint on Peak Oil Production in China

Scenario	Low	Medium	High	Ultra high
Annual oil production by 2000, 10^6 ton/yr.	175	185	190	200
Peak Annual Production, 10^6 ton/yr.	200	225	250	300
Peak time, Year	2010–2020	2010–2020	2010–2020	2010–2020
Total production, 10^9 ton	12.46	13.52	16.97	19.12
Proven reserve required, 10^9 ton	46.45	50.34	62.95	70.82
Reserve/resource ratio	0.59–0.76	0.64–0.82	0.80–1.02	0.90–1.15
Confidence level	0.94	0.72	0.33	0.11

Table 12.6 Share of Energy Investment in Total Industrial Investment (%)

	China		India	
	1976-80	1981-85	1980-85	1985-90
Energy sector share of total investment	20.9	20.4	27.8	30.5
Share of various energy sources in energy investment				
Coal	28.0	30.0	12.4	13.5
Oil	27.0	21.5	27.6	23.0
Electricity	45.0	48.5	59.5	62.5
Nonconventional/renewable energy sources	—	—	0.5	1.0

Table 12.7 Domestic Energy Production and Import/Export (1,000 toe)

	China			India		
	Production	Consumption	Export	Production	Consumption	Import
1970	216,713	204,832	565	51,609	131,870	12,570
1975	340,937	317,657	10,639	69,257	146,663	13,141
1976	352,028	334,483	9,870	72,265	152,505	15,492
1977	394,378	366,112	10,990	73,799	157,221	17,855
1978	438,951	399,608	13,285	78,402	159,072	16,813
1979	451,483	409,706	17,598	78,497	163,943	20,631
1980	445,699	421,504	19,446	83,252	165,257	21,805
1981	442,146	415,713	20,697	95,771	171,672	17,896
1982	466,979	438,084	22,194	104,199	174,034	11,840
1983	498,392	461,818	22,328	112,868	180,505	13,588
1984	544,440	495,832	30,283	123,124	185,366	12,653
1985	598,223	538,601	39,512	127,548	191,435	17,743
1986	616,252	571,084	36,720	137,070	196,338	17,480

nese commodities enter the world market to replace crude oil, more revenue could be earned and the domestic energy situation would be better. Thus the oil export policy in China is always a topic of internal controversy. In figure 12.8 the annual variations of China's oil exports are shown, with an abrupt rise of Chinese oil exports in 1984 and 1985, to a peak of 35 million tons, followed by a drop to 28.5 million tons in 1986 and, further, to 27.2 million tons in 1987.

12.5 ENERGY SUPPLY

12.5.1 COAL

China and India are the two largest countries where the share of coal in total energy consumption exceeds 50 percent. In fact, China gets three-fourths of its energy from coal, and this proportion is still rising. The share of coal in India's energy mix fluctuates at around 55 percent. Both countries have relatively abundant indigenous coal resources, though in India the proven reserve is only one percent of China's, and the quality of India's coal is poor. A comparison of coal production in these countries is shown in table 12.8.

China has all varieties of coal for industrial use, but India has fewer types. High-quality anthracite is virtually absent in India, and Indian coking coal is very poor, with high ash content. Hence India must import a sizable quantity of coal for its industry. In both countries the distribution of coal reserves is uneven, and great transportation difficulties have been encountered. It is particularly interesting to see

Fig. 12.6 Energy Exports of China and India

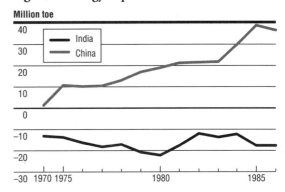

Fig. 12.7 Net Energy Imports of India

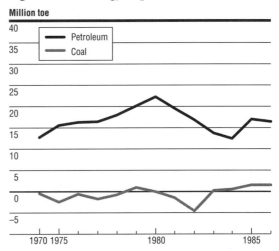

that 97 percent of the coal in India is produced by central government-owned mines, while this figure in China is only 46.5 percent. Most Chinese coal is produced in provincial, collective, and privately owned coal mines, and this institutional arrangement makes Chinese coal production more flexible and capable of steady growth. The achievement of the Chinese coal industry demonstrates the effectiveness of the policy of "walking on two legs." Local and privately owned coal mines need less capital investment and can be constructed faster. However, the recovery rate of coal resources in these small mines is much lower, and worker fatality rates are high due to the poorer safety measures.

The proportion of coal washed in both countries is very low, and it is noted that the ash content of Indian coal after washing is still much higher than the Chinese counterpart (almost double the latter's value).

The Chinese coal industry is more advanced than its Indian counterpart. In table 12.9 a comparison of the current status of mines in these two countries is made, and great differences are seen. First, the size of coal mines in China is much larger than those in India. Eleven mines in China have an annual production greater than 10 million tons, while no mines of such size exist in India. Most Indian coal mines are much smaller, with an annual

Fig. 12.8 Net Energy Exports of China

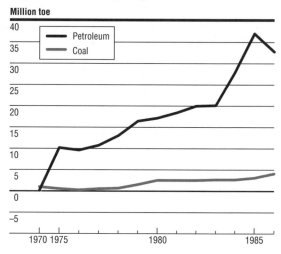

Million toe

Table 12.8 Coal Production in China and India, 1985

	China	India
Total coal output (Mt)	872.28	161.6
Anthracite	182.28	0
Bituminous coal	657.78	154.3
Coking coal	391.09	35.7
Non-coking coal	266.69	118.6
Lignite	32.22	7.3
Number of provinces/states where coal is produced	27	8
Output by ownership (%)		
Collieries under central government	46.5	97
Collieries owned by provinces	21.0	0
Collieries owned by collectives	30.6	—
Collieries owned by private enterprises	1.9	3
Coal washing (Mt)	141.58	21.1
Coking coal (Mt)	105.79	21.1
Washed coking coal production (%)	58.3	12.2
Recovery rate (%)	55.01	57.8
Ash content in coking coal (%)	19.78	26-32
Ash content in washed coal (%)	10.27	19-22
Non-coking coal (Mt)	35.79	0
Washed non-coking coal production (Mt)	15.68	—
Recovery rate (%)	43.81	—

Table 12.9 Coal Mines in China and India

	China	India
Production capacity (Mt/yr.)	554	251
Production size of mines:		
> 10 Mt	11	0
5–10 Mt	16	8
3–5 Mt	21	9
1–3 Mt	40	53
< 1 Mt	—	330 (est.)
Output by mining method		
Underground	377.2	74.1
Long-wall/stopping (Mt)	329.4	2.6
Board and pillar/tunneling (Mt)	34.9	71.5
Open-cast	19.4	87.5
Others	9.6	0
Total	406.3	161.6
Level of mechanization in underground long-wall faces		
Total number of long-wall faces	2,341	33
Mechanized faces	659	8
Overall mechanization	172	—
Normal mechanization	465	—
Hydraulic coal mining	22	0
Non-mechanized faces	1,682	25
Average monthly production (1,000 t)		
Per overall mechanized face	35.8	15
Per non-mechanized face	9.0	4
Labor productivity (ton per man-shift)		
Overall mechanized face	14.8	9
Non-mechanized face	3.9	2
Energy consumption per ton output of coal (underground mines)		
Electricity (kWh)	37.5	11–24
Overall labor productivity, all mines (t/man-shift)	0.94	0.91

throughput of less than a million tons. On the other hand, 54.1 percent of the Indian coal was open-cast, while this method produces only 8.6 percent of the total in China. Instead, 97.4 percent of Chinese coal from the central government's large mines is produced underground with a higher level of mechanization using long-wall/stopping technology. Electricity consumption per ton of coal output in China is therefore much higher than in India, roughly 37.5 kWh as compared with 11 to 24 kWh in India. Since most of Indian coal is open-cast, the average labor productivity of all mines in these two countries is almost the same: 0.94 and 0.91 tons per man-shift.

12.5.2. PETROLEUM

The production of indigenous oil increased very rapidly during the past two decades in both countries. China produced 30.58 million tons of crude oil in 1970, 105.95 million tons in 1980, and 124.90 million tons in 1986, or an average growth rate of 13.2 percent from 1970 to 1980, and 2.8 percent from 1980 to 1986. On the other hand, Indian oil production increased from 6.8 million tons in 1970 to 10.51 million tons in 1980 and 30.17 million tons in 1986, corresponding to average growth rates of 4.5 percent and 19.2 percent, respectively. While China's oil production growth rate has slowed down in recent years due to resource depletion, India's petroleum

Table 12.10 Petroleum and Natural Gas Industries in China and India

	China		India	
	1980	1985	1980/81	1985/86
Crude oil exports/imports				
1,000 t	13,309	28,760	16,248	14,616
US dollars, 10^6	—	5,014.9	4,255	2,919
Refined products net export/imports				
1000 t	4,203	6,830	7,253	1,902
US dollars, 10^6	—	1,594.9	2,426	628
Net crude oil and products exports/imports as percentage of				
Total exports, %	—	24.2	78.4	41.6
Total imports, %	—	15.6	41.9	23.5
Refinery losses and own-use in refineries, %	8.19	6.68	6.63	7.06
Total consumption of petroleum products, 1,000 t	72,179	80,150	30,896	40,286
Total crude oil produced, 1,000 t	105,950	124,895	10,507	30,168
Losses in oil field, %	1.64	1.52	—	—
Own use in oil field by oil enterprises, %	2.27	1.65	—	—
Net gas production, $10^6\,m^3$	14,270	12,930	1,522	4,950
Refining capacity, 1,000 t	—	10,500	31,800	45,550
Crude oil throughput, 1,000 t	78,291	86,622	25,836	42,910
Total production, 1,000 t	72,797	80,836	24,123	39,881
Production of				
LPG, 1,000 t	1,290	1,600	366	1,230
Gasoline, 1,000 t	10,490	14,382	1,519	2,306
Kerosene, 1,000 t	3,990	4,050	2,396	4,030
Diesel, 1,000 t	18,280	19,842	8,479	15,801
Fuel oils, 1,000 t	31,420	28,600	6,120	7,955
Consumption of				
LPG, 1,000 t	1,200	1,550	405	1,228
Gasoline, 1,000 t	9,986	13,963	1,522	2,264
Kerosene, 1,000 t	3,659	3,855	4,228	6,200
Diesel, 1,000 t	16,632	19,344	11,467	15,836
Fuel oils, 1,000 t	30,737	28,374	7,473	7,713

growth is accelerating. However, China had become self-reliant in the supply of nearly all kinds of petroleum products since the mid-sixties and was able to avoid the impact of the global oil crisis, while India has continued to depend on imported oil, though the degree of its dependence is decreasing. The share of petroleum supplied from indigenous resources in India has increased from 34 percent in 1980 to 74.7 percent in 1986 (see table 12.10).

The efficiency of the refineries in these two countries seems to be comparable. However, more detailed analysis reveals that the refinery efficiency and the complexity of the Indian plants are higher than the Chinese: the fraction of fuel oil in the Indian refineries has been reduced to 18.5 percent, compared to 32.5 percent in the Chinese plants. There is no data for the comparison of the utilization efficiencies of resources in oil exploitation and exploration. The per capita proven reserve of oil in India, however, is far less than that in China, though the potential resources of the latter are considered insufficient for its long-term development. It is therefore believed that India also faces a less-than-rosy future for its indigenous oil supply.

12.5.3. ELECTRICITY

The growth rates of power generation in the two countries could match or even surpass their GDP growth. However, the average elasticity of electricity consumption in China from 1973 to 1986 was just 1.034, while that of India from 1970 to 1986 amounted to 1.934. The difference may explain the more acute power shortage and the more serious waste of industrial capacity in China.

Another discrepancy exists in the obviously larger share of hydroelectricity in India. The proportion of installed hydropower capacities is the same in the two countries — that is, around 30 percent — but the hydroelectricity generated in India is

greater by 33.3 percent (table 12.1). However, the potential of hydropower plants in India is less than that in China. The reason for the higher proportion of hydroelectricity generated lies in the relatively lower performance of Indian fossil-fueled plants. The rate of exploitation of hydropower resources, on the other hand, is much higher in India: 19.7 percent versus 7.9 percent in China.

The average power generation efficiency in Chinese thermal plants is about 20 percent higher than that in Indian plants: in 1985 the rates of fuel consumption per GWh were 0.312 tons oil equivalent in China versus 0.378 tons oil equivalent in India. The reasons are twofold: the excessive power demand caused very high load factors in Chinese power plants, and the poorer management caused frequent outages in Indian plants. The obvious difference in transmission/distribution losses as between India and China is also striking — 21.7 percent in India and 8.2 percent in China. The high figure for India is considered due not only to technical considerations but also because of poor management, particularly in rural areas.

Presently India is more advanced in nuclear power generation. Nuclear power plants with a capacity of about 1,330 megawatts were operating by 1986, and indigenous technology in heavy water power reactors has been developed. Long-term development programs such as the exploration of fast breeder reactor technology has commenced. In China the first two commercial nuclear power plants based on pressurized water reactor (PWR) technology are still under construction, and some of the technologies for the first commercial plants have been purchased from foreign companies, though China has already built a number of nuclear submarines. It is planned that by the end of this century some nuclear plants generating 6 to 10 gigawatts will be put into operation in both China and India. Long-term development of more advanced reactor types such as nuclear heating devices has begun in China, but fast breeder technologies are still in very early stages. (Nuclear power in Taiwan is not included in this analysis.)

12.6. ENERGY CONSUMPTION

Energy consumption by sectors in the two countries is shown in table 12.12 as well as in figures 12.9A and 12.9B. In contrast to previous tables containing only commercial energy, in this table both commercial and noncommercial data are included.

Table 12.11 Power Industries of China and India

	China 1985	India 1985/86
Capacity (MW)	86,493.3	46,563
% hydro	30.2	33.2
Gross generation (GWh)	410,695	170,037
% hydro	22.5	30
Capacity utilization (kWh/KW per annum)		
Hydro	3,537	3,295
Others	5,272	3,850
Transmission/distribution losses (%)	8.2	21.7

Fig. 12.9A Energy Consumption by Sector in India

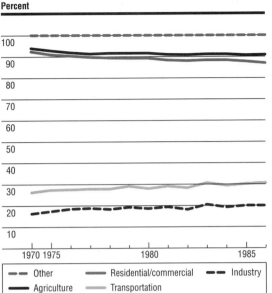

Fig. 12.9B Energy Consumption by Sector in China

The prominent role of the residential sector is thus emphasized since most of the energy used in this sector is from noncommercial traditional fuels. In the long run this sector will consume more and more commercial energy, and this transition may become one of the major energy issues of the near future.

12.6.1. AGRICULTURAL SECTOR

Agriculture plays a very important role in both countries, not only because agricultural production constitutes about a third of their GDPs, but also because the majority of their huge populations still live in rural areas and rely on the agricultural economy. However, the actual energy consumption in agricultural production is difficult to estimate. The measurements and the data collection of rural energy present some technical problems. Also, the complicated nature of the agricultural production processes themselves makes such statistics unreliable. First of all, different climates and natural conditions cause the output of each crop obtained per unit energy input from each unit area of land to vary substantially in successive years, even on the same piece of land, before even attempting a comparison of

Table 12.12 Energy Consumption by Sectors (%)

	China					India				
	Industrial	Trans-portation	Residential/commercial	Agricultural	Other	Industrial	Trans-portation	Residential/commercial	Agricultural	Other
1970	—	—	—	—	—	16.02	9.92	66.90	1.12	6.04
1975	—	—	—	—	—	17.49	9.83	64.22	1.86	6.59
1976	—	—	—	—	—	18.37	9.35	62.89	1.93	7.46
1977	—	—	—	—	—	18.75	9.35	61.81	2.00	8.10
1978	—	—	—	—	—	18.47	9.54	61.80	2.26	7.93
1979	—	—	—	—	—	19.52	9.42	60.83	2.44	7.79
1980	66.21	6.10	19.44	8.25	0	18.81	9.68	61.19	2.56	7.76
1981	65.20	6.20	20.50	8.10	0	19.64	9.46	59.97	2.57	8.36
1982	65.00	6.30	21.40	7.30	0	18.76	9.80	60.23	2.88	8.34
1983	64.80	6.20	21.70	7.30	0	20.75	9.83	58.84	2.89	7.69
1984	63.51	6.27	22.19	8.04	0	17.14	9.55	50.76	2.69	6.96
1985	62.44	6.51	23.44	7.61	0	20.40	10.22	57.85	3.24	8.28
1986	—	—	—	—	—	20.31	10.56	57.26	3.53	8.34

Table 12.13 Agricultural Production in China and India (1980/85)

	Rice	Wheat	Maize	Sorghum	Gram*	Total	Cotton	Jute	Sugarcane	Peanuts	Total
			Food grains						**Non-food grains**		
Gross cropped area, million ha.											
China: 1980	33.9	29.9	20.4	2.5	—	117.2	4.9	0.31	0.48	2.34	15.89
1985	32.1	29.2	17.7	1.9	—	108.8	5.1	0.99	0.96	3.32	22.38
% change	−5.3	0	−13.24	−24.0	—	−7.17	4.08	219.35	100	41.88	40.8
India: 1980/81	40.2	22.3	6.01	15.81	6.38	126.61	7.82	0.94	2.67	6.8	18.32
1985/86	40.9	23.1	5.88	15.79	7.65	127.06	7.58	1.15	2.86	7.31	18.9
% change	1.9	3.6	−2.16	−0.13	16.26	0.36	−3.07	22.34	7.12	7.5	3.68
Share of gross cropped area, %											
China: 1980	23.2	19.9	13.9	1.8	—	80.1	3.4	0.2	0.3	1.6	10.9
1985	22.4	20.3	12.3	1.4	—	75.8	3.6	0.7	0.7	2.3	15.6
India: 1980/81	23.2	12.9	3.5	9.1	3.8	73.14	4.52	0.54	1.54	3.93	—
1985/86	21.0	11.8	3.0	8.1	4.24	70.39	4.2	0.64	1.59	4.05	—
Productivity, t/ha.											
China: 1980	4.14	1.89	1.1	2.52	—	1.41	0.56	3.5	47.57	1.55	—
1985	5.25	2.94	1.37	2.89	—	1.8	0.81	4.16	53.43	2.01	—
% change	26.81	55.56	24.55	14.68	—	27.66	44.64	18.86	12.32	29.66	—
India: 1980/81	1.34	1.63	1.16	0.66	0.66	1.02	0.15	1.25	57.84	0.74	—
1985/86	1.56	2.03	1.17	0.64	0.74	1.18	0.19	1.72	59.99	0.76	—
% change	16.42	24.54	0.86	−3.03	12.12	15.69	26.67	37.6	3.72	2.7	—

*Chick peas

Table 12.14 Mechanization of Agricultural Production (Quantity per 1,000 hectares)

	China 1980	China 1985	% changed	India 1980/81	India 1985/86	% changed
Tractor	5.09	5.93	16.50	0.02	3.81	26.16
Tractor-drawn equipment	12.95	8.09	−37.53	15.25	25.50	67.21
Pumps	38.46	42.91	11.57	38.46	42.91	11.57
Power tillers	—	—	—	—	—	—
Total hp employed/hectare	—	1.98	—	—	1.09	—

various kinds of crops bred in different countries. Second, the relationship between the energy input and various kinds of agricultural activities (plowing, weeding, cropping, drying, irrigating, fertilizing, applying pesticides) and the output of each crop is highly non-linear and is very sensitively time/space-dependent. As a result, qualitative rather than quantitative results would be available, even if very detailed case studies were carried out.

In order to make possible the comparison study of the energy consumption in the agricultural sector, the agricultural production level and the level of mechanization of both China and India are first analyzed. The basic results are listed in tables 12.13 and 12.14, respectively. The patterns of plantation or shares of gross cropping of various food-grains (in which maize, sorghum, and gram are considered as one group — in Chinese referred to as "miscella-neous grains") bear great resemblance in the two countries, but the patterns of cultivation of the non-food grain crops differ much more and depend strongly on local conditions.

The productivity of the same crop per unit cultivated land in China and India, however, differ substantially (see table 12.13). The energy input per hectare in the Chinese agricultural economy amounts to 26,889 gigajoules, but in India this figure is only 5,906 gigajoules per hectare, just one-fifth of China's. Thus the energy input-output ratio, taking account of grain products alone (in table 12.15 the energy output in straw is also included), is roughly the same in the two countries: 0.48 in China and 0.52 in India. It can be concluded that Chinese agriculture is much more energy intensive than Indian agriculture, but the specific energy input per unit output is almost the same. It is thus

Table 12.15 Energy Intensities in Agricultural Production (1985, GJ/ha)

	China	(%)	India	(%)
Energy input				
Farm machinery	2,079	7.73	244.4	4.14
Diesel	1,576	5.86	1,003.2	16.99
Electricity	327	1.22	436.4	7.39
Chemical fertilizers	9,025	33.56	2,348.8	39.77
Pesticides/agrochemicals	4.7	1.75	128.2	2.17
Total nonorganic energy	13,477	50.12	4,161	70.46
Labor	4,350	16.18	196.6	3.33
Animal power	7,222	26.90	328.2	5.55
Seeds	1,840	6.84	328.2	5.55
Total organic energy	13,412	49.88	1,745.1	29.54
Total energy input	**26,889**	**100.00**	**5,906.1**	**100.00**
Energy output (MJ/ha)				
Grain	55,680		11,342.5	
Straw	46,980		9,645	
Total output	**102,660**		**20,987.5**	
Energy output-input ratio	3.82		3.55	
Organic-nonorganic ratio	0.995		0.419	
Organic fertilizer (kg/ha)	2,332		743.7	
Output + organic fertilizer (MJ/ha)	44.02		28.22	

anticipated that if Indian agriculture moved from its current labor-intensive technology to a more energy-intensive one, the per hectare production and hence the total production would be increased substantially.

In order to make the comparison more reasonable, a consistent set of energy equivalents for each of the most important inputs and outputs has been generated (see table 12.16).

The total energy consumed in agricultural production by sources is shown in table 12.17. The rate of increase of total energy consumption in Indian agriculture is higher, and even more striking are the differences in the growth rate of consumption of petroleum products between these two countries (0.70 percent versus 43.5 percent). However, in this table the Chinese statistics include also non-agricultural production activities, and the Indian figures are not directly comparable. The share of the agricultural energy consumption decreased by 1.2 percent from 1980 to 1985 in China, but in the meantime a corresponding drop is observed in the proportion of agricultural products in the total national product.

Considering all these elements, the following comments may be made:

1. For direct input to farm processes, the share of commercial energy — diesel and electricity —
   is higher in India than in China: 16.99 percent and 7.39 percent compared to 9.76 percent and 2.02 percent, respectively.

2. The amount of farm machinery and use of chemical fertilizers in Chinese agriculture are greater than in India: 12.87 percent and 55.87 percent compared to 4.14 percent and 39.77 percent, respectively.

3. The non-organic energy intensity per hectare is much higher in China than in India: 13,477 million joules per hectare versus 4,161 million joules per hectare, a ratio of 324 percent in this case.

4. The organic energy intensity difference is also greater between China and India: 2,677.8 gigajoules per hectare compared to 1,745.1 gigajoules per hectare.

5. The energy output/input ratio in China is greater, however, since the output (including both grains and straw, the latter being considered an important source of rural energy) is much more in China. The relevant ratios are 6.36 in China and 3.55 in India.

6. It may therefore be concluded that comparatively better energy management prevails in the farming systems in China. In India there is more potential for increasing the yields of crops

Table 12.16 Energy Equivalents of Agricultural Production Inputs

	China		India	
	Unit	Equivalent	Unit	Equivalent
Nonorganic energy input				
Farm machinery:				
Tractor	MJ/yr	8,000	MJ/yr	210
Diesel pump-set	MJ/set/yr	1,900	—	—
Electric pump-set	MJ/set/yr	1,250	—	—
Hand tools	MJ/tool/yr	30	—	—
Animal-drawn tool equipment	MJ/equipment/yr	110	—	—
Power-driven tool equipment	MJ/equipment/yr	2,000	—	—
Diesel oil	MJ/kg	46.3	MJ/kg	45
Electricity	MJ/kWh	3.6	MJ/kWh	3.6
Chemical fertilizer:				
Nitrogen	MJ/kg	60	MJ/kg	91
P_2O_5	MJ/kg	14	MJ/kg	13.3
K_2O	MJ/kg	6	MJ/kg	9
Insecticides	MJ/kg	250	MJ/kg	102
Organic energy input				
Labor	MJ/worker/yr	270	MJ/capita/yr	270
Animal power	MJ/head/yr	800	MJ/head/yr	800
Seed	MJ/ha	1,350	MJ/kg	16
Organic fertilizer	MJ/t	300	MJ/kg	10
Energy output				
Grains	MJ/kg	14.7	MJ/kg	16
Straw	MJ/kg	12.5	MJ/kg	13.5

and improving the existing farming methods. Experiences could be profitably transferred from China to India in many areas of the agricultural economy.

12.6.2. INDUSTRIAL SECTOR

The industrial sector consumes the major part of commercial energy in both countries, that is, 61.5 percent in China and 57.6 percent in India. Although the share of industrial energy consumption has decreased slowly in recent years, the absolute quantity increased very rapidly despite the efforts made in energy conservation. The energy intensity of industry based on U.S. dollar value output is much higher in China than in India, 1.83 versus 1.28 kilograms oil equivalent per dollar. However, the differences in prices of commodities in these two countries make these figures less significant — even meaningless. It is interesting to note that the net conservation effect is almost nil in India (see table 12.18), while it attains 74.40 million tons oil equivalent in China, a quite remarkable record corresponding to a 26.43 percent saving per unit value added in the Chinese industrial sector.

In order to facilitate the inter-country comparison, the actual energy intensity per unit physical quantity produced in each country was first identified. The consequences of energy conservation measures were investigated on-site by a group composed of representatives from relevant industries in China and India. The power generation sector as well as four energy-intensive manufacturing sectors — iron and steel, cement, fertilizer, and paper-making industries — were chosen for this case study. Detailed reports are available elsewhere, and a summary of the outcomes is shown in table 12.19.

It is interesting to note that, in four out of the five sectors investigated, the specific energy consumption based on physical units is lower in China than in India. For the steel industry, the specific energy consumption figures in China and India are 1.00 and 1.32 tons oil equivalent per ton crude steel, or 24 percent less in China; for the fertilizer industry, 9.5 and 12.3 gigacalories per ton ammonia (from natural gas), or 22.7 percent less in China; for the paper industry, 0.88 and 0.95 kilograms oil equivalent per ton paper, or 7.4 percent less in China; and for the power sector, 2,786 and 3,201 kilocalories per

Table 12.17 Commercial Energy Consumption in Agricultural Production (Mtoe)

	China 1980	1985	Change (%)	India 1980/81	1985/86	Change (%)
Coal	13.06	18.77	43.72	—	—	—
Coke	0.13	0.3	130.77	—	—	—
Oil and petroleum products	7.14	7.19 (5.43)	0.7	3.02	4.32	43.05
Electricity	2.85	3.58 (1.13)	5.61	1.25	2.03	62.4
Total	**24.08**	**29.84 (6.56)**	**23.9**	**4.27**	**6.37**	**48.71**
Sectoral share of agriculture in total commercial energy (%)	8.7	7.5	−1.2	6.16	7.23	1.07

Table 12.18 Energy Consumption and Conservation in Industry (1980 prices)

	Gross value added (billions RMB)	Final energy consumed (Mtoe)	Energy consumption per unit gross value added (Mtoe/billions RMB)	Energy conservation (Mtoe)
China				
1980	195.80	169.64	0.87	—
1985	320.10	204.09	0.64	74.40
India				
1980	200.16	36.577 (2)	0.18	—
1985	256.88	46.535 (2)	0.18	0.40

Table 12.19 Specific Energy Consumption of Some Energy-Intensive Products

	China	India
Industrial energy consumption, Mtoe	28.8	60.6
Industrial energy consumption intensity, toe/1,000 US dollars	1.83	1.28
Crude steel, toe/ton steel	1	1.32
Coke consumption, kg coke/ton metal	558	723–1,056
Cement (average), kcal/kg clinker	1,400	1,330
Wet process, kcal/kg clinker	1,480	1,500
Dry process, kcal/kg clinker	1,340	1,100
Paper and paperboard, kgoe/ton	0.88	0.95
Ammonia: Feed stock—Natural gas, Gcal/ton ammonia	9.5	12.3
Naphtha, Gcal/ton ammonia	10.2	13.4
Fuel oil, Gcal/ton ammonia	11.7	17.2
Electricity generation, kcal/kWh	2,786	3,201

kilowatt-hour, or 12.9 percent less in China. In only one sector, cement manufacturing, is energy intensity in China marginally higher than in India: 1,400 compared to 1,330 kilocalories per ton clinker, or 5 percent more. Since the energy intensities per unit product of most commodities in these two countries are comparable, or even lower in the case of China, the much higher per capita industrial energy consumption in China should be attributed to the much higher per capita physical quantity of various industrial products consumed by Chinese as compared with that consumed by Indians. In fact, Chinese industry has made great progress in energy conservation. The Indian delegation did find many useful experiences in China, and their Chinese counterparts also learned much from the Indian side during their mutual visits.

12.6.2.1. IRON AND STEEL PRODUCTION
Iron- and steel-making is the most energy-intensive industrial sector in both countries. About 15.4 percent of the energy consumed in Chinese industry was used by this sector, and a similar situation exists in India. Our study naturally begins with this sector, and a number of interesting findings have been acquired.

Table 12.20 Capacity, Production, and Capacity Utilization of Steel Industry (Crude Steel)

	China				India		
Year	Capacity Mt/yr	Production Mt/yr	Utilization %	Year	Capacity Mt/yr	Production Mt/yr	Utilization %
1960	20.0	18.7	93.3	1970/71	8.9	6.3	—
1970	19.0	17.8	93.6	1980/81	10.6	9.4	—
1980	40.0	37.1	92.8	1983/84	15.5	10.4	67.3
1985	50.6	46.8	92.5	1986/87	19.1	12.0	63.0

Table 12.21 Production, Import/Export, and Consumption of Finished Steel Products (Mt)

	China				India			
Year	Production	Import	Export	Consumption	Year	Production	Import	Export	Consumption
1960	11.75	0.87	0.09	12.53	—	—	—	—	—
1970	12.23	2.67	0.22	14.68	1970/71	4.79	0.63	0.51	4.91
1980	27.16	5.01	0.40	31.27	1980/81	7.90	1.02	0.05	8.87
1985	36.92	19.67	0.18	56.38	1985/86	10.03	1.06	0.02	11.07

The trends in capacity, production, and utilization of plants are listed in table 12.20. It is rather striking that the Chinese steel mills have maintained an extraordinarily high utilization factor since 1960, always exceeding 92 percent over the past two and a half decades. In contrast, Indian plants were operated at far less efficiency: 67.3 percent in 1983/84 and 63.0 percent in 1985/86, for example.

Still more interesting is the abrupt increase of imported steel products in China, as shown in table 12.21. The import/production ratio of finished steel products increased from 7.3 percent in 1960 to 53.2 percent in 1985, which means that more than one of every three tons of steel consumed in China is imported. For a country in which over a long period the motto was "Steel in Command," that is, where steel production was the backbone of the whole industrial system, the importation of such a large proportion of steel clearly indicates a change from the former general economic line. In fact, it is one of the outcomes of Chinese energy policy: to import energy-intensive products in order to save indigenous energy. By contrast, the import/production ratio in India decreased from 12.6 percent in 1960/61 to 10.6 percent in 1985/86.

Detailed surveys and analysis of all the important manufacturing processes in the iron and steel industry have been carried out in order to identify the process parameters concerned and to evaluate the energy conservation potential of each process. In table 12.22 the process parameters of iron production in China and India are compared. It is seen here that coke consumption is generally lower in China, where the ash content of coal is also low, but ore consumption in China is higher. The spe-

Table 12.22 Process Parameters of Iron-making (1985/86)

	China	India
Coke consumption, kg/t hot metal	608	723–1,056
Iron ore consumption, kg/t hot metal	1,789	631–1,430
Sinter consumption, kg/t hot metal	—	0–1,112
Iron input, kg/t hot metal	—	971–1,026
Ash in coke, %	10.27	23.1–28.5
Hot blast temperature, °C	760	653–965

cific energy consumptions of steel-making in these two countries are summarized in table 12.23. This parameter decreased from 1980 to 1985 by 14.1 percent in China and 7.3 percent in India, but China consumed only 0.997 toe per ton steel as compared with 1.321 toe per ton in India, or about 25 percent less. The higher quality of Chinese coking coal is one reason for this difference, but it should be noted also that a number of energy conservation measures have already been implemented in China while they remain in the proposal stage in India. Detailed descriptions of the conservation steps can be found in country reports of this study, but the most important ones are summarized as follows:

1. Operational improvements
   - Minimizing leakages of oil, air, steam, and so on
   - Making flue gas analysis to maintain appropriate air-fuel ratios
   - Maintaining proper quality and quantity of all input raw materials
   - Strictly following thermal regimes of furnaces
   - Operating optimum number of furnaces

Table 12.23 Specific Energy Consumption in Iron and Steel Industry (toe/ton steel)

	China		India	
	1980	1985	1980/81	1985/86
Coking coal	0.730	0.616	1.141	1.035
Non-coking coal	0.223	0.222	0.195	0.199
Petroleum fuel	0.111	0.075	0.042	0.046
Natural gas	0.024	0.013	—	—
Electricity	0.073	0.071	0.046	0.041
Total	**1.161**	**0.997**	**1.425**	**1.321**

Table 12.24 Capacity, Production, and Capacity Utilization of Cement Industry

	China		India	
	1980	1985	1980/81	1985/86
Capacity, Mt/yr	26*	32*	26.8	44.3
Production, Mt/yr	25.6*	30.8*	18.7	33.1
Utilization, %	>95	>95	69.8	75.2

*Figures from large and medium-size plants only. Total annual production, including small kilns, in 1980 and 1988 were 79.86 and 145.95 Mt, respectively.

2. Equipment improvements
   - Insulating cold blast main
   - Minimizing leakages of hot blast
   - Improving combustion system
   - Using ceramic fiber insulation
   - Modifying water-cooled skids in reheating furnaces
   - Introducing waste heat recovery systems
3. Modernization measures
   - Stamp-charging/partial briquette-making of coal charge
   - Intensifying blast furnaces
   - Replacing open-hearth furnaces with oxygen converters
   - Adopting continuous casting methods
   - Introducing walking beam furnaces
   - Modernizing rolling mills
   - Introducing computerized control systems
   - Introducing waste energy recovery processes, such as coke dry quenching, heat recovery systems in sintering plants, power generation using blast furnace top gas pressure

12.6.2.2. CEMENT MANUFACTURING

The building materials manufacturing sector consumes as much energy as the iron and steel industry in China. In fact, the energy consumption of the Chinese building materials sector has exceeded even that of the iron and steel sector in recent years. Brick-making and cement manufacturing are the two major energy consumers in this sector. However, cement manufacturing is more easily analyzed than brick-making, though the latter constitutes the major part of the total energy consumption in this sector.

In table 12.24 the trend of increase of the capacity, production, and utilization factors of cement plants in China and India are compared. Once again, it is clear that the Chinese plants are operated with a very high utilization factor — more than 95 percent from 1980 to 1985 — while the Indian utilization factor increased from 69.8 percent to 75.2 percent during the same period. This implies a much better performance on the part of India's cement industry than for Indian steel mills, but it is still far less than the Chinese counterpart.

Although the growth rate of capacity and production of cement in India is much greater than that in China (65.3 percent and 77 percent, respectively, in India compared to 23.1 percent and 20.4 percent in China), the increase of production in Chinese local small kilns is not included here. These tendencies are shown in table 12.24. Taking into account the total production from all kind of kilns in China, the growth rate becomes 82.8 percent over five years, which is much higher than India's. This again demonstrates the success of the Chinese policy of "walking on two legs."

A shortcoming of Chinese policy also becomes obvious in table 12.25. The specific energy consumption of the cement industry in China is higher than that in India, though the margin seems to be comparatively small (only 3.1 percent). The reason is also clear from table 12.26: the fraction of the more energy-intensive wet process in China rose from 55 percent in 1960 to 58 percent in 1985, while the proportion of production using the more efficient dry process decreased from 32 percent to 25 percent. The rapidly proliferating smaller kilns (the smallest ones are not included in this table) are responsible for this trend.

The most important energy conservation measures identified as needed in China and India are summarized as follows:
1. Dry process instead of wet process in cement production. This change would result in a net energy saving of about 400 kilocalories per kilogram clinker, or 26.7 percent over the wet process. In the meantime, a specific kiln output increase of 20 percent could be achieved.
2. Adoption of suspension preheaters. In a rotary kiln with a suspension preheater, it is possible to preheat the raw meal up to a temperature of 700° to 800° C. As a result of excellent heat

Table 12.25 Specific Energy Consumption in Cement Production

Process	China (1985) Heat (kcal/kg)	China (1985) Electricity (kWh/t)	China (1985) Total (kcal/kg)	India (1983/84) Heat (kcal/kg)	India (1983/84) Electricity (kWh/t)	India (1983/84) Total (kcal/kg)	World range Heat (kcal/kg)	World range Electricity (kWh/t)
Dry	1,340	105.4	1,430	977	155	1,100	762–812	110–112
Wet	1,480	101.4	1,567	1,657	114	1,755	1,197–1,296	70–104
Semi-dry	1,190	116.4	1,290	996	123	1,102	752–895	90–95
All plants	**1,400**	**102.3**	**1,488**	**1,330**	**130**	**1,442**	—	—

Table 12.26 Profile of Cement Manufacture (Percentage of total capacity)

Process	China 1960	China 1970	China 1980	China 1985	India 1950	India 1970	India 1981	India 1985
Wet	55	59	60	58	97.3	69.5	56	34
Dry	32	23	22	25	—	21.5	36	63
Semi-dry	13	18	18	17	2.7	9	7.8	3
Total	**100**	**100**	**100**	**100**	**100**	**100**	**100**	**100**

transfer, raw meal is partially calcined up to 30 to 40 percent (except in the two-stage suspension preheater). It is estimated that about 300 to 350 kilocalories per kilogram clinker could thus be saved.

3. Improvements in raw materials preparation and handling. For instance, energy savings can be achieved through monitoring raw meal composition, fineness, and moisture, and through use of belt conveyors instead of pneumatic conveyor devices.
4. Better coal preparation and handling. The segregation of shale, stones, and other impurities from the fuel would improve efficiency.
5. Improvements in kiln operation. Energy can be saved by monitoring and control of the coal and air feeds, for example.
6. Other improvements such as installation of instrumentation for process control, including microprocessor-based systems.

12.6.2.3. FERTILIZER MANUFACTURING

The fertilizer manufacturing sector consumes a great amount of fossil fuel not only for processes but also for feedstocks. Hydrogen is needed as a raw material in many products, and it has to be produced from hydrocarbons or coal. The production of fertilizer has increased steadily in China and India due to the ever-growing demand for agricultural products. As a result, in both China and India the fertilizer industry has expanded rapidly since 1960 (see table 12.27). Nitrogen fertilizer production increased 58.6 times in China and 38.6 times in India from 1960 to 1985.

In addition to what is produced domestically, both countries have imported a considerable amount of fertilizer in the past two and half decades. Although the proportion of imports in the total fertilizer consumption has been decreasing (table 12.28), the import of nitrogen fertilizer still accounted for 27.8 percent in India and 13.5 percent in China in 1985.

Ammonia fertilizer production is the most energy-intensive, requiring about 10 to 17 gigacalories per ton. The specific energy consumption varies substantially with different feedstocks: with natural gas the energy consumption is the lowest, and with fuel oil it is the highest (see table 12.29). In fact, the coal-based process is the most energy-intensive one, but it is not included in this table since very little data is available. For the same feedstock, the energy consumption in India is much higher than that in China — about 13 percent for light feedstocks and as high as 47 percent for fuel oil.

A number of measures have been addressed for conservation of energy in the fertilizer industry in both countries. They include:

1. Short-term measures
   - Checking insulation on steam lines
   - Checking steam leakages from valve glands, pipe joints, and steam traps
   - Checking proper depressurization on high-pressure steam and loss of steam from vent valves
   - Checking cleanliness of heat exchangers
   - Checking combustion and draft control in steam boilers and fire heaters
2. Medium- and long-term measures
   - Recovery of purge gas in ammonia synthesis

Table 12.27 Capacity, Production, and Capacity Utilization in Fertilizer Industry (Mt nutrients/yr)

	Nitrogen (N)			Phosphates (P_2O_5)		
	Capacity (1,000 ton/yr)	Production	Utilization (%)	Capacity (1,000 ton/yr)	Production	Utilization (%)
China						
1960	—	0.196	—	—	0.193	—
1970	—	1.532	—	—	0.907	—
1980	10	9.993	99.9	—	2.308	—
1985	15	11.483	76.6	—	2.359	—
India						
1960/61	0.162	0.112	69.0	0.096	0.054	56
1970/71	1.349	0.833	62.0	0.434	0.228	53
1980/81	4.357	2.164	50.0	1.334	0.842	63
1985/86	5.924	4.323	73.0	1.774	1.430	81

Table 12.28 Production, Imports and Consumption of Fertilizer (Mt Nutrients)

	China				India			
	1960	1970	1980	1985	1960	1970	1980	1985
Nitrogen (N)								
Production	0.196	1.532	9.993	11.438	0.112	0.833	2.164	4.323
Imports	0.250	1.348	1.875	1.632	0.399	0.477	1.510	1.616
Consumption	0.465	2.497	9.800	12.050	0.212	1.479	3.678	5.815
Phosphates (P_2O_5)								
Production	0.193	0.907	2.308	2.359	0.054	0.228	0.842	1.430
Imports	0.013	—	0.080	0.046	—	0.032	0.452	0.805
Consumption	0.156	0.991	2.601	3.109	0.053	0.541	1.214	2.068
Potassium salts (K_2O)								
Production	0.016	0.005	0.020	0.024	—	—	—	—
Imports	—	—	0.150	0.248	0.020	0.120	0.797	−0.894
Consumption	0.041	0.024	0.030	0.080	0.029	0.236	0.624	0.854

Table 12.29 Specific Energy Consumption of Ammonia Production (Gcal/ton NH_3)

	China (1985)		India (1981-83)	
	Range	Average	Range	Average
Natural gas	8.5–10.5	9.5	9.8–14.9	12.3
Naphtha	9.4–10.9	10.2	9.2–15.7	13.4
Fuel oil	—	11.7	16.7–18.1	17.2

- Use of low-energy systems for CO_2 removal
- Use of better catalysts
- Adopting co-generation systems
- Replacing low-efficiency compressors, turbines, and drives with high-efficiency ones
- Adopting microprocessor-based instrumentation for efficient and reliable process control

12.6.2.4. THE PAPER INDUSTRY

The paper industry is an energy-intensive sector, ranking third among light industries, just below the

Table 12.30 Capacity, Production, and Capacity Utilization in Paper Industry

	China		India	
	1980	1985	1980/81	1985/86
Paper and paperboard				
Capacity, Mt/yr	5.938	10	1.538	2.349
Production, Mt/yr	5.346	9.112	1.059	1.5
Utilization factor, %	90	91.1	69.8	63.9
Pulp				
Capacity, Mt/yr	5.331	7.204	—	—
Production, Mt/yr	4.263	6.153	—	—
Utilization factor, %	80	85.4	—	—

food processing and textile sectors. It consumes even more energy than the non-ferrous metals sector in Chinese heavy industry. Production of paper products in both China and India increased very rapidly from 1980 to 1985, by 70.4 percent in China and 41.6 percent in India (see table 12.30). The utiliza-

199

tion factor of paper factories in India is again seen to be lower than for those in China (63.9 percent compared to 91.1 percent), as also in the above-indicated three heavy industry sectors.

The differences in specific energy consumptions is striking in the papermaking sector (table 12.31). The consumption of total energy averaged over the whole sector in newsprint production is about 50 percent higher in India and for other paper products amounts to 60 percent more. For large units, the Chinese plants consume 5.8 gigacalories per ton, while the Indian ones use 9.78 gigacalories per ton, 68.6 percent higher. Such a great discrepancy can be attributed to the following causes in India, as identified by Indian experts participating in this survey:

- Old and inefficient boilers
- Poor heat recovery systems
- Low-efficiency turbines
- Low capacity factors of turbo-generators
- Poor quality of Indian coal
- Frequent interruptions in power, oil, and coal supply
- Obsolete plants
- Low capacity utilization of plants
- Heat loss due to improper insulation, steam leakage, etc.
- Large variances in physico-chemical characteristics of raw materials
- Lack of proper housekeeping measures
- Lack of incentives for energy conservation and penalties for abuses

Even in the relatively more efficient Chinese paper factories, the specific energy consumption is still below that of most advanced plants in developed countries. The following energy conservation measures for paper mills are therefore proposed by the group of experts in this study:
1. Better housekeeping
2. Short-term measures such as
   - Increasing boiler efficiency
   - Upgrading insulation
   - Pump-motor matching
   - Introducing flash steam recovery
   - Using variable speed drives
   - Improving black liquor recovery boiler operation and combustion
   - Improving multi-effect evaporator performance
   - Optimizing compressor operation
   - Replacing plain presses by suction presses in paper machines

Table 12.31 Specific Energy Consumption of Pulp and Paper Products

	China 1986	India 1983/84	1985/86
Newsprint			
Thermal energy, Mcal/t	3.04	6.36	5.43
Electricity, kWh/t	400–770	1,995	1,825
Total energy (Average), Gcal/t	4.7	8.08	7
Paper products			
Thermal energy, Mcal/t	4.5–8.5*	9.1	8.37
Electricity, kWh/t	330–850*	1,638	1,642
Total energy (average), Gcal/t	6*		

* For writing paper only.

- Selecting proper pump sizes
- Improving blow heat recovery systems
- Adopting more-efficient lighting
3. Long-term measures
   - Increasing the number of effects of evaporators
   - Replacing obsolete equipment such as old boilers
   - Modifying processes in paper machine/stock preparation
   - Introducing vapor recompression systems
   - Promoting water conservation
   - Adopting vapor absorption refrigeration systems
   - Adopting waste heat recovery systems
   - Improving the power factor
   - Replacing oil with coal in boilers
   - Using cogeneration with back pressure boilers
   - Introducing microprocessor controls in paper machines

12.6.3. TRANSPORTATION SECTOR
The transportation sector in India consumes a much larger share of commercial energy than does its Chinese counterpart — that is, 22.7 percent compared to 5.0 percent, or about 4.4 times more in India. Besides the different proportion of the transportation sector in total GDP for the two countries, there is a significantly different structure of the transportation sector in China and India. As shown in table 12.32, railway transportation predominates in both countries, constituting 50.8 percent of the transportation sector in China and 61.6 percent in India. However, waterways transport plays an important role in China, and road transport is more important in India. These two modes of transportation account for 37.0 percent

Table 12.32 Specific Energy Consumption of Transportation

	China 1985	India 1985/86
Total traffic, billion ton-km (%)	2,076	971.1
Rail	1,054 (50.8)	598.3 (61.6)
Road	193 (9.3)	325.4 (33.5)
Water	767 (37)	46.7 (4.8)
Air	1.32 (0.06)	0.67 (0.07)
Pipeline	60.3 (2.9)	—
Energy use, Mtoe	35.29	18.60
Rail	12.85	5.82
Road	15.73	12.04
Water	4.92	0.42
Air	0.56	0.32
Pipeline	1.50	—
Average energy intensity, kgoe/1000 ton-km	17.00	19.15
Rail	11.94	9.72
Road	81.50	36.98
Water	6.41	8.92
Air	424.00	477
Pipeline	24.9	—

Table 12.33 Specific Energy Consumption in Urban Households (kgoe per capita)

	Commercial Energy	Non-commercial Energy	Total
China (1985)			
Cooking and water heating	163.59	0	163.59
Space heating	142.48	0	142.48
Light and appliances	5.10	0	5.10
All end-uses	311.16	0	311.16
India (1984/85)			
Cooking and water heating	25.77	61.32	87.09
Space heating	0.74	0.26	1.00
Light and appliances	5.24	0	5.24
All end-uses	31.75	61.58	93.33

China. During the recent economic reform, the Chinese automobile industry began to adopt new designs and look for technology transfer from various Western countries. However, the much higher share of energy-saving waterway transportation gives China a lower average energy intensity in the transportation sector as a whole: 17.00 versus 19.15 kgoe/1,000 ton-km in India.

and 9.3 percent of the sector in China and 4.8 percent and 33.5 percent in India, respectively. The magnitudes of the shares of these two modes seem to be reversed in the two countries.

Since coal-fired locomotives are still used extensively in railway transportation in both countries, the average energy intensity of this mode of transportation is rather high, 11.94 and 9.72 kgoe/1,000 ton-km in China and India, respectively. However, the energy intensities in road transportation differ significantly in these two countries, 81.50 compared to 36.98 kgoe/1,000 ton-km, respectively, more than twice as much in China as in India. The major reason lies in different fuel efficiencies and modes of management in these two countries. Freight transportation constitutes the major part of Chinese road use, but most of the trucks used in China are manufactured domestically following a Russian 1950s model which has not been improved in thirty years. This obsolete design uses gasoline instead of diesel as fuel, so the specific fuel consumption is much higher than in modern trucks in other countries. On the other hand, nearly all the passenger cars in China are government- or public- (or institution-) owned and run basically on a noncommercial basis at a very low efficiency. These two crucial factors determine the high energy intensity in the transportation sector of

12.6.4. RESIDENTIAL ENERGY CONSUMPTION

At first sight household energy consumption also differs greatly between China and India (see table 12.1, above) — that is, 24.0 percent and 12.5 percent, respectively — and the quantity of commercial energy consumed in this sector in China is five times as much as in India. However, since a vast amount of noncommercial energy is used in the households of both countries, particularly in the rural regions, the actual energy situation is different than it appears. When all kinds of energy consumption are combined, the share of residential energy consumption becomes 40.45 percent in China and 57.85 percent in India (in 1985), the former figure obviously smaller than the latter. The per capita energy consumed in the residential sector then amounts to 270 kilograms oil equivalent in China and 155.6 in India, or less than twice as much in China as compared with India.

The reasons for such differences have been identified in more detailed surveys. In tables 12.33 through 12.36, a summary of the outcomes of these surveys is given. In urban areas, the energy consumed (end-use) for cooking (water heating included as a small portion) is seen to be about twice as much in China as in India, and energy for space heating is virtually nil in India. Hence each urban

Table 12.34 Per Capita Energy Consumption for Urban Households

	China 1985	India 1984/85
Coal, kg	554.0	31.3
LPG, kg	4.4	2.2
Natural gas, kg	2.1	—
Kerosene, kg	0.7	11.6
Electricity, kWh	59.5	35.0
Charcoal, kg	—	3.8
Firewood, kg	—	82.8
Dung, kg	—	35.7
Other biomass fuels, kg	—	41.5

Table 12.35 Specific Energy Consumption in Rural Households (kgoe per capita)

	Commercial Energy	Non-commercial Energy	Total
China (1985)			
Cooking, water and space heating	55.83	183.96	239.79
Light and appliances	2.46	0	2.46
All end-uses	58.28	183.96	242.24
India (1984-85)			
Cooking and water Heating	1.84	98.35	100.19
Space heating	0.07	0.43	0.50
Light and appliances	5.43	0	5.43
All end-uses	7.34	99.78	107.12

Table 12.36 Per Capita Energy Consumption in Rural Households

	China 1985	India 1984/85
Coal, kg	106.25	2.26
LPG, kg	—	0.01
Kerosene, kg	1.42	5.11
Electricity, kWh	11.92	4.90
Charcoal, kg	—	0.15
Firewood, kg	194.38	40.07
Dung, kg	15.51	133.02
Other biomass fuels, kg	292.97	176.81

resident in China consumed more than three times as much energy as his Indian counterpart did in 1985. On the other hand, each Chinese peasant consumed almost two and a half times as much energy as an Indian peasant did (in terms of end-use), of which 99 percent was for cooking and space heating. (In Chinese rural houses, the stove is often built to serve the dual purposes of cooking and house-heating.) It is thus reasonable to attribute the difference in specific energy consumption in the two countries' residential sectors to variations in cooking styles and climate.

Additional surveys indicate that the energy efficiencies of various appliances are rather similar in these two countries (see table 12.37), though the shares of use of various devices in these two countries differ. Hence residential energy consumption could hardly be reduced from the Chinese side without making great changes in eating habits or improvements in house insulation, both of which are long-term strategic measures.

12.7. ENERGY FORECAST

The energy future of these two largest developing countries is of major concern to energy economists and environmentalists since it will have profound effects on global prosperity and stability, and may influence catastrophic environmental changes. Long-term energy forecasts in China and India are therefore under way in order to discern the trends of energy demand and supply potential for early in the next century and beyond.

It is extremely difficult to predict the energy demands of the distant future in the volatile world of today. Political and even military confrontations, economic competition, technical innovation, cultural evolution, and other factors could invalidate many types of forecasts even within the time horizon of a couple of years. However, some common patterns of development emerge when the profile of a group of countries at different developmental stages is analyzed. It is therefore possible to make trend forecasts for the less-developed countries based on the interpolation of current multi-country data instead of extrapolating from one country's data alone.

A summary of the available recent forecast exercises in China and India is shown in tables 12.38 and 12.39. The Chinese forecast was made recently for the purpose of evaluating future strategies in energy supply, in particular the roles of oil and nuclear energy. The total energy demand is expected to increase 3.6 times in the next fifty years or so, corresponding to a 2.5 percent annual growth rate. The per capita annual energy consumption is expected to reach 2.57 toe, a moderate figure as compared with the current per capita consumption of 6.5 toe per year for the United States, 4.15 for West Germany, and 2.58 for Japan (in 1985). It is predicted

Table 12.37 Average Efficiency of Utilization of Different Fuels in Residential Sector (%)

	China	India
Traditional wood stove	10 – 12	14
Improved wood stove	25 – 33	20 – 25
Straw- and stalk-burning stove	8 – 10	8–10
Traditional coal stove	15 – 18	18
Improved coal stove	35 – 40	—
Dung-burning stove	—	8
LPG stove	55 – 60	55 – 60
Kerosene stove	40 – 45	35 – 50
Kerosene lamp	—	1
Electric cooker	—	85
Electricity for lighting	—	10
Electric heater	—	35

Table 12.38 Long-term Energy Demand/Supply Forecast for China

	2000		2020		2050	
	Mtce	%	Mtce	%	Mtce	%
Coal	736	70.1	1,138	67.7	2,184	60.0
Nuclear	7	0.7	44	2.6	735	20.7
Oil	200	19.0	250	14.9	116	3.2
Natural gas	37	3.5	94	5.6	186	5.1
Hydropower	70	6.7	147	8.8	224	6.2
Other renewable sources	0	0.0	7	0.4	175	4.8
Total	**1,050**	**100.0**	**1,680**	**100.0**	**3,640**	**100.0**

Table 12.39 Long-term Energy Demand/Supply Forecast for India

	1989/1990		1999/2000		2009/2010	
	Mtce	%	Mtce	%	Mtce	%
Coal	109.0	48.5	164.5	46.7	220.9	41.7
Oil	79.0	35.1	100.2	28.5	122.3	23.1
Natural gas	3.1	1.4	12.1	3.4	35.4	6.7
Electricity	33.8	15.0	75.3	21.4	151.2	28.5
Total	**224.7**	**100.0**	**352.1**	**100.0**	**529.8**	**100.0**

that the Chinese indigenous oil supply will reach its peak output around 2020 (about 250 million tons) and drop to 116 million tons in 2050, then constituting only 3.2 percent of the total primary energy supply. As seen in this table, oil will account for the smallest proportion of all kinds of primary energy in China by 2050.

On the other hand, nuclear energy is expected to increase to a strikingly high share of 20.17 percent, corresponding to 563 gigawatts installed capacity and 33.78 tetrawatt-hours per year. Even in this case, coal consumption will still rank first in the Chinese energy system, accounting for 60 percent of the total primary energy supply. If nuclear energy fails to attain this high goal, coal will occupy over 80 percent of the total supply. Such a huge amount of coal, corresponding to 5.88 billion tons raw coal, will give rise to very serious transportation and environmental problems.

The available forecast for India (table 12.39) cannot be used for direct comparison with the Chinese forecast. Only the demand of delivered energy (including both primary and secondary energy forms) is estimated in the Indian work, and the possibility of meeting this demand is left to further study. The types and amounts of different fuels for power generation are also left undefined. However, the rapid growth rate of energy demand in India expected in the two decades after 1990 will attain 235.7 percent, or average 4.38 percent per year — much higher than that in the Chinese case. The potential supply of indigenous primary energy has been evaluated in a separate study for the year 2004/05. The issue of the shortage of domestic oil supply in India has been addressed: for the total demand of 77 million tons, only 50 million tons can be pro-

duced in India; the remaining 27 million tons will have to be imported. Further analysis demonstrates the deficit in the liquid fuel supply could be partly filled with natural gas — about 6 Mt. The pattern of power generation in 2004/05 is also estimated in the study; it is as follows: coal, 56.9 percent; lignite, 1.9 percent; hydropower, 30.8 percent; nuclear power, 9.5 percent; and natural gas, 0.8 percent. This analysis presents a very similar picture for the coal-predominant energy systems of both India and China.

12.8. POLICY RECOMMENDATIONS

Policy recommendations based on the comparison of the energy situations in India and China are integrated into this study. Many concrete policy suggestions have already been addressed in the analyses above, but some additional general policy recommendations are offered below.

12.8.1. CONTROL OF POPULATION GROWTH

Population policy is the basis of all economic policies in developing countries since all natural resources and national products will be divided by the total number of the people before they are consumed; hence the growth rate of the population will have a major bearing on all economic factors. Because of the existing large populations and the moderately high growth rates in both China and India, the energy future (and the economic future as a whole) depends critically on the size of their future populations. China's population is now increasing by more than 15 million people per year, corresponding roughly to the creation of one Malaysia, one east Germany, one Czechoslovakia, or one Australia annually. By 2000 the Chinese population will have grown by 250 million over that of 1985, corresponding to twice the population of Japan or the population of theUnited States. India has an even higher population growth rate, and its population will surpass China's by the middle of the twenty-first century. Thus, ceteris paribus, though the energy situations in both countries will be more critical in the next century than today, India will face an even more serious challenge than China does. Effective population control or family planning policy is thus of first importance for both countries, in particular for India.

Rural areas of both countries will be the most troublesome. The population growth rates are generally higher in the countryside, and the modernization of the rural economy or urbanization (even "local" urbanization) requires the substitution of commercial energy sources for traditional ones. Thus the rural energy problem will be threefold: faster population growth, large-scale energy transition, and increasing energy intensity.

12.8.2. RATIONALIZATION OF ECONOMIC POLICIES

A rational economic policy will be the basis of any successful energy policy. Although feedback from the economy will have a strong influence on policy, the effect will be rather immediate and limited. For example, the abrupt rise of energy import costs may eventually be balanced by increasing commodity exports, as already shown by the experiences of many developed and newly developed countries, since the cost of energy in most products constitutes only a small fraction of the total. Moreover, the structure of the economy has significant impact on energy demand, as mentioned above. Thus, a rational economic policy could substantially alleviate the pressure of energy shortages. On the other hand, due to the combined energy conservation efforts of many countries, the global oil demand has been cut back and oil prices have fallen almost to the real value

before the 1973 crisis. It can therefore be concluded that a rational economic policy and a successful energy policy would reinforce each other.

The energy situation of China has been improved during the past decade of radical economic reform, and very great success in both areas has been achieved. Presently Chinese economic reforms face a crisis for political reasons, but no one in China could deny the fact that without successful economic reform, no other policies, including energy policy, can be implemented effectively. For instance, distorted energy prices in China have seriously retarded the development of the energy industry. Further institutional reforms in the energy sector will be required to promote the vitality of the industry. The bold "open policy" and the successful development of the export-oriented coastal Special Economic Zones could eventually allow replacement of Chinese oil exports by more benign commodity exports.

Different political-social systems give rise to distinct economic policies. However, some policies are considered essential in any economic system, even more obviously where they concern universal economic factors. Several important economic policies related to energy issues are (1) rationalizing energy pricing, (2) self-financing of energy enterprises, (3) balancing of foreign exchange, (4) efficiently utilizing all kinds of resources, and (5) establishing equilibrium in development of all economic sectors.

Detailed steps for implementing these policies may be radically different in China and India. For instance, in the Chinese central planning system, energy prices cannot be rationalized. China tried to improve the situation by introducing a dual pricing system, but many negative effects have been experienced. Thorough price reforms would require certain changes in institutional arrangements or ownership transfers, and the latter again will depend upon the political environment.

12.8.3. EMPHASIZING ENERGY CONSERVATION

Energy conservation should be taken as a long-term strategic vector in energy policy. Unless the energy consumption elasticity can be kept far below unity, no developing economy can ever afford the tremendous energy demands seen in the developed countries. If the three billion people of China and India combined in the mid-twenty-first century consume as much energy per capita as Americans do today, a total energy consumption of about 28 billion tons coal equivalent will be needed for them alone, corresponding to more than three times the total world consumption today! Leaving aside the limitations of natural resources, the huge capital investment for supplying such a tremendous amount of energy will be far beyond the reach of even any developed economy, let alone the developing countries, in which capital is badly needed for the development of all economic sectors.

On the other hand, the potential of energy conservation in China and India is quite high due to the rapidly developing nature of their economies. By 2000, about three-quarters of the production capacity of Chinese industry will come from newly added or technologically updated plants. If the managers and decisionmakers are kept aware of the importance of energy conservation, less energy-intensive equipment and processes will be introduced and substantial reduction of energy consumption can be realized. In the case of India, where the economic growth rate is slower than in China, retrofitting existing industry with energy-saving technologies could also result in great energy conservation, though more investment may be needed per unit energy saved.

In non-productive sectors, there is also great conservation potential in the rational choice of life styles in these countries. Neither India nor China can afford the huge demand of liquid fuel for transportation required by most Western developed countries. Mass transportation and other energy-efficient modes should be chosen in these two countries, and significant saving of liquid fuel will result.

The major areas of energy conservation success foreseen in China and India will be (1) choice of an energy-saving economic structure, (2) promotion of energy-saving life styles, (3) application of energy-saving equipment and processes, (4) improvements in energy efficiencies, (5) substitution of renewable energy sources for exhaustible energy sources, (6) monitoring and management of energy demand, and (7) training and education in energy conservation.

12.8.4. BETTER UTILIZATION OF ENERGY RESOURCES AND DEVELOPMENT OF ALTERNATIVE ENERGIES

Both India and China have all kinds of primary energy resources, though the relative abundance of each kind varies substantially. Rational utilization of these resources will be important, since some of them will be quickly depleted in the coming decades.

Large-scale transitions in the primary energy supply are expected to take place in the two countries since in the long term the existing fossil energy resources will never meet the huge energy demand. First of all, great amounts of traditional energy, mainly consumed in the rural regions, will be gradually replaced by modern commercial energy. As a result, not only will millions of tons oil equivalent of commercial energy have to be provided for this purpose, but also very complicated large-scale infrastructures will have to be developed for the transportation and distribution of energy in the vast rural areas. Secondly, in both countries the indigenous supply of oil will be more and more reduced in next century, and alternative energy sources will have to be developed to replace oil in many applications. Thirdly, even though the extensive coal resources in these countries will not in themselves present a restriction, the large-scale consumption of coal will result in adverse environmental impact, unacceptable in the long run. A transition to clean coal and/or post-coal energy is unavoidable. The major forms of alternative energy under consideration include synthetic liquid fuel, nuclear energy, and other renewables. Technological and financial provisions should be therefore provided in advance and great efforts made to promote such transitions.

The major policies on energy resource utilization and development are summarized as follows:

1. Petroleum resources are the most critical issue and deserve particular attention. The present proven reserves in India and China are far from enough to support their future economic development. India needs to intensify its exploration efforts in order to reduce oil imports in the future. China will put more emphasis on offshore and nonconventional oil exploitation to meet the fast-growing demand. Enhanced recovery processes will need to be implemented to increase the utilization factor of the diminishing oil resources.

2. Natural gas could partially replace oil and is considered a promising energy source in the coming decades. Unfortunately, the present natural gas reserves in both countries are so limited that the prospects are still uncertain. For the time being natural gas cannot be considered a reliable future major energy source. In any case, it would better be used as a raw material for producing fertilizer and other chemical products if the supply is limited.

3. Coal is the most abundant energy source in both countries. In China it is virtually limitless for the coming decades. However, both local and global environmental impact will make its

use increasingly unacceptable. If future technology cannot solve the problems of air pollution, acid rain, and global "greenhouse" effects, coal use will eventually be ruled out. The improvement of coal utilization with FBB boilers, combined cycle, fuel cells, coal gasification and coal liquefaction, among other technologies, will be inevitable if coal continues to be used as a major fuel.

In China, it is expected that liquefied coal will provide the most likely substitute for petroleum, either by direct hydrogenation processes or indirect synthesis. But in India, liquefaction from natural gas is considered the potential replacement for liquid fuel, though the potential reserves of natural gas are still uncertain.

4. Hydropower is abundant in both countries, the total exploitable potential amounting to 380 GWe in China and 89 GWe in India, of which only 7.9 percent and 19.7 percent, respectively, had been exploited by 1987. Further exploitation of hydropower is unquestionable, but a series of problems must be solved besides the huge investment and long lead-time required. The environmental and social impacts of major projects are always formidable, and the difficulties will increase with the passage of time.

In addition, considering the astronomical figures of future electricity demand in the distant future, the proportion that can be provided by hydropower, even fully exploited, will become smaller and smaller. New energy sources other than fossil fuels must be developed to meet the ever-growing power demands.

6. The role of nuclear energy is already emphasized in both countries, and both have sufficient indigenous resources for its development. Comparatively large-scale programs are under way, and ambitious targets have been declared. However, the international anti-nuclear atmosphere does create some suspicions on this option. Inherently safe reactors should be developed to replace current power reactors, the latter being vulnerable to core melt-down accidents of the kind which led to the catastrophic consequences at Chernobyl and the controversy at Three Mile Island. The technical and economic problems of fuel reprocessing and radioactive waste disposal have not been fully solved. Efforts must be made if the nuclear option is to become the primary choice in these countries. The tremendous capital investment needed will be another formidable barrier in nuclear development. A safe and economical reactor design must be developed.

Solar energy is considered a safer and cleaner candidate, but there still exist considerable technical and economic obstacles to be overcome. Present designs for solar devices are much more material-intensive than other commercialized energy sources, and hence are too expensive for large-scale application. However, the situation is improving rapidly, as in the development of amorphous thin film solar cells. Energy storage is considered another challenging problem in large-scale solar energy application. Hence, it is expected that the commercialization of hard solar energy is still decades away. In both China and India the nuclear and the solar technologies are being pursued in parallel, though the former is considered more mature at present and ready for commercialization on a large scale.

12.8.5. LONG-TERM INTEGRATED PLANNING

Long-term integrated planning taking into consideration energy, economy, environment, and social development, as well as policy options, seems indispensable to every rapidly developing economy. The successes of many newly industrialized countries have demonstrated the importance of such an approach. The experiences of China and India themselves also support the necessity of such an effort. Huge investments, long lead-times, and complex interactions among economic, social, and environmental factors may render any major energy program unsuccessful unless it is thoroughly considered in an integrated plan giving due weight to all these crucial factors. The decades-long contention over the mammoth Three Gorges Hydropower Station project in China is not the only example. The recent concern over global CO_2 issues has a direct bearing on the energy future in India and China. It is estimated that, without timely introduction of non-fossil fuels on a very large scale, the CO_2 emissions from China and India by 2010 would constitute at least a third of the world total. Thus the long-term integrated planning of these two countries will have global impact apart from their important influence on domestic energy policies.

The comparative study carried out in ITEESA/ INET and TERI has been successful. The five major general policy recommendations discussed above and many other concrete suggestions, along with the detailed outcomes of this study, have been submitted directly to the senior decisionmakers in the governments of both India and China. The cooperation initiated by this comparative study is continuing, and its scope is being broadened. It is believed that the successful solution of energy supply and consumption problems of the two most populous countries in the world will have a profound impact on the global energy and environmental future.

BIBLIOGRAPHY AND REFERENCES

*1. An, Yupei. "Policy Retrospection and Suggestions for Further Perfection of Petroleum Industry." *Energy of China*, 5(1989).

*2. Bureau for Energy Conservation. *The Development and Application of Energy Forecasting Models.* Beijing: China's Planning Press, 1988.

*3. Chen, Wangxiang, et al. "Retrospect of the Past, Prospects for the Future." *Energy of China*, 5(1989).

*4. Chen, Weiping, et al. "A Two-Level Planning Model for Regional Agriculture and Its Application in XinJiang Area." *Proceedings of First International Conference on Agricultural System Energy*, Changchun, August 1987.

*5. *China's Coal Industry Yearbook, 1988.* Beijing: China's Coal Industry Press, 1989.

*6. *China's Energy Statistics Yearbook, 1989.* Beijing: China's Statistics Press, 1990.

*7. *China's Metallurgy Industry Yearbook, 1988.* Beijing: China's Metallurgy Press, 1989.

8. *China Statistical Yearbooks, 1980-1989.* Beijing: International Center for the Advancement of Science and Technology Ltd., 1989.

*9. Deng, Keyun, et al. *China's Rural Energy by 2000.* Beijing: Institute for Agricultural Energy Research and Development (IAERD), 1984.

*10. Economy-Technology-Social Development Research Center of the State Council, ed. *China's Economic Development and Its Modeling.* Beijing: China's Financial and Economic Press, 1990.

11. Edmond, J. A., et al. *An Analysis of Possible Future Atmosphere Retention of Fossil Fuel CO_2.* Springfield, Virginia: DOE/OR-21400-1, NTIS, 1984.

*12. *Electric Power Industry in China (In Celebration of National Installed Generating Capacity Over 100 GW).* Beijing: China's Water Research and Electric Power Press, 1988.

13. Energy Information Administration. *The Petroleum Resources of China.* Washington, D.C.: U.S. Government Printing Office, 1987.

14. *Energy Statistics.* Chicago: Gas Research Institute, 1980.

15. Fridley, David, et al. *China and the Changing Global Energy Industry.* A report of the China Energy Study, Resources Study Institute (RSI), East-West Center, Honolulu, 1987.

16. Ghirad, David, et al. *Greenhouse Gas Emissions and the Developing Countries: Strategic Options and the U.S.A.I.D. Response, A Report to Congress.* Washington, D.C.: U.S. Agency for International Development, July 1990.

17. Goldemberg, Jose, et al. "An End-Use Oriented Global Energy Strategy," *Annual Review of Energy,* 10(1985), pp. 613–88.

*18. Gu, Jiajun. "The Comprehensive Utilization of Oil Shale and Its Prospects." Paper presented at the Fifth Annual Meeting of China's Energy Research Society, Beijing, October 1985.

*19. Gu, Jian. "Issues of the Development of New Energy in China." *New Energy* 11, 12(1989).

*20. Gu, Peiliang. *The Long-Term Strategy for Energy Supply in China and the Measures for Energy Supply by 2000.* Tianjin: Institute for System Engineering, 1984.

*21. Gu, Shuhua. *Diffusion of Biogas and Small Hydropower Stations in China.* Interim Report. Beijing: Institute of Nuclear Energy Technology, July 1986.

*22. ———. "The Diffusion of Fuel-Saving Stoves and Conservation." Proceedings of the National Conference on Energy Management and New Techniques of Energy Conservation, Nanjing, September 1988.

23. ———. "Diffusion of Improved Firewood Stove in China, International Network on Evaluation and Diffusion of Rural Energy Technology." Paper presented at the International Network on Evaluation and Diffusion of Rural Energy Technology, Bariloche, November 1988.

24. Gu, Shuhua, et al. "Assessment and Innovation of Improved Firewood Stoves in China." Internal Report of Institute of Nuclear Energy Technology, February 1990.

---

* Published in Chinese

*25. ———. "Comprehensive Benefits of Biogas Project in China." *Journal of Rural Engineering*, 2(1988).

26. ———. "Diffusion and Innovation in Rural Energy Technology in China." Presented at the International Network on Evaluation of Rural Energy Technology, Manila, November 1986.

27. ———. "Diffusion of Improved Firewood Stoves in China." Report to International Development Research Center (Canada), February 1990.

28. ———. *Integrated Assessment of Rural Energy Technologies in Demonstrative County in China.* Final report to Commission on the European Community, March 1989.

*29. ———. *The Methodology of Comprehensive Planning for Rural Energy, the Application in 12 Pilot Counties.* Beijing: Institute of Nuclear Energy Technology, 1988.

30. ———. "Popularization of Firewood-, Coal-Saving Stoves and Energy Conservation." *Proceedings of the International Workshop on Energy Management and Conservation Technology*, Nanjing, September 1988.

*31. ———. "Regional Energy and Supply Structure Forecast Model for Beijing." A Collection of Research and Applications of *New Technology*, Volume 1. Beijing: Tsinghua Press, 1986.

*32. ———. "A Survey Report for Rural Energy and Its Technologies in Tong Liang County of RETAIN Project in China." October 1986.

*33. Gu, Shuhua, and Zhang, Zhengming, eds. *The Comprehensive Planning of Rural Energy Development and Its Applications.* Beijing: Beijing Press, 1990.

*34. Guo, Xiying. "Current Status of Biogas Development in China and Relevant Proposals." *New Energy* 10, 4(1988).

*35. He, Dexing. "Current Status and Strategy of Wind Energy Development in China." *New Energy* 11, 12(1989).

*36. He, Jiankun. "Comprehensive Evaluation Methodology for Rural Energy Projects." Paper presented at Third National Conference on Rural Energy, Hefei, November 1987.

*37. ———. "Objective Planning Model for the Development of Water Resources in Xingjiang Region." *China's Agriculture Science* 5, 1985.

38. ———. "Optimizing the Energy Demand-Supply System in a Rural Region in North China." FAO Environment and Energy Paper 5. New York: United Nations Food and Agriculture Organization, 1985.

*39. He, Jiankun, et al. "The Evaluation of Methodologies for Long-Term Forecast of Rural Productivity." *Journal of Tsinghua University* 28, special issue, 2(1988).

*40. ———. "Model for Ecological Protection in Boqitung Lake and Equilibrium of Water Resources in Yanqi Basin." *China's Agriculture Science,* 3(1985).

*41. ———. "Optimal Planning for Nuclear Energy Development." *Nuclear Science and Engineering* 2, 2(1982).

42. ———. "Optimization of the Energy Demand-Supply System in a Rural Region in North China." Paper presented at Seminar on Evaluation of National and Rural Energy Planning and Technology, Athens, July 1988.

*43. ———. "System Analysis of Ecological Agriculture System of Hainan." *Journal of Ecology* 4, 3(1984).

*44. Hu, Angang, et al. *Survival and Development.* Beijing: Scientific Press, 1989.

45. Huang, Joe. "Potential and Barriers to Building Energy Conservation in China." Paper presented at the Western Economic Association's International Annual Meeting, June 18-22, 1989, Lake Tahoe.

*46. Huang, Kun, et al. "Report of Investigation on the Popularization of Improved Firewood Stove in Zunhua County, Hebei Province." October 1988.

47. ———. "Report of Investigation on the Popularization of Improved Firewood Stove in Zunhua County, Hebei Province." Paper presented at the International Network on Evaluation and Diffusion of Rural Energy Technology, Bariloche, November 1988.

*48. Huang, Yicheng. "About the Medium-Term Strategies of Energy Industry of China." *Energy of China,* 1(1989).

*49. ———. "Give the Superiority of the Coal Resources of China Full Play," *Energy of China,* 4(1989).

---

* Published in Chinese

*50. ———. "Make a Good Job of Management and Rectification of Energy Industry Conscientiously and Try in Every Possible Way to Tap the Labor Productivity and Economic Results." *Energy of China*, 1(1990).

*51. Institute for Agricultural Engineering Research and Design. *The Comprehensive Rural Energy Planning of Wuhua County.* Guangdong: Office of Rural Energy of Wuhua County, 1988.

*52. ———. *Report on China's Rural Energy Policy Issues.* Beijing: Institute for Agricultural Energy Research and Development, 1982.

*53. ———. *Atlas of Excellent Fuel-Saving Stoves in China.* Beijing: Agricultural Engineering Journal, 1983.

*54. Institute for Agricultural Energy Research and Development, et al. "The Report on Comprehensive Rural Energy Planning in Pilot Counties." Paper presented at the Third National Symposium on Rural Energy, 1987.

*55. Jiang, Xiangrong. "Retrospection and Prospects of Energy Conservation in China." *Energy of China*, 5(1989).

*56. Jiang, Xingxiong. "Speed Up the Development of the Nuclear Power Industry." *Energy of China*, 6(1989).

57. Levine, Mark D., and Liu, Xueyi. *Energy Conservation Programs in the People's Republic of China*, LBL 29211. Berkeley: Lawrence Berkeley Laboratory, 1990.

*58. Li, Junfeng, et al. "Temporary Crisis or Long-Term Defect?" *Energy of China*, 3(1989).

59. Li, Yourun, et al. "Preliminary Report on Energy Auditing in Shijiazhuang Chemical Fertilizer Plant." Report to Asian Development Bank, July 1989.

60. Li, Zhinai, et al. "Preliminary Report on Energy Auditing in Datong Cement Mill." Report to Asian Development Bank, July 1989.

61. Lieberthal, K., and M. Oksenberg. *Bureaucratic Politics and Chinese Energy Development.* Washington, D.C.: U.S. Government Printing Office, 1986.

62. Lippit, V.D. *The Economic Development of China.* New York: M.E. Sharpe, Inc., 1987.

63. Liu, Deshun. "Analytic Hierarchy Process (AHP) Multiple Goal Programming Linking Model." Paper presented at International Symposium on Urban Development Strategy, Beijing, August 1986.

64. ———. "Present Energy Situation and Energy Policy in China." Paper presented at the Third Seminar on Energy Planning, Kuala Lumpur, May 1986.

*65. Liu, Deshun, et al. "The Application of Multi-Objective Coupling Model in Urban Energy-Environmental System Planning." *Journal of Tsinghua University* 28, 2(1988), special issue.

66. ———. "Assessment of Impact of Economy-Energy Development on Environment in Harbin." Paper prepared for International Association of Energy Economists (IAEE) Twelfth International Annual on Energy-Environment and Development, January 1990, New Delhi.

67. ———. "The Key Issues Facing Electricity System of Developing Countries: A 21st Century Perspective Country Study: China." Final report to Commission on the European Community, March 1990.

68. Liu, Fang. *The Energy Efficiency of Steel Industry of China.* Berkeley: Lawrence Berkeley Laboratory, 1989.

*69. Liu, Zhizhen. "Prospects of and Measures for China's Rural Electrification." Paper presented at the Third National Symposium on Rural Energy, Beijing, 1987.

70. Lu, Yingyun. "Regional Energy Environment System Analysis and the Role of Low-Temperature Nuclear Heat in North China." Paper presented at the International Symposium on Risk and Benefit of Energy System, Julich, April 1984.

71. Lu, Yingyun, et al. "A Practical Short- and Medium-Term Model for Regional Demand-Supply Analysis." *Proceedings of the China-U.S. Conference on Energy, Environment and Resources*, Beijing, September 1982.

*72. ———. "Regional System Planning Model for Beijing." *Proceedings of the Conference on National Energy Forecast Models and Their Application*, Beijing, June 1987.

*73. ———. "Research and Application of Regional Energy System Planning Model for Beijing." *A Collection of Research and Applications of New Technology*, Volume 1. Beijing: Tsinghua Press, 1986.

74. Lu, Yingzhong. "Alternative Nuclear Strategy and the Role of HTGRs." Paper presented at the Summer Meeting of American Nuclear Society, June 1980, Las Vegas. The summary was published in the *Transactions of American Nuclear Society 1980 Summer Meeting*.

*75. ———. "An Analysis of the Substitution of Coal with Nuclear Energy." *Research in Econometrics and Technoeconomics*, 10(1983).

76. ———. "Carbon Dioxide Issues and Energy Policy in the PRC." *International Journal of Global Energy Issues* 1, 2(1989).

77. ———. "The Challenge and the Hope — the Status and Prospects of Nuclear Energy in Asia." Paper presented at the Plenary Meeting of the 1990 Annual Meeting of American Nuclear Society, June 10-14, 1990, Nashville.

78. ———. *Comparison of the Energy Supply, Consumption, and Policy of the PRC and Some Developing Countries*. Washington, D.C.: Washington Institute for Values in Public Policy, 1989.

79. ———. "Current Status and Prospects of District Heat in PRC." *Proceedings of the International Association of District Heating*, June 1984, Bretton Woods, New Hampshire.

80. ———. "Current Status and Prospects of District Heat in PRC." *Energy* 9, 9/10(1984).

81. ———. "The Development of LTR for District Heating in the PRC." Paper presented at a seminar held at Japanese Atomic Energy Research Institute (JAERI), Tokyo, September 25, 1985.

82. ———. "The Development of Nuclear Energy in China." Article written for the Energy Research Group Series, International Development Research Center (Canada), September 1984.

83. ———. "Economic Development and Energy Use in PRC." Paper presented at Roundtable on Energy, Technology and the Economy, International Institute for Applied System Analysis (IIASA), Luxembourg, October 1986.

84. ———. "The Economic Reform and Energy Future of the PRC," and "Environmental Issues of Urban Energy in the PRC." *Proceedings of the Tenth Annual Conference of International Association of Energy Economists* (IAEE), July 4-7, 1988, Luxembourg.

85. ———. "Energy Conservation in China — Experience and Potential." Paper presented at the International Energy Workshop, June 7-8, 1990, Honolulu.

86. ———. "The Energy Data System in PRC." *Proceedings of the International Conference on Energy Data Systems*, December 1982, New Delhi.

*87. ———. "The Energy Forecast and Energy Models in the PRC." Paper presented at the Conference of Henan Energy Research Society, Zhengzhou, August 1981.

*88. ———. "The Energy Forecast in the PRC and the Relevant Issues in Energy Strategies." Paper presented at the Fifth Annual Meeting of China's Energy Research Society, October 1984, Chongqing.

89. ———. "Energy Planning Methodologies and Application in PRC." Paper presented at Seminar on Energy at Lawrence Berkeley Laboratory, Berkeley, April 1986.

90. ———. "Energy Planning Methodologies and Applications in the PRC." Paper presented at the Commission on the European Communities, Seminar on Energy Planning, September 1986, Luxembourg.

91. ———. "Energy Prospects and Policies in PRC." *Energy Journal* 7, 3(1986).

92. ———. "Energy System Development and Energy Training in the PRC." Paper presented at the Senior Experts' Meeting, Economic and Social Committee for the Asian Pacific (ESCAP), March 16-17, 1987, Bangkok.

93. ———. "Environmental Impact of the Energy System in PRC." Paper presented at the Annual Conference of International Association of Energy Economists (IAEE), Bonn, June 1985.

94. ———. "Environmental Issues and Relevant Policies of the Energy System in the PRC." Paper presented at the Annual Meeting of Commission on the European Community, Network on Energy in Developing Countries, May 25-29, 1987, Brighton, England.

95. ———. "Experience in Energy Planning in the PRC." Paper presented at the Annual Meeting of the Commission on the European Community, Network on Energy in Developing Countries, April 12-16, 1986, Bariloche.

---

* Published in Chinese

96. ———. "The Food-Energy System in the PRC." Paper presented at the International Conference on the Unity of the Sciences, Atlanta, November 26-29, 1987.

*97. ———. "Important Role of Nuclear Energy in Energy Forecasting of China." *Nuclear Science and Engineering* 1, 1(1981).

98. ———. "The Important Role of Nuclear Energy in the Future Energy System of China." *Energy* 9, 9/10(1984), pp. 761–71.

99. ———. "Lectures on Energy in Developing Countries: 1. Energy Policy Issues in Europe: How Relevant for ADCs? 2. The Energy Situation and Relevant Policy in the PRC. 3. Manpower Needs in Energy Planning and Management." Paper presented at Workshop on Experience of Energy Planning and Management in European and Developing Countries, Ispra, June-July 1984.

100. ———. "Long-Term Energy Demand and the CO_2 Issues in the PRC." Paper presented at the International Association of Energy Economists' Twelfth International Conference, New Delhi, January 4-6, 1990.

101. ———. "The Long-Term Energy Demand Forecast in PRC." Paper presented at the International Energy Workshop, Luxembourg, June 1985.

102. ———. "Long-Term Energy Forecast and the Strategies in the Development of Nuclear Energy." Working paper at the Institute for Energy Analysis/Oak Ridge Associated Universities, Oak Ridge, December 1986.

103. ———. "A Methodology for Energy Supply and Demand Evaluation: a Dynamic Rural Energy Model and a Study of Energy Management and Conservation in Industry." Final Report to Commission on the European Community, October 1984.

104. ———. "Non-Renewable Energy Resources." In *Manual of Integrated Energy Planning*, edited by Asia-Pacific Development Center, Kuala Lumpur, July 1983.

105. ———. "The Ordeals of Chernobyl and the Rejustification of the Inherently Safe Reactors." *Proceedings of the Conference of International Scientific Forum on Fueling the 21st Century*, September 30-October 6, 1987, Moscow.

106. ———. "The Potential of Non-Carbon Energy Sources in Developing Countries — the Case of China." Paper presented at the International Workshop on Reducing Carbon Dioxide Emissions from the Developing World, October 4-6, 1990, Lawrence Berkeley Laboratory, Berkeley.

*107. ———. "A Proposal on the Energy Planning in the PRC," submitted to the State Science and Technology Commission, December 1979.

*108. ———. "The Prospect of Energy in the PRC." Paper presented at the Training Program on Energy Planning and Management at the State University of New York, Stony Brook, October 1980. The Chinese translation was published in *Scientific American* (Chinese Edition), Beijing, August 1982.

109. ———. "The Prospects and Development of HTGR in the PRC." Paper presented at a seminar held at the Japanese Atomic Energy Research Institute, Tokyo, September 25, 1985.

110. ———. "The Prospects of Rural Energy in the PRC." Paper presented at the Annual Meeting of International Association of Energy Economists, January 1984, New Delhi.

111. ———. "Reflection on Market Economy in PRC." Paper presented at Seminar in International Strategy Institute, Stanford University, May 1986.

112. ———. "A Regional Energy Planning Application: The Energy Flow Analysis of the Beijing Region." Paper presented at the Commission on the European Community, Seminar on Energy Planning, October 13-16, Marseille.

*113. ———. "The Role and the Prospects of Nuclear Heat in the Energy System of China." Article written for the Study of Nuclear Energy Strategies in China, sponsored by State Science and Technology Commission, May 1988.

*114. ———. "The Second Nuclear Era and the Prospects of Nuclear Power Development." Paper presented at the First Annual Meeting of China's Nuclear Power Society, April 22-27, 1985, Wuxi. Published in *Nuclear Power Engineering* 7, 1/8(1986).

115. ———. "Some Comments on the CO_2 Issue in the PRC." Paper presented at a seminar held by the U.S. Department of Energy, February 10, 1987, Washington, D.C.

116. ———. "A Survey of Several Asian Countries on the Situation of Training on Energy Planning and Management." Paper presented at United Nations Development Program, Network on Energy Training, New York, October 1981.

117. Lu, Yingzhong, et al. "Application of National Energy Demand Model and Some Policy Suggestions." Paper presented at Seminar on Evaluation of National and Rural Energy Planning and Technology, Athens, July 1988.

118. ———. "Comparative Study of Energy Supply, Energy Consumption and Policies in the People's Republic of China and India." Final Report to Commission on the European Community, May 1989.

119. ———. "Comprehensive Assessment of Impact of Energy on Environment in Harbin." Final Report to Commission on the European Community, March 1989.

120. ———. "An Elementary Model for Energy Forecast and Optimization in PRC." *Proceedings of the China-U.S. Conference on Energy, Environment and Resources*, Beijing, September 1982.

*121. ———. "Energy Forecast of China in 2000." *A Collection of Research on 'China in 2000.'* Beijing, 1988.

122. ———. "Integrated Assessment of Rural Energy Technologies in Demonstrative County in China." Final Report to Commission on the European Community, March 1989.

123. ———. "A Methodology for Energy Supply and Demand Evaluation: Dynamic Rural Energy Model." Final Report to Commission on the European Community, October 1985.

124. ———. "A Methodology for Energy Supply and Demand Evaluation: The Industrial Sectoral Energy System Model in Connection with Environment Impacts." Final Report to Commission on the European Community, February 1984.

125. ———. "A Methodology for Energy Supply and Demand Evaluation: The Rural Energy Model in Connection with the Ecological Equilibrium Issues in the PRC." Final Report to Commission on the European Community, February 1984.

126. ———. "A Methodology for Energy Supply and Demand Evaluation: A Survey and Methodology of Energy Management and Conservation in Industrial Enterprises." Final Report to Commission on the European Community, October 1985.

127. ———. "Non-Industrial Energy: Consumption and Supply in Cities of China." Report to International Development Research Center (Canada), December 1982.

*128. ———. "Prospects of Low-Temperature Heating Reactor." *Nuclear Power Engineering* 5, 6 (1984).

129. ———. "The Study of HTGR Technology and Its Industrial Applications." *Proceedings of the Sixth Pacific Basin Nuclear Conference*, September 7-11, 1987, Beijing.

130. ———. "Urban Household Energy Survey (China)." Progress Report to International Development Research Center (Canada), August 1985.

131. ———. "Urban Household Energy Survey (China)." Report to International Development Research Center (Canada), November 1986.

132. Manne, Alan, et al. "Global CO_2 Emission Reduction — the Impacts of Rising Energy Costs." Paper presented at the International Energy Workshop, June 7-8, 1990, Honolulu. *Energy Journal* 12, 1 (1991).

*133. Meng, Zhaoli. "Modernization and Energy." *Modernization*, 11(1988).

*134. Meng, Zhaoli, et al. "Analysis Methodology of Energy Conservation in Paper Mill." *Proceedings of the National Conference on Energy Management and New Techniques of Energy Conservation*, Nanjing, September 1988.

135. ———. "The Energy Audit of Qiqihar Paper Mill and the Information System of Energy Management for Enterprises." *Proceedings of the International Workshop on Energy Management and Conservation Technology*, Nanjing, September 1988.

*136. ———. "Industrial Energy Management Information System." *Proceedings of the National Conference on Energy Management and New Techniques of Energy Conservation*, Nanjing, September 1988.

137. ———. "Industry Energy Conservation in China: Overseas Study Tours Report for Pulp-Paper Making Industry." Report to Asian Development Bank, July 1989.

* Published in Chinese

138. ———. "Preliminary Report on Energy Auditing in Qiqihar Paper Mill." Report to Asian Development Bank, July 1989.

*139. ———. "The Structure and Application of Information System on Enterprise Energy Management." *Energy,* 3(1987).

*140. Miao, Tianjie. "Train of Thoughts on the Approach to Resource Conservation and Comprehensive Utilization in 8th FYP." *Energy of China,* 1(1990).

*141. Ministry of Energy. *Energy in China* (1989). Beijing: Ministry of Energy, 1990.

142. Qiu, Daxiong. *Energy Strategy and Plan in China.* Report to Asian Development Bank Network on Evaluation of Energy Strategy and Planning, May 1987.

143. ———. *Food-Energy Nexus in China.* Report to Asia-Pacific Development Center Research Network, Kuala Lumpur, 1986.

144. ———. *Integrated Assessment of Rural Energy Technologies in Demonstrative County in China.* Final Report to Commission on the European Community, March 1989.

145. ———. "Role of New and Renewable Sources of Energy in Integrated Rural Development in China." Paper presented at the UN Group of Experts on the Role of New and Renewable Sources of Energy in Integrated Rural Development, Stockholm, June 1990.

146. ———. "Rural Energy Data Base Development Program and Project Level." Paper presented at the Seminar on Regional Rural Energy Planning, Kuala Lumpur, October 1987.

147. ———. "Rural Energy Model in Connection with Agriculture Production and Ecological Equilibrium." Paper presented at European Community Workshop on Methodologies in Research on Energy Demand and Supply, Mexico City, October 1983.

*148. ———. "Study on Rural Energy Model." Special volume of *Journal of Power,* 1985.

*149. Qiu, Daxiong, et al. "Analysis of Energy Conservation in Five Trades in China." *Proceedings of the National Conference on Energy Management and New Techniques of Energy Conservation,* Nanjing, September 1988.

150. ———. "The Application of Rural Energy Model in Xinjiang Autonomous Region — Energy Survey and Policy Analysis in Fu Kang County." Final Report to Commission on the European Community, October 1986.

151. ———. "The Application of Rural Energy Model in Xinjiang Autonomous Region — A Survey of Rural Energy and Its Model Research in Qi Tai County." Final Report to Commission on the European Community, December 1987.

152. ———. "Assessment and Innovation of Improved Firewood Stoves in China." Final Report to Commission on the European Community, February 1990.

153. ———. "Diffusion and Innovation in the Chinese Biogas Program." Paper presented at the Seminar on Evaluation of National and Rural Energy Planning and Technology, Athens, July 1988.

154. ———. "Energy Conservation in Enterprises in Industry Sectors." *Proceedings of the International Workshop on Energy Management and Conservation Technology,* Nanjing, September 1988.

*155. ———. *Energy in China by 2000 (A Special Report on Energy Forecast).* Beijing: Institute for Nuclear Energy Technology, 1984.

156. ———. *Energy Program: Food-Energy Nexus in China.* Final Report to Asia-Pacific Development Center, Kuala Lumpur, July 1986.

157. ———. "Experience on Rural Energy Planning and Technology Assessment in China." Paper presented at Seminar on Evaluation of National and Rural Energy Planning and Technology, Athens, July 1988.

*158. ———. *First Training Course on National Energy Training.* Beijing: Institute of Nuclear Energy Technology, June 1986.

159. ———. "Improvement of National and Provincial Energy Statistics — Application of Energy Flow Analysis Model (EFLOW) in China." Final Report to Commission on the European Community, March 1989.

160. ———. *Industry Energy Conservation in China: Overseas Study Tours Report for Cement Industry.* Report to Asian Development Bank, July 1989.

161. ———. "Industry Energy Conservation in China: Preliminary Report on Energy Auditing in Five Demonstrative Plants." Report to Asian Development Bank, July 1989.

162. ———. "Methodology of Energy-Environment System in Urban Area." Paper presented at the Commission on the European Community, Network on Energy Environmental System, Hangzhou, February 1987.

*163. ———. "The National Energy Demand Model and Its Policy Implications." *Soft Science Study,* 1(1986).

164. ———. "Rural Energy Planning Methodology and Application." Paper presented at South Asia Seminar on Energy Planning, Goa, March 1987.

165. ———. "Rural Energy Technology Assessment and Innovation (China)." Final Report to International Development Research Center (Canada), July 1987.

166. ———. "Urban Household Energy Survey (China)." Paper presented at the International Symposium on Urban Energy, Beijing, May 1987.

*167. Ren, Hongshen, et al. "A Review of Ten Years' Development of Solar Cookers in China." *New Energy* 11, 10 (1989).

168. Sathaye, Jayant, et al. "Energy Demand in Developing Countries: A Sectoral Analysis of Recent Trends." *Annual Review of Energy,* 12(1987): 253-281.

169. Selden, M. *The Political Energy of Chinese Socialism.* New York: M.E. Sharpe, Inc., 1988.

*170. Shen, Hangjiang. "The Status of Small Fossil Power Plants and Their Role in the Development of Rural Economy." Paper presented at the Third National Symposium on Rural Energy, 1987.

171. Shen, Youting, et al. "Preliminary Report on Energy Auditing in Beijing Dongfanghong Refinery." Report to Asian Development Bank, July 1989.

172. Shirk, Susan. "The Acquisition of Foreign Technology in China: the Bargaining Game." Paper presented at the Fall Regional Seminar of the Case of China Studies, October 29, 1988, Berkeley.

*173. Shu, Guoguang, et al. "Energy and Air Pollution in Urban Beijing." *Energy and Conservation,* 2(1985): 55-66.

*174. *Small Hydropower Development in China.* Beijing: China's Water Resources and Electric Power Press, 1986.

175. Smil, V. *Energy in China's Modernization, Advances and Limitations.* New York: M.E. Sharpe, Inc., 1988.

*176. Song, Jian, et al. *Population Cybernetics.* Beijing: Scientific Press, 1985.

177. State Science and Technology Commission. *Guide to China's Science and Technology Policy (1986) — White Paper on Science and Technology.* Beijing: China Academic Publishers, 1987.

178. ———. *China's Technology Policy: Energy (Blue Paper No.4).* Beijing: State Science and Technology Commission, English version in press.

*179. *A Statistical Survey of China, 1990.* Beijing: China's Statistics Press, 1990.

*180. Sun, Yongguang. "Double Decomposition Algorithm of Large-Scale Linear Programming Problems." *Computational Physics* 2, 3(1984).

*181. Training Center on Energy Planning and Management, ed. *Energy Planning and Energy System Modeling.* Beijing: Tsinghua University Press, 1986.

182. Wan Chunrong, et al. "Industrial Energy Conservation in China: Overseas Study Tour Report for Chemical Fertilizer Industry." Report to Asian Development Bank, July 1989.

183. ———. "Industrial Energy Conservation in China, Preliminary Report on Energy Auditing in Shijiazhuang Chemical Fertilizer Plant." Report to Asian Development Bank, July 1989.

*184. Wang, Bingzhong, et al. "Solar Energy Resources in China." *Acta Energiae Solaris Sinica* 1, 1(1980).

185. Wang Dazhong, et al. "The Energy Forecast and Nuclear Energy Prospect in China." Paper presented at the Conference on CO_2 Minimization with Nuclear Energy, March 1990, Aachen, West Germany.

*186. Wang, Jingwu. "Feasibility Studies of Pipeline Transportation of Coal Mash in China." *Energy of China,* 4(1990).

*187. Wei, Zhihong, et al. "Dual Level Regional Energy-Economic Planning Model for Beijing Industry." *A Collection of Research and Applications of New Technology,* volume 1. Beijing: Tsinghua Press, 1986.

* Published in Chinese

188. World Bank. *China: the Energy Sector.* Washington, D.C.: World Bank, 1985.

189. Wu, Ming. "The Chinese Economy at the Crossroads." *Communist Economies* 2, 3(1990).

190. Wu, Zongxin. "The Effects of Energy Policies on Demand Management." Paper presented at the Seminar on Structural Change and Energy Policy, Economic and Social Committee on the Asian Pacific (ESCAP), Bangkok, 1987.

*191. Wu, Zongxin, et al. *China's Energy Demand by 2050.* Beijing: Institute of Nuclear Energy Technology, 1988.

192. ———. "Energy Demand and CO_2 Greenhouse Effect in China." Report to Lawrence Berkeley Laboratory, Berkeley, December 1989.

193. ———. "Energy Demand Forecasting in China for the Year 2030." Final Report to Commission on the European Community, March 1989.

194. ———. "Energy Demand Scenarios and CO_2 Emission to 2020 in China." Paper presented at the Energy Information Advisory (EIA) Meeting, Third Plenary Conference, Intergovernmental Panel for Climate Change (IPCC), Washington, D.C., February 1990.

*195. ———. "National Energy Demand Forecast Model." *Proceedings of the Conference on National Energy Forecast Models and Their Application,* Beijing, June 1987.

196. ———. "Research of Market and Price of Coal in China." Final Report to Commission on the European Community, December 1987.

*197. ———. "Study on Dual-Level Planning Model for National Economy and Energy System." Special issue of *Journal of Power,* 1985.

*198. Xu, Haixing. "The Development and Progress of New Energy in China." *New Energy* 10, 2(1988).

*199. Yang, Jike. "The Strategy and Measures of Rural Energy under New Situation." Paper presented at the Third National Symposium on Rural Energy, 1987.

*200. Yang, Yaoxian. "The Consumption of Fuel-Woods and the Development of Forest Energy Source." Paper presented at the Third National Symposium on Rural Energy, 1987.

201. Yang, Zhirong, et al. "Preliminary Report on Energy Auditing in Beijing No. 2 Cotton Textile Plant." Report to Asian Development Bank, July 1989.

*202. Ye, Qing. "Summary of the Fifth Official Meeting on Energy Conservation of the State Council." *Energy of China,* 5(1989).

*203. Yi, Chu. "Retrospection of the 10 Years Restructuring and Development of Coal Industry." *Energy of China,* 5(1989).

*204. Yu, Suhua. "The Application of Decomposition Algorithm of Large System Linear Programming in Energy Planning." Paper presented at the National Conference of Optimization Methodology in Computational Mathematics, Beijing, 1983.

*205. ———. "Computer Program for Decomposition Algorithm for Large-Scale Linear Programming." Special issue of *Journal of Power,* 1985.

*206. Yu, Suhua, et al. "Rural Development Planning Model Generator." *Proceedings of the Third National Conference on Optimization Methodology in Computation Mathematics,* July 1987.

207. Yu, Tzong-Shian. *The Demand and Supply of Primary Energy in Mainland China.* Taipei: Chung Hua Institute for Economic Research, 1984.

*208. Yue, Lingkang, et al. "National Input-Output Model — A Study on the Macro-Economical Model." Paper presented at the Fourth Annual Meeting of China's Energy Research Society, Chongqing, October 1984.

*209. Zhang, Yingwu, ed. *The Chronicle of China's Science and Technology Development (1949-1988).* Beijing: Scientific Literature Press, 1989.

210. Zhao, D., et al. "Air Pollution and Acid Rain in China." *AMBIO,* 1(1985).

*211. Zhao, Shuying. "From the Rise of the Small-Sized Power Station to Discuss the Pooling Fund for Electricity in Shangdong Province." *Energy of China,* 3(1989).

212. Zhao, Xue, et al. "New Methods for Long-Term Agricultural Yields Forecasting." *Proceedings of the First International Conference on Agricultural System Engineering,* Changchun, August 1987.

*213. Zheng, Guangchang. "Retrospection of the 10 Years Development of Energy Industry." *Energy of China,* 5(1989).

214. Zhou, Dadi, et al. "The Experience and Prospects of Energy Conservation in China." Paper presented at a seminar held at the Lawrence Berkeley Laboratory, Berkeley, December 1989.

*215. Zhou, Fengqi. "On the Progress of Energy Conservation Issue of China." *Energy of China,* 1(1989).

216. ———. "The Status and Prospects of Energy in China to 2005." Paper presented at a seminar at Lawrence Berkeley Laboratory, Berkeley, December 1989.

*217. Zhou, Fengqi, et al. "Countermeasures on Alleviation of the Overall Tightness of National Energy Supply." *Energy of China,* 3(1990).

*218. Zhou, Xianming, et al. "The Application of Monte-Carlo Method in Forecasting the Agricultural Production." Paper presented at the Conference on Agricultural System Engineering, Taiyuan, July 1985.

*219. ———. "Dynamic Optimization Model for Rural Energy." Paper presented at the Fourth Annual Conference of China's Energy Research Society, Chongqing, October 1984.

*220. ———. "Dynamic Planning Model for Forestry in Xingjiang." *Forestry Economics,* May 1987.

*221. ———. "Rural Energy Dynamic Model and Its Applications." *Journal of Tsinghua University,* 5(1987).

*222. ———. "Simulation Model for Agricultural Production Forecasting." *Agricultural Techno-Economics,* December 1985.

*223. ———. "Simulation Model for Rural Economic Structure in Xinjiang." Paper presented at the Seminar on Development Strategy, Shenzheng, December 1987.

224. ———. "The Xinjiang Agricultural Development Planning Model." *Proceedings of the International Conference on System Science and Engineering,* July 1988.

*225. Zhu, Liangdong. "Promote the Energy Conservation and Decrease the Energy Consumption of the Whole Society by Raising the Understanding and the Implementation of the Measures." *Energy of China,* 2 (1990).

APPENDIXES

APPENDIX A

THE ENERGY TECHNOLOGY POLICY OF CHINA

SOURCE: State Science and Technology Commission, Guide to China's Science and Technology Policy (1986). White Paper on Science and Technology. Beijing: China Academic Publishers, 1987. In order to preserve the originality, this Appendix is directly copied from the *Guide to China's Science and Technology Policy (1986) — White paper on Science and Technology* [177] without further editing. Any ambiguity of the text due to inadequacy of the original translation may be clarified by referring to the relevant chapters in this book.

I. TO INCREASE PRODUCTION OF PRIMARY ENERGY SOURCES AND IMPROVE STRUCTURE OF PRIMARY ENERGY SOURCES

(1) To try our best to increase production of primary energy sources is the key to the tackling of energy problem. There must be a mutual coordination between national economy and primary energy sources; between various kinds of primary energy sources; between primary and secondary energy sources, especially primary source and the power; between production, transmission, and consumption of energy sources; and between energy sources; and between energy sources and environmental protection with regard to the speed of development, scale, distribution, and time series.

(2) Coal is the main energy source of our country. It is vital to expand as rapidly as possible the scale of construction of coal mines, shorten construction cycles, and enhance equipment level.

(3) The first important task is to increase the reservation of the oil deposit. It is necessary to speed up the survey, prospecting, and opening-up of oil resources to increase the yield considerably.

(4) To develop water power for the improvement of the structure of primary energy sources is the most practical course to follow. In this country, there is a great potential for tapping water power. Therefore, it is important to determine for the vigorous development of water power generation.

(5) To actively develop nuclear energy and build nuclear plants with considerable size in regions which are worth to develop but short of energy.

(6) To view natural gas as an important energy source in our country. Its survey, prospecting, and opening up are to be strengthened to strive for an increase in the proportion of natural gas in primary energy sources.

II. TO MAKE ECONOMIC DIVISION OF ENERGY SOURCES, SET UP REGIONAL COMPLEXES OF ENERGY SOURCES, AND READJUST THE DISTRIBUTION OF PRODUCTIVE FORCES

In our country, the distribution of productive forces is not suited to the dispersion of energy resources. There is a need to break down the barriers of departments and regions and reasonably divide economic zones of energy sources in terms of local conditions of resources, links between production and selling, and reasonable flow of energy sources.

(1) To concentrate our efforts on the planning and formation of some regional complexes of energy sources, and tap energy resources in line with local conditions.

(2) To readjust the distribution of productive forces. To coordinate the relationship between energy production and consumption, and to formulate optimized plans for inter-regional transmission of energy sources. New high energy consuming enterprises are to be built as closely as possible to the places where the energy resource is located.

III. TO SPEED UP THE OPENING UP OF COAL MINES

(1) To plan in a unified manner the prospecting and opening up of coal resources with the most promising ones opened up first. To increase the intensity of opening and construction scale of new mines in the eastern area; to intensify the prospecting and opening of coal resources in the western area. As regards the construction of coal mines, the

policy of "combining large, medium, and small sizes" is to be implemented.

(2) To use high-efficiency drilling techniques, advanced digital devices for physical exploitation, data processing systems, remote sending technology, and techniques of mathematical geology in order to speed up comprehensive prospecting of coal basins.

(3) To build large size open mines in Shanxi Province, Inner Mongolia, and Shaanxi Province, etc.

(4) To shorten the construction period of mines, it is important to conduct reforms of mine design; to a good job of the preparation of building shafts; employ advanced technologies and matched high-efficiency construction equipment; to actively develop comprehensive mechanization of the construction of shafts and drifts; to intensify organization and management of construction and make synchronous building of matched projects.

(5) To conduct technical transformation and reasonable centralized production, renovate mining technology, enhance equipment level, and increase comprehensive production capability and recovery rate of resources as far as existing coal mines are concerned.

(6) To perform comprehensive mechanization of mining and drifting and matched auxiliary operations in large pits.

(7) To strictly carry out the safety precautions in all coal mines. To use advanced techniques of comprehensive prevention and control against disasters and injuries in coal shafts and drifts.

(8) To actively develop locally-administered state coal mines and small coal mines which belong to collectives. It is necessary to strengthen scientific management and technical guidance and offer support to them. As for the locally-administered state mines, technical transformation will be made with the priority given to those with the most promising conditions. The technology applicable to small coal mines should be researched and popularized. To reasonably divide resources and prohibit disorderly building of small coal mines within the coal pits or fields being built or to be built.

IV. To Put the Survey and Prospecting of Oil Resources in theFirst Place and Enhance Economic Results of the Tapping of Oil Fields

(1) To strengthen regional comprehensive survey and prospecting and to employ advanced comprehensive prospecting technologies as far as possible.

(2) To develop techniques of optimal drilling and directional drilling and utilize high-grade mud to raise the speed and quality.

(3) To develop and perfect secondary recovery technologies, research third recovery technologies and fairly enhance the exploiting speed under the prerequisite of increasing the oil recovery rate. To research recovery technologies of low permeable oil deposit and dense oil deposits.

(4) To make full recovery of associated gas and oil- condensate fields, and perfect technologies of collection, transport, and treatment of oil and gas.

(5) To master as rapidly as possible technologies of prospecting and opening-up of off-shore oil and gas resources.

(6) To develop technologies of closed transport of oil. To research technologies of high-pressure pipeline transport, and technologies of unheated pipeline transport of high wax-bearing oil so as to decrease energy consumption and transport losses.

(7) To intensify prospecting of oil shales, and to support and develop production of oil shales. To research and improve processing technologies of oil shales and to carry out comprehensive utilization.

V. Tapping Priority Must Be Given to Water Power Because It is a Renewable Energy Source

(1) To strengthen the earlier stage project in constructing hydroelectric power stations, making comprehensive planning, and effect consecutive ladle-type tapping. To build power stations with the adjustment by reservoir, runoff river plant and pumping stations for energy reservation in accordance with local conditions.

(2) To utilize water resources in a comprehensive way. The tapping of water power must be planned in an overall way with due consideration for navigation, irrigation, water supply, flood control, draining of waterlogged fields, aquatic culture, tourism, ecological environment, etc. in accordance with the principle of being beneficial to various fields and reasonable sharing of the investment.

(3) To expand the scale of the construction of hydroelectric stations as far as possible. In the building of hydroelectric station, large projects must be made to be the mainstay. It is necessary to choose a group of large projects with remarkable economic benefits for an early start of construction. With the medium size hydroelectric stations, unified planning should be made to encourage local governments and enterprises to finance the construction with support from the state, and benefits belong to the contribu-

tors. Construction priority should be given to the building of medium size hydroelectric stations in the eastern area which is short of energy.

(4) To employ small hydroelectric stations which are able to make full use of scattered water resources and play an important role in the electrification of rural areas. They must be actively developed, implementing the policy of self-building, self-management, and self-utilization.

(5) To actively develop high earth and stone dams and light-duty concrete dams. To make breakthrough in technologies of large-span underground projects, long tunnels, and foundations with deep covering for the building of dams.

(6) To establish matched construction machinery. A contingent of specialized construction and construction bases should be built up so as to increase the construction speed.

(7) To research and develop large size water turbo-generators, turbine sets of high-head impact type and mixed-flow type, turbine sets of pumping accumulation type, turbine sets of low-head tubular type, and other large water engineering machinery and equipment.

VI. To Build Nuclear Plants in Regions Which Are Economically Developed but Short of Energy

(1) To develop pressurized water reactors in first-generation nuclear plants in China.

(2) To make full use of existing domestic technical foundations. To introduce advanced technology from abroad; to realize as early as possible domestication and to form the system of the nuclear power industry.

(3) To speed up the survey and prospecting of uranium resources. To intensify research of the technology of after- treatment of fuel elements and disposal of the "three wastes" (waste gas, waste water, and industrial residue).

(4) To formulate decrees, standards, and approval procedures concerning nuclear power.

(5) To actively conduct feasibility studies and experiments involved with nuclear heat supply and nuclear thermal plants.

(6) To strengthen the research of new-type reactors.

VII. To Put the Opening Up of Natural Gas in the Same Important Place as Oil

(1) To intensify the survey and prospecting of natural gas, especially coal-forming gas.

(2) To develop technologies for the prospecting, exploitation, treatment, transport, and storage of natural gas, especially seismic, geophysical well-logging, and gas testing technologies necessary for probing shallow and deep natural gas. To research the underground gas storage technologies.

(3) To formulate as far as the exploitation of natural gas fields, comprehensive plans and matched facilities built in order to guarantee balanced production and utilization.

VIII. To Increase the Electric Power Development Speed

(1) To push ahead electric power development. As regards the construction of power stations, large stations serve as the mainstay and small and medium size stations are to be developed in accordance with local conditions. To increase the proportion of hydroelectric power and actively use new energy sources.

(2) To locate, if possible, new large heat power plants adjacent to mines. When large heat power plants are built in the center of the load, economic, reasonable and environmental requirements must be satisfied. Thermal power stations will be built in medium and large cities and in industrial centers where central heat supply is needed.

(3) To research and develop advanced equipment necessary for large heat power stations. To actively adopt the air-cooling technology and dry ash removal technology at stations situated in districts which are rich in coal resources but in acute shortage of water resources. To develop comprehensive utilization of ash and slag.

(4) To strengthen regional transmission networks and make interconnections and expansion gradually. To conduct optimized planing, set up unified control systems and adopt advanced technologies to exercise optimized control as far as large transmission networks are concerned. To master the 500 Kv AC transmission technology, develop the 500 Kv DC transmission technology and research the transmission technology with a higher voltage level.

IX. To Actively Tap and Use New Energy Sources

(1) To tap and use new energy sources such as solar energy, biomass energy, wind energy, geothermal energy, tidal energy, marine energy, etc. and to make up the deficiency of conventional energies. The research and demonstration of new energy sources concerned must be strengthened. To actively popularize research achievements and set up the new energy industry step-by-step.

(2) To develop household methane pits in the southern area. To improve fermenting technologies and equipment; to develop central gas supply technologies and small power generation by using marsh gas. To research new technologies for gasification of agricultural and forest residues.

(3) To actively tap and make use of solar energy, develop and popularize solar stoves, solar water heaters, solar cells, passive solar houses, and solar driers in those districts which are rich in sunshine but in acute shortage of energy sources.

(4) To develop small power generation and sail boat by using wind energy in those districts which are rich of wind energy sources.

(5) To strengthen the investigation and evaluation of geothermal resources. Low-temperature geothermal energy will be used directly and medium-and-high temperature geothermal energy is to be used for geothermal power generation.

X. TO INCREASE ENERGY UTILIZATION RATE AND STRICTLY ENFORCE ENERGY CONSERVATION

(1) To bring about comprehensive utilization plans for the rational processing, efficient utilization, and optimized distribution of energy.

(2) To intensify the research of energy conservation so as to develop and popularize new technologies, facilities and materials for conserving energy.

(3) To speed up the technological transformation of energy conservation. To eliminate low-efficiency, high energy consumption equipment within a fixed period. To renew such machinery and electric devices extensively used in large quantities such as industrial boilers, water pumps, fans, electric motors, internal combustion engines,etc.; to renovate industrial kilns and furnaces; to renew consecutively low and medium pressure generating sets; to establish the system of issuing permits for the manufacture and utilization of equipment with high energy consumption, and to organize specialized production; to restrict production mode and transport mode that results in an enormous waste of energy, especially in the production of coke using the indigenous method; to improve conditions of urban roads and highways; to reduce oil consumption of mobile vehicles.

(4) To re-adjust the structure of industrial products with high energy consumption. To decease the iron-steel ratio; to vigorously develop potash and phosphorous fertilizers; to spread heat preservation and thermal insulation materials and energy- conservation type wall body materials.

(5) To develop energy conservation technologies at coal mines, oil fields, gas fields, refineries, and power plants; to decrease the proportion of self-consumption of energy industries.

(6) To design and spread energy conservation-type houses. To heighten thermal insulation performance of building; to make full use of natural energy sources; to enhance energy utilization rate of equipment.

(7) To save energy in commerce. To renovate the structure of frozen foods. To adopt new technologies for conserving energy in freezers.

(8) To actively develop the recovery and re-use of energy; to make rational use of the industrial after-heat and inflammable emitted gas.

(9) To speed up the research, development, production, and energy measuring meters, instruments and devices.

(10) To intensify scientific management of energy. To formulate energy-conservation decrees and laws; to improve management systems; to work out unified systems of energy conservation indexes; to undertake survey of energy utilization and tests of energy balances; to conduct forecasting and planning of energy conservation; to formulate energy consumption quota and inspection procedures; to perfect energy standards.

XI. TO MAKE REASONABLE USE OF OIL AND NATURAL GAS RESOURCES AND TO PROMOTE THE PROCESSING OF OIL AND DISTRIBUTION OF OIL PRODUCTS

(1) To give major place to the production of fuels for mobile internal combustion engines, chemical materials and lubricating oils, and give a rational distribution of the product. With the exception of special cases, it is prohibited to burn crude oil directly. The practice of oil-burning reduced gradually.

(2) To determine kinds and specifications of oil products in the light of requirements, and to work out product standards and raise the quality of all products.

(3) To develop heavy fuel oils used for high-efficiency, medium and low speed, and large size diesel engines.

(4) To develop such deep processing technologies as catalysis, cracking, hydrogenation, solvent-handling of heavy oil in order to raise the output rate of light oil, and increase the output of diesel, petrochemical raw materials, road bitumen, acicular tar, etc.

(5) To make a comprehensive utilization of natural gas, associated gas in oil fields, and refinery gas. To develop the production technologies of cheap hydrogen and high octane value petrol.

(6) To research and develop new high-efficiency and multi-function catalysts. To improve the production technologies and quality of various additives.

(7) To construct large oil refineries and processing enterprises. Indigenous rude refineries should be eliminated. Small refineries and petrochemical plants should be shut down, merged, or shifted to a new production orientation within a fixed period, unless they are turning out specific products with remarkable economic benefits or products for use in scientific experiments.

(8) To determine the distribution of refineries and the amount to be processed according to the comprehensive optimization of exploiting, transport, refining, and marketing.

XII. To Promote the Technologies of Processing, Burning and Conversion, to Improve the Distribution of Coal and Coal Products, and to Carry Out the Effective Comprehensive Utilization of Coal

(1) To develop coal screening and dressing by washing so as to enhance commodity coal quality and increase varieties. To employ advanced technologies of coal dressing, coal quality inspection, and power dosing of coal. Mines producing coal on a monopoly basis are required to gradually supply commodity coal in accordance with resource conditions and requirements of chief users at fixed supply points, with fixed quantity and fixed quality. To effect a system that the measurement should be made based on dressed or screened commodity coal.

(2) To formulate coal quality criteria and coal consumption quotas required by various coal users.

(3) To do an adequate job of comprehensive optimization of production, transport, and marketing of coal.

(4) To vigorously intensify research into coal characteristics and burning technologies. To raise thermal efficiency of various combustion equipment, especially that of industrial boilers, kilns, furnaces, and household stoves. To research new combustion technologies such as fluidized-bed combustion and the application of water coal slurry.

(5) To make on-the-spot comprehensive utilization of such fuels as brown coal, medium coal after washing, coal sludge, gangue, stone coal and oil shale with low heat value below 3500 Kcal/kg.

(6) To build, in light of the principle of specialized cooperation and economic rationalization, combines of various types such as coal, electric power, gas, chemical engineering, coking and chemical engineering, building materials, etc. to bring about comprehensive utilization of coal resources in mining areas.

(7) To actively develop coal gasification and coal chemical engineering. To centrally process coal tar and increase varieties of products; to strengthen research into production technologies of coal gasification for supplying synthetic raw materials gas, city gas, and industrial gas (including new technologies of joint production of methanol while turning out gas). To develop new technologies of coal liquefaction to extract motor fuels.

XIII. To Establish a Reasonable Rural Energy Structure and Bring About a Rapid Change in the Acute Energy Shortage Situation in Rural Areas

(1) To adopt the policy of being in line with local conditions, mutual supplement of various energies, comprehensive utilization, and attaching importance to economic returns as far as the energy construction in rural areas is concerned.

(2) To give first place to commodity energy for the production of energy in rural areas. Commodity energy supply for rural areas should be augmented gradually. To actively develop small hydroelectric stations and small coal mines. To fairly develop small power plants in localities which are rich in coal sources, but short of electricity supply or insufficient in electricity supply. To spread step by step electric power for rural use and raise the reliability of rural electric supply.

(3) To give priority to biomass energy for the energy demand for livelihood in rural areas. To work hard to increase firewood resources and popularize firewood-saving stoves with a thermal efficiency higher than 25%. To develop commercialized household methane pits with a gas generation rate above 0.2%, and to develop small and medium size methane supply stations. To research the conversion technology of biomass energy.

(4) To develop forest energy resources. To change conventional low-efficiency mode of afforestation, and make great efforts to select and spread quick-growing, high-yielding, and high-heat-value tree seeds.

(5) To develop energy conservation agricultural machinery and high-efficiency machinery operated by man or animal.

(6) To research and spread energy conservation technologies for rural areas.

XIV. TO PROMOTE CIVILIAN ENERGY STRUCTURE IN URBAN AREAS AND SATISFY RATIONAL REQUIREMENT FOR LIVING ENERGY OF RESIDENTS AS FAR AS POSSIBLE

(1) High-grade clean energy sources should be supplied as far as possible for civil use in urban areas.

(2) To increase electricity supply for municipal life. To develop electric appliances with low energy consumption. To adequately increase electricity for cooking use in areas with necessary conditions.

(3) To make reasonable use of various gas sources and develop town gas. To actively develop coal generating gas in cities with suitable conditions. It is required to make full use of gas from coking furnaces and from coal mines. As for natural gas and liquified oil gas, besides being used as petrochemical raw materials, priority should be given to civil use.

(4) To make great efforts to improve the technology of utilizing coal for civil use. To actively research and develop high-efficiency, multi-purpose and low-contamination new-type stoves and ranges for civil use. To develop shaped coal products such as honeycomb briquette, etc. To strictly restrict the burning of coal in bulk.

(5) To develop central heat supply in urban areas. To determine rational heat supply plans in accordance with heat load conditions and overall urban planning.

XV. TO WORK HARD TO ENHANCE THE QUALITY AND TECHNICAL LEVEL OF ENERGY EQUIPMENT

(1) To make energetic efforts to develop advanced energy equipment. The manufacturing of energy equipment should be coordinated with the development of the energy industry with regard to the speed, scale and time series; and there must become leading period.

(2) To implement the principle of taking quality as the first consideration. To adopt the universal international standards gradually.

(3) To effect the principle of combining domestic research and development with the introduction of technology from abroad on the basis of self reliance. To form a system of energy equipment characteristic of the situation of our country, ranging from research, design, manufacture, service to renewal.

XVI. TO PREVENT AND CONTROL THE ENVIRONMENTAL POLLUTION IN THE PRODUCTION AND UTILIZATION OF ENERGY

(1) To take into consideration environmental factors in the exploitation, conversion, transport and utilization of energy. To analyze gains and losses, ascertain optimized plans symbolizing environmental objectives, and incorporate relevant measures into plans of social and economic development proceeding from the comprehensive benefits to the whole society.

(2) To make energy environment models and work out regional energy-environment comprehensive plans.

(3) To formulate decease and laws for the prevention and control of environmental pollution by energy.

(4) To note that the focal point in preventing the environment from being polluted by energy is promote the technology of coal distribution and utilization.

ENERGY BALANCE IN CHINA, 1980 – 1988

SOURCE: *China's Energy Statistics Yearbook, 1989* (Beijing, China's Statistics Press, 1990).

Table B-1 Energy Balance of China, 1980

	Coal 10⁴ ton	Coke 10⁴ ton	Crude oil 10⁴ ton	Fuel oil 10⁴ ton	Gasoline 10⁴ ton	Kerosene 10⁴ ton	Diesel 10⁴ ton	LPG 10⁴ ton	Refinery gas 10⁴ ton	Natural gas 10⁸ m³	Coal gas 10⁸ m³	Other oil products 10⁴ ton	Other coke products 10⁴ ton	Heat 10¹² kJ	Electricity 10⁸ kWh	Total 10⁴ tce
Energy supply	62,601.0	−27.7	9,222.9	−45.9	−79.6	−39.5	−164.6	—	—	142.7	—	−98.8	—	—	582.1	61,556.9
Primary energy production	62,015.0	—	10,594.6	—	—	—	—	—	—	142.7	—	—	—	—	582.1	63,734.7
Imports	199.0	—	36.6	39.0	—	5.0	2.1	—	—	—	—	—	—	—	—	260.6
Exports (−)	−632.0	−27.1	−1,330.9	−45.4	−117.8	−46.8	−166.5	—	—	—	—	−98.8	—	—	—	−3,058.0
Stock change	1,019.0	−0.6	−77.4	−39.5	38.2	2.3	−0.2	—	—	—	—	—	—	—	—	619.6
Conversion	−22,205.3	4,334.7	−8,443.0	1,686.2	1,079.0	398.5	1,755.5	122.5	—	−2.4	109.3	1,217.7	233.0	30,910.7	2,424.2	−1,357.8
Power generation (thermal)	−12,648.4	—	−574.0	−1,419.1	—	—	−72.3	—	—	−2.4	−8.9	—	—	30,910.7	2,424.2	—
Heat generation	—	—	—	—	—	—	—	—	—	—	—	—	—	—	—	—
Coal washing loss	−2,743.7	—	—	—	—	—	—	—	—	—	—	—	—	—	—	−588.0
Coke making	−6,682.2	4,256.2	—	—	—	—	—	—	—	—	106.5	—	229.3	—	—	−644.5
Petroleum refining	—	—	−7,869.0	3,142.0	1,079.0	398.5	1,827.8	122.5	—	—	—	1,217.7	—	—	—	−112.6
Gasification	−131.0	78.5	—	−36.7	—	—	—	—	—	—	11.7	—	3.7	—	—	−12.7
Transportation and transmission losses	—	—	262.4	—	—	—	—	0.4	—	1.6	1.5	—	—	9.2	242.9	1,409.6
Final consumption	38,804.2	4,294.7	499.6	1,617.9	998.6	365.9	1,590.9	119.2	—	136.6	107.8	1,118.9	233.0	30,901.5	2,763.4	57,507.6
Material production sectors	26,139.0	4,290.0	493.5	1,610.8	804.9	50.4	1,533.2	76.1	—	134.1	94.1	1,118.9	233.0	26,101.4	2,589.4	46,099.3
Agriculture, forests, husbandry, fisheries	1,550.3	10.6	8.0	2.3	53.3	2.3	749.0	—	—	—	—	—	—	—	270.0	3,471.0
Industry	21,643.1	4,258.4	429.7	1,481.6	273.2	15.7	385.1	76.1	—	128.0	94.1	1,118.9	233.0	24,365.9	2,229.0	38,292.9
Construction	556.0	11.9	28.8	15.0	54.1	0.8	76.5	—	—	6.0	—	—	—	18.4	47.1	956.6
Transportation and communication	1,934.4	8.2	27.0	109.0	404.9	31.4	316.1	—	—	0.1	—	—	—	17.2	26.5	2,860.8
Commerce and services	455.2	0.9	—	2.9	19.4	0.2	6.5	—	—	—	—	—	—	1,699.9	16.8	518.0
Non-material production sectors	1,091.2	4.7	6.1	7.1	193.7	216.7	57.7	—	—	0.5	—	—	—	228.6	68.8	1,825.7
Residential sector	11,674.0	—	—	—	—	98.8	—	43.1	—	2.0	13.7	—	—	4,571.5	105.2	9,582.6
Urban	—	—	—	—	—	—	—	—	—	—	—	—	—	—	—	—
Rural	—	—	—	—	—	—	—	—	—	—	—	—	—	—	—	—
Statistical difference	1,591.5	12.3	17.9	22.4	6.8	−6.9	—	2.9	—	2.1	—	—	—	—	—	1,281.7

Table B-2 Energy Balance of China, 1981

	Coal (10⁴ ton)	Coke (10⁴ ton)	Crude oil (10⁴ ton)	Fuel oil (10⁴ ton)	Gasoline (10⁴ ton)	Kerosene (10⁴ ton)	Diesel (10⁴ ton)	LPG (10⁴ ton)	Refinery gas (10⁴ ton)	Natural gas (10⁸ m³)	Coal gas (10⁸ m³)	Other oil products (10⁴ ton)	Other coke products (10⁴ ton)	Heat (10¹² kJ)	Electricity (10⁸ kWh)	Total (10⁴ tce)
Energy supply	62,430.0	39.4	8,751.0	31.5	-167.3	-29.4	-133.2	—	—	127.4	111.8	-124.9	—	—	658.5	60,906.4
Primary energy production	62,164.0	—	10,122.1	—	—	—	—	—	—	127.4	—	—	—	—	655.5	63,226.4
Imports	193.0	—	7.0	53.2	—	8.0	2.8	—	—	—	—	—	—	—	3.0	252.0
Exports (-)	-657.0	-20.3	-1,375.4	-48.3	-131.6	-44.8	-159.2	—	—	—	—	-124.9	—	—	—	-3,177.8
Stock change	730.0	59.7	-2.7	26.6	-35.7	7.4	23.2	—	—	—	—	—	—	—	—	605.8
Conversion	-21,394.8	3,886.6	-8,016.9	1,430.9	1,111.9	367	1,657.4	110.7	—	-2.4	111.8	1,221.1	209.1	32,056.4	2,437.2	-1,137.2
Power generation (thermal)	-12,699.0	—	-540.9	-1,350.4	—	—	-120.5	—	—	-2.4	-8.6	—	—	32,056.4	2,437.2	—
Heat generation	—	—	—	—	—	—	—	—	—	—	—	—	—	—	—	—
Coal washing loss	-2,650.4	—	—	—	—	—	—	—	—	—	—	—	—	—	—	-568.0
Coke making	-5,908.9	3,806.5	—	—	—	—	—	—	—	—	107.4	—	205.5	—	—	-459.8
Petroleum refining	—	—	-7,476.0	2,818.0	1,111.9	367.0	1,777.9	110.7	—	—	—	1,221.1	—	—	—	-100.4
Gasification	-136.5	80.1	—	-36.7	—	—	—	—	—	—	13.0	—	3.5	—	—	-9.0
Transportation and transmission losses	—	—	249.3	—	—	—	—	1.1	—	2.4	1.1	—	—	9.6	255.0	1,434.9
Fuel consumption	39,189.0	3,917.4	459.5	1,462.2	940.1	347.0	1,524.2	108.3	—	119.7	110.7	1,096.2	209.1	32,046.8	2,840.7	56,875.4
Material production sectors	25,990.6	3,913.9	454.1	1,455.7	748.0	52.9	1,469.4	62.8	—	116.9	96.4	1,096.2	209.1	27,068.4	2,648.9	45,019.6
Agriculture, forests, husbandry, fisheries	1,569.3	8.8	6.9	4.1	57.6	2.8	704.8	—	—	—	—	—	—	—	281.6	3,459.4
Industry	21,452.2	3,884.9	385.5	1,322.2	260.6	13.7	377.0	62.8	—	111.8	96.4	1,096.2	209.1	25,268.4	2,272.5	37,274.7
Construction	359.0	15.0	32.6	14.8	49.3	0.6	72.6	—	—	5.0	—	—	—	19.3	46.6	786.8
Transportation and communication	2,085.9	4.3	28.9	111.9	360.9	35.6	303.3	—	—	0.1	—	—	—	17.6	29.1	2,910.3
Commerce and services	524.2	0.9	0.2	2.7	19.6	0.2	11.7	—	—	—	—	—	—	1,763.1	19.1	588.4
Non-material production sectors	1,109.0	3.5	5.4	6.5	192.1	178.6	54.8	—	—	0.6	—	—	—	237.3	73.8	1,792.2
Residential sector	12,089.4	—	—	—	—	115.5	—	45.5	—	2.2	14.3	—	—	4,741.1	118.0	10,063.6
Urban	—	—	—	—	—	—	—	—	—	—	—	—	—	—	—	—
Rural	—	—	—	—	—	—	—	—	—	—	—	—	—	—	—	—
Statistical difference	1,846.2	8.6	25.3	0.2	4.5	-9.4	—	1.3	—	2.9	1.1	—	—	—	—	1,458.8

Table B-3 Energy Balance of China, 1982

	Coal 10⁴ ton	Coke 10⁴ ton	Crude oil 10⁴ ton	Fuel oil 10⁴ ton	Gasoline 10⁴ ton	Kerosene 10⁴ ton	Diesel 10⁴ ton	LPG 10⁴ ton	Refinery gas 10⁴ ton	Natural gas 10⁸ m³	Coal gas 10⁸ m³	Other oil products 10⁴ ton	Other coke products 10⁴ ton	Heat 10¹² kJ	Electricity 10⁸ kWh	Total 10⁴ toe
Energy supply	65,874.5	−14.1	8,736.1	22.2	−122.0	−45.4	−159.3	−0.1	—	119.3	—	−164.0	—	—	747.3	63,465.1
Primary energy production	66,633.0	—	10,212.3	—	—	—	—	—	—	119.3	—	—	—	—	744.0	66,777.8
Imports	219.0	—	64.4	79.7	—	9.0	4.1	—	—	—	—	—	—	—	3.3	394.8
Exports (−)	−644.0	−47.2	−1,520.4	−44.9	−142.2	−55.2	−162.9	−0.1	—	—	—	−164.0	—	—	—	−3,484.6
Stock change	−333.5	33.1	−20.2	−12.6	20.2	0.8	−0.5	—	—	—	—	—	—	—	—	−222.9
Conversion	−22,442.7	4,010.2	−8,013.1	1,439.7	1,114.1	384.1	1,673.8	124.0	—	−2.1	112.3	1,305.7	215.7	32,678.4	2,532.8	−1,195.1
Power generation (thermal)	−13,427.3	—	−480.1	−1,320.8	—	—	−72.5	—	—	−2.1	−9.1	—	—	32,678.4	2,532.8	—
Heat generation	−2,798.4	—	—	—	—	—	—	—	—	—	—	—	—	—	—	−599.7
Coal washing loss	−6,077.4	—	—	—	—	—	—	—	—	—	—	—	—	—	—	−494.0
Coke making	—	3,928.2	—	—	—	—	—	—	—	—	106.9	—	212.1	—	—	—
Petroleum refining	—	—	−7,533.0	2,798.8	1,114.1	384.1	1,746.3	124.0	—	—	—	1,305.7	—	—	—	−93.4
Gasification	−139.6	82.0	—	−38.3	—	—	—	—	—	—	14.5	—	3.6	—	—	−7.9
Transportation and transmission losses	—	—	246.6	—	—	—	—	1.4	—	2.5	1.0	—	—	9.6	262.3	1,454.
Final consumption	41,683.1	3,988.4	428.6	1,451.7	993.1	341.2	1,514.5	119.9	—	114.4	111.3	1,141.7	215.7	32,669.0	3,017.8	59,417.3
Material production sectors	28,031.4	3,985.6	427.8	1,447.3	798.5	58.1	1,471.8	70.9	—	112.1	96.5	1,141.7	215.7	27,593.8	2,815.7	47,243.0
Agriculture, forests, husbandry, fisheries	1,714.1	9.2	4.7	3.4	60.6	2.9	654.3	—	—	—	—	—	—	—	286.4	3,502.9
Industry	23,164.6	3,954.4	362.5	1,296.5	274.8	15.2	396.9	70.9	—	106.9	96.5	1,141.7	215.7	25,758.6	2,429.1	39,172.1
Construction	414.0	16.4	33.1	11.8	54.9	0.8	79.4	—	—	5.1	—	—	—	19.7	50.0	857.2
Transportation and communication	2,173.2	4.6	27.4	132.2	385.2	39.1	330.8	—	—	0.1	—	—	—	18.0	29.9	3,082.4
Commerce and services	565.5	1.0	0.1	3.4	23.0	0.1	10.4	—	—	—	—	—	—	1,797.5	20.3	628.4
Non-material production sectors	1,194.7	2.8	0.8	4.4	194.6	182.8	42.7	—	—	0.3	—	—	—	242.0	81.6	1,861.7
Residential sector	12,457.0	—	—	—	—	100.3	—	49.0	—	2.0	14.8	—	—	4,833.2	120.5	10,312.6
Urban	—	—	—	—	—	—	—	—	—	—	—	—	—	—	—	—
Rural	—	—	—	—	—	—	—	—	—	—	—	—	—	—	—	—
Statistical difference	1,748.7	7.7	47.8	10.2	−1.0	−2.5	—	2.6	—	0.3	—	—	—	−0.2	—	1,398.6

Table B-4 Energy Balance of China, 1983

	Coal 10^4 ton	Coke 10^4 ton	Crude oil 10^4 ton	Fuel oil 10^4 ton	Gasoline 10^4 ton	Kerosene 10^4 ton	Diesel 10^4 ton	LPG 10^4 ton	Refinery gas 10^4 ton	Natural gas 10^8 m^3	Coal gas 10^8 m^3	Other oil products 10^4 ton	Other coke products 10^4 ton	Heat 10^{12} kJ	Electricity 10^8 kWh	Total 10^4 tce
Energy supply	69,759.0	−66.9	9,110.0	−9.4	−157.4	−61.2	−256.4	−0.2	—	122.1	—	−185.9	—	—	867.9	66,921.6
Primary energy production	71,453.0	—	10,606.8	—	—	—	—	—	—	122.1	—	—	—	—	863.6	71,270.1
Imports	214.0	—	37.0	83.7	—	9.8	4.4	—	—	—	—	—	—	—	4.3	363.4
Exports (−)	−656.0	−35.0	−1,519.4	−62.2	−138.0	−55.7	−131.2	−0.2	—	—	—	−185.9	—	—	—	−3,481.9
Stock change	−1,252.0	−31.9	−14.4	−30.9	−19.4	−15.3	−129.6	—	—	—	—	—	—	—	—	−1,230.0
Conversion	−23,839.4	4,211.3	−8,436.6	1,503.5	1,264.4	410.2	1,848.8	150.1	—	−2.0	124.3	1,343.6	226.4	33,421.0	2,650.8	−1,225.1
Power generation (thermal)	−14,310.8	—	−395.6	−1,355.5	—	—	−54.7	—	—	−2.0	−9.8	—	—	33,421.0	2,650.8	—
Heat generation	—	—	—	—	—	—	—	—	—	—	—	—	—	—	—	—
Coal washing loss	−2,986.7	—	—	—	—	—	—	—	—	—	—	—	—	—	—	−640
Coke making	−6,393.5	4,122.3	—	—	—	—	—	—	—	—	118.9	—	222.3	—	—	−482.1
Petroleum refining	—	—	−8,041.0	2,896.7	1,264.4	410.2	1,903.5	150.1	—	—	—	1,343.6	—	—	—	−96.5
Gasification	−148.4	89.0	—	−37.7	—	—	—	—	—	—	15.2	—	4.1	—	—	−6.5
Transportation and transmission losses		—	263.5	—	—	—	—	2.4	—	2.8	1.7	—	—	10.0	274.6	1,526.9
Final consumption	44,873.6	4,141.5	379.7	1,463.3	1,094.9	368.1	1,592.4	144.6	—	116.5	122.6	1,157.7	226.4	33,411.0	3,244.1	63,287.7
Material production sectors	30,510.5	4,139.1	379.3	1,458.4	885.4	60.9	1,532.0	84.1	—	114.8	107.7	1,157.7	226.4	28,220.8	3,017.3	50,359.5
Agriculture, forests, husbandry, fisheries	1,835.0	7.8	0.2	1.9	72.1	2.6	665.3	—	—	—	—	—	—	—	286.4	3,608.1
Industry	25,381.6	4,118.0	318.9	1,305.4	306.1	16.4	395.0	84.1	—	108.6	107.7	1,157.7	226.4	26,344.2	2,618.5	41,872.6
Construction	467.0	8.0	41.6	12.1	61.6	0.7	94.7	—	—	6.1	—	—	—	20.1	52.7	956.1
Transportation and communication	2,191.8	4.9	18.5	135.9	421.0	41.0	365.6	—	—	0.1	—	—	—	18.4	35.8	3,222.4
Commerce and services	635.1	0.4	0.1	3.1	24.6	0.2	11.4	—	—	—	—	—	—	1,838.1	23.9	700.3
Non-material production sectors	1,299.0	2.4	0.4	4.9	209.5	182.7	60.4	—	—	0.3	—	—	—	247.4	89.5	2,018.2
Residential sector	13,064.1	—	—	—	—	124.5	—	60.5	—	1.4	14.9	—	—	4,942.8	137.3	10,910.0
Urban	—	—	—	—	—	—	—	—	—	—	—	—	—	—	—	—
Rural	—	—	—	—	—	—	—	—	—	—	—	—	—	—	—	—
Statistical difference	1,046.0	2.9	30.2	30.8	12.1	−19.1	—	2.9	—	—	—	—	—	—	—	881.8

Table B-5 Energy Balance of China, 1984

	Coal 10⁴ ton	Coke 10⁴ ton	Crude oil 10⁴ ton	Fuel oil 10⁴ ton	Gasoline 10⁴ ton	Kerosene 10⁴ ton	Diesel 10⁴ ton	LPG 10⁴ ton	Refinery gas 10⁴ ton	Natural gas 10⁸ m³	Coal gas 10⁸ m³	Other oil products 10⁴ ton	Other coke products 10⁴ ton	Heat 10¹² kJ	Electricity 10⁸ kWh	Total 10⁴ tce
Energy supply	76,768.7	−125.9	9,214.6	23.5	−130.8	−35.0	−193.8	−1.2	—	124.3	—	−205.3	—	—	875.5	72,251.8
Primary energy production	78,923.0	—	11,461.3	—	—	—	—	—	—	124.3	—	—	—	—	867.8	77,855.3
Imports	249.0	—	24.6	72.1	—	12.0	3.8	—	—	—	—	—	—	—	8.0	371.0
Exports (−)	−695.5	−37.0	−2,229.3	−56.8	−116.1	−49.5	−210.5	−1.2	—	—	—	−205.3	—	—	−0.3	−4,620.8
Stock change	−1,707.8	−88.9	−42.0	8.2	−14.7	2.5	12.9	—	—	—	—	—	—	—	—	−1,353.7
Conversion	−26,187.8	4,548	−8,586.2	1,462.4	1,350.1	408.0	1,876.5	154.2	—	−2.0	125.9	1,468.3	244.6	35,452.1	2,902.1	−1,361.8
Power generation (thermal)	−15,935.1	—	−335.2	−1,354.5	—	—	−70.0	—	—	−2.0	−10.2	—	—	35,452.1	2,902.1	—
Heat generation	—	—	—	—	—	—	—	—	—	—	—	—	—	—	—	—
Coal washing loss	−3,127.0	—	—	—	—	—	—	—	—	—	—	—	—	—	—	−670.1
Coke making	−6,963.4	4,446.2	—	—	—	—	—	—	—	—	120.5	—	239.7	—	—	−587.1
Petroleum refining	—	—	−8,251.0	2,857.0	1,350.1	408	1,946.5	154.2	—	—	—	1,468.3	—	—	—	−97.6
Gasification	−162.3	101.8	—	−40.1	—	—	—	—	—	—	15.6	—	4.9	—	—	−7.0
Transportation and transmission losses	—	—	240.2	—	—	—	—	3.6	—	3.0	1.3	—	—	10.5	293.6	1,566
Final consumption	48,780.5	4,422.1	383.6	1,484.5	1,199.7	384.3	1,682.7	146.7	—	121.2	124.6	1,263.0	244.6	35,441.6	3,484.0	67,975.9
Material production sectors	33,343.3	4,419.6	383.5	1,481.1	969.9	72.6	1,632.4	85.8	—	116.2	108.3	1,263.0	244.6	29,935.7	3,224.4	54,051.1
Agriculture, forests, husbandry, fisheries	2,017.6	23.9	0.2	2.2	89.2	2.9	705.0	—	—	—	—	—	—	—	288.4	3,844.1
Industry	27,841.9	4,381.7	300.6	1,319.7	351.5	17.0	419.5	85.8	—	109.6	108.3	1,263.0	244.6	27,944.9	2,808.2	44,975.7
Construction	471.0	7.6	50.4	14.9	64.2	0.9	107.1	—	—	6.5	—	—	—	21.3	57.7	1,021.3
Transportation and communication	2,279.6	5.5	32.2	140.4	440.2	51.7	390.7	—	—	0.1	—	—	—	19.7	41.4	3,414.5
Commerce and services	733.2	0.9	0.1	3.9	24.8	0.1	10.1	—	—	—	—	—	—	1,949.8	28.7	795.5
Non-material production sectors	1,454.2	2.5	0.1	3.4	229.8	163.5	50.3	—	—	0.5	—	—	—	262.5	100.5	2,162.3
Residential sector	13,983.0	—	—	—	—	148.2	—	60.9	—	4.5	16.3	—	—	5,243.4	159.1	11,762.5
Urban	—	—	—	—	—	—	—	—	—	—	—	—	—	—	—	—
Rural	—	—	—	—	—	—	—	—	—	—	—	—	—	—	—	—
Statistical difference	1,800.4	—	4.6	1.4	19.6	−11.3	—	2.7	—	−1.9	—	—	—	—	—	1,348.1

Table B-6 Energy Balance of China, 1985

	Coal	Coke	Crude oil	Fuel oil	Gasoline	Kerosene	Diesel	LPG	Refinery gas	Natural gas	Coke oven gas	Other coal gas	Other oil products	Other coke products	Heat	Electricity	Total
	10^4 ton	10^4 ton	10^4 ton	10^4 ton	10^4 ton	10^4 ton	10^4 ton	10^4 ton	10^4 ton	10^8 m^3	10^8 m^3	10^8 m^3	10^4 ton	10^4 ton	10^{12} kJ	10^8 kWh	10^4 tce
Energy supply	82,776.6	-112.4	9,516.5	12.2	-72.3	-22.1	-79.1	-2.4	—	129.3	—	21.7	-159.1	249.7	—	934.4	77,603.2
Primary energy production	87,228.4	—	12,489.5	—	—	—	—	—	—	129.3	—	—	—	—	—	923.7	85,545.7
Imports	230.7	2.1	—	70.0	0.3	15.2	4.5	—	—	—	—	—	—	—	11.1	—	340.4
Exports (-)	-777.0	-36.9	-3,003.0	-64.9	-129.9	-46.0	-225.6	-1.9	—	—	—	—	-159.1	—	—	-0.4	-5,774.1
Stock change	-3,905.5	-77.6	30.0	7.1	57.3	8.7	142.0	-0.5	—	—	—	—	—	—	—	—	-2,508.8
Conversion	-28,898.6	4,790.3	-8,929.7	1,539.7	1,471.9	405.3	1,914.6	159.6	218.1	-2.9	117.3	21.7	1,362.0	249.7	38,207.7	3,183.2	-1,490.9
Power generation (thermal)	-16,440.7	—	-279.5	-1,042.3	—	—	-103.6	-0.1	—	-2.7	-9.3	—	—	—	—	3,183.2	—
Heat generation	-1,462.3	—	-61.3	-219.3	—	—	-5.0	—	—	-0.2	—	—	—	—	38,207.7	—	—
Coal washing loss	-3,501.2	—	—	—	—	—	—	—	—	—	—	—	—	245.3	—	—	-797.8
Coke making	-7,303.8	4,690.9	—	—	—	—	—	—	—	—	126.6	5.3	—	—	—	—	-572.4
Petroleum refining	—	—	-8,588.9	2,835.8	1,471.9	405.3	2,023.2	159.7	218.1	—	—	—	1,362.0	4.4	—	—	-110.3
Gasification	-190.6	99.4	—	-34.5	—	—	—	—	—	—	—	16.4	—	—	—	—	-10.4
Losses	—	—	229.4	2.5	5.0	0.9	3.4	1.1	4.7	2.7	0.4	0.2	—	—	13.0	304.3	1,605.4
Transportation and transmission losses	—	—	24.1	—	—	—	—	—	—	0.7	0.4	0.2	—	—	13.0	304.3	1,258.9
Final consumption	52,704.4	4,677.9	350.4	1,538.8	1,391.3	384.6	1,827.4	154.5	213.4	123.7	116.2	21.4	1,202.9	249.7	38,195.8	3,813.3	73,586.3
Material production sectors	35,500.5	4,652.9	350.0	1,532.8	1,142.4	80.1	1,751.6	60.3	212.3	118.9	109.2	12.6	1,202.9	249.7	31,747.9	3,469.1	57,803.5
Agriculture, forests, husbandry, fisheries	2,208.6	20.8	0.8	3.1	122.3	3.3	629.2	—	—	—	—	—	—	—	—	317.4	4,044.8
Industry	29,714.7	4,615.9	254.9	1,363.6	446.3	19.2	532.1	59.8	212.3	104.7	109.0	12.4	1,202.9	249.7	31,664.9	2,979.1	48,020.7
Construction	531.9	7.8	74.0	18.9	73.0	1.3	125.0	—	—	14.1	—	—	—	—	23.4	71.2	1,301.9
Transportation and communication	2,307.1	5.7	20.0	144.1	477.4	56.2	454.4	—	—	0.1	0.2	—	—	—	20.9	63.4	3,669.8
Commerce and services	738.2	2.7	0.1	3.1	23.4	0.1	10.9	0.5	—	—	—	0.2	—	—	38.7	38.0	766.3
Non-material production sectors	1,579.5	2.0	0.4	6.0	238.3	182.9	74.0	3.4	—	0.5	2.2	0.3	—	—	796.8	121.7	2,464.4
Residential sector	15,624.4	23.0	—	—	10.6	121.6	1.8	90.8	1.1	4.3	4.8	8.5	—	—	5,651.1	222.5	13,318.4
Urban	8,744.6	10.0	—	—	8.0	6.2	0.4	90.8	1.1	4.3	4.8	8.5	—	—	4,857.0	122.5	7,548.9
Rural	6,879.8	13.0	—	—	2.6	115.4	1.4	—	—	—	—	—	—	—	794.1	100.0	5,769.5
Statistical difference	1,173.6	—	7.0	10.6	3.3	4.7	4.7	1.6	—	—	0.7	0.1	—	—	-1.1	—	920.4

Table B-7 Energy Balance of China, 1986

	Coal 10^4 ton	Fine washed coal 10^4 ton	Ordinary washed coal 10^4 ton	Coke 10^4 ton	Crude oil 10^4 ton	Fuel oil 10^4 ton	Gasoline 10^4 ton	Kerosene 10^4 ton	Diesel 10^4 ton	LPG 10^4 ton	Refinery gas 10^4 ton	Natural gas 10^8 m^3	Coke oven gas 10^8 m^3	Other coal gas 10^8 m^3	Other oil products 10^4 ton	Other coke products 10^4 ton	Heat 10^{12} kJ	Electricity 10^8 kWh	Total 10^4 tce
Energy supply	87,594.8	−263.1	−8.8	−26.5	10,217.4	26.9	−184.6	−30.8	119.2	1.5	—	137.6	—	—	−171.3	—	—	957.0	81,855.8
Primary energy production	89,403.9	—	—	—	13,068.8	—	—	—	—	—	—	137.6	—	—	—	—	—	945.3	88,123.7
Imports	194.2	52.9	—	—	45.6	129.5	9.9	16.2	148.9	1.8	—	—	—	—	—	—	—	12.1	740.7
Exports (−)	−682.9	−298.8	—	−46.0	−2,849.8	−17.3	−108.4	−46.4	−213.0	−0.3	—	—	—	—	−171.3	—	—	−0.4	−5,745.3
Stock change	−1,320.4	−17.2	−8.8	19.5	−47.2	−31.3	−86.1	−0.6	55.1	—	—	—	—	—	—	—	—	—	−1,263.3
Conversion	−35,151.5	991.4	2,634.5	5,267.1	−9,571.1	1,650.4	1,684.8	416.4	2,170.4	201.9	238.8	−5.0	140.6	37.3	1,343.3	213.1	41,320.4	3,550.0	−1,687.6
Power generation (thermal)	−17,295.0	−61.0	−656.4	—	−245.8	−1,045.9	—	—	58.8	0.1	−2.9	−4.7	−11.3	−3.4	−5.0	−0.1	—	3,550.0	—
Heat generation	−1,605.7	—	−19.2	—	−65.4	−252.0	—	—	1.3	—	−1.5	−0.3	−1.5	−3.5	−1.1	−0.1	41,320.4	—	—
Coal washing loss	−13,973.4	6,986.8	3,398.3	—	—	—	—	—	—	—	—	—	—	—	—	—	—	—	−886.0
Coke making	−2,146.5	−5,836.9	−73.5	5,185.0	—	—	—	—	—	—	—	—	151.3	12.3	—	207.9	—	—	−645.9
Petroleum refining	—	—	—	—	−9,259.9	2,986.2	1,684.8	416.4	2,230.5	202	243.2	—	—	—	1,349.4	—	—	—	−126.9
Gasification	−131.0	−97.5	−14.7	82.1	—	−37.9	—	—	—	—	—	—	2.1	31.9	—	5.4	—	—	−28.8
Losses	—	—	—	232.1	—	—	—	—	—	0.3	3.7	4.1	0.4	0.5	—	—	—	332.1	1,718.5
Transmission and transmission losses	—	—	—	—	28.1	—	—	—	—	0.3	—	0.7	0.4	0.5	—	—	—	332.1	1,376.0
Final consumption	51,677.9	640	2,171.6	5,240.6	407.4	1,672.4	1,500.2	385.6	2,056.6	200.1	232.5	128.5	139.5	36.5	1,172.0	213.1	41,320.5	4,174.9	77,444.3
Material production sectors	34,635.6	638.8	1,720.6	5,205.0	407.3	1,667.6	1,217.4	78.6	1,993.3	81.5	230.2	121.5	130.9	27.7	1,172.0	213.1	33,826.3	3,800.2	61,321.5
Agriculture, forests, husbandry, fisheries	2,274.2	5.2	17.5	49.8	0.6	1.3	142.4	2.3	671.3	—	—	—	—	—	—	—	—	321.9	4,238.2
Industry	28,950.4	587.3	1,588.1	5,128.2	317.9	1,476.1	456.4	20.5	575.1	81.1	230.2	107.0	130.5	27.6	1,172.0	213.1	33,710.3	3,316.7	51,088.6
Construction	486.0	—	12.3	11.0	56.5	15.3	79.3	1.8	150.1	0.1	—	14.2	—	—	—	—	26.4	53.5	1,223.4
Transportation and communication	2,174.0	46.0	75	6.6	32.2	173.0	508.5	53.0	580.8	—	—	0.3	—	—	—	—	42.7	66.9	3,945.9
Commerce and services	751.0	0.3	27.7	9.4	0.1	1.9	30.8	1.0	16.0	0.2	—	—	0.4	0.1	—	—	46.9	41.2	825.4
Non-material production sectors	1,560.4	1.2	111.2	1.7	0.1	4.8	271.5	172.6	61.2	4.3	—	0.5	1.8	1.7	—	—	898.3	126.8	2,539.4
Residential sector	15,481.9	—	339.8	33.9	—	—	11.3	134.4	2.1	114.3	2.3	6.5	6.8	7.1	—	—	6,595.9	247.9	13,583.4
Urban	8,718.3	—	234.7	14.7	—	—	7.9	10.1	2.1	114.3	2.3	6.5	6.8	7.1	—	—	6,595.9	144.3	7,856.6
Rural	6,763.6	—	105.1	19.2	—	—	3.4	124.3	—	—	—	—	—	—	—	—	—	103.6	5,727.4
Statistical difference	765.4	88.3	454.1	—	6.8	4.9	—	—	5.4	—	—	—	0.7	0.3	—	—	−0.1	—	1,005.3

Table B-8 Energy Balance of China, 1987

	Coal (10^4 ton)	Fine washed coal (10^4 ton)	Ordinary washed coal (10^4 ton)	Coke (10^4 ton)	Crude oil (10^4 ton)	Fuel oil (10^4 ton)	Gasoline (10^4 ton)	Kerosene (10^4 ton)	Diesel (10^4 ton)	LPG (10^4 ton)	Refinery gas (10^4 ton)	Natural gas (10^8 m³)	Coke oven gas (10^8 m³)	Other coal gas (10^8 m³)	Other oil products (10^4 ton)	Other coke products (10^4 ton)	Heat (10^{12} kJ)	Electricity (10^8 kWh)	Total (10^4 tce)
Energy supply	93,529.1	−271.2	3.8	−84.1	10,695.8	−9.7	−112.9	−36.4	24.6	1.9	—	138.9	—	—	−160.7	—	—	1,012.6	87,144.8
Primary energy production	92,796.5	—	—	—	13,414.0	—	—	—	—	—	—	138.9	—	—	—	—	—	1,000.1	91,265.5
Imports	171.7	22.4	—	—	—	103.3	12.8	22.1	170.6	—	—	—	—	—	14.6	—	—	12.9	660.8
Exports (−)	−995.1	−357.9	—	−61.3	−2,722.5	−78.1	−116.5	−53.8	145.9	1.7	—	—	—	—	−175.3	—	—	−0.4	−5,794.9
Stock change	1,556.0	64.3	3.8	−22.8	4.3	−34.9	−9.2	−4.7	49.3	0.2	—	—	—	—	—	—	—	—	1,013.4
Conversion	−38,725.6	1,082.9	2,716.4	5,766.2	−10,058	1,819.1	1,737.0	418.2	2,273.0	214.7	245.5	−7.9	122.9	39.7	1,482.8	206.5	46,372.0	3,972.6	1,828.2
Power generation (thermal)	−19,559.2	−42.9	−687.0	—	−258.8	−1,018.6	−0.2	−0.1	−92.3	−0.4	−4.4	−7.6	−8.9	−2.8	−0.1	−0.1	—	3,972.6	—
Heat generation	−1,885.7	—	−7.7	—	−48.6	−225.9	—	—	−0.4	−0.2	−2.8	−0.3	−21.5	−1.6	−0.4	—	46,372.0	—	—
Coal washing loss	−14,495.0	7,279.8	3,461.2	—	—	—	—	—	—	—	—	—	—	—	—	—	—	—	−917.4
Coke making	−2,688.7	−6,049.4	−27.9	5,739.1	—	—	—	—	—	—	—	—	150.5	4.8	—	198.9	—	—	−711.3
Petroleum refining	—	—	—	—	−9,775.0	3,130.6	1,737.2	418.3	2,365.7	215.3	252.7	—	—	—	1,483.3	—	—	—	−166.7
Gasification	−97.0	−104.6	−22.2	27.1	—	−37.0	—	—	—	—	—	—	2.8	39.3	—	7.7	—	—	−32.8
Losses	—	—	—	—	—	—	—	—	—	0.4	1.7	2.8	0.1	0.3	—	—	—	361.2	1,799.0
Transportation and transmission losses	—	—	—	—	27.1	—	—	—	—	—	—	0.2	—	—	—	—	—	361.2	1,475.4
Final consumption	54,487.0	810.2	2,575.5	5,692.0	401.5	1,809.4	1,624.1	381.9	2,221.3	212.4	243.8	128.2	122.8	39.1	1,322.1	206.5	46,372.0	4,624.0	83,004.8
Material production sectors	36,736.0	808.3	2,111.0	5,657.1	398.1	1,802.3	1,306.4	96.4	2,140.3	82.2	241.1	119.4	114.0	27.3	1,322.1	206.5	37,344.1	4,188.4	65,934.0
Agriculture, forests, husbandry, fisheries	2271.2	1.8	13.7	48.0	0.7	4.0	146.3	2.8	729.7	—	—	—	—	—	—	—	3.0	359.6	4,471.6
Industry	31,068.8	799.8	1,980.0	5,583.5	275.1	1,574.7	505.2	22.9	584.0	81.1	241.1	110.5	113.5	27.2	1,322.1	206.5	37,186.3	3,644.6	55,211.3
Construction	441.3	0.7	11.4	11.7	98.8	45.3	88.2	1.7	154.9	0.9	—	8.6	—	—	—	—	44.9	58.4	1,259.6
Transportation and communication	2,158.3	5.9	77.3	4.9	23.1	176.1	532.5	67.7	650.0	—	—	—	—	—	—	—	20.9	76.7	4,084.4
Commerce and services	796.4	0.1	28.6	9.0	0.4	2.2	34.2	1.3	21.7	0.2	—	0.3	0.5	0.1	—	—	89.0	49.1	907.1
Non-material production sectors	1,608.4	1.9	120.9	2.0	3.4	7.1	303.1	157.6	78.1	5.8	—	1.1	1.8	1.8	—	—	1,212.4	149.1	2,748.1
Residential sector	16,142.6	—	343.6	32.9	—	—	14.6	127.8	2.9	124.4	2.7	7.7	7.0	10.0	—	—	7,815.5	286.5	14,322.7
Urban	8,844.5	—	238.0	11.3	—	—	11.8	9.0	0.8	124.3	2.7	7.7	7.0	10.0	—	—	7,815.5	162.3	8,116.8
Rural	7,298.1	—	105.6	21.6	—	—	2.8	118.8	2.1	0.1	—	—	—	—	—	—	—	124.2	6,205.9
Statistical difference	316.5	1.5	144.7	−9.9	10.3	—	—	—	27.1	—	—	—	—	0.3	—	—	—	—	512.8

Table B-9 Energy Balance of China, 1988

	Coal 10⁴ ton	Fine washed coal 10⁴ ton	Ordinary washed coal 10⁴ ton	Coke 10⁴ ton	Crude oil 10⁴ ton	Fuel oil 10⁴ ton	Gasoline 10⁴ ton	Kerosene 10⁴ ton	Diesel 10⁴ ton	LPG 10⁴ ton	Refinery gas 10⁴ ton	Natural gas 10⁸ m³	Coke oven gas 10⁸ m³	Other coal gas 10⁸ m³	Other oil products 10⁴ ton	Other coke products 10⁴ ton	Heat 10¹² kJ	Electricity 10⁸ kWh	Total 10⁴ tce
Energy supply	99,912.2	−218.9	−25.5	−83.1	11,202.0	19.3	−102.0	−27.2	123.6	0.9	—	142.6	—	—	−113.2	—	—	1,106.2	93,234.8
Primary energy production	97,987.6	—	—	—	13,704.6	—	—	—	—	—	—	142.6	—	—	—	—	—	1,091.5	95,800.8
Imports	169.3	—	—	0.1	85.5	108.3	18.2	22.3	245.2	—	—	—	—	—	28.9	—	—	15.1	912.4
Exports (−)	−1,240.5	−324.1	—	−103	−2,804.5	−80.8	−111.2	−56.4	145.8	1.5	—	—	—	—	−142.1	—	—	−0.4	−5,767.3
Stock cchange	2,995.8	105.2	−25.5	19.8	16.4	−8.2	−9.0	6.9	24.2	0.6	—	—	—	—	—	—	—	—	2,288.9
Conversion	−42,042.2	1,156.0	3,070.9	6,069.0	−10,486.3	1,832.3	1,892.4	385.4	2,263.7	229.9	242.9	−5.8	141.0	45.4	1,585.1	227.3	47,714.2	4,360.6	−1,822.9
Power generation (thermal)	−22,124.2	−1.2	−708.5	—	−234.2	−1,072.5	−0.2	—	−195.9	−0.7	−9.3	−5.7	−6.7	−1.9	—	−6.2	—	4,360.6	—
Heat generation	−2,095.4	−0.1	−20.5	—	−12.7	−276.4	—	—	−0.3	−1.2	−6.6	−0.1	−12.2	−0.4	−26.2	−4.9	47,714.2	—	—
Coal washing loss	−15,063.8	7,531.8	3,825.1	—	—	—	—	—	—	—	—	—	—	—	—	—	—	—	−886.0
Coke making	−2,657.7	−6,213.2	−8.4	6,006.1	—	—	—	—	—	—	—	—	155.9	6.3	—	211.7	—	—	−711.0
Petroleum refining	—	—	—	—	−10,239.4	3,218.7	1,892.4	385.4	2,459.9	231.8	258.8	—	—	—	1,611.3	—	—	—	−181.4
Gasification	−101.1	−161.3	−16.8	62.9	—	−37.5	—	—	—	—	—	—	4.0	41.4	—	26.7	—	—	−44.5
Losses	—	—	—	262.5	—	—	—	—	—	0.5	0.3	2.7	0.5	—	—	—	452.1	379.5	1,939.9
Transportation and transmission losses	—	—	—	—	27.7	—	—	—	—	—	—	0.6	—	—	—	—	—	379.5	1,554.2
Final consumption	57,705.2	839.6	2,993.8	5,988.1	453.1	1,851.6	385.2	358.2	2,379.0	228.5	242.6	135.1	139.9	45.4	1,471.9	227.3	47,244.8	5,087.3	89,233.9
Material production sectors	38,893.8	838.6	2,373.9	5,954.4	453.0	1,848.2	97.3	97.3	2,194.9	91.7	239.8	119.4	124.7	40.1	1,471.9	227.3	38,290.9	4,578.7	70,559.2
Agriculture, forests, husbandry, fisheries	2,354.7	1.1	21.7	59.1	1.0	4.3	2.9	2.9	767.2	—	—	—	—	—	—	—	—	378.9	4,709.2
Industry	33,043.7	832.8	2,215.4	5,879.0	365.8	1,630.6	22.7	22.7	563.4	90.2	239.8	111.1	124.2	39.1	1,471.9	227.3	38,119.5	3,985.1	59,328.2
Construction	432.1	0.5	12.6	5.8	64.4	26.9	1.2	1.2	142.4	0.5	—	7.6	—	—	—	—	87.3	62.7	1,158.7
Transportation and communication	2,163.2	4.1	92.1	4.3	21.6	183.8	68.6	68.6	690.0	0.1	—	0.6	—	—	—	—	37.3	89.5	4,281.3
Commerce and services	900.1	0.1	32.1	6.2	0.2	2.6	1.9	1.9	31.9	0.9	—	0.1	0.5	1.0	—	—	46.8	62.5	1,081.8
Non-material production sectors	1,774.5	1.0	131.5	1.9	0.1	3.4	140.6	140.6	178.2	5.3	0.3	0.4	2.2	1.1	—	—	1,224.9	165.3	3,141.0
Residential sector	17,036.9	—	488.4	31.8	—	—	120.3	120.3	5.9	131.5	2.5	15.3	13.0	4.2	—	—	7,729.0	343.3	15,533.7
Urban	9,081.6	—	269.7	10.2	—	—	10.8	10.8	5.9	131.5	2.5	15.3	13.0	4.2	—	—	7,729.0	194.4	8,647.8
Rural	7,955.3	—	191.7	21.6	—	—	109.5	109.5	2.9	—	—	—	—	—	—	—	—	148.9	6,885.9
Statistical difference	164.8	97.5	51.6	−2.2	0.1	—	—	—	8.3	—	—	−1.0	0.6	—	—	—	17.3	—	238.1

APPENDIX C

ENERGY BALANCE BY FUELS IN CHINA

SOURCE: *China's Energy Statistics Yearbook, 1989,* (Beijing, China's Statistics Press, 1990).

Table C-1 Total Energy Balance Sheet (10^4 tce)

	1980	1985	1986	1987	1988
Total supply	61,557	77,603	81,856	87,145	93,235
Production	63,735	85,546	88,124	91,266	95,801
Imports	261	340	741	661	912
Exports (−)	3,058	5,774	5,745	5,795	5,767
Stock change	619	−2,509	−1,264	1,013	2,289
Total consumption by sectors	60,275	76,682	80,850	86,632	92,997
Material production sectors	48,857	60,894	64,723	69,556	74,317
Agriculture, forests, husbandry, fisheries	3,471	4,045	4,238	4,471	4,709
Industry	41,010	51,068	54,441	58,792	63,040
Light industry	—	10,156	10,891	12,401	13,311
Heavy industry	—	40,912	43,550	46,391	49,729
Construction	956	1,302	1,223	1,260	1,159
Transport and communication	2,902	3,713	3,996	4,126	4,327
Commerce	518	766	825	907	1,082
Non-material production sectors	1,835	2,470	2,544	2,753	3,146
Residences	9,583	13,318	13,583	14,323	15,534
Final consumption, total	57,508	73,586	77,444	83,005	89,234
Industrial consumption	38,293	48,021	51,089	55,211	59,328
Conversion losses	1,358	1,491	1,688	1,828	1,823
Coke making losses	644	572	646	711	711
Oil refining losses	113	110	127	167	181
Losses	1,409	1,605	1,718	1,799	1,940
Oil fields losses	375	328	332	323	375
Transmission and distribution losses	1,003	1,211	1,322	1,434	1,507
Statistical difference	1,282	920	1,006	513	238

Table C-2 Coal Balance Sheet (10^4 ton)

	1980	1985	1986	1987	1988
Total supply	62,601.0	82,776.6	87,322.9	93,261.7	99,667.8
Production	62,015.0	87,228.4	89,403.9	92,796.5	97,987.6
Imports	199.0	230.7	247.1	194.1	169.3
Exports (−)	632.0	777.0	981.7	1,353.0	1,564.6
Stock change	1,019.0	−3,905.5	−1,346.4	1,624.1	3,075.5
Total consumption by sectors	70.5	81,603.0	86,015.1	92,799.0	99,353.9
Material production sectors	48,344.3	64,399.1	68,520.6	74,581.6	79,921.6
Agriculture, forests, husbandry, fisheries	1,550.3	2,208.6	2,296.9	2,286.7	2,377.5
Industry	43,848.4	58,613.3	62,651.4	68,774.9	73,907.2
Light industry	—	8,522.2	9,165.6	10,529.6	11,169.8
Heavy industry	—	50,091.1	53,485.8	58,245.3	62,737.4
Construction	556.0	531.9	498.3	453.4	445.2
Transport and communication	1,934.4	2,307.1	2,295.0	2,241.5	2,259.4
Commerce	455.2	738.2	779.0	825.1	932.3
Non-material production sectors	1,091.2	1,579.5	1,672.8	1,731.2	1,907.0
Residences	11,574.0	15,624.4	15,821.7	16,486.2	17,525.3
Interim consumption	19,461.6	25,397.4	27,937.4	31,172.3	34,108.4
Power generation	12,648.4	16,440.7	18,012.4	20,289.1	22,833.9
Heat generation	—	1,462.3	1,624.9	1,893.4	2,116.0
Coke making	6,682.2	7,303.8	8,056.9	8,766.0	8,879.3
Gas production	131.0	190.6	243.2	223.8	279.2
Final consumption, total	38,804.2	52,704.4	54,489.5	57,872.7	61,538.6
Final industrial consumption	21,643.1	29,715.0	31,126.0	33,849.0	36,091.9
Washing losses	2,743.7	3,501.2	3,588.2	3,754.0	3,706.9
Statistical difference	1,591.5	1,173.6	1,307.8	462.7	313.9

Table C-3 Coke Balance Sheet (10^4 ton)

	1980	1985	1986	1987	1988
Total supply	4,315.3	4,689.7	5,249.0	5,711.0	6,024.9
Production	4,343.0	4,802.1	5,275.5	5,795.1	6,108.0
Imports	—	2.1	—	—	0.1
Exports (−)	27.1	36.9	46.0	61.3	103.0
Stock change	−0.6	−77.6	19.5	−22.8	19.8
Total consumption by sectors	4,303.0	4,689.7	5,249.0	5,720.9	6,027.1
Material production sectors	4,298.3	4,664.7	5,213.4	5,686.0	5,993.4
Agriculture, forests, husbandry, fisheries	10.6	20.8	49.8	48.0	59.1
Industry	4,266.7	4,627.7	5,136.6	5,612.4	5,918.0
Light industry	—	126.9	175.2	188.2	183.8
Heavy industry	—	4,500.8	4,961.4	5,424.2	5,734.2
Transportation and communication	11.9	7.8	11.0	11.7	5.8
Construction	8.2	5.7	6.6	4.9	4.3
Commerce	0.9	2.7	9.4	9.0	6.2
Non-material production sectors	4.7	2.0	1.7	2.0	1.9
Residences	—	23.0	33.9	32.9	31.8
Interim consumption	8.3	11.8	8.4	28.9	39.0
Gas production consumption	8.3	11.8	8.4	28.9	39.0
Final consumption, total	4,294.7	4,677.9	5,240.6	5,692.0	5,988.1
Final industrial consumption	4,258.4	4,615.9	5,128.2	5,583.5	5,879.0
Losses	—	—	—	—	—
Statistical difference	12.3	—	—	−9.9	−2.2

Table C-4 Crude Oil Balance Sheet (10^4 ton)

	1980	1985	1986	1987	1988
Total supply	9,222.9	9,516.5	10,217.4	10,695.8	11,202.0
Production	10,594.6	12,489.5	13,068.8	13,414.0	13,704.6
Imports	36.6	—	45.6	—	85.5
Exports (−)	1,330.9	3,003.0	2,849.8	2,722.5	2,604.5
Stock change	−77.4	30.0	−47.2	4.3	16.4
Total consumption by sectors	9,205.0	9,509.5	10,210.6	10,685.5	11,201.9
Material production sectors	9,198.9	9,509.1	10,210.5	10,682.1	11,201.8
Agriculture, forests, husbandry, fisheries	8.0	0.8	0.6	0.7	1.0
Industry	9,112.0	9,389.9	10,093.0	10,532.0	11,086.9
Light industry	—	232.0	248.8	262.0	271.1
Heavy industry	—	9,157.9	9,844.2	10,270.0	10,815.8
Construction	28.8	74.0	56.5	98.8	64.4
Transport and communication	50.1	44.3	60.3	50.2	49.3
Commerce	—	0.1	0.1	0.4	0.2
Non-material production sectors	6.1	0.4	0.1	3.4	0.1
Residences	—	—	—	—	—
Interim consumption	8,443.0	8,929.7	9,571.1	10,085.1	10,486.3
Power generation	574.0	279.5	245.8	258.8	234.2
Heat generation	—	61.3	65.4	24.3	12.7
Refining	7,869.0	8,588.9	9,259.9	9,775.0	10,239.4
Final consumption, total	499.6	350.4	407.4	401.5	453.1
Final industrial consumption	429.7	254.9	317.9	275.1	365.8
Losses in oil fields	262.4	229.4	232.1	225.9	262.5
Statistical difference	17.9	7.0	6.8	10.3	0.1

Table C-5 Fuel Oil Balance Sheet (10^4 ton)

	1980	1985	1986	1987	1988
Total supply	3,096.1	2,848.0	3,013.1	3,120.9	3,238.0
Production	3,142.0	2,835.8	2,986.2	3,130.6	3,218.7
Imports	39.0	70.0	129.5	103.3	108.3
Exports (−)	45.4	64.9	71.3	78.1	80.8
Stock change	−39.5	7.1	−31.3	−34.9	−8.2
Total consumption by sectors	3,073.7	2,837.4	3,008.2	3,120.9	3,238.0
Material production sectors	3,066.6	2,831.4	3,003.4	3,113.8	3,234.6
Agriculture, forests, husbandry, fisheries	2.3	3.1	1.3	4.0	4.3
Industry	2,937.4	2,662.2	2,811.9	2,886.2	3,017.0
Light industry	—	296.0	342.8	395.2	354.6
Heavy industry	—	2,366.2	2,469.1	2,491.0	2,662.4
Construction	15.0	18.9	15.3	45.3	26.9
Transport and communication	109.0	144.1	173.0	176.1	183.8
Commerce	2.9	3.1	1.9	2.2	2.6
Non-material production sectors	7.1	6.0	4.8	7.1	3.4
Residences	—	—	—	—	—
Interim consumption	1,455.8	1,296.1	1,335.8	1,311.5	1,386.4
Power generation	1,419.1	1,042.3	1,045.9	1,018.6	1,072.5
Heat generation	—	219.3	252.0	255.9	276.4
Gas production	36.7	34.5	37.9	37.0	37.5
Final consumption, total	1,617.9	1,538.8	1,672.4	1,809.4	1,851.6
Final industrial consumption	1,481.6	1,363.5	1,476.1	1,574.7	1,630.6
Losses	—	2.5	—	—	—
Statistical difference	22.4	10.6	4.9	—	—

Table C-6 Gasoline Balance Sheet (10^4 ton)

	1980	1985	1986	1987	1988
Total supply	999.4	1,399.6	1,500.2	1,624.3	1,790.6
Production	1,079.0	1,471.9	1,684.8	1,737.2	1,892.6
Imports	—	0.3	9.9	12.8	18.2
Exports (−)	−117.8	−129.9	−108.4	−116.5	−111.2
Stock change	38.2	57.3	−86.1	−9.2	−9.0
Total consumption by sectors	998.6	1,396.3	1,500.2	1,624.3	1,789.9
Material production sectors	804.9	1,147.4	1,217.4	1,306.6	1,412.4
Agriculture, forests, husbandry, fisheries	53.3	122.3	142.4	146.3	153.6
Industry	273.2	451.3	456.4	505.4	560.5
Light industry	—	139.1	135.3	158.3	177.9
Heavy industry	—	312.2	321.1	347.1	382.6
Construction	54.1	73.0	79.3	88.2	87.1
Transport and communication	404.9	477.4	508.5	532.5	565.4
Commerce	19.4	23.4	30.8	34.2	45.8
Non-material production sectors	193.7	238.3	271.5	303.1	361.2
Residences	—	10.6	11.3	14.6	16.3
Statistical difference	0.8	3.3	—	—	0.7

Table C-7 Kerosene Balance Sheet (10^4 ton)

	1980	1985	1986	1987	1988
Total supply	359.0	383.2	385.6	381.9	358.2
Production	398.5	405.3	416.4	418.3	385.4
Imports	5.0	15.2	16.2	22.1	22.3
Exports (−)	−46.8	−46.0	−46.4	−53.8	−56.4
Stock change	2.3	8.7	−0.6	−4.7	6.9
Total consumption by sectors	365.9	385.5	385.6	381.9	358.2
Material production sectors	50.4	81.0	78.6	96.5	97.3
Agriculture, forests, husbandry, fisheries	2.3	3.3	2.3	2.8	2.9
Industry	15.7	20.1	20.5	23.0	22.7
Light industry	—	5.1	5.6	6.8	7.6
Heavy industry	—	15.0	14.9	16.2	15.1
Construction	0.8	1.3	1.8	1.7	1.2
Transport and communication	31.4	56.2	53.0	67.7	68.6
Commerce	0.2	0.1	1.0	1.3	1.9
Non-material production sectors	216.7	182.9	172.6	157.6	140.6
Residences	98.8	121.6	134.4	127.8	120.3
Statistical difference	−6.9	−2.3	—	—	—

Table C-8 Diesel Balance Sheet (10^4 ton)

	1980	1985	1986	1987	1988
Total supply	1,663.2	1,944.1	2,111.3	2,341.1	2,583.5
Production	1,827.8	2,023.2	2,230.5	2,365.7	2,459.9
Imports	2.1	4.5	148.9	170.6	245.2
Exports (−)	−166.5	−225.6	−213.0	−145.9	−145.8
Stock change	−0.2	142.0	−55.1	−49.3	24.2
Total consumption by sectors	1,663.2	1,939.4	2,116.7	2,314.0	2,575.2
Material production sectors	1,605.5	1,863.6	2,053.4	2,233.0	2,391.1
Agriculture, forests, husbandry, fisheries	749.0	629.2	671.3	729.7	767.2
Industry	457.4	644.1	635.2	676.7	759.6
Light industry	—	116.9	128.6	127.8	145.9
Heavy industry	—	527.2	506.6	548.9	613.7
Construction	76.5	125.0	150.1	154.9	142.4
Transport and communication	316.1	454.4	580.8	650.0	690.0
Commerce	6.5	10.9	16.0	21.7	31.9
Non-material production sectors	57.7	74.0	61.2	78.1	178.2
Residences	—	1.8	2.1	2.9	5.9
Interim consumption	72.3	108.6	60.1	92.7	196.2
Power generation	72.3	103.6	58.8	92.3	195.9
Heat generation	—	5.0	1.3	0.4	0.3
Final consumption, total	1,590.9	1,827.4	2,056.6	2,221.3	2,379.0
Final industrial consumption	385.1	532.1	575.1	584.0	563.4
Losses	—	3.4	—	—	—
Statistical difference	—	4.7	−5.4	27.1	8.3

Table C-9 Natural Gas Balance Sheet (10^8 m^3)

	1980	1985	1986	1987	1988
Total supply	142.7	129.3	137.6	138.9	142.6
Production	142.7	129.3	137.6	138.9	142.6
Total consumption by sectors	140.6	129.3	137.6	138.9	143.6
Material production sectors	138.1	124.5	130.6	129.9	127.8
Agriculture, forests, husbandry, fisheries	—	—	—	—	—
Industry	131.4	109.6	115.4	120.8	119.0
Light industry	—	9.0	8.3	5.5	8.3
Heavy industry	—	100.6	107.1	115.3	110.7
Construction	6.0	14.1	14.2	8.6	7.6
Transport and communication	0.7	0.8	1.0	0.5	1.1
Commerce	—	—	—	—	0.1
Non-material production sectors	0.5	0.5	0.5	1.3	0.5
Residences	2.0	4.3	6.5	7.7	15.3
Statistical difference	2.1	—	—	—	-1.0

Table C-10 Electricity Balance Sheet (10^8 kWh)

	1980	1985	1986	1987	1988
Total supply	3,006.3	4,117.6	4,507.0	4,985.2	5,466.8
Total production	3,006.3	4,106.9	4,495.3	4,972.7	5,452.1
Hydropower	582.1	923.7	945.3	1,000.1	1,091.5
Thermal power	2,424.2	3,183.2	3,550.0	3,972.6	4,360.6
Import	—	11.1	12.1	12.9	15.1
Export	—	0.4	0.4	0.4	0.4
Total consumption by sectors	3,006.3	4,117.6	4,507.0	4,985.2	5,466.8
Material production sector	2,832.3	3,773.4	4,132.3	4,549.6	4,958.2
Agriculture, forests, husbandry, fisheries	270.0	317.4	321.9	359.6	378.9
Industry	2,471.9	3,283.4	3,648.8	4,005.8	4,364.6
Light industry	—	655.7	723.8	815.6	930.5
Heavy industry	—	2,627.7	2,925.0	3,190.2	3,434.1
Construction	47.1	71.2	53.5	58.4	62.7
Transport and communication	26.5	63.4	66.9	76.7	89.5
Commerce	16.8	38.0	41.2	49.1	62.5
Non-material production sectors	68.8	121.7	126.8	149.1	165.3
Residences	105.2	222.5	247.9	286.5	343.3
Final consumption, total	2,763.4	3,813.3	4,174.9	4,624.0	5,087.3
Final industrial consumption	2,229.0	2,979.1	3,316.7	3,644.6	3,985.1
Transmission and distribution losses	242.9	304.3	323.1	361.2	379.5

ENERGY CONSUMPTION BY SECTORS, 1980–1985

SOURCE: Wu, Zongxin, et al, *Energy Demand Forecasting in China for the Year 2030,* Final Report to CEC, March, 1989.

Table D-1 Energy Consumption By Sectors in China (Million tce)

	1980	1981	1982	1983	1984	1985
Total	602.75	594.47	626.46	660.40	709.04	770.20
Material production sectors	480.55	465.66	487.33	512.84	547.22	586.45
Agriculture, forestry, husbandry, fisheries	46.92	47.73	48.88	50.37	54.67	56.11
Industry	389.86	374.76	392.51	413.29	440.02	471.73
Metallurgy	77.84	71.52	73.01	77.03	82.64	88.06
Power	18.75	19.36	19.91	20.68	22.13	25.11
Coal and coke	25.96	24.78	25.86	27.21	29.42	32.65
Petroleum	24.20	21.46	21.15	21.56	22.04	25.00
Chemicals	83.94	80.74	83.75	87.78	91.93	90.90
Machine building	36.50	33.65	35.86	37.20	40.21	42.23
Building materials	42.65	42.05	47.92	51.44	55.51	63.21
Forest products	3.90	3.91	3.78	4.42	4.25	4.56
Food processing	14.78	15.53	16.62	18.13	19.45	21.44
Textiles	19.92	21.57	22.49	23.86	24.80	26.78
Clothing	0.51	0.57	0.62	0.63	0.69	0.91
Leather	0.88	0.94	0.95	0.89	0.90	1.04
Papermaking	8.94	8.45	8.98	9.61	10.29	11.80
Cultural,educational and arts articles	0.80	0.85	0.90	1.01	1.07	1.24
Others	13.03	12.64	13.34	14.14	15.41	18.15
Construction	9.57	7.87	8.57	9.56	10.21	13.01
Transport and communication	29.02	29.42	31.03	32.62	34.36	37.15
Commerce, restaurants and service	5.18	5.88	6.29	7.00	7.95	8.45
Non-material production sector	12.05	11.70	11.90	13.03	13.66	15.94
Residential	110.15	117.11	127.23	134.53	148.17	167.81

Table D-2 Coal Consumption by Sectors in China (Million ton)

	1980	1981	1982	1983	1984	1985
Total	610.10	605.04	649.03	687.13	749.68	816.03
Material production sectors	422.71	460.25	489.32	519.26	564.31	608.35
Agriculture, forestry, husbandry, fisheries	29.05	29.75	30.97	32.33	37.03	37.54
Industry	414.20	400.81	426.83	453.99	493.44	535.04
Metallurgy	59.61	54.93	56.71	59.42	65.52	69.96
Power	119.46	119.94	126.56	134.53	149.20	164.56
Coal and coke	64.36	60.08	62.79	66.88	71.89	74.34
Petroleum	0.84	0.75	0.87	0.81	1.03	1.06
Chemicals	48.06	46.09	49.10	53.16	56.56	57.08
Machine building	21.17	21.92	23.83	24.25	26.18	27.11
Building materials	45.86	45.37	52.05	55.01	59.02	68.50
Forest products	3.68	3.61	3.60	3.77	4.11	4.81
Food processing	14.67	15.27	16.58	18.02	19.33	21.19
Textiles	14.33	15.13	15.75	16.65	17.51	19.66
Clothing	0.35	0.39	0.41	0.41	0.47	0.69
Leather	0.88	0.93	0.97	0.96	0.95	1.06
Paper-making	7.82	7.24	7.92	8.62	9.48	11.21
Cultural,educational and arts articles	0.83	0.88	0.92	1.01	1.05	1.16
Others	8.49	8.29	8.77	9.70	10.27	12.58
Construction	5.56	3.59	4.14	4.67	4.71	5.32
Transport and communication	19.35	20.86	21.73	21.92	22.80	23.07
Commerce, restaurants and services	4.55	5.24	5.65	6.35	7.33	7.38
Non-material production sector	2.47	2.66	2.82	3.23	3.65	4.40
Residential	134.92	142.93	156.89	164.64	180.72	203.28

Table D-3 Coke Consumption by Sectors in China (Million ton)

	1980	1981	1982	1983	1984	1985
Total	43.03	39.26	39.97	41.50	44.31	46.90
Material production sectors	42.98	39.22	39.94	41.48	44.29	46.88
Agriculture, forestry, husbandry, fisheries	0.20	0.19	0.20	0.20	0.40	0.44
Industry	42.59	38.84	39.53	41.14	43.75	46.28
Metallurgy	30.33	26.68	27.11	28.88	31.00	33.57
Power	0.01	0.01	0.03	0.02	0.04	0.03
Coal and coke	0.21	0.19	0.07	0.25	0.28	0.29
Petroleum	0.05	0.06	0.22	0.06	0.06	0.09
Chemicals	8.35	8.51	8.41	7.89	8.00	7.27
Machine building	2.82	2.48	2.68	2.91	3.15	3.37
Building materials	0.58	0.48	0.53	0.60	0.70	0.96
Forest products	0.01	0.01	0.01	0.01	0.01	0.01
Food processing	0.06	0.08	0.09	0.09	0.10	0.12
Textiles	0.10	0.10	0.12	0.14	0.14	0.17
Clothing	0.01	0.003	0.002	0.002	0.003	0.001
Leather	0.003	0.002	0.003	0.01	0.01	0.01
Paper-making	0.01	0.01	0.01	0.01	0.004	0.01
Cultural, educational and arts articles	0.01	0.01	0.01	0.01	0.01	0.01
Others	0.33	0.21	0.24	0.27	0.26	0.36
Construction	0.12	0.15	0.16	0.08	0.08	0.08
Transport and communication	0.08	0.04	0.05	0.05	0.06	0.06
Commerce, restaurants and services	0.01	0.01	0.01	0.004	0.01	0.03
Non-material production sector	0.05	0.04	0.03	0.02	0.03	0.02
Residential	—	—	—	—	—	—

Table D-4 **Crude Oil Consumption by Sectors in China** (Million ton)

	1980	1981	1982	1983	1984	1985
Total	92.05	87.26	86.88	90.8	92.10	95.10
Material production sectors	91.99	87.20	86.88	90.79	92.10	95.10
Agriculture, forestry, husbandry, fisheries	0.08	0.07	0.05	0.002	0.002	0.01
Industry	91.12	86.35	86.09	89.98	91.19	93.90
Metallurgy	2.50	2.28	2.34	0.53	0.47	0.40
Power	5.74	5.41	4.80	3.96	3.34	3.41
Coal and coke	—	—	—	—	—	—
Petroleum	68.46	65.64	65.87	71.65	72.96	76.40
Chemicals	10.83	9.45	9.59	10.58	11.27	10.22
Machine building	0.20	0.15	0.12	0.11	0.09	0.10
Building materials	0.16	0.13	0.10	0.07	0.06	0.07
Forest products	0.002	0.01	0.003	0.001	—	0.001
Food processing	0.10	0.14	0.08	0.05	0.04	0.02
Textiles	2.85	2.90	2.93	2.85	2.80	3.15
Clothing	—	—	—	—	—	—
Leather	0.002	0.002	0.002	0.002	0.002	0.002
Paper-making	0.12	0.12	0.06	0.04	0.04	0.03
Cultural, educational and arts articles	—	—	0.002	0.001	0.004	0.001
Others	0.16	0.13	0.20	0.16	0.12	0.11
Construction	0.29	0.33	0.33	0.42	0.50	0.74
Transport and communication	0.50	0.46	0.41	0.39	0.41	0.44
Commerce, restaurants and services	—	0.002	0.001	0.001	0.001	0.001
Non-material production sector	0.06	0.05	0.01	0.004	0.001	0.004
Residential	—	—	—	—	—	—

Table D-5 **Fuel Oil Consumption by Sectors in China** (Million ton)

	1980	1981	1982	1983	1984	1985
Total	30.74	28.49	28.11	28.57	28.79	28.37
Material production sectors	30.67	28.43	29.06	28.52	28.76	28.31
Agriculture, forestry, husbandry, fisheries	0.02	0.04	0.03	0.02	0.02	0.03
Industry	29.37	27.10	26.56	26.99	27.14	26.62
Metallurgy	4.14	3.41	3.36	3.57	3.62	3.47
Power	11.07	10.32	10.15	10.43	10.37	9.54
Coal and coke	0.37	0.38	0.39	0.38	0.40	0.60
Petroleum	2.74	2.45	2.26	2.25	2.24	2.61
Chemicals	4.60	4.44	4.29	4.23	4.20	4.06
Machine building	1.52	1.14	1.14	1.09	1.11	1.05
Building materials	1.47	1.40	1.45	1.40	1.52	1.53
Forest products	0.07	0.10	0.05	0.02	0.03	0.04
Food processing	0.24	0.20	0.19	0.18	0.17	0.16
Textiles	1.76	1.83	1.84	0.90	1.88	1.97
Clothing	—	—	—	—	—	—
Leather	0.01	0.01	0.01	0.01	0.004	0.01
Paper-making	0.46	0.39	0.35	0.35	0.34	0.32
Cultural, educational and arts articles	0.01	0.01	0.01	0.01	0.02	0.03
Others	0.91	1.01	1.07	1.10	1.24	1.23
Construction	0.15	0.15	0.12	0.12	0.15	0.19
Transport and communication	1.09	1.12	1.32	1.36	1.40	1.44
Commerce, restaurants and service	0.03	0.03	0.03	0.03	0.04	0.03
Non-material production sector	0.07	0.07	0.04	0.05	0.03	0.06
Residential	—	—	—	—	—	—

Table D-6 Gasoline Consumption by Sectors in China (Million ton)

	1980	1981	1982	1983	1984	1985
Total	9.99	9.40	9.93	10.95	12.00	13.96
Material production sectors	8.05	7.40	7.99	8.85	9.70	11.47
Agriculture, forestry, husbandry, fisheries	0.72	0.77	0.02	0.97	1.22	1.67
Industry	2.55	2.41	2.54	2.81	3.19	4.06
Metallurgy	0.25	0.20	0.20	0.23	0.30	0.34
Power	0.07	0.06	0.06	0.07	0.08	0.09
Coal and coke	0.18	0.18	0.19	0.21	0.25	0.26
Petroleum	0.23	0.21	0.18	0.20	0.12	0.38
Chemicals	0.39	0.33	0.36	0.40	0.47	0.57
Machine building	0.66	0.61	0.64	0.69	0.72	0.93
Building materials	0.23	0.21	0.25	0.28	0.35	0.39
Forest products	0.20	0.22	0.23	0.25	0.25	0.28
Food processing	0.20	0.22	0.23	0.25	0.25	0.26
Textiles	0.08	0.10	0.10	0.12	0.14	0.19
Clothing	0.01	0.01	0.01	0.01	0.01	0.02
Leather	0.02	0.02	0.02	0.02	0.02	0.03
Paper-making	0.03	0.03	0.03	0.04	0.04	0.06
Cultural, educational and arts articles	0.02	0.02	0.02	0.03	0.03	0.06
Other	0.11	0.12	0.09	0.11	0.12	0.17
Construction	0.45	0.49	0.55	0.62	0.64	0.73
Transport and communication	4.05	3.61	3.85	4.21	4.40	4.78
Commerce, restaurants and service	0.19	0.20	0.23	0.25	0.25	0.23
Non-material production sector	1.94	1.92	1.95	2.10	2.30	2.38
Residential	—	—	—	—	—	0.11

Table D-7 Kerosene Consumption by Sectors in China (Million ton)

	1980	1981	1982	1983	1984	1985
Total	3.66	3.47	3.41	3.68	3.84	3.86
Material production sectors	0.50	0.53	0.58	0.61	0.73	0.80
Agriculture, forestry, husbandry, fisheries	0.02	0.03	0.03	0.03	0.03	0.03
Industry	0.16	0.14	0.15	0.16	0.17	0.19
Metallurgy	0.01	0.01	0.01	0.01	0.01	0.01
Power	0.001	0.001	0.001	0.001	0.001	0.001
Coal and coke	0.02	0.02	0.02	0.02	0.02	0.02
Petroleum	0.01	0.01	0.01	0.01	0.01	0.01
Chemicals	0.02	0.02	0.02	0.01	0.02	0.02
Machine building	0.08	0.06	0.08	0.09	0.09	0.09
Building materials	0.01	0.01	0.01	0.01	0.01	0.01
Forest products	—	—	—	—	—	—
Food processing	0.001	0.001	0.001	0.001	0.001	0.01
Textiles	0.01	0.01	0.01	0.01	0.01	0.01
Clothing	—	—	—	—	—	0.001
Leather	—	—	—	—	—	0.001
Paper-making	0.001	0.001	0.001	0.001	0.001	0.001
Cultural, educational and arts articles	0.003	0.003	0.003	0.003	0.004	0.01
Others	0.01	0.01	0.01	0.01	0.01	0.01
Construction	0.01	0.01	0.01	0.01	0.01	0.01
Transport and communication	0.31	0.36	0.39	0.41	0.52	0.55
Commerce, restaurant and service	0.002	0.002	0.001	0.002	0.001	0.001
Non-material production sector	2.17	1.79	1.83	1.83	1.64	1.84
Residential	0.99	1.16	1.00	1.25	1.40	1.22

Table D-8 Diesel Consumption by Sectors in China (Million ton)

	1980	1981	1982	1983	1984	1985
Total	16.63	16.45	15.87	16.47	17.53	19.39
Material production sectors	16.06	15.9	15.44	15.97	17.02	18.64
Agriculture, forestry, husbandry, fisheries	7.90	7.59	7.09	7.18	7.58	7.12
Industry	4.08	4.44	4.15	3.98	4.37	5.58
Metallurgy	0.27	0.26	0.26	0.27	0.31	0.35
Power	0.72	1.21	0.73	0.55	0.70	1.30
Coal and coke	0.08	0.08	0.08	0.10	0.11	0.17
Petroleum	0.34	0.31	0.27	0.27	0.32	0.32
Chemicals	1.37	1.32	1.48	1.46	1.49	1.53
Machine building	0.61	0.54	0.54	0.53	0.59	0.69
Building materials	0.23	0.22	0.28	0.29	0.30	0.30
Forest products	0.16	0.17	0.17	0.18	0.16	0.16
Food processing	0.08	0.08	0.11	0.11	0.14	0.23
Textiles	0.09	0.13	0.09	0.09	0.12	0.19
Clothing	0.002	0.003	0.004	0.004	0.01	0.02
Leather	0.003	0.004	0.003	0.003	0.004	0.01
Paper-making	0.03	0.02	0.02	0.02	0.02	0.04
Cultural, educational and arts articles	0.01	0.01	0.01	0.01	0.01	0.03
Others	0.11	0.09	0.18	0.10	0.10	0.14
Construction	0.77	0.73	0.79	0.95	1.07	1.25
Transport and communication	3.16	3.03	3.31	3.66	3.91	4.58
Commerce, restaurant and service	0.07	0.12	0.10	0.11	0.10	0.11
Non-material production sector	0.58	0.55	0.43	0.60	0.50	0.74
Residential	—	—	—	—	—	0.02

Table D-9 Natural Gas Consumption in China (Billion m³)

	1980	1981	1982	1983	1984	1985
Total	14.06	12.45	11.90	12.13	12.62	12.93
Material production sectors	13.81	12.17	11.57	11.96	12.10	12.43
Agriculture, forestry, husbandry, fisheries	—	—	—	—	—	—
Industry	13.14	11.60	11.00	11.27	11.37	10.96
Metallurgy	1.04	0.82	0.77	0.76	0.72	0.64
Power	0.07	0.06	0.06	0.06	0.10	0.58
Coal and coke	—	—	—	—	—	0.02
Petroleum	6.40	5.26	4.97	5.11	5.08	3.95
Chemicals	4.31	4.21	3.98	3.99	4.19	4.37
Machine building	0.51	0.48	0.49	0.58	0.57	0.61
Building materials	0.07	0.06	0.06	0.08	0.06	0.18
Forest products	—	—	—	—	0.01	—
Food processing	0.31	0.26	0.22	0.20	0.20	0.18
Textiles	0.34	0.35	0.30	0.36	0.32	0.04
Clothing	—	—	—	—	—	—
Leather	—	—	—	—	—	—
Paper-making	0.02	0.02	0.07	0.03	0.02	0.03
Cultural, educational and arts articles	—	—	—	0.01	0.01	—
Others	0.07	0.08	0.08	0.09	0.09	0.36
Construction	0.60	0.50	0.51	0.68	0.72	1.46
Transport and communication	0.07	0.07	0.06	0.01	0.01	0.01
Commerce, restaurants and service	—	—	—	—	—	—
Non-material production sector	0.05	0.06	0.03	0.03	0.05	0.05
Residential	0.20	0.22	0.30	0.14	0.47	0.45

Table D-10 Electricity Consumption by Sectors in China (TWh)

	1980	1981	1982	1983	1984	1985
Total	300.63	309.57	328.01	351.87	377.76	411.76
Material production sectors	283.23	290.39	307.00	329.19	351.80	377.34
Agriculture, forestry, husbandry, fisheries	33.14	34.68	37.52	38.38	38.99	41.62
Industry	241.05	246.23	260.26	279.57	300.03	318.46
Metallurgy	45.99	45.06	46.84	50.73	54.07	57.04
Power	43.85	46.08	47.61	49.93	53.57	58.78
Coal and coke	17.37	17.72	18.77	20.11	21.28	22.06
Petroleum	8.57	8.68	9.10	9.70	10.78	12.35
Chemicals	52.88	52.86	56.03	59.32	62.24	63.76
Machine building	23.08	23.15	24.44	26.44	29.53	30.57
Building materials	11.21	11.42	13.31	14.59	19.96	17.60
Forest products	1.42	1.50	1.58	1.62	1.69	1.72
Food processing	7.04	8.09	8.70	10.07	11.07	11.42
Textiles	12.17	14.28	15.52	16.68	17.24	20.02
Clothing	0.55	0.63	0.72	0.76	0.77	0.83
Leather	0.43	0.46	0.45	0.47	0.54	0.63
Paper-making	5.63	5.80	6.20	6.80	7.15	7.81
Cultural, educational and arts articles	0.35	0.40	0.47	0.51	0.54	0.58
Others	10.51	10.10	10.52	11.84	12.60	13.29
Construction	4.71	4.66	5.00	5.27	5.77	7.12
Transport and communication	2.65	2.91	2.99	3.58	4.14	6.34
Commerce, restaurants and services	1.68	1.91	2.03	2.93	2.87	3.80
Non-material production sector	6.88	7.38	8.16	8.95	10.05	12.17
Residential	10.52	11.80	12.05	13.73	15.91	22.25

SAMPLE SURVEY OF URBAN HOUSEHOLD EXPENDITURE ON ENERGY

SOURCE: Wu, Zongxin, et al, *Energy Demand Forecasting in China for the Year 2030*, Final Report to CEC, March, 1989.

Table E-1 Sample Survey of Urban Household Income and Expenditures, 1981

	All households	Per capita monthly income (yuan)					
		<20	20-25	25-35	35-50	50-60	>60
Number of households surveyed	8,715	179	476	2,772	3,685	1,037	566
Average number of persons per household	4.24	5.60	5.22	4.66	4.00	3.70	3.20
Annual income per capita (yuan)	458.07	210.60	270.48	364.56	492.96	646.68	804.00
Annual living expenditure per capita (yuan)	456.84	226.20	276.24	369.60	491.04	629.76	762.12
Energy expenditures							
Coal							
kg	240	222	211	228	246	294	312
yuan	8.88	7.24	6.85	7.43	8.02	9.58	10.17
Electricity, yuan	4.07	2.15	2.99	3.62	4.19	5.14	6.50
LPG, kg	6.12	2.04	4.05	5.54	6.56	7.68	8.68
Gas, yuan	0.84	0.24	0.60	0.72	0.84	0.96	1.44
Non-energy expenditures							
Food, yuan	258.84	150.12	170.52	216.84	274.20	343.08	402.36
Clothing, yuan	67.56	26.16	37.80	51.60	72.72	102.60	117.72
Articles for daily use, yuan	43.68	12.72	18.24	30.24	47.88	70.56	92.64
Other, yuan	72.97	27.13	38.89	53.38	82.09	96.62	129.58

Table E-2 Sample Survey of Urban Household Income and Expenditures, 1982

	All households	Per capita monthly income (yuan)					
		<20	20-25	25-35	35-50	50-60	>60
Number of households surveyed	9,020	83	332	2,312	4,095	1,281	917
Average number of persons per household	4.14	5.88	5.22	4.62	4.02	3.80	3.34
Annual income per capita (yuan)	500.28	231.24	296.40	401.40	538.44	697.08	877.68
Annual living expenditure per capita (yuan)	471.05	227.62	269.08	362.05	473.53	598.97	742.11
Energy expenditures							
Coal							
kg	230	247	198	220	228	248	292
yuan	8.80	8.04	6.79	8.08	8.78	9.97	11.56
Electricity, yuan	4.53	2.69	3.13	3.76	4.47	5.57	6.84
LPG, kg	7.08	4.39	4.10	6.23	7.14	8.70	10.28
Gas, yuan	0.92	0.11	0.92	0.77	0.88	1.03	1.40
Non-energy expenditures							
Food, yuan	276.23	143.53	171.99	220.34	277.48	340.18	409.62
Clothing, yuan	67.66	29.27	33.20	48.69	68.69	93	115.93
Articles for daily use, yuan	43.41	11.70	16.10	27.03	42.28	64.37	84.03
Other, yuan	69.53	32.28	36.95	53.38	70.95	84.85	112.73

Table E-3 Sample Survey of Urban Household Income and Expenditures, 1983

	All households	Per capita monthly income (yuan)					
		<20	20-25	25-35	35-50	50-60	>60
Number of households surveyed	9,060	55	269	1,841	4,218	1,488	1,189
Average number of persons per household	4.06	5.49	5.13	4.52	3.99	3.75	3.55
Annual income per capita (yuan)	525.96	216.72	277.68	372.24	501.96	651.96	828.24
Annual living expenditure per capita (yuan)	505.92	230.16	282	371.76	487.08	614.04	759.60
Energy expenditures							
Coal							
kg	230	234	232	240	233	225	233
yuan	8.76	7.20	7.20	7.92	8.76	9.12	10.44
Electicity, yuan	5.00	2.40	3.16	3.82	4.69	6.00	7.66
LPG, kg	8.16	4.68	4.56	6.12	8.40	9.36	9.24
Gas, yuan	0.96	—	0.24	0.72	0.96	1.32	1.44
Non-energy expenditures							
Food, yuan	299.52	142.08	178.922	227.16	290.64	355.80	432.60
Clothing, yuan	73.56	24.08	38.20	52.80	71.52	92.16	107.52
Articles for daily use, yuan	45.72	13.68	19.44	28.44	42.72	59.16	81.60
Other, yuan	72.64	30.72	34.76	50.90	67.79	90.33	118.56

Table E-4 Sample Survey of Urban Household Income and Expenditures, 1984

	All households	Per capita monthly income (yuan)					
		<20	20-25	25-35	35-50	50-60	>60
Number of households surveyed	12,500	209	1,315	4,861	2,834	1,601	1,680
Average number of persons per household	4.04	5.77	4.84	4.19	3.80	3.71	3.48
Annual income per capita (yuan)	607.56	261.12	375.36	511.92	654.60	775.44	1,004.04
Annual living expenditure per capita (yuan)	559.44	263.52	361.56	479.76	601.80	705.12	887.04
Energy expenditures							
Coal,							
kg	255	326	258	266	245	242	233
yuan	9.24	9.36	8.28	9.24	9.36	9.72	9.96
Electricity, yuan	5.24	3.04	3.62	4.58	5.39	6.60	8.12
LPG, kg	6.84	1.32	3.24	6.24	8.16	12.60	9.24
Gas, yuan	0.84	0.12	0.36	0.60	1.08	1.32	1.8
Non-energy expenditures							
Food, yuan	324.24	161.88	220.92	285.12	348.60	398.88	486
Colthing, yuan	86.88	39.36	54.24	75.60	94.92	110.04	133.08
Articles for daily use, yuan	50.64	13.92	24.24	39.12	55.56	69.00	99.6
Other, yuan	82.49	35.84	49.90	65.60	86.89	109.56	149.32

Table E-5 Sample Survey of Urban Household Income and Expenditures, 1985

	All households	Per capita monthly income						
		Lowest	Low	Lower medium	Medium	Upper medium	High	Highest
Number of households surveyed	17,143	1,714	1,714	3,429	3,429	3,429	1,714	1,714
Average number of persons per household	3.82	4.47	4.16	3.99	3.80	3.62	3.48	3.24
Annual income per capita (yuan)	752.40	437.40	546.72	632.88	737.28	861.96	1,012.32	1,276.20
Annual living expenditure per capita (yuan)	732.24	455.64	551.28	626.88	724.20	830.28	963.24	1,162.92
Energy expenditures								
Coal								
kg	253.92	239.52	245.64	245.52	267.60	319.08	342.24	306.12
yuan	10.08	9.12	9.36	9.48	10.08	10.80	10.80	12.12
Electicity, yuan	5.76	4.32	4.68	5.28	5.40	6.24	6.96	8.40
LPG, kg	6.72	3.98	5.18	5.60	6.46	7.80	9.06	10.71
Gas, yuan	0.96	0.60	0.72	0.84	0.84	0.96	1.32	1.68
Non-energy expenditures								
Food, yuan	390.36	278.88	319.56	352.44	392.76	430.80	473.88	546.12
Clothing, yuan	112.32	60.00	81.36	95.76	113.52	130.56	152.64	178.68
Articles for daily use, yuan	81.48	35.76	51.12	62.88	77.16	96.36	118.44	167.04
Other, yuan	131.28	66.96	84.48	100.20	124.44	154.56	199.20	248.88

Table E-6 Sample Survey of Urban Household Income and Expenditures, 1986

	All households	Per capita monthly income						
		Lowest	Low	Lower medium	Medium	Upper medium	High	Highest
Number of households surveyed	27,024	2,702	2,703	5,405	5,405	5,405	2,702	2,702
Average number of persons per household	3.82	4.05	4.48	4.07	3.82	3.63	3.47	3.19
Annual income per capita (yuan)	827.88	446.41	507.36	663.26	772.94	905.09	1,054.52	1,347.08
Annual living expenditure per capita (yuan)	798.96	469.79	573.97	650.91	747.37	855.21	987.47	1,263.83
Energy expenditures								
Coal								
kg	304.29	308.34	393.65	269.26	281.36	287.5	291.36	323.7
yuan	12.00	11.28	11.70	12.15	12.76	13.11	14.41	16.94
Electicity, yuan	6.96	4.70	5.51	5.96	6.33	7.15	7.75	9.6
LPG, kg	6.35	2.92	2.40	3.99	4.71	5.12	6.36	6.71
Gas, yuan	0.96	0.70	0.76	1.00	1.18	1.26	1.4	1.84
Non-energy expenditures								
Food, yuan	418.92	275.56	323.95	356.29	395.76	434.7	482.33	572.16
Clothing, yuan	113.03	58.67	75.38	91.81	108.29	124.47	141.27	166.35
Articles for daily use, yuan	88.92	36.65	53.03	63.35	77.65	98.63	120.22	160.56

APPENDIX F

SAMPLE SURVEY OF RURAL HOUSEHOLD EXPENDITURE ON ENERGY

SOURCE: Wu, Zongxin, et al, *Energy Demand Forecasting in China for the Year 2030,* Final Report to CEC, March, 1989.

Table F-1 Sample Survey of Rural Household Income and Expenditures

	1981	1982	1983	1984	1985	1986
Number of households surveyed	18,529	22,775	30,427	31,375	66,642	66,836
Average number of persons per household	5.50	5.46	5.43	5.37	5.12	5.07
Annual net income per capita (yuan)	223.44	270.11	309.77	355.33	397.60	423.76
Annual living expenditure per capita (yuan)	190.81	220.23	248.29	273.80	317.42	356.95
Fuel expenditures (yuan/yr.)						
Commercial energy	1.92	2.77	3.01	3.33	4.04	4.07
Non-commercial energy	7.67	9.59	10.46	11.71	14.12	14.50
Non-fuel expenditures (yuan/yr.)						
Food	113.83	133.20	147.24	161.52	183.33	201.17
Clothing	23.57	24.77	27.65	28.33	31.34	33.74
Housing	18.67	22.58	27.65	32.12	39.46	51.23
Others	24.15	27.32	32.37	36.79	45.13	52.24

APPENDIX G

OFFICIAL ENERGY PRICE, 1988

SOURCE: Wu, Zongxin, et al, *Energy Demand Forecasting in China for the Year 2030,* Final Report to CEC, March, 1989.

Table G-1 Energy Price in China, 1988 (Official prices only)

Energy	Unit	Price	Energy	Unit	Price
1. Raw coal			**6. Gasoline**		
Coking coal			For aviation	yuan/ton	720
No. 1–10 grades	yuan/ton	31.9	For vehicles		
No. 11–16 grades	yuan/ton	24.5	Nos. 56 and 61	yuan/ton	550
No. 17–22 grades	yuan/ton	18	Nos. 70 and 75	yuan/ton	580
Bituminous coal			Nos. 80, 82 and 85	yuan/ton	660
No.1–10 grades	yuan/ton	27	**7. Kerosene**		
No. 11–16 grades	yuan/ton	21.9	For lighting	yuan/ton	430
No. 17–22 grades	yuan/ton	14.8	For aviation	yuan/ton	430
Hard coal			Nos. 240, 260 and special No.1	yuan/ton	600
No. 1–10 grades	yuan/ton	29.8	**8. Light diesel**		
No. 11–16 grades	yuan/ton	23.5	Nos. 0, 10 and 20	yuan/ton	240
No. 17–22 grades	yuan/ton	16.2	Nos. 30, 35 and 50	yuan/ton	460
2. Washing coal			**9. Heavy diesel**	yuan/ton	140
High grade furnace coal	yuan/ton	52.3	**10. Fuel oil**		
Other washing coal	yuan/ton	7.3–45.0	No. 0-200	yuan/ton	150–200
Lump washing coal	yuan/ton	35	No. 250 and others	yuan/ton	50
Mixture	yuan/ton	20	**11. LPG**	yuan/ton	80
3. Electricity	yuan/kWh	0.065	**12. Coke**		
4. Crude oil			Furnace coke		
Natural oil	yuan/ton	110	> 40 mm	yuan/ton	90
Condensate oil	yuan/ton	450	25–40 mm	yuan/ton	76
Artificial oil	yuan/ton	140	10–25 mm	yuan/ton	65
5. Natural gas	yuan/m³	0.05	< 10 mm	yuan/ton	40
			Fuel coke		
			< 25 mm	yuan/ton	80

APPENDIX H

ENERGY FLOW DIAGRAM OF CHINA, 1986

Modified Energy Flow Analysis Model (EFLOW) is used in the development of this energy flow diagram, which has been adopted by the State Planning Commission as a standard tool for improving national and provincial energy statistics. For detailed information, see Qiu Daxiong, et al., "Improvement of National and Provincial Energy Statistics — Applications of Energy Flow Analysis Model (EFLOW) in China," final report to the Commission on the European Community, March 1989.

Energy Flow Analysis, People's Republic of China, 1985

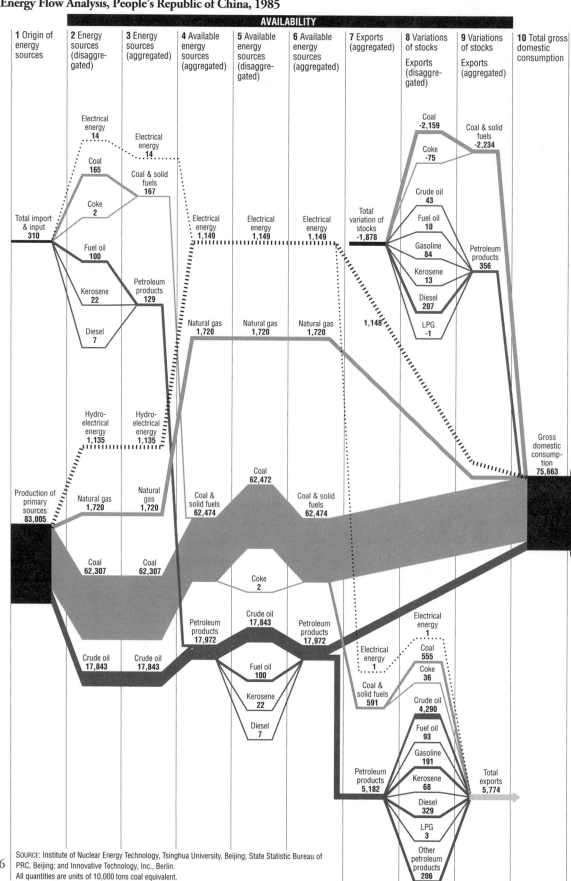

SOURCE: Institute of Nuclear Energy Technology, Tsinghua University, Beijing; State Statistic Bureau of PRC, Beijing; and Innovative Technology, Inc., Berlin.
All quantities are units of 10,000 tons coal equivalent.

Energy Flow Analysis, People's Republic of China, 1985 (continued)

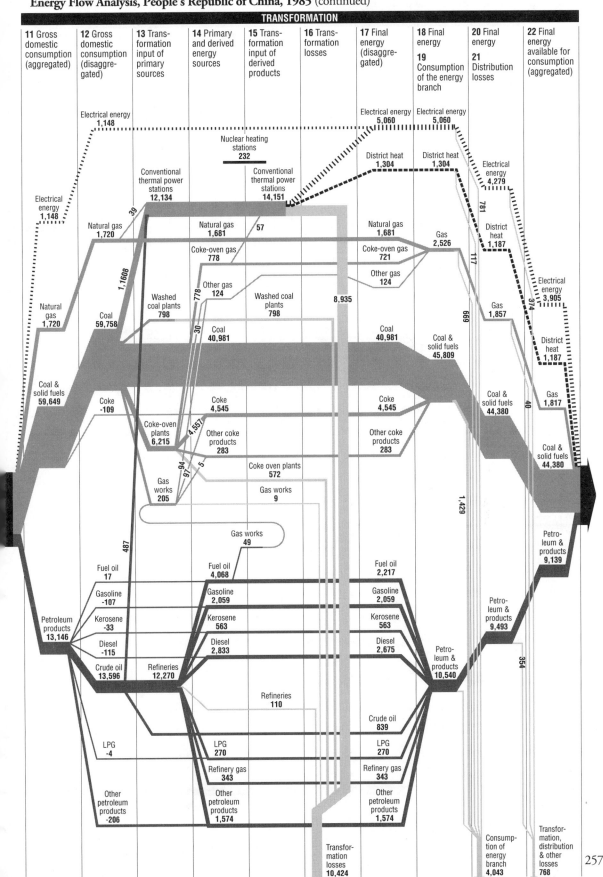

257

Energy Flow Analysis, People's Republic of China, 1985 (continued)

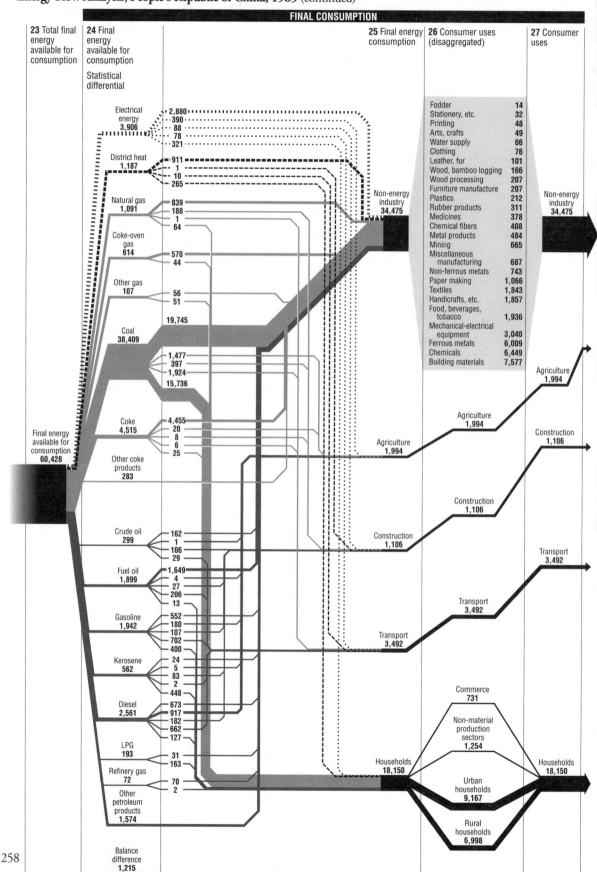

Energy Flow Analysis, People's Republic of China, 1985 (continued)

FINAL CONSUMPTION (continued)

28 Non-energy consumption **29** Applied energy	**30** Applications	**31** Energy losses during final consumption	**32** Total energy losses in use	**33** Useful energy (disaggregated)	**34** Useful energy (aggregated)	**35** Total useful energy

Non-energy consumption **4,748**

Applied energy	Application	Loss		Useful		
Light oil 1,203	Piston engines 1,203			Piston engines 324		
Coal 6,613	Cement kilns 7,524	879		Cement kilns 3,010		
Heat 911	Radiation furnaces 11,381	4,514		Radiation furnaces 2,283		
Coal 10,579		9,098	Losses in non-energy industries 17,124			
Fuel oil 778						
Light oil 24						
Fuel oil 778	Furnace boilers, steamcrackers 3,614	1,446		Furnace boilers, steamcrackers 2,168	Non-energy industry 12,622	
Coal 2,035						
Natural gas 120	Blast furnaces 3,145	629		Blast furnaces 2,516		
Coal 3,145						
Electricity 2,592	Electric motors 2,592	518		Electric motors 2,074		
Electricity 288	Lighting 288	40		Lighting 248		
Coal 382	Boilers 382			Boilers 229		
Light oil 1,097	Piston engines 1,097	40	Losses in agriculture 1,091	Piston engines 311		
Electricity 312	Electric motors 312	153		Electric motors 250	Agriculture 902	
Electric 39	Lighting 39	62		Lighting 35		
Other energy 163	Other appliances 336	4 / 86		Other appliances 77		
Gas 94	Boilers 412			Boilers 238		
Coal 316	Piston engines 289	174		Piston engines 77		
Light oil 289	Electric motors 61	212 / 12	Losses in construction 596	Electric motors 49	Construction 510	
Electricity 61	Lighting 9	1		Lighting 8		
Electricity 9						
Other energy 336	Other appliances 336	198		Other appliances 138		
Coal 1,379	Steam engines 1,379			Steam engines 110		Useful energy 25,850
Light oil 1,447	Piston engines 1,447	1,269		Piston engines 367		
Electricity 35	Electric motors 35	1,080		Electric motors 28		
Electricity 35	Electric rail haulage 35	7		Electric rail haulage 9	Transport 952	
Coal 178	Furnace boilers, steamcrackers 179	12	Losses in transport 2,540	Furnace boilers, steamcrackers 107		
Fuel oil 235		72				
Coal 171	Space heating 407	84		Space heating 323		
District heat 1	Lighting 15	1		Lighting 7		
Electricity 8						
Light oil 527	Piston engines 527			Piston engines 118		
Gas 159	Cookers 984	409		Cookers 336		
Petroleum products 343	Water heaters 161	648		Water heaters 80		
Coal 482		81	Losses in households 7,049			
Coal 161						
District heat 274	District heating 13,140	3,914		Space heating 10,277	Households 11,099	
Coal 12,853						
Oil 13	Stoves 977	733				
Coal 977	Boilers 1,621	814				
Coal 1,621						
Electricity 376	Electric motors & appliances 376	226		Electric motors & appliances 150		
Electricity 94						
Kerosene 270	Lighting 364	225		Lighting 139		

Losses in use **28,400**

259

INDEX